MACROECONOMICS AFTER KEYNES

A
Reconsideration of
the *General Theory*

VICTORIA CHICK

The MIT Press
Cambridge, Massachusetts

Second printing, 1984
First MIT Press edition, 1983

First published 1983 by
PHILIP ALLAN PUBLISHERS LIMITED

Library of Congress Cataloging in Publication Data

Chick, Victoria
  Macroeconomics after Keynes.

  Bibliography: p.
  Includes index.
  1. Macroeconomics. 2. Keynes, John Maynard, 1883–1946.
  General theory of employment, interest and money.
  I. Title
  HB172.5.F5   1983   339   83-844
  ISBN 0-262-03095-0 (hard)
  ISBN 0-262-53045-7 (pbk.)

CONTENTS

PREFACE

The Purpose of this Book

This is a book about a book: J.M. Keynes's *The General Theory of Employment, Interest and Money.* It is the outcome of several years' experience using the *General Theory* as the core of my macroeconomics courses for undergraduates at UCL. I believe it sheds new light on Keynes's book, and in that respect my intended audience is my fellow-academics, but it is also meant for students: I feel strongly that the current practice of separating one's audience, reserving new thinking for the professionals and giving students only what is generally accepted, is both patronising to students and inimical to the vitality and progress of our subject.

Therefore I hope to encourage others, by means of this book, to bring the *General Theory* back into mainstream teaching — not because there is anything sacrosanct about Keynes, but because I would argue (*do* argue, in this book) that the *General Theory* gives a far richer understanding of the structure of macroeconomic interactions and methods of analysing them than much of what has been written since.

The macroeconomics that has been developed after Keynes, though claiming inspiration from the *General Theory*, in my view has not, with some outstanding exceptions, been macroeconomics after the *manner* of Keynes — with the method and perspective and insight of Keynes. My title is intended to indicate this jarring fact: that the macroeconomics which has followed the *General Theory* in time has not followed it in spirit. It is the latter we need.

I would go so far as to argue not only that Keynesian economics is not Macroeconomics After Keynes, but that it is not even macroeconomics! Consider the approach in any textbook. One is told that there are three central behavioural equations in Keynes: the consumption function, the investment equation and liquidity preference. That is not unreasonable. Much detailed exposition of these three functions then ensues, based entirely on principles relevant to individual behaviour. There is nothing wrong with choosing the individual level: that is where these decisions are made. But then, flying in the face of what is (usually) said in introducing macroeconomics about the fallacy of composition, the equations representing individual behaviour are regarded as relating to aggregates and given the simultaneous-solution treatment.

The approach of the neoclassical synthesis is one of splitting up the theory into components, tinkering with the parts and never quite enquiring whether they still legitimately fit together into a coherent theory at the macroeconomic level. Nor is the method of simultaneous equations challenged.

In contrast, Keynes set out with the objective of providing a theory of, as he called it, 'output-as-a-whole', one which would admit the possibility of unemployment which was neither voluntary nor transitory. The components were seen as crucial elements in that whole picture. The difference is one between a 'holistic' and a 'reductionist' attitude to theory.

I believe passionately that the urge to simplify a theory, to reduce it to its component parts chiefly because these are easy to handle mechanically, is largely responsible for the unhappy state of the subject and of economic policy.

Consider, for example one effect of presenting 'macroeconomics' as the three behavioural equations mentioned above (substitute a saving function for consumption for greater familiarity, though I argue in the book that the substitution has been disastrous) and an exogenous money supply. Separate the 'monetary' from the 'real' in an *LM* and an *IS* curve, respectively. Then it is easy to talk of fiscal policy without regard to the consequences of the mode of its financing, as if any 'monetary' effects operate solely through the *demand* for money. For a long time this was standard 'Keynesian' theorising, which ignored what Keynes *did* say about the effects of financing and was insensitive to what he, not envisioning intervention on such a scale, did *not* say. Thus the way was left wide open for monetarism's challenge, and the enfeebled theory was too weak to combat it effectively.

It was my dissatisfaction with conventional macroeconomics which first prompted me, in a search for something better, to go back to the *General Theory* and to use it instead of a textbook in my macroeconomics courses for second-year undergraduates. There seems to me to be no point at all in perpetuating the present state of affairs by teaching students about the 'Monetarist-Keynesian Debate', or latter-day alternatives such as New Cambridge and the New Classical economics, on the basis of the oversimplifications and algebraic manipulations which dominate the textbooks, for they are not thereby given any criteria for evaluating the theories or choosing between them. It is my experience that students end up by saying no more than 'X's theory is this' and 'Y's theory is that', making no attempt at evaluation and choosing, if they choose at all, on the basis of their political preferences for some policy prescription associated with a particular theory. If the policy conclusions do not *follow* from the theory (which is all too often the case) the student is, it seems to me, in a worse intellectual state than if he had never learnt any economics at all.

So this is not a particularly easy book, and for that I make no apologies. Macroeconomics by its very nature requires that one keep track of a fair number of things at once, and a holistic vision is something every reader must construct for himself, from the 'clues to your thought which you are trying to throw him'.*

Students do not find the *General Theory* particularly easy either: it is all words, for a start, with only one diagram and few equations to seize upon. The analysis is often far from clear and particularly difficult to penetrate after learning some 'Keynesian economics'. (Students are quite stunned to see how different the two are, and often quite excited by the discovery.)

Initially, therefore, I conceived this book as an aid to understanding the *General Theory*, sharing what I had learned in returning to it — an exercise, if you like, in restoration, stripping off layers of 'Keynesian' varnish so that the original object could be seen. Leijonhufvud (1968) had also done this of course, but I felt he had still more layers to go. So, it turned out, had I.

The first attempt, in 1974(!), came unstuck on its way round the circular flow of income. Later I came to realise that the circular flow and Keynes's treatment of finance and money were not really compatible. It was right that I should come unstuck.

As first conceived it was also largely an 'anti-text', critical in detail of textbook macroeconomics. I found however that the Keynesians kept getting in the way of my trying to say what I thought Keynes was about. And I wanted also to rework and extend parts of the theory and to point the way to necessary changes. These aims took precedence, so with some exceptions where I felt that prevailing conceptions needed to be dealt with explicitly, I have left the Keynesians more or less in peace. In any case there were more sinister foes around by the time I came back to the project.

This is not a book in the history of economic doctrine as such, which is concerned with illuminating the author's point of view as brightly as possible on his own terms. I hope at several points to have done that, though I do not claim that this book reveals 'what Keynes really meant'. It is obviously important when reading *anyone* to use one's sympathy and intuition to approach as closely as possible the author's point of view, to attempt to understand him or her to the best of one's ability. That effort, and basic respect, is necessary even to make effective criticism — one does not have to agree. But it is a philosophical impossibility to *know* what someone else 'really meant'; what matters is to make coherent sense for oneself of what an author says and to evaluate its relevance to the problem at hand.

The question of relevance ultimately dominates the book, whether evaluating Keynes's ideas vis-à-vis those of his predecessors and their modern representatives or the applicability of his ideas to the present. Theory is all too often presented as if its origins were totally abstract. This helps to foster the idea that later ideas are better, as Truth gradually

* Keynes's *Collected Writings*, Vol. XIII, p. 470.

overcomes Error. When theories are presented for what they are —
products of living human minds, with their particular interests, strengths and
failings, working in a particular place at a particular time — students can
understand that certain minds capture the essence of a problem better than
others and even the best theory is only provisional. It is unfortunate that in
macroeconomics a very good theory has been superseded by much more
limited ones, but even when the better theory has been understood one must
not stop there. The book ends by suggesting areas where substantial,
perhaps radical, revision is needed.

It follows that the student looking for the Truth here will not merely be
disappointed; the disturbing idea will have been put to him that there really
is no such thing. Theories are rarely True or False, but they may be judged
more or less relevant to the place and time to which they are applied.

Having said that, it will strike the reader as odd, to say the least, that there
is precious little in this book on the international aspects of the economy, or
on government outside the frame of reference of stabilisation policy. This is
the case despite the urgings of many who have seen the manuscript at various
stages to include these matters. Let me say immediately that I agree with
them that it is a matter of great importance, even urgency, to develop a
macroeconomic model which fully incorporates these aspects. It is thus with
regret and apologies that I have not followed their advice; very simply, I do
not feel I have the depth of understanding required to treat these aspects on
the same level as what does appear here and to integrate them with the rest
of the analysis rather than merely tacking them on, and I feel strongly that
'tacking-on' is not good enough. At points there are some suggestions in
these directions which others might like to follow. One does what one feels
one can, and leaves the rest to others.

Thanks

One cannot even do what one can without the help and support of others,
and I have many debts.

Some of my debts go back a long way, to my student days at Berkeley.
There, David Alhadeff and Harvey Leibenstein taught me microeconomics
in a way which allowed me to see more in supply and demand analysis than
the point where two curves cross. That perception is the fulcrum on which
almost all the theoretical argument of this book rests.

Also at Berkeley, Hyman Minsky tried to teach me *The General Theory*,
but I didn't really see the point then. I wish to thank him for trying and to
apologise for being so obtuse at the time.

I have had the marvellous opportunity of trying out many of the ideas in
this book in seminars at many British and several Italian universities and at
greater length while a visitor to McGill University and the University of
Aarhus. I am most grateful for these invitations and for the stimulating
discussions which resulted.

There are many people to thank for reading part or all of the manuscript at various stages. Susan Howson, David Laidler and a student on the course, Hyginus Leon, read almost all the manuscript and Richard Lipsey a great chunk of it. Comments on particular chapters were also forthcoming from Michael Danes, Sheila Dow, Peter Earl, Nicolas Rau, Colin Rogers, Kerry Schott, Thanos Skouras, John Sutton, Christopher Torr, Valeria Termini, and Claus Vastrup. I thank them all for giving so generously of their time and offering me their expertise and their criticisms. They are not to be held responsible for the result.

Those who helped the book take physical shape are also to be thanked. Too many have been involved in the typing at various stages to name them all. I am grateful to all of them, but particularly to Celia Rhodes. Celia, a former student (so she knew what I was about) undertook not only a vast amount of typing in the final stages but also editorial tasks including most of the responsibility for the index. Not only was her nearly faultless typing and intelligent editorial work a boon, but she was always calm, greatly alleviating the stress of such a project. I was very lucky — indeed I wonder if this book would have seen the light of day without her.

I wish also to thank Philip Allan, first for his patience and then, equally, for knowing exactly when and how to lose it. Both were vital, as were his constant support and enthusiasm. Thanks are due him also for organising the book's almost alarmingly rapid production. I should particularly like to thank Ann Hirst, who was both a superb copy-editor and such fun to work with. Geoffrey Harcourt and Basil Moore also spotted some late errors.

Notes on Reading this Book

Keynes was a skilful tactician: he stated the main outline of his theory and drew the lines of dissent with existing theory after a first chapter of only half a page. In retrospect I might have been wise to follow that format. My Chapter 4 corresponds to his Chapter 3 and the three preceding chapters can be pretty heavy going in places. My advice is to have a go but feel free to skip to Chapters 4, 5 and 7 and then come back. (But *do* come back: too much is built on those early chapters.)

I have brought forward the analysis of changes in money-wages (*G.T.* Ch. 19) to Chapter 8; other topics are fairly clearly indicated by the chapter titles. There is a table of correspondences between chapters of the *General Theory* and this book following the Table of Contents.

For teaching purposes there will undoubtedly be a need to make cuts. I cut or skim over different material every year. Any cut damages coherence, but it is not obvious what is most dispensable. (If I knew, the book would be shorter.) My view is that the balance should be determined by what does and does not turn the students and the lecturer on. Students will probably need further background for Chapter 9 than I was able to provide without distorting the shape of the book.

Acknowledgement

The author gratefully acknowledges the permission of the Royal Economic Society and Harcourt Brace Jovanovich to quote from Keynes's writings.

Bibliographical Note

Although other references are indicated by author and date, the *General Theory* and items for which Keynes's *Collective Writings* are the only or most convenient source have been indicated by *G.T.* and *C.W.* (with volume number following) respectively. Page references to the *General Theory* are to the original (1936) edition.

Chapters of the *General Theory* Relevant to Each Chapter of this Book

Macroeconomics after Keynes	*The General Theory*
Part I	
1	1,2
2	–
3	4,6,7
Part II	
4	3,5
5	3,20
6	8,9,11,12
7	2,19
8	–
Part III	
9	13,14,16
10	13,15
11	13
12	–
13	18
Part IV	
14	10
15	20,21
16	22
17	17
Part V	
18	–
19	–
20	–

Part *I*
PRELIMINARIES AND FUNDAMENTALS

Chapter 1

KEYNES AND MACROECONOMICS

A Monetary Theory of Production

In some sense, Keynes's *General Theory of Employment, Interest and Money is* macroeconomics and in another, very real, sense modern macroeconomics has gone a long way toward restoring the theory that existed before Keynes wrote and which he thought he had overturned.

All theory is simplification, abstraction, stylisation. Theory does not mirror reality; it extracts the salient features that convey the essence of that reality, the way an artist may use only a few lines to suggest both form and feeling.

Good theories are relevant abstractions, and relevance alters as history moves on. In economics, old theories are seldom wrong; they have just become irrelevant. Surveying the economic theory in which he had been trained, Keynes felt that the theory was not relevant to the world which he knew:

> ... [W]e lack a monetary theory of production. An economy, which uses money but uses it merely as a neutral link between transactions in real things and real assets and does not allow it to enter into motives or decisions, might be called — for want of a better name — a *real-exchange economy* ... Most treatises on the principles of economics are concerned mainly, if not entirely, with a real-exchange economy; and — which is more peculiar — the same thing is also largely true of most treatises on the theory of money. ...The theory which I desiderate would deal, in contradistinction to this, with an economy in which money plays a part of its own and affects motives and decisions and is, in short, one of the operative factors in the situation, so that the course of events cannot be predicted, either in the long period or in the short, without a knowledge of the behaviour of money between the first state and the last. And it is this which we ought to mean when we speak of a *monetary economy*. ... Everyone would, of course, agree that it is in a monetary economy in my sense of the term that we actually live. ...

> Nevertheless it is my belief that the far-reaching and in some respects fundamental differences between the conclusions of a monetary economy and those of the more simplified real-exchange economy have been greatly underestimated by the exponents of the traditional economics; with the result that the machinery of thought with which real-exchange economics has equipped the minds of practitioners in the world of affairs, and also the economists themselves, has led in practice to many erroneous conclusions and policies. The idea that it is comparatively easy to adapt the hypothetical conclusions of a real wage economics to the real world of monetary economics is a mistake. It is extraordinarily difficult to make the adaptation. ... Accordingly I believe that the next task is to work out in some detail a monetary theory of production. ... [T]hat is the task on which I am now occupying myself, in some confidence that I am not wasting my time.

(C.W. XIV, pp. 408–411)

The student might think it extraordinary that a theory of real exchange would be applied to an industrialised nation. One might even think it odd that such a theory would have been constructed in the first place. Consider, however, what sort of economics one would write if one lived in a society which was largely agricultural, in which much domestic trade was not monetised.

A theory of direct exchange of labour-time for 'corn', the representative commodity, would not be unreasonable. Money would enter the picture in the section on international trade. If one's work is good enough, one might capture the minds of succeeding generations so completely that the analysis and habits of mind appropriate to one situation continue to be brought to bear long after the situation to which they are applied has altered enough to require a change of theory. The laws of inertia apply to thought as to the material world.

The economy that Keynes observed was nothing like that. It was a world which, in broad outline, is similar to our own, (though of course there are differences, some of them important). He saw, and so do we, an industrial economy, capitalist[1] in form, with a sophisticated financial system to bridge the gap between the ownership of capital by a few and the need for a broad source of funds to finance that ownership: a monetary, production economy.

Of course, one might think. But what is the fuss about *now*? Surely Keynes succeeded in his task and the issue is settled? No, it is *not* settled. In some bizarre and tragic way, although the result of his efforts is still counted amongst the three or four most important books yet produced in economics, it was, or it has so far been, a waste of time. By three steps, much of the old real-exchange theory has been restored. One wonders what it is that is so deeply appealing about it.

The first, the biggest step was the 'neoclassical synthesis', based on the *IS–LM* framework, in which Keynes's theory was retained in outward form but lost in substance. The three essential behavioural elements are there — the consumption function, the marginal efficiency of capital and liquidity preference — but they are put together in a framework of simultaneous equations — a method only suitable to the analysis of exchange[2] — and everything, even the liquidity-preference function, is 'real'.

The restoration of the method appropriate to real-exchange theory was the major step, but monetarism provided two more: first, the distinction between consumption and investment, already weakened in *IS–LM* analysis, was virtually obliterated,[3] returning us to the 'corn' economy; second, the development of 'rational expectations', while making the analysis *seem* to deal with uncertainty and forecasting, takes the analysis back almost to the model of perfect certainty; only random errors, which are not forecastable, remain.

In Keynes's theory, shifts in investment are a major source of disturbance (for good or ill) to the economy. The effect of restoring a theory of undifferentiated output is to remove this source of disturbance, leaving government policy as the main cause of fluctuations. This is a major step toward restoring the theorem, prevalent before Keynes, that the economic system was 'self-righting': fluctuations were temporary and self-reversing and the best policy was to leave the economy alone. The introduction of rational expectations reinforces this conclusion, since expenditure plans are no longer based, as Keynes's investment plans are, on long-range, very uncertain forecasts and government expenditures are nullified in their effect by the knowledge that they are matched by future tax liabilities, We have moved from the economics of Keynes to the 'economics of Dr. Pangloss'.[4] The *status quo ante* is virtually restored, and that, I believe, is tragic both for theory and for policy.

How did it happen? Most of the trouble lay, perhaps, in the complexity of the *General Theory* and the desire of interpreters to simplify its message rather than taking pains to understand its complexity. Part of the trouble lies in the fact that the assumptions of today's real-exchange model are tacit, as they were in the version Keynes attacked. One can thus be fooled by the words one uses — note his remark about the 'real' character of *monetary* theory, and I have asserted that the standard textbook theory of output is really a theory of exchange. (One cannot see others' assumptions clearly if one does not know one's own. For this reason, we shall pay much attention to *method*.)

So although on some points the world to which Keynes's theory most closely pertains differs from our own, the difference is far less than the gulf that separates the reality of the modern industrial economy from the nearly-perfectly-certain, one-commodity exchange economy of modern macro-economics. This fact — it is a fact as I see it — is the *raison d'être* of this book.

Money

Macroeconomics has never really come to terms with money.

(Microeconomics hasn't either.) Few have seen with this kind of clarity what
the shift to a monetary theory entails:

> [T]he task of monetary theory is a much wider one than is commonly assumed; ...
> its task is nothing less than to cover a second time the whole field which is treated
> by pure theory under the assumption of barter, and to investigate what changes in
> the conclusions of pure theory are made necessary by the introduction of indirect
> exchange.
>
> (von Hayek, 1935, p. 110)

Money, as is well known, permits the separation of the act of selling goods
from the act of purchasing them: that is, indirect exchange. In much
economic theory even today this attribute of money is treated as a pure
convenience. In such theory the presumption is that the existence of money
does nothing to change the nature of transactions; in its absence the same
sales would simply take place with greater awkwardness and higher real
cost. Relative prices are unchanged; money is neutral. Goods exchange for
goods: the real-exchange economy.

Indirect exchange means a separation in time between actions involving
real goods. The real value of a sales transaction, therefore, cannot be known
for certain. In that sense, every transaction is a speculation (Hicks, 1939)
and in the possibility that the gap between transactions may be quite long in
aggregate, Marx finds an explanation of the 'crisis'.[5] Even a theory of a
monetary exchange economy can give important results.

Production

Production also, in the nature of things, takes time.

The time-consuming nature of production places upon producers the
necessity to make decisions based on an *estimate*, a forecast, of the demand
for their product: the goods must be placed on the market before people can
buy them, and thus before demand can be known.[6] The existence of money
can enhance the difficulty of making that estimate, for when people save for
future purchases, they need not place specific orders even if they know what
they will want and when. They can hold money instead, or one of the many
claims on future money that a developed financial system provides. This
action gives producers no clue as to their future plans.

These are the basic facts which Keynes's theory incorporates, and using
them he attacks the prevailing orthodoxy. The attack was at one and the
same time a declaration of all-out war and a battle for a specific objective.
The specific objective, one manifestation of the prevailing orthodoxy, was
the theory of employment. Events determined his specific objective, for
while Keynes knew that his theory was a full scale critique of Real-Exchange
Economics, the condition of the British economy in the 1930s was too dire to
permit a lofty, disengaged approach, even if Keynes's temperament would
have allowed it.

Historical Background

All books are products of their place and time. And the place and time that
stand as backround to the *General Theory* are extraordinary. The time, the
early 1930s;[7] the place, Cambridge. These influenced both the form and the
content of the book.

First, form. Styles change. Economics today is couched in a technical (or
seemingly technical) language, infiltrated by mathematics. The *General
Theory* is almost entirely verbal. Words whose meanings were taken as given
were those in agreed usage in Cambridge at the time. There were other
words, whose meaning is now (wrongly, I think) taken as agreed, which
were even then (and there) the subject of heated controversy — saving, for
example. A full understanding of the book, to which I do not lay claim,
requires a knowledge of the particular language current in that closely-knit
group of economists amongst whom Keynes was working. At the least, one
must be alert to the 'fallacy of common language'[8] and the need to exercise
interpretive imagination. Cambridge Economics was (and still is) a distinct
intellectual tradition. The reader of the *General Theory* must make a
translation from the language of Cambridge in the 1930s to the language of
the present.

More important, content. It is necessary to view the *General Theory* in the
context of history, both the history of the British economy and the history of
economic thought. The *General Theory* is a direct reaction to established
doctrine. A famous passage in Keynes's preface describes the book as:

> a long struggle of escape ... — a struggle of escape from habitual modes of thought
> and expression ... . The difficulty lies, not in the new ideas, but in escaping from
> the old ones, which ramify ... into every corner of our minds.
>
> (*G.T.* p.viii)

I cannot possibly give a full exposition of macroeconomic theory as it existed
before Keynes,[9] much less list the contents of Keynes's mind before he
began the train of thought that resulted in this work.[10] But a sketch of the
more important ideas is in order, for his opposition to the prevailing
orthodoxy shapes the entire argument. It is an orthodoxy which has by no
means died, though it has changed its form slightly.[11]

Keynes was anxious to refute a particular manifestation of orthodox
theory, namely Say's Law and the theorem which derives from it: that
involuntary unemployment is impossible. This was hard to believe in Britain
in the early 1930s, when Keynes began working on his new ideas.

From 1921, when reasonable data became available, rates of
unemployment in the UK were not a pretty sight. The percentage of insured
workers unemployed was 15.6 per cent in that year. It fell to 9.7 per cent in
1927 and reached its peak of 22.1 per cent in 1932: 2.8 million people. The
registered unemployed numbered over two million until late 1935.

These are data for the country as a whole; they are given in full in Table

Table 1.1

Wages, Prices and Unemployment in Interwar Britain

Year	Average Weekly Wage Rate 1958 = 100 (1)	Retail Prices 1958 = 100 (2)	Real Wage Index (1)÷(2)	Unemployment per cent (4)
1920	(47)*	58	(0.81)	2.5
1921	(46)	53	(0.87)	15.6
1922	(36)	43	(0.84)	14.3
1923	(32)	41	(0.78)	11.7
1924	32	41	0.78	10.3
1925	32	41	0.78	11.3
1926	32	40	0.80	12.5
1927	32	39	0.82	9.7
1928	32	39	0.82	10.8
1929	32	39	0.82	10.4
1930	32	37	0.86	16.0
1931	31	35	0.89	21.3
1932	31	34	0.91	22.1
1933	30	33	0.91	19.9
1934	30	33	0.91	16.7
1935	31	34	0.91	15.5
1936	31	35	0.89	13.1
1937	33	36	0.92	10.8
1938	34	37	0.92	12.9

Source: London and Cambridge Economic Service, *Key Statistics of the British Economy, 1900–1962*, Table F.
* Brackets indicate 'particularly rough' estimates.

1.1. Regional data make terrifying reading.

So when Keynes was writing, a depressed economy had been a familiar feature of the UK for a very long time, for particular reasons — some would say for *one* particular reason: a determination to restore the gold standard in Britain at the pre-war rate of exchange. If this was to happen, prices and costs had to be brought down to levels consistent with those in the United States, at the prewar exchange rate. To achieve this, deliberately deflationary policies were pursued. Once achieved (in 1925) the overvalued rate did its own work: the deflation continued partly because exports were too expensive, thus depressing sales and income.

The *global* slump appeared later, as America too suffered depression, aided or precipitated by the Wall Street collapse of 1929.[12] Between 1929 and the trough in 1933, net national product in current prices fell by more than 50 per cent, in constant prices by more than a third.[13] Unemployment rose from 3.2 per cent in 1929 to 23.6 per cent at the trough: nearly 13 million people.[14] Banks failed, and the depositors were not insured. None of this did anything for world trade: America, a major source of demand, had fallen on hard times.

Pre-Keynesian economists had seen slumps and financial collapses before, and had theories of business fluctuations. But they supposed that the system, like a well-built boat, would without undue delay right itself. What was new was the *persistence* of the slump. And it is from this perspective that Keynes's demonstration of the possibility of underemployment equilibrium should be understood.[15] It is a theorem which has got lost in the resurgence of neoclassical theory and concentration on Keynes's policy conclusions.

The Self-Righting Economy

Economists in the 1930s had a different world-view from those brought up after the war. The fundamental vision of economic systems was that they tended toward stability. This vision was embodied in the theory of the stationary state. Around a stable level of performance there were cycles and irregular aberrations due to special factors such as crop failures.[16] Today we think of growth as the norm, with fluctuations around a rising trend. It is hard for us to understand their way of thinking.

Unemployment was seen as a consequence of the fluctuations around the stable norm. The exogenous fluctuations were not predictable but the cycles were amenable to analysis. Explanations of unemployment therefore were part of the theory of the trade cycle.

Fluctuations are by their nature transitory. It was a central tenet of pre-Keynesian orthodoxy that there could never emerge for any substantial period of time a general excess supply of output (a 'general glut'). Industry might need to slacken temporarily in order to adjust to some change in the pattern of demand. This would create 'frictional' unemployment as workers looked for new jobs — clearly only a transitory phenomenon.

The Classical presumption was that labour would not offer itself for employment if it did not wish to use the income so obtained to purchase what it had produced. This is the simplest version of Say's Law.[17] The other strand of the argument is that flexible prices are always able to eliminate excess demands or supplies — in this case an excess supply of labour. Thus the cause or causes of unemployment, and steps which might be taken to alleviate or correct it, were not questions of much interest to the Classical economists; they were chiefly concerned with the long run, not transitory fluctuations.

If an excess demand or supply is to be eliminated, whether by policy or by 'natural forces', it is plausible to look to the own-price to do it. The own-price of labour time is the 'real wage': the purchasing power, in terms of wage goods, of the money wage. The prices of wage goods are set as the outcome of a wide range of economic activities, with no direct link to the process of obtaining or agreeing to take a job. Hence attention becomes focused on the money wage as the adjusting variable. At any point of time, in any case, a change in the money wage *is* a change in the real wage.

So it is appealing to argue, that since unemployment meant that there must be an excess supply of labour, its price was too high. The wage, in terms of what it would buy, was higher than that necessary to obtain the work force actually employed; the real wage being greater than the marginal disutility of work, additional people sought work. When wages fell, as they were confidently expected to do, the disequilibrium situation would normally correct itself: the lower wages would simultaneously reduce the numbers of those seeking work and make it profitable to offer more jobs.

Belief in the automaticity of such an adjustment mechanism was challenged by the events in the UK of the 1920s and 30s.

Money wages fell drastically between 1920 and 1923[18] and real wages fell markedly less as a consequence of the government's deliberate policy of deflation in preparation for a return to the gold standard. It is plain from Table 1.1 that deflation of demand had more influence on unemployment rates than deflation of wages. After 1922, money wages steadied for eight years and fell only 6 per cent from 1930 to the trough in 1933–34. Real wages during this period, for those lucky enough to keep their jobs, were actually rising. (Observe column (2) of Table 1.1 carefully. It is difficult these days to take in the fact that prices can actually fall.)

Theory and Policy

The persistence of unemployment made it clear that something needed to be done. A good deal of the discussion [19] involved the question of whether the real wage was too high. Pigou believed this (1927), but was less sure that a policy to reduce the real wage could be carried through.

There are two ways for real wages to fall — either money wages fall or prices rise. On the face of it, either ought to work. Lower money wages mean lower costs to firms and cheaper labour ought to be more employable. And there is a certain logic to the view that disequilibrium in the labour market should be eliminated by altering the own-price of labour.

As a theoretical matter, Keynes questioned the validity of generalising the results of a single-market, partial-equilibrium approach to an aggregate such as 'the labour market'. Changes in real wages can be expected to have repercussions on other parts of the system and to be affected by variables which at first sight seem rather remote. One cannot look at the labour market in isolation.

As a practical matter, he argued that a policy of encouraging wage-reduction would not be as useful as the partial-equilibrium approach suggests and might even be counterproductive.

Keynes therefore proposed a radical change in perspective to one enquiring into the *causes* of changes in wages and prices. The components are the level of demand and costs, where labour income figures in both.

From this new perspective comes the astonishing conclusion that the chief cause of unemployment is not so much that the real wage is too high, but that the *rate of interest* is too high. What an implausible thing to say. What relationship could there possibly be between unemployment, the most human of problems, and the rate of interest, the driest of economic variables? That is a major theme of the *General Theory*. It derives directly from the clash of theory and events in the 1920s and 30s, and the new theory produced, in turn, the new policy prescriptions which are all many people understand by 'Keynesianism'.

Concentration on the immediate historical antecedents of the *General Theory* is not intended to suggest that the relevance of the theory is restricted to that time or to periods of unemployment generally. There would be insufficient justification for paying so much attention to it if this were true. In many ways it *is* 'depression economics' — ways which are often extremely subtle, ways which this book is at pains to point out, so that modifications may be made where necessary. But its scope is far broader than the short-period analysis of unemployment, as it is often characterised. It embodies a theory of cyclical fluctuations and their long-term consequences. Its analysis can be turned to the problem of inflation as well as depression.

Time, Uncertainty, Money and Say's Law

It is not, however, in the length of the list of problems to which the *General Theory* can be applied that the measure of its power lies. The primary purpose of the *General Theory*, and the chief justification for describing its message as a Revolution, was its destruction of Say's Law, the idea that there was no reason for production to stop short of the full-employment level and therefore unemployment was only a transitory phenomenon.

Keynes used money as the instrument to break Say's Law — or so, at any rate, it appears. It is in his insistence on a realistic basis to the theory of employment — labour is paid a money wage and can only *estimate* its real value — that he is most explicit about the repercussions for Say's Law. In reality, Keynes breaks Say's Law at *all* the points where households and firms interact — in the market for labour, through the saving-investment nexus, and in the market for output — and it is not really money that causes the trouble, but time — the sheer fact that commitments are based on *future* demands, costs and prices. These cannot be known for certain, but commitments must be made regardless.

The necessity for commitment is just as pressing in an economy that gets along without much use of money, and penalties for unwise production commitments are equally or more unpleasant. Money, in contrast, gives the *impression* of a fairly certain claim on resources. This illusion of security or liquidity heightens problems created by essential uncertainty by acting to disguise that uncertainty, to some degree, from market participants.

Money and delayed claims on money also give little indication of future wants.[20].

The philosophical niceties of pinpointing exactly what it was that broke Say's Law — money, time or uncertainty — were not really Keynes's concern. He was interested more in the disease of a particular economy, an industrial economy in which all three were present, and he took this reality as his starting point. The introduction of any one of them would have constituted a break with classical and neoclassical theory.

Money has been chosen as the culprit partly due to Keynes's own emphasis. He was writing, throughout, about an economy that was intensely monetary. All transactions with which he was concerned involve the use of money. That is not to say that barter, gifts and unpaid labour are of no economic significance; it is just that those transactions do not play a significant role in the problem at hand — the nature of the relations between producers and consumers, hirers and the hired, borrowers and lenders, and how those relations can create a situation which, while unsatisfactory to practically everyone, can be sustained virtually indefinitely.

Latter-day Keynesians have stressed the role of money in the labour market; the inflexibility of money wages is held responsible for Keynes's results. I shall argue that time is the key: that the *General Theory* is a static model of a dynamic process, the process of production. And it is as thoroughly monetary as the economy it attempts to explain. I shall show that the disruption caused by the impossibility, in the nature of things, of striking a real wage bargain is a mirror image of the dislocation caused by untimely attempts to save and by speculative action designed to enhance the value of one's wealth. Keynes's model leads one to conclude that when prices are uncertain, the sheer *fact* of a money-wage bargain could break Say's Law. Inequality of planned saving and investment (whatever that may mean) also breaks Say's Law. Exactly the same mechanism operates in the second case as in the first. The fact that saving takes place by declining to spend *money* on commodities, channelling it into financial assets instead, is just as crucial a fact as is the money-wage bargain.

In its preoccupation with 'real' magnitudes, modern 'Keynesian' macroeconomics has almost completely forgotten that money is also real: in a money economy the pursuit of income, profits and wealth all at some time take monetary form. 'Real' values are in the future, are uncertain, and can surprise.

Articles by the dozen are written wondering why plans of different economic agents fail to mesh. It would be astonishing if they did. The mystery is that the economy, viewed as a whole, does usually exhibit some kind of coherent — though not always attractive — behaviour.

Elaborating these remarks is the task ahead of me. But first we must look at the *method* Keynes used in his analysis, for it is the method which is the most robust of Keynes's creations in the *General Theory*. By understanding the method we stand a chance of retaining or recapturing the capacity to see the relevance of Keynes's reasoning to changed historical circumstances and to adapt it to events not yet foreseen.

Notes

1. The term 'capitalist' is used in a highly emotive fashion in some Marxist literature; however its technical usage refers to ownership of productive capital equipment by a group of persons not co-extensive with the group which works with that equipment to produce the economy's output. One antonym is 'cooperative', denoting a system in which workers jointly own the equipment. There is no obvious label for the state of affairs, only sustainable where the amount of capital is not large, in which every family owns its own means of production. Keynes calls the first an 'entrepreneur economy', the second a 'real-wage' or 'cooperative' economy. (*C.W.* XXIX, especially pp. 76–87)

2. This fact is acknowledged by Hicks (1980/81), who should know.

3. Brunner refers to this as 'lack of allocative detail'. See, e.g., Brunner (1970).

4. This description of 'the new macroeconomics' is Willem Buiter's (1980).

5. Marx (1867), p.128.

6. Producing to order is of course an exception to this, an exception which is more important in the capital-goods industries than in industries producing consumer goods, but not in Keynes's view important enough presumably, to require special treatment in the context of a theory of 'output as a whole'.

7. The *General Theory* was published in 1936, but the development of its ideas began as early as 1931. See the articles by Patinkin, Moggridge and Johnson in Patinkin and Leith (1977) and for a first-hand appreciation, browse in *C.W.* XIII.

8. Usually raised in connection with conversation with English-speaking people from other countries, but equally applicable in this context — 'The past is another country; they do things differently there'. (L.P. Hartley, *The Go-Between*)

9. For guidance, see Sowell (1972 and 1974) and Eshag (1963), as well as *C.W.* XIII.

10. His *Treatise on Money* (1931) and the early parts of *C.W.* XIII are the obvious things to consult.

11. The new version of orthodoxy constitutes *my* background, from which I in turn have had a long struggle of escape.

12. Whether the financial crisis caused the American depression of the 1930s or was merely a symptom of the American economy's underlying weakness is still a subject of considerable debate, but is not at issue here.

13. Friedman and Schwartz (1963), p. 2.

14. *Historical Statistics of the United States*, Table D46–47; US Bureau of the Census, *Statistical Abstract, Supplement.*

15. It is not the *only* outcome of Keynes's theory; there is no need to panic. Nor is there any need, by serious economists, to dismiss this analytical conclusion as a 'slogan' (Mayer, 1978).

16. Jevons was not prepared to leave these as random, but connected agricultural fluctuations to cyclical variations in solar activity (sunspots).

17. For a corrective to this simplification see Sowell (1972) and/or Baumol (1977).

18. Moggridge (1969), p. 16, using Routh's data (1965), says by almost 40 per cent. The data in Table 1.1 indicate somewhat less, but quite enough.

19. Hancock (1960) and Winch (1969) give interesting accounts.

20. Compare a bilateral claim on an individual's production of specific commodities which arise. Claims directly on commodites do not commit the creditor to final consumption of those commodities, but from the producer's point of view sales are virtually assured.

Chapter 2

THE METHOD OF THE GENERAL THEORY

The most difficult thing to grasp about the *General Theory* is its analytical method. So accustomed have we become to economic models consisting of a set of equations, with or without lags, to be manipulated to find their simultaneous solution, which we call equilibrium, that it is now virtually impossible to see what Keynes's method was. Much controversy exists, in print and in discussion papers, over whether Keynes's method was partial or general equilibrium, statics or dynamics, temporary equilibrium or disequilibrium. This controversy is taking place among economists whose conception of theory is firmly based on simultaneous equation systems, whether these be the supply and demand equations of Marshallian partial equilibrium or the grand design of General Equilibrium.

Neither of these methods would have served Keynes's purpose. His aim was to analyse the effects on the economy as a whole of a number of crucial decisions taken by individual firms and households, interacting. So partial equilibrium would not do. And for reasons that have now become evident, thanks to the insistence of Mrs Robinson and Professor Shackle and the admissions of Frank Hahn, general equilibrium would not do either.

It is even debatable whether the structure of his analysis should be called a method at all — it is rather in the nature of an expedient. Shackle's characterisation may be closest to the truth. He terms Keynes's method Kaleidostatics, trying to create an image of a method which freezes temporarily a continually shifting picture. A kaleidoscope's picture, however, changes randomly. Keynes's method is more like a film, a moving picture, made from snapshots (as films are), each snapshot systematically related to what has gone before. It is a story full of flashbacks — and flashes forward.

Subject Dictates Method

In both general and partial equilibrium the goods and services up for sale are many in number and each is viewed as relatively trivial from the standpoint of the economy as a whole. Marshall's method used this feature to analyse the behaviour of a single market, not allowing what happened in that market to impinge on the economy as a whole. This was the method that Keynes had been taught, but it was not suited to his purpose: to analyse markets where macroeconomic repercussions could not be ignored — the markets for labour, money, and major aggregates of produced commodities. Marshall's method was ruled out. General equilibrium was ruled out also, but not chiefly for its disaggregated nature — it was its freezing of *time* that would not do. The fundamental feature of a production economy, that production takes time and production decisions must be made in ignorance of the conditions which will prevail when the output comes to be sold, is removed from general equilibrium analysis. To Keynes, the necessity of producers to take a leap into an unknown future, committing resources as they go, was fundamental.

General equilibrium analysis embodies a principle essential to Keynes's subject: the concept of the interaction of economic decisions. Interaction places the analysis sharply at variance with the isolation of markets which characterised Marshall's method. Yet the abrogation of time and uncertainty in general equilibrium leave it incapable of explaining how an economy might exhibit fluctuations, except as a result of exogenous shocks. Such a result is appealing, psychologically — one can blame outside events — but that is neither healthy nor particularly useful, especially if it is not correct.

Keynes's method is something of a compromise, using the partial equilibrium method to analyse a market taken in isolation, then feeding the result back into the mainstream of economic events, which were themselves moving meanwhile. There is a distinct time-stream of events, in sharp contrast to general equilibrium, where everything happens at once, or partial equilibrium, where everything happens in the market being analysed and nothing is allowed to happen in other markets, while the economist's back is turned.

Consider as an analogy trying to explain the propulsion of a motor car. It is a valid method to explain first the steering mechanism, then the electrical system, and finally the pistons and drive shaft. In practice a car moves because of the interaction, more or less well-timed, of all these factors. But clarity is gained by describing major subsystems in isolation, recognising all the while that there is no point to a well-timed distributor and clean plugs if one is out of petrol and that it is useless knowing in principle how to steer the vehicle if it is not going anywhere. (The steering is different when the car is in motion than it is 'in principle', because of the camber of the roads on which the car is travelling.) Keynes proceeded in a similar fashion, analysing the main components of the economy and then fitting them together to give a theory of output as a whole. No one had done it quite like that before, and I daresay no one has done it since.

Statics, Dynamics and Process Analysis

The *General Theory* can hardly be said to be concerned with a static economy. Yet paradoxically the method used was statics. Mrs Robinson (1952) resolves the paradox thus: 'Past history is put into the initial conditions, so that the analysis is static in itself, and yet is part of a dynamic theory.'

Benavie (1972) has shown the formal relation between comparative statics and the discrete form of what is commonly understood by dynamic analysis, which incorporates various lags in the behavioural equations: it is the static method which is used to trace out the paths of the variables from their starting point to final equilibrium, period by period. The solution of the system for any given period may be called a temporary equilibrium — temporary because the inherent dynamics will move the system to another position in the next period.

Keynes could not use this form of dynamic analysis, however, for the lag structure he was attempting to describe and analyse was too complex; Keynes's system is one in which things happen at different speeds and behaviour may alter in response to events. The system cannot be conveyed all at once, in words any more than equations. Furthermore, standard dynamic analysis considers the effect of one change in an exogenous variable, allowing this change to work its way through to equilibrium on the basis of behavioural reactions which are represented by stable functions. For Keynes it was not enough to consider the effects of one change in 'the system', allowing this change to work its way through, for this would prevent the introduction of new information from other parts of the system as it progressed through time. Instead, events are permitted, sometimes, to create in their wake new initial conditions for subsequent periods, while conditions in markets which changed less often were fixed for a longer time. In those markets which are affected by the initial event, decisions are altered on the basis of outcomes along the way. This is the essence of process analysis. What Keynes created was an uneasy compromise between the method of comparative statics and the concerns of process dynamics.

Time Horizons

The choice of what to vary and what to keep constant was dictated by the different time horizons and speeds of adjustment inherent in the many decisions of an advanced capitalist economy. The time horizons appropriate to different conditions of production were well entrenched in Cambridge economics as part of the Marshallian tradition: production using the capital stock already in one's possession was called the short run. Opportunities to produce using an expanded or more efficient plant which would only be available some time in the future constituted the long run.

Although time is involved in obtaining new plant and equipment, these 'runs' should not be identified with a length of calendar time; the salient characteristic is the fixity of capital equipment in the short period from the point of view of production.

All production takes place in the short run: one must produce with the capital one has. One can, however, enquire at the same time whether this is the capital stock one wants, or whether one should take steps to alter it. The production decision and the investment decision are conceptually separate, although they may be taken simultaneously.

When an investment decision is made, equipment is ordered and building undertaken; these are contributions to demand, though current production cannot yet take advantage of the new capital's potential contribution to the efficiency of supply; that can only come later, when the capital goods have been produced, delivered to those who bought them, and installed. The first aspect of investment is entirely consistent with the short run. Later, when investment is allowed to affect cost conditions, the previous short-run conditions no longer obtain. Keynes's analysis (with the exception of Chapter 17, which is long-run) acknowledges the first, demand, aspect of investment and suppresses the latter, supply, aspect.

Perhaps it would be helpful to adopt the perspective of a producer of capital equipment. His firm gets orders: there is a demand for investment. The goods are produced with existing capital equipment. He is in the short run. His customers made their investment with regard to long-run profitability. When they install and use the equipment, they move through a portion of their long-run production possibilities to, somewhat paradoxically, another short run (because their equipment is once again fixed). The capital-goods producer may, meanwhile, improve his own plant as well.

In practice, of course, the capital stock is being altered continuously as earlier investment decisions reach fruition and ageing equipment wears out or is scrapped. So the long-run/short-run distinction cannot be made empirically; it is an intellectual device for preventing everything happening in time.[1]

The Marshallian distinction rests on the character of the production possibilities open to the entrepreneur. In Keynes, while the distinction is preserved, there co-exists another use of the terms short-run and long-run, in which they pertain to the horizon of the expectations that motivate production decisions and investment decisions respectively. Both decisions depend on estimates of future demand, but investment involves a long-term

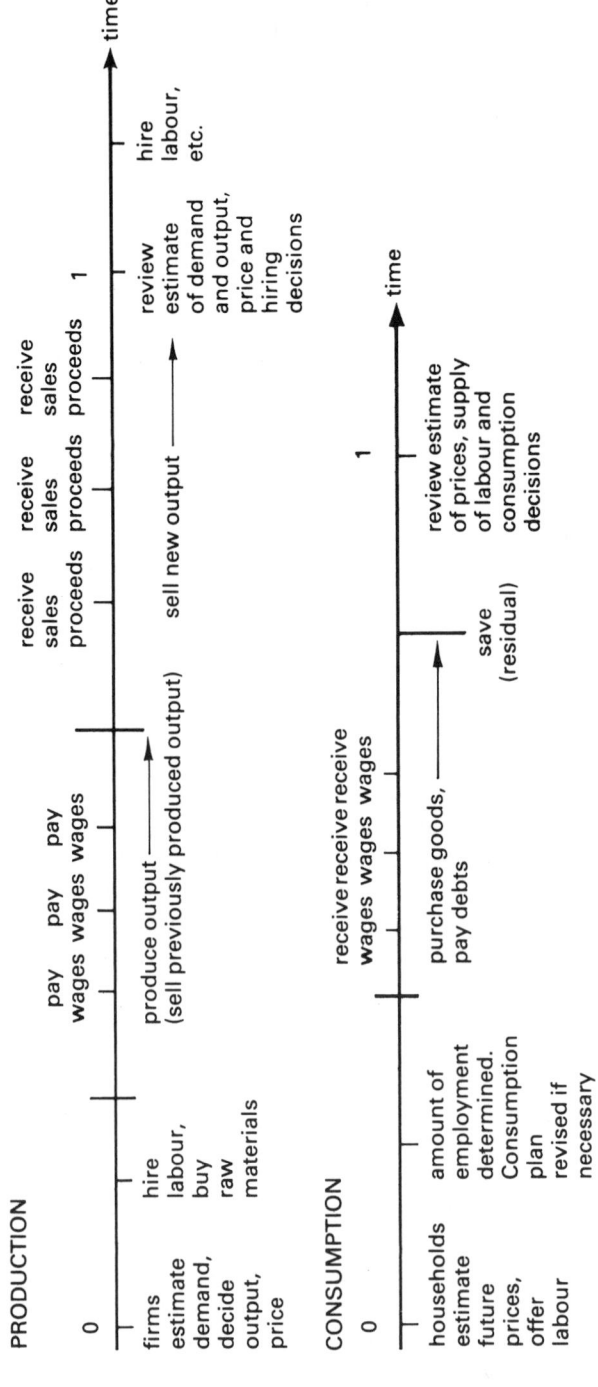

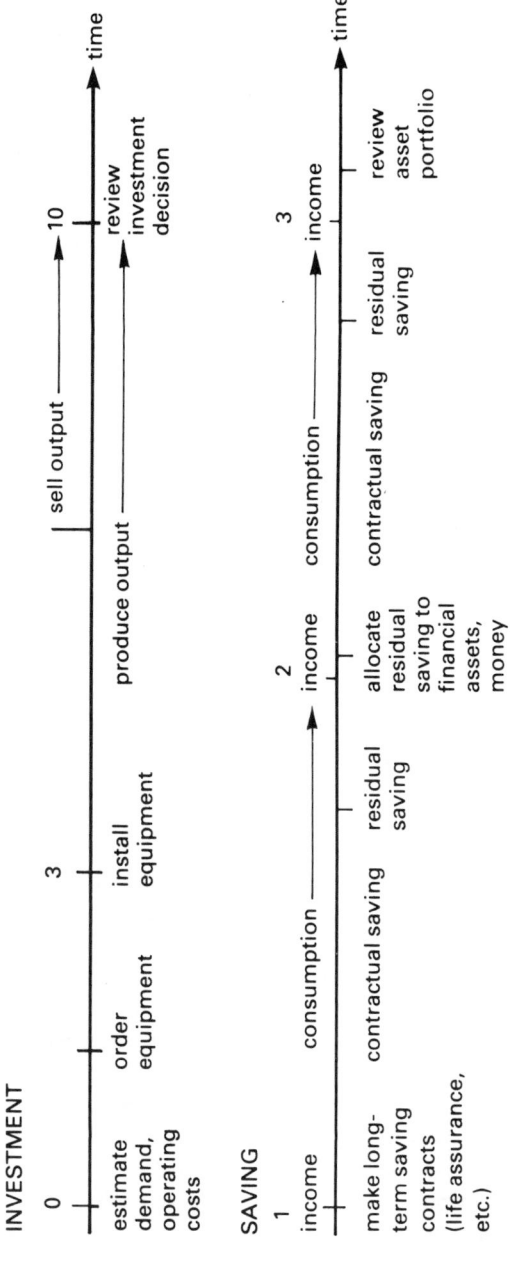

Figure 2.1

commitment to a plant with particular operating characteristics, including an optimal output. Meanwhile (in a shorter space of time), outputs may be varied by altering the variable factors which combine with capital to produce output: chiefly, labour.[2] Thus the expectations relevant to investment encompass many production decision-periods.

Let us formalise these ideas (a dangerous procedure) with the help of a diagram indicating, horizontally, the passage of time. Refer to the schemes labelled PRODUCTION and INVESTMENT in Figure 2.1. Let time begin at 0, with a board meeting to decide production levels and pricing policy and (as a corollary) labour needs. These policies must be based on an estimate of demand, and we take the horizon of that estimate as the length of what we shall call the *production period*, and to which we assign unit length: at time 1, these decisions are reviewed. The rest of the diagram should be self-explanatory, although it does not do justice to the overlapping nature of sales and wage payments.

The levels of demand and costs which must be estimated in making the investment decision are not those immediately ahead, but beginning only after the equipment is actually used in production (i.e. outside the confines of the short run) and lasting for the life of the equipment. In the figure, we have (arbitrarily) assumed that the gestation period encompasses three production periods and that the equipment lasts seven production periods (look for the numbers 3 and 10).

In terms of this scheme, Keynes's 'short-period expectations' pertain to sales expected at the end of the current production period and 'long-period expectations' refer to sales expected in periods 3 to 10.

Although Keynes did not make much explicit use of similar concepts for consumers, they also conduct their affairs with different time horizons in view. A life-time, or even inter-generational, horizon is appropriate to contractual savings arrangements and major capital expenditures (e.g. housing, training for an occupation) while the repetitive purchases of life are made, and plans concerning them changed, with much greater frequency. Keynes's concept of saving, which is essentially aggregative in character, is congruent with only the shorter-run aspects of individual saving, if it is congruent at all.[3] Aggregate saving in the *General Theory* is a residual from income after consumption. If this concept were applied to individual behaviour, it implies a sum saved as it were by accident which is then allocated chiefly among financial assets. No allowance is made for the pre-emptive quality of contractual saving, which limits the freedom with which current income can be disposed.[4]

The important horizons pertaining to consumer behaviour in the present context are the income period, which for most purposes it will be convenient to assume is the same length as the production period or shorter, and the asset-holding decision-period. In the figure, saving is allocated to assets according to a plan which is only re-evaluated after three income periods.

Exactly the opposite relationship between those two horizons pertains to a class of people called speculators, who review their asset portfolio many times within an income period.

Equilibrium

Keynes's method necessitates a rethinking of our notion of equilibrium. There are two concepts of equilibrium extant in economics:
1. Equilibrium is a point of rest; forces leading to change are either absent or countervailing.
2. Equilibrium is a point at which supply equals demand.

The second definition is a subset of the first. It pertains to the special cases in which either excess demand or excess supply creates a force leading to a change (e.g. in prices) which will eliminate the excess demand or supply, and the adjusting variable(s) will be stable when equality of supply and demand is established. In both a Marshallian single market and a Walrasian general equilibrium system the two definitions coincide.

The dominance of these two models has led to the conflation of the two concepts of equilibrium. The complete identification of equilibrium with the achievement of utility and profit maximisation is powerfully expressed by Hicks (1973):

> There is an equilibrium when all individuals are choosing the quantities, to produce and consume, which they prefer. To a conception of equilibrium that is of this type we must hold fast.[5]

It is a mistake however, so to identify equilibrium with universal profit and utility maximisation in the system devised by Keynes. The presumption that excess demand and excess supply constitute equally strong forces for change does not apply in the labour market, where firms decide at the beginning of the period how much employment to offer at the going wage, and labour is given no opportunity to recontract if at that wage fewer are employed than would like to be. Had recontracting been possible, firms might have preferred more labour at a lower wage, but the offer has been made and accepted by the fortunate. The rest go away unemployed, and there the position remains until entrepreneurs have reason to change their minds. If at the end of the production period entrepreneurs sell all the output they expect to sell, they will have no reason to change their minds. There is no change. That is a position of equilibrium, even though the marginal disutility of work lies well below the going wage, even though workers expected a higher level of employment.[6]

There will be disequilibrium if and only if the party whose expectations are falsified has power to *effect* change. If firms' expectations are disappointed — if they cannot get enough labour at the expected wage or their sales surprise them (in either direction) — wage and job offers will change at the next opportunity. That is disequilibrium.

Expectations and Equilibrium

It is clear from the above that expectations play a major role in determining equilibrium: when expectations are falsified there is a *desire* for change. Where that desire is combined with the power to effect changes we have disequilibrium. Which expectations *are* relevant *depends on the activity*. Hence equilibrium, which, like the 'period' or 'run', is an intellectual construct, is defined with reference to the constraints imposed in order to analyse the activity.

Equilibrium of prices, output and employment in the short run is defined in terms of the expectations of profit to be gained by production: expected demand and expected costs. The costs pertain to production with a given capital stock. Workers' expectations of reward for their labour affect the position of equilibrium if they affect firms' expected costs.

Equilibrium of output and prices, assuming labour is available at the wage expected, depends on the sales forecasts made at the beginning of the period being met at the end of the period. It follows that objective *evidence* that the decision made at $t = 0$ was an equilibrium decision requires observation of a firm's decisions at at least two points: the decision itself is observed at the beginning of a production period and the outcome is observed at the end.

In general, one would not wish to define equilibrium so precisely, and in a one-period context, for random variations in demand are bound to occur. Inventories are held to meet random variations, and revision of production decisions is likely to require considerably more evidence than one period's observation. Costs of adjustment may also delay adjustment, even where fluctuations are not random. It would be tedious to qualify every statement to allow for these factors; that burden is shifted onto the reader.

Equilibrium relating to the investment decision would imply, by analogy, that long-term expectations are met.[7] This does not figure in our story, for three reasons. One is that even if the relevant expectations were precise, they would take a long time to be confirmed or falsified. To consider them would require extending the analysis beyond the short run. The second is that these expectations cannot be judged before the new plant and equipment are working, by which time the firm can do little to reverse its decision (the doctrine of sunk costs notwithstanding). The third is that the success of an investment has little bearing on the calculation of whether to repeat it later on; too many factors will have changed in the interim.

The approach taken in this chapter to the definition of equilibrium in Keynes is rather different from the conventional wisdom, in which two equilibria are distinguished, not by the two activities production and investment, but rather as pertaining to stocks or flows. Evidence for equilibrium is that the values of the relevant variables are not changing. While net investment is positive — or negative — the capital stock is changing; therefore the economy cannot be in equilibrium in the sense that the magnitudes of all the variables, stocks as well as flows, are stationary. However, if one is *approaching* the desired capital stock at a rate such that the flow of saving equals the rate of investment, one could be said to be in flow equilibrium in the sense that the level of income — a flow variable — is not changing. This is what is usually understood by short-run equilibrium.

From this perspective, investment equilibrium in the sense of long-term expectations being satisfied actually pertains to the equilibrium capital stock, not the equilibrium rate of investment, and there is some point to that. However, that is not a debate we need to enter, for the important thing is that there is, within the time horizon of the short run, no question of ascertaining whether long-period expectations are met or not. If long-run expectations are underfulfilled, it is just hard luck; a pleasant surprise is no more useful: it comes too late. Stock equilibrium as defined by $\Delta K = 0$ is not at issue in the *General Theory*.

Organising one's ideas around stocks and flows might be thought harmless enough. But there is a significant difference between the equality of planned saving and planned investment and the equality of planned purchases and anticipated sales. Firms and their expectations (of sales) have no role to play in the former definition. There is the additional misfortune that Keynes's definitions of saving and investment are such as to make them identical (an old charge, revived here in Chapters 3 and 9), so that equilibrium and disequilibrium do not arise. A further consequence is that the borderline between the short and long runs is thought to be due to the quantitative insignificance of investment relative to the capital stock, which is to miss the point entirely.

Expectations and Models

Since producers have two sets of decisions to make, based on different expectations, one might predict that there would be different models to explain these things. There are, however, more than two possible models, for the two problems are not independent as regards the *explicandum*: the level of employment.

The models can be distinguished by what is being assumed about expectations. Kregel (1976) distinguishes three models as follows:
  (i) both short- and long-run expectations are stable. This implies that short-run expectations are met and that the economic and non-economic factors that influence long-term expectations are stable;
  (ii) long-run expectations are stable but short-period expectations may not be fulfilled;
  (iii) long-run expectations are not stable, either
    (a) because they are affected by disappointed short-period expectations, or
    (b) because the autonomous influences on them are changing.

Kregel (1976) calls (i) the static model, (ii) the stationary model, and (iii) the shifting model.

The first two models are really two aspects of the same problem: the determination of output and employment when the climate of long-term expectations is given. 'Model (i)' refers to the determination of equilibrium output and employment and 'Model (ii)' refers to adjustment to disequilibrium. Long-term expectations always impinge, because investment is determined by them, but it is important to prevent them from varying while analysing the influence of short-term expectations, or there will be too much happening for there to be a coherent result. Thus it is also important from the standpoint of the method of the *General Theory* that long-term expectations be allowed to persist unchanged even when shorter-term expectations are not met: it helps to preserve the separation of the short run and long run.

The independence of long-term expectations may also be reasonable empirically. It is a matter of common experience that the further into the future we attempt to forecast, the less we feel able to form specific judgements. It was Keynes's view that long-term investment proceeds more on hunch and gambling instinct than on precise calculation. This view might be extreme, but it is likely that the firm's expectations will be based more on forecasts of the general state of the economy or industry and its foreign competition than on specific levels of demand twenty years hence, and that the factors that enter into the forecasts and the evaluation of them will include non-economic and subjective factors. Sales results in the recent past may not have much effect.

Short-term expectations can and must be more precise: these expectations are constantly tested. If these results were always allowed to affect long-run demand forecasts and thus investment decisions, little investment would ever get done. In the jargon, the investment function would be highly unstable.

It may, however, not always be useful to maintain separation, but to permit long-term expectations to be affected by surprises to short-term expectations (Model iii(a)), or to permit exogenous variations in long-term expectations (Model iii(b)), so that the effects on output and employment might be analysed.

It is in the 'shifting model' (Model iii) that investment is allowed the volatile behaviour which some would say was the essence of Keynes's theory. But all three sets of assumptions are in fact important to the analysis.

Characterisation of the Firm

Firms' decisions are central to the *General Theory*. A fairly lengthy discussion of the sort of firm assumed is necessary, for Keynes's representative firm is an anomaly from the point of view of established thinking: it is a small 'polypolistic' or atomistic firm which operates under uncertainty and therefore is not a price taker.

Interpreters and commentators have often expressed dismay at Keynes's choice of the small firm on the empirical grounds that the market situation described by perfect competition exists, if at all, only rarely, e.g. on the stock exchange or the primary commodity markets (wheat, cocoa, etc.). Others wish, implicitly or otherwise, to deny the small-firm basis of the *General Theory,* because of the association of this market form with models which only hold in a static, timeless equilibrium and perfect knowledge or foresight. These models are not at all congruent with Keynes's analysis or his concept of equilibrium and are unable to produce 'underemployment equilibrium', a possible outcome (indeed Keynes thought the most *likely* outcome) of the General Theory of employment.

Even though the small firm is no longer the dominant market form, it is well that Keynes took it as his model, for in doing so he met the neoclassical theory on its own ground. Only the assumption of perfect knowledge was changed. Those who wish to claim greater realism for the theory by introducing monopolistic elements into it do not seem to recognise that by doing so they undermine the power of Keynes's argument: Keynes showed that, even *taking the assumption* of neoclassical analysis, he could produce non-neoclassical results. Monopoly elements then strengthen the argument, but the argument does not depend on them.

The choice of a polypolistic market has aroused great *puzzlement:* how can the theory be based on the small firm, yet be a theory about the consequences of producing when the market for output is *uncertain?*[8] In the usual representation of the small firm, once the price is determined, there is no uncertainty about the marketability of output at that price. Price *represents* demand in this system, and having been 'given' the price by the market, there is no need for firms to forecast demand. It is 'known'. The only decision that firms must make is how much output to produce, and that decision is made on the basis of costs which are also presumed to be known, given the wage and a known technology.

This story is coherent in a world where prices are stable and have been stable for quite some time — in other words, if we have and have had equilibrium. However, unless the assumption of perfect knowledge or foresight is made, the prices, or demands, firms face cannot be treated as known or given if market demand is liable to change — for the information has to be collected afresh every time a change is a possibility. Modern theory adopts the assumption of perfect foresight, often implicitly, thus appearing to legitimise the use of the theory for the analysis of changes in demand. But Keynes insisted that the fundamental feature of production was the necessity of committing resources to production for a market which in the nature of things exists in the future and is therefore uncertain. The

assumption of perfect foresight would rob the *General Theory* both of its
subject and of its major contribution, for the difference of its conclusions
from those of neoclassical analysis stems from the properties of production
under uncertainty.

So, how does a small firm which is *not* a price-taker behave? Inescapably,
it must form *expectations* of the demand for its product (short-run
expectations). The expected position of the demand curve it faces in the near
future will determine the price it should set for its product and the quantity it
should produce. The estimated (expected) demand curve for the firm may
be drawn as horizontal,[9] just like the demand curve of the price-taker.[10] The
only difference is that the curve is based on expectations, both of market
demand and of other firms' supply responses. The latter is necessary for
determining the position of the industry supply curve. If consumers are
indifferent as to their sources of supply and other firms forecast the 'correct'
price, then for a firm that sets the price too high actual sales are zero that
period and the price and output are subsequently revised. If it sets the price
too low, it sells its entire production and such stocks as it may have. The
unexpected change in stocks and perhaps other information not involving
actual sales, e.g. number of enquiries, customers turned away, etc., give a
signal to change the price-output strategy subsequently. These are outcomes
and do not determine production within the period.

The implications of this model of the firm and associated problems of
aggregation will be raised again in Chapters 3 and 5.

The Role of Empirical Judgement

Every theory is based, at its roots, on empirical judgement. One tends to
forget this: so antiseptic has theory become that it is natural to acquiesce to
the view that the demand and supply functions that characterise our models
are derived from rational behaviour postulates with no intervention on the
part of the economist except to discover what rational behaviour entails.
Empirical work is then channelled into evaluating the quantitative
importance of the variables which enter the equations. Empirical judgement
in fact enters much earlier: the very choice of aggregates, on which the
formal structure of macroeconomics depends, must be decided on empirical
grounds.

There are no rules to guide one's choice of significant aggregates. The
General Theory is based on the belief, derived from observation, that the
interaction of employers and employed, producers and consumers, is what
drives the economy along its path, for good or ill. The division of output into
two commodity aggregates, consumption and investment, though dictated
more by the speed which sales expectations would be falsified, also
conveniently fits the sectoral division between households and firms, as we

shall see later.

The choice of aggregates is fundamental, but there are two other empirical assumptions, two key points on which the argument of the *General Theory* is based: that capital is not, and will not in the foreseeable future, be abundant, and that while producers can always get the labour they require, workers can take no action to promote their own employment. Without these assumptions the argument of the *General Theory* might have been lost in taxonomy; it is these assumptions that permitted the number of possibilities left open by the theory's sequential nature to be cut down to a manageable size.

These are assumptions particularly well suited to the period within which Keynes was writing. In present day conditions, the relevance of both assumptions can be (and has been) questioned. The emergence of periods of scarce labour and the practice of labour hoarding, not to mention labour's increased bargaining power and government's concern with levels of employment, surely require a re-examination of the theory of wages and employment in the *General Theory*. This has, of course, been done by specialists in that subject. What is missing is the integration of their ideas into macroeconomic theory.

Less easy to assess is the abundance of capital. To my eye, it is becoming increasingly obvious that while capital as a whole (whatever that may mean) may yet be less than optimal (however defined), certain forms of investment have now become unduly wasteful methods of maintaining the level of economic activity.

Without demonstrating the role of these assumptions in the *General Theory*, my statement that they are crucial can be no more than assertion. The point is made at this early stage to alert the reader to what follows, not to convince him — yet.

Style and Structure

The *General Theory* is a complicated and subtle book, covering vast territory in remarkably few pages. Keynes did not regale his reader with long lists of assumptions and qualifications — they are often dealt with in a mere phrase. And ideas which have developed into major areas of research are dealt with in a sentence or two; for example, the distinction between short-run and long-run consumption behaviour, later developed at length by Duesenberry (1959) and Friedman (1957), is the subject of a short paragraph (p. 97). A somewhat elliptical style was, Keynes thought, inevitable:

> It is, I think, of the essential nature of economic exposition that it gives, not a complete statement, which, even if it were possible, would be prolix and complicated to the point of obscurity but a sample statement, so to speak, out of

all the things which could be said, intended to suggest to the reader the whole bundle of associated ideas, so that, if he catches the bundle, he will not in the least be confused or impeded by the technical incompleteness of the mere words which the author has written down, taken by themselves.

(*C.W.* XIII, p. 470)

There may be still more to it than that. Fouraker (1958) has argued that Keynes shared with Marshall the desire to reach a wider, non-academic public, who would be put off by lengthy proofs and lists of qualifications. With this in view, Fouraker says:

... they employed a curious device when it came to recording the results of their pursuits. Instead of leading the reader through the intricate analytical processes that their own minds had recently traversed, they would provide a short cut, in the form of an assumption whose purpose was to eliminate consideration of the difficult problem they had faced and solved.

(p. 66)

And Shackle (1961) comments: 'If all Keynes's critics had possessed Mr. Fouraker's insight, what seas of ink could have been saved.'

Indeed. However, it is not right to take an author on faith. It is therefore incumbent on the reader to satisfy himself that the problem *was* faced, and solved correctly. Much of past controversy and of the present book is concerned with these gaps, and at times, I fear, the latter illustrates Keynes's remark about exposition 'prolix and complicated to the point of obscurity'. On the other hand, it is well to remember that logic is never enough: continuing the earlier passage Keynes goes on:

[A]n economic writer requires from his reader much goodwill and intelligence and a large measure of co-operation; ... there are a thousand futile, yet verbally legitimate, objections which an objector can raise.
... [I]f there is a defect in your own powers of persuasion and exposition or if his head is already ... filled with contrary notions ... he cannot catch the clues to your thought which you are trying to throw to him.

(loc. cit.)

The economic system is a devilish thing to write about, whoever your audience, because the parts are interconnected but have to be analysed or described in sequence, as one word follows another. Earlier I drew on the analogy of a motor car, but to make clear the structure of the *General Theory,* it might be helpful to compare the book to a play. When characters go off-stage in the theatre, you do not presume them to be dead — they are likely to pop back at any time. The *General Theory* is rather like that. Early on (*G.T.* Chapter 3) you are given a sketch of the plot, but it is only much later (*G.T.* Chapters 19–21) that the full story is revealed. For those brave enough to read the *General Theory* for themselves (and how else can you evaluate what I say about it?), Table 2.1 is your playbill. The present book follows a similar structure.

Table 2.1
The *General Theory*: Synopsis

The *General Theory* can be likened to a lengthy and complex play, with many changes of scene. While action proceeds in one area of the economy, the rest is held off-stage. The actors enter and leave the stage, dominating one scene, absent from the next. Finally, in Chapter 18, the whole cast is on-stage, the elements of the plot pulled together. The next three chapters take up questions which the structure of the exposition required to be left aside until the 'whole story was out'. The following scheme is an attempt to clarify the structure of the book by defining the spheres of action (scenes) and the subject matter (action) of each chapter. An alternative is to look upon Book I (Chapters 1 to 3) as a trailer (though compulsory even for those prepared to watch the full show) and Book II (Chapters 4 to 7) as the prologue, the main action beginning in Book III.

Chapter; Section	Dramatis Personae	Scene	Action	Backdrop (Assumptions and things kept constant)
1: The General Theory			PROLOGUE	
2: The Postulates of the Classical Economics	Entrepreneurs and Workers	The Labour Market	Involuntary unemployment; The supply of labour	Perfect competition (mainly) Given organisation, equipment and technique
3: The Principle of Effective Demand	Entrepreneurs	The Board Room	The determination of output and offers of employment	Given technique, resources, and factor costs per unit
4: The Choice of Units			INTERLUDE (The audience to remain in their seats)	
5: Expectation as Determining Output and Employment	Entrepreneurs	The Board Room	Formulation and revision of expectations. How changes in expectations affect output and employment	

Chapter; Section	Dramatis Personae	Scene	Action	Backdrop (Assumptions and things kept constant)
6: The Definition of Income, Saving and Investment				
7: Saving and Investment, Further Considered				
SECOND INTERLUDE (The audience to remain in their seats)				
8: The Propensity to Consume: I				
I, II	Workers and Rentiers	Private households	Consumption plans	The labour market has not yet opened; income is hypothetical
III, IV	Full cast	The economy as a whole	The multiplier; net and gross investment and income	Given rate of investment
9: The Propensity to Consume: II				
I	Workers and Rentiers	Private households	Consumption plans	
II	Full cast	The Economy	The effect on saving and investment of an income-induced change in the rate of interest	mec constant
10: The Mpc and the Multiplier				
I-III	Entrepreneurs, Consumers	Goods and Labour markets	The multiplier effects of changing rates of investment	Consumption and investment goods industries advance together.
IV			Changes in the relative prices of consumption and investment goods	Investment rises, but not consumer-goods output

V	Consumers	Households	The marginal propensity to consume in boom and slump	Given market rates of interest
VI	Government	Whitehall, Threadneedle Street	Policies to counter unemployment	
11: The Marginal Efficiency of Capital	Entrepreneurs, Engineers, Sales Forecasters	The Board Room	The Investment Decision	The rate of interest is given
12: Long-term Expectation	Investors and Speculators	Stock Market	Evaluation of long-term prospects; speculation. Short-period changes in long-term expectations	
13: The Rate of Interest	Households	Banks, the Bond Market	Liquidity preference and the rate of interest	Given expected profits (*mec* given). Given normal rate of interest. Given level of financial wealth
14: The Classical Theory of the Rate of Interest		A DIVERSION (An Interval may be taken)		
15: Incentives to Liquidity	Speculators and Investors	Markets for financial assets	An examination of motives: speculation and liquidity preference	Financial wealth, the supply of money, and the rate of saving are given
16: On the Nature of Capital I, II	Savers, Entrepreneurs	Markets for consumption and investment goods	Thrift, capital accumulation	
III, IV			Euthansia of the rentier	

Chapter; Section	Dramatis Personae	Scene	Action	Backdrop (Assumptions and things kept constant)
17: The Essential Properties of Interest and Money				The long run
		EXCURSUS		
18: The General Theory Restated	Full cast	All markets	Output and employment	The state of the arts, resources, and the degree of competition are given
19: Changes in Money Wages	Labour and Entrepreneurs	The Labour and goods markets. The 'money market'	Changes in money wages and some remarks on income distribution	
		A DIVERSION		
Appendix				
20: The Employment Function				
I, II	Labour and	The Economy	Employment	No capacity constraints
III	Entrepreneurs (not clearly visible)		Employment and prices. 'True inflation'	Full capacity
IV			Asymmetry between inflation and deflation	
21: The Theory of Prices	Full Cast, off-stage	The Economy	Prices	
22: Notes on the Trade Cycle				
23: Notes on Mercantilism, etc.				
24: Notes on the Social Philosophy				
		THREE EPILOGUES		

Notes

1. Cf. 'Time is a device for preventing everything happening at once' (Bergson).

2. Labour is traditionally contrasted with capital on the grounds that firms have no long-term commitment to labour. Since the Second World War this contrast has become less marked than even in Keynes's time and certainly than before the 1914–18 War. Both social conscience and union pressure for severance pay have given labour more of the attributes of fixed factors. Employment may be expected to be less closely related to variations in output as a result; particularly in temporary downturns firms may simply carry the excess labour. But employment figures do vary with the level of economic activity. The distinction is not entirely useless yet.

3. See Chapters 3 and 9.

4. The saving behaviour of different social classes was very much more marked in Keynes's day; my remarks, treating households as if they conformed to some roughly middle-class norm, are to a considerable extent inappropriate to the 1930s, when working-class households' access to financial assets was very limited in range, if those households managed to save at all.

5. 'Equilibrium' conveys misleading overtones of a satisfactory state of affairs: everyone is getting what he 'prefers'. But to let us not forget that all transactors are maximising subject to *constraints* — in Walras, their initial wealth (including human wealth), in Marshall income. (Note that Hicks does not mention these constraints.) For the situation to be truly satisfactory, transactors must, at some level, accept the constraints within which they are operating. It is not helpful to a peasant scratching a subsistence from poor soil on the edge of a rich land-owner's estate to know that he is doing the best he can with what he has, unless he accepts his lot. If he and others like him do not accept it, then the system may be poised on the edge of a very profound disequilibrium indeed.

6. These assertions are substantiated in Chapter 7.

7. This is the subject of Classical theory. The criterion of long-run equilibrium is that profit rates in different uses of capital resources must be equalised, otherwise the allocation of these resources to different kinds of production will change. Hence modern classicists (Garegnani, Eatwell) insist that the *General Theory* says nothing about equilibrium, for this is the only equilibrium they acknowledge.

8. See, for example, the discussion and the paper by Hahn at the Conference on the Microfoundations of Macroeconomics (Harcourt, 1977), for the sense of incongruity of these ideas.

9. Strictly, the curve consists of two discontinuous segments, a vertical segment along the zero axis above the correct price and the market curve below, connected, if one must, by a dotted horizontal line. The horizontal demand curve is a misrepresentation of demand, which states the *maximum* amount demanded at each price.

10. Arrow (1959) handles the problem differently. He describes the firm out of equilibrium (i.e. not at the market-clearing price) as having a degree of 'monopoly power', because it has some control over prices. This reflects the identification of polypoly with price-taking, referred to earlier, and obscures the issues arising from the uncertainty inherent in production for market sale.

Chapter 3

THE AGGREGATIVE
FRAMEWORK

A modern industrial economy presents a chaotic appearance. A multitude of businesses, under a variety of legal arrangements and market structures, produce commodities and services of every description. These are bought by households, other firms, institutions, governmental authorities. A complex financial system which facilitates the finance of these purchases has evolved. The process by which decisions are made within any one of these institutions — even a single household — is complex and subtle, and a study of the system as a whole is concerned with all of them and their many interactions. Clearly a simplifying device is essential: aggregation.

The appropriateness of a choice of aggregates depends on the purpose which it will serve: the basis of aggregation is some useful unifying principle, inherent in the characteristics or the behaviour of the things or actors to be aggregated.

There are two dimensions of aggregation in the *General Theory,* and these are not unconnected: there is aggregation by type of economic unit, and aggregation by type of product. The aggregates are neither precise nor exhaustive: they are instead *suggestive,* of the most significant features of an industrialised, capitalist, Western economy. Each dimension of aggregation highlights an important feature of such an economy: the basis of the first type of aggregation is the unit's economic *function*, ultimately resting on the ownership structure; the basis of the second lies in the role of the goods in question — whether they satisfy the wants of households or whether they are instrumental in providing for those wants. And there are further salient characteristics which will come out in the discussion which follows.

The Aggregation of Economic Agents

In capitalist economies, production and consumption activities are separated; production is carried out by specialist institutions to which people hire out their labour and from which perhaps through the mediation of wholesalers and retailers, they buy the output. This arrangement reflects the form of organisation of productive activity in which the control of the means of production is vested in fewer hands than those who engage in production. The single proprietorship or partnership was the earlier form of capitalist ownership, now superseded by the joint stock company. The joint stock company, or corporation, owns capital equipment and makes production and investment decisions with the (usually nominal) approval of its shareholders who, collectively, are the ultimate owners of the company through the claims represented by their equity shares. The aggregation of economic agents is chosen such that the likely response of members of an 'aggregate' to various economic incentives will display more similarity than difference. In a capitalist system, households are consumers of goods and sellers of labour, while the chief concern of business firms is production. These two groups are the basic aggregates of Keynes's system.

There are potential ambiguities, such as how to treat the owner of a firm, entrepreneur at work and consumer at home. These two activities are treated, in effect, as independent: the subtleties of the difference between consumption financed from business profits and from labour income, while important in Keynes's *Treatise on Money* (1930) and made much use of in the post-Keynesian theory of income distribution and growth,[1] does not figure prominently in the *General Theory*. And there are additional aggregates, which become important from time to time as the theory unfolds: government, of course, when questions of policy are raised, and speculators and rentiers,[2] when discussing the rate of interest. But the main elements of the theory are based on the aggregates of households and firms.

Their chief differences can be portrayed in a balance sheet and an income statement for a typical member of each aggregate. The balance sheet indicates ownership structure and the limitations on action that this imposes. Firms are distinguished by their ownership of productive capital. They cannot own labour services, for the 'ownership' of labour is vested solely in the individual. Households, on the other hand, own labour but can only provide direct services or engage in 'cottage industry' forms of production which require little capital. In an industrial society, therefore, households' chief source of income is the rental of their labour. The results of the two groups' activities are indicated in their income statements. These follow as Tables 3.1 and 3.2.

Table 3.1
Balance Sheets

Balance Sheet of a Firm		*Balance Sheet of a Household*	
bank loans	cash	overdraft	cash
bonds (debentures)	bank deposits	unpaid portion of mortgage	bank deposit
wages and other accounts payable	liquid assets e.g. Govt. bonds	other outstanding consumer credit	accounts receivable (chiefly accrued wages)
	stocks of raw materials		
Total Liabilities	work in progress	Total Liabilities	life assurance
	stocks of finished goods		equity shares
	capital equipment		other financial assets
	plant and office premises		clothing
			household maintenance equipment
Assets less Liabilities	Total Assets		consumer durables e.g. furniture, car
= NET WORTH			house
			the 'human capital' of members of the household
			Total Assets

Table 3.2
Income Statements

Income Statement of a Firm*	Income Statement of a Household
Sales of finished product	Labour income
less labour and raw material costs	Income from rent, interest etc.
maintenance and replacement	
(actual expenditures)	
	Total income
indirect taxes	less interest payments
	income tax
Gross profits	contractual saving
less interest and rent	
depreciation	Discretionary income
	less current consumption
Profits before tax	
less dividends	Residual (non-contractual saving)
profits tax	
Retained profits	

* This income statement follows accounting principles; its structure differs significantly from the methods used to define profits later in this chapter.

Aggregates and Decentralised Decisions

Aggregation, though a powerful simplifying device, is somewhat at variance with the facts of an economy in which decisions are taken by individual firms and consumers. Aggregates are to be chosen for the similarity of their constituents in some way deemed to be significant. In aggregation by agent the constituents have similar interests and may be expected to react in similar ways to the same stimulus — say to a fall in the rate of interest or a rise in expected demand. Although aggregation implies a kind of coherence, it emphatically does *not* imply collusion or even consultation. The postulated similarity of behaviour is only approximate: it only needs to be similar for agents within an aggregate in comparison to the behaviour of agents across aggregates.

The relationship of the observed behaviour of an aggregate like Firms or Households is not easily related to the plans or actions of its component agents.[3] One problem arises from the potential conflicts between agents within an aggregate, for, obviously, the behaviour of the aggregate will depend on the manner in which those conflicts are resolved. (In the absence of the impossibly detailed information required, some simplifying assumptions can be made.) Nevertheless, a great deal can be done to relate the aggregate behaviour to decision processes: Chapters 5, 6 and 10 will be concerned with this question. Just now, there is a need to explore the general principle involved.

Consider an example: suppose households budget for the coming year to spend some fraction of their expected income during the year. Since the year is in the future, there is nothing that guarantees that income: even if the wage or salary bargain is firm, the earner may die or some other disaster befall. But let us just suppose that all incomes *are* guaranteed. There is still nothing to guarantee that at the prices they expect to pay, the goods that all these households have decided to buy will in fact be available. Since households do not make their plans in consultation, there is no reason to expect that all plans can be met. If not, households will find themselves competing for goods, which may be rationed or their prices may rise. If goods are rationed, *actual* aggregate consumption in both real and money terms will be determined not by the plans of the demanders but by supply. If prices rise to clear the market, some purchasers drop out and others pay more than they had anticipated: the money *spent* on goods may be given by the aggregate of households' plans, if when faced with unexpectedly high prices they adjust their *real* consumption to somewhere else on their demand schedules. The amount of aggregate real consumption originally planned, a single quantity, is irrelevant because it was formulated on the assumption that yesterday's prices would prevail.[4]

If in the same situation the excess demand were resolved by rationing, the outcome bears *no* relation to consumers' plans, rather it is determined by supply.

So we see that unless the plans of the decision-makers comprising an aggregate are in perfect harmony with each other (which would only be accidental) the aggregate outcome cannot be inferred from — in particular does not equal the sum of — individuals' plans. Some plans, certainly in real terms and possibly in money terms, will be frustrated.

What meaning should we attach, then, to 'planned aggregate output' or 'planned aggregate consumption' if these magnitudes cannot be related to the sum of individual agents' plans except when the plans do not conflict? A satisfactory answer to this question does not seem to exist at the conceptual level. At the practical level however, if it is assumed that the intra-aggregate conflict is far less important than the conflict between aggregates, aggregate planned magnitudes may still be related to the plans of a *representative* member of the aggregate. Indeed, it is the art of aggregation to choose aggregates for which the above condition holds, so that the important interaction is between the chosen sectors.

Aggregation and the Theory of the Firm

Problems of reconciling individual and aggregate consumption are minor when compared to the difficulties posed for the theory of the firm. It does no great violence to common sense to assume that consumers make their plans 'atomistically', though as we have just seen, the aggregate behaviour ignores any conflict arising from the attempt to implement those plans without regard for the probable impact of other consumers' purchases on the market. In the context of the small firm, which Keynes adopted, the identical problem exists and is immediately visible in the graphical exposition of the theory of the atomistic firm. A moment's reflection reveals that the individual firms' demand curves are *derived* from the market outcome and that the process *cannot be reversed:* the sum of many horizontal demand curves does not give the downward-sloping market curve!

Similarly, an individual firm may face a perfectly elastic supply — of labour, of raw materials, of capital equipment (especially things not made to order), of borrowed funds. One cannot infer from that, however, that the aggregate supplies of those things are price-invariant. This is an exact analogue of the consumer problem.

The demand example is more complex. The horizontal demand curve is said to arise from the fact that small firms can sell all they like without affecting their competitors or the market price. Strictly speaking, however, the theory of perfect competition does not say that, and it is important to see clearly what it does say.

The standard theory of perfect competition says that once the equilibrium price is established, firms can sell all they like without altering that equilibrium, where 'all they like' *is already determined* for the industry as a whole and is taken into account in deriving that equilibrium price. It is true that the supply curve of each firm is based on an answer to the question, 'What is the most you would be willing to sell at each possible hypothetical price *assuming* you could sell all you supplied' — the small-firm assumption. Then the aggregate of the answers to this question, the 'market supply curve', is confronted with demand as determined by consumers and the actual price which will clear the market is found. This price determines the *level* at which the demand facing each firm, which the individual producer perceives as perfectly elastic, is supposed to be established by 'market forces'. In contrast to reality, where even small firms are not price-takers, perfectly-competitive (i.e. perfectly-informed) firms need not make assessments of other firms' likely supplies at each price, and hence how much of the market is left over for them, because (but only because) this information in effect is collected by some Almighty Accountant and distributed to all firms as 'the equilibrium price', or the level of demand. Firms' output responses to this demand wait, as it were, until all the returns are in: sales are assured.

So, it is no good pretending that the theory of the perfectly-competitive firm is free from assumptions about supply responses of other firms. This fact will create difficulty in dealing, as we must, with atomistic firms which do not have perfect information, but it should salve our conscience when we assert (in Chapter 5) the theoretical validity of supply curves for less-than-perfect competitors. It is usually said that interaction between firms rules out a supply curve for firms which are not independent of each other (as small firms are supposed to be). But as it happens there is nothing special about market forms for which interdependence has always been recognised; the atomistic firm, once price-taking is seen for what it is — the consequence of an assumption of full information — poses exactly similar problems once the assumption is dropped and uncertainty introduced.

Commodity and Financial Aggregates

The second dimension of aggregation in the *General Theory* — and in postwar interpretations the dominant dimension — rests on the properties of *things*. An advanced economy deals in two types of 'things': goods and financial assets. Goods are distinguished from financial assets by the property that their production and sale generates income. In Keynesian textbooks goods are broken down into two aggregates, Consumption and Investment. These words actually refer to *processes* — the acts of consumption and investment. The acts involve the things that households buy and the things producers buy, respectively; hence the connection of the acts with things. There is also an obvious relationship to the first scheme of aggregation.

Sales of financial assets, in contrast, do not generate incomes;[5] they are dealings in various sorts of *claims*. They involve the transfer of purchasing power from one person or firm to another. Viewed from the point of view of the issuer, these instruments are claims on the issuer's ability to generate income; to him they are a liability, entered into because the expected profitability of money borrowed by means of the sale of these instruments exceeds the costs of such borrowing. Insofar as the act of borrowing (or increasing the outstanding volume of financial claims) results in increased production, there will be increased income, but the increase will be counted on the 'real' side, as output of consumption or investment goods. Variations in the outstanding stock of these assets are not, therefore, included in aggregate income.

In Keynes's framework, the crucial distinction to be drawn amongst financial assets is between an asset or group of assets whose aggregate supply is not controlled by either households or firms and whose value is not affected by variations in interest rates, and claims on future sums of money, which bear interest[6] and whose market value[7] varies with the rate of interest.[8]

The above remarks constitute only an introduction; a further discussion of the significance of these aggregates awaits the further exploration of the concept of income which now follows.

Income and its Components

Income and its component aggregates, consumption and investment, are central concepts in macroeconomics, though they commonly receive far less attention than they deserve. The lack of discussion is particularly regrettable since there are several competing concepts of income about; in the absence of debate about them the relevant place of each has become obscure. After reviewing some of the complexities involved in defining these aggregates, one may sympathise with Marshall, who 'decided to take refuge in the practices of the Income Tax Commissioners and — broadly speaking — to regard as income whatever they, with their experience, chose to treat as such' (*G.T.* p. 59).

The first problem to tackle is that of perspective: several perspectives are possible.

    (i) One may take an eagle's-eye view; from that perspective income is usually thought of as the sum of newly produced goods available to be distributed amongst the community (whether through markets or by other means).

    (ii) There is the matter of what the individual perceives as his income. (ii) may be sharply at variance with (i).

    (iii) One may relate income to motivation. This is the perspective of (*G.T.*) Chapter 6, where, although income is defined as an aggregate, its reference point is the *motivating force* of the two sectors — households and firms.

The Eagle's Perspective

When taking a macroeconomic overview of the concept of income, the first thing to say is that none of the theoretical notions we shall review bears a close resemblance to National Income statistics. These *ex post* data have their uses but not for forming concepts; the concepts come first and the data approximate (well or badly) to them.

Traditionally, income has been defined with reference to wealth:[9] income is that which may be consumed while leaving wealth intact. This definition only shifts the burden onto what is meant by wealth and consumption. A number of possibilities are outlined in Table 3.3. Let us concern ourselves first with consumption.

Perhaps the most intuitive notion of consumption is 'that which is used up' or physically disappears, as food is consumed when eaten. This idea of

Table 3.3
Concepts of Income and Wealth

	'Utility' Approach	*'Durability' Approach*	*'Productivity' Approach*	*'Sectoral' Approach*
WEALTH	The aggregate of existing goods, infrastructure, etc. which yield utility directly or which can be used to produce other goods which do yield utility to final consumers. Usually includes human wealth and the stock of knowledge. May also include such intangibles as the social structure.	Actual physical stocks, not used up at the end of the period, of all final and intermediate goods, whether in the hands of final consumers or of producers.	Physical stocks of raw materials, capital equipment and buildings used to produce final goods. Could include infrastructure. Valuation would take account of expected sales of the output; may become obsolete (valueless) before wearing out.	Value of the stocks of capital equipment, buildings, raw materials, work in progress and finished output owned by the business sector. (The general level of infrastructure is taken as given.)
INCOME	Total utility enjoyed this period. Narrowly, utility from economic activity. Broadly, comprising also the utility derived from the possession of knowledge (e.g. greater enjoyment of the arts) and the utilities (and disutilities) associated with the physical environment (e.g. clean air, sunshine) and from membership in the social structure.	The amount of goods, equipment and structures which could be used up within the income period, while leaving wealth intact.	Goods and services newly produced within the period (gross income). Gross income less depreciation = net income. Depreciation may reflect economic obsolescence as well as physical deterioration.	Income of households (wages, salaries, rent and interest) ± profits (losses) of the business sector. Equal to the proceeds of sales of goods and services produced in the period. The value of any increment, intended or unintended, in stocks of financial goods less user cost.

INVEST-MENT	Changes in productive capacity (capacity to produce future utility).	New durable goods less the portion of the old stock which has worn out. (Includes producers' and consumers' durable goods and structures.)	New producers' goods and structures (gross investment) less depreciation of existing stock (net investment). Gross or net additions to the infra-structure may be included. In National Income accounts, household expenditure on housing is treated as investment, the imputed rent taken as the consumption component. This convention is usually incorporated into all approaches but is not strictly compatible with the 'productivity' or 'sectoral' approaches.	As in productivity approach, but in value terms, and without infrastructure.
CONSUMP-TION	Consumption is equivalent to income in this approach.	The goods, equipment and structures worn out during the period, whether produced within the period or pre-existing.	Current output of consumers' goods, whether durable or non-durable (but see note under Investment).	Consumers' expenditure or goods and services (but see note under Investment).
SAVING	Accumulation of goods which yield future utility, less the utility enjoyed this period (e.g. the future utility from consumer durables, including housing).	Accumulation of financial assets, including money.	Accumulation of financial assets, including money.	Accumulation of financial assets (including money) by households. A separate category of business saving may be added to account for the business sector's acquisition of such claims (= unspent retained profits and depreciation).

consumption is part of what is called in Table 3.3 the 'durability' approach, which is unambiguous in the case of perishable goods but poses problems when durable goods are produced or held (as they always are). Only a portion of any durable, whether capital equipment or a consumer good, wears out in the perod. 'Consumption' becomes, for those goods, a matter of estimating depreciation — something business firms do regularly but households do only rarely.

It follows that 'investment' in this frame of reference is equivalent to the production of any new durable good, whether it is destined for purchase by households or firms and regardless of its purpose — the provision of final services or the facilitation of production of other goods. The distinction by purpose is a feature of the 'productivity' and 'sectoral' approaches.

I have spoken of production rather than purchase because of the macroeconomic perspective adopted. From the standpoint of individual firms and households the 'durability' criterion bears a fairly close correspondence to the purchases of the two sectors: firms buy many durable machines and few fish and eggs. On this criterion, however, a private individual's purchase of a motor car or a refrigerator counts as 'investing', because these things are expected to last. House purchase, usually the largest and most durable consumer outlay, is officially regarded (in National Income statistics) as investment; only the imputed rent of owner-occupied houses counts as consumption. Firms' purchases of relatively perishable items (raw materials destined to be transformed in production, office supplies, electric power) would count as firms' consumption; on other definitions they would be 'working capital'. While internally consistent, the 'durability' definitions contrast sharply with Keynes's, as we shall see.

The idea of consumption as physical disappearance is easy to integrate with the idea of 'leaving wealth intact', where wealth is defined as the stock of physical assets in existence. Income is what is *available* for consumption; investment represents a decision to add to wealth rather than consume.

Conceptually, it is equally easy to think of this income in real terms, as a list of goods, or in terms of some numeraire (e.g. money), as an aggregate value. Practically, of course, it would be impossible to compare one year's income with another with precision unless the composition of output were constant and the composition of the capital stock were unchanged at the end of the period as compared to the beginning. These are examples of the index number problem inherent in dealing with heterogeneous goods, a problem which is in principle insoluble, though in practice there exist different indexes each of which tells one something useful.

The usual definition of income in macroeconomics textbooks is 'newly produced goods and services'. A distinction is made between gross and net income to allow for depreciation of capital held by firms, but not depreciation of consumer durables. The 'net' version bears some resemblance to the idea of income as what may be consumed while leaving capital intact, but capital or wealth is now restricted to producers' goods — machinery and building which serve the productive process.

The subdivision into consumption and investment is also determined functionally: consumption goods are those destined for final buyers (by assumption, households) while a commodity destined for use in production is an intermediate or instrumental good, and its purchase is 'investment', even if it is not durable. Equipment which is of no particular use *except* as an instrument of production is by definition always bought by firms, but many commodities present ambiguities which are well known. For example, coal used to heat a house is a consumption good; used to heat a blast furnace it becomes an instrumental good, a raw material, working capital.

Income in this 'productivity' approach can be conceived in either physical or value terms. The difference is not merely one of pricing output; the important distinction concerns the treatment of capital. On the 'durability' criterion, depreciation is physical wear and tear. In the productivity approach, allowance may be made for losses of value due to economic obsolescence as well as physical deterioration. The value of productive capital may be defined to reflect the anticipated earnings stream associated with existing equipment. Similarly, if stocks of finished goods are revalued with changes in their actual or anticipated market value, changes in stocks reflect more than physical investment or disinvestment.

A third set of concepts begins from the reasons for goods' desirability: their utility. Here, consumption is of the services of goods. This concept divorces consumption from both production and puchasing, for one can 'consume the services of' — i.e. enjoy — a painting over many years while only buying it once and without the object suffering any more or less physical deterioration whether looked at or ignored.

At the opposite extreme, the separations between purchase, use (destruction) and utility are minimised. Even with most durable goods, the divorce is not always complete; some goods cannot be enjoyed, provide no services, unless they are used in a way that exposes them to depreciation in addition to that due to the passage of time. Running a motor car is an obvious example. On the other hand, depreciation and utility could be viewed as antithetical: as Boulding (1950) nicely puts it, the less his motor car is 'consumed' in the sense of wearing out, the more services it provides.

On a slightly broader canvas, it can be seen that it is the utility criterion which economists have in mind when they assert that consumption is the end purpose of economic activity; they could hardly be expected to mean that the whole economic machine exists chiefly to be worn out! However, income on the utility criterion is completely intangible and subjective: income is satisfaction. In other words, it is identical with the notion of consumption in the same approach.

Such a definition is not very useful for the purpose to which Keynes addressed himself: the determination of output and employment. These are determined as a result of profit-seeking by firms, and profits are made by selling. A firm selling television sets is more or less indifferent as to whether you watch TV or not; the only significance use can have is its correlation with wear and tear and thus the timing of replacement. (Most firms have relied on persuading people that their equipment is old-fashioned rather than waiting for genuine replacement needs, so even this connection is tenuous.)

It is a notable feature of the durability, productivity and utility concepts of consumption and investment just outlined that they have to do with inherent properties of the goods themselves — how suitable they are for inclusion in the productive process or private final use and how quickly they wear out. Keynes's criterion, at least in (*G.T.*) Chapter 6, however, is — who *buys* them. Thus I have called it in Table 3.3 a *sectoral* approach: consumption is what consumers buy, investment is what firms buy. It is also a monetary approach: it is expenditure, not utility, that motivates firms to produce.

The four approaches to income have been discussed from what I have called an eagle's perspective. Before returning to that perspective to discuss Keynes's concept of income in detail, a word needs to be said about income from an individual's point of view.

Individual Income

An individual is likely to understand by income what he can spend while leaving his wealth intact, but this concept is not likely to 'add up' to aggregate income from a social perspective, nor is it easy to imagine this concept, even in principle, in real terms.

While the economy's real income is what is produced and is (if capital is unchanged) unambiguous, an individual's real income depends on what subset of these goods he chooses to buy, which is itself likely to vary with the level of his income. If the 'individual' is a firm, the concept of real profits is even more ambiguous.

The disparity between individual and social wealth is even more acute. Some of the individual's wealth will be held in the form of financial assets — a bank deposit at least. These financial assets, while wealth to the individual, are not part of the productive wealth of the economy. Thus they constitute a major source of divergence between aggregate wealth evaluated directly at the aggregate level and the aggregate of individuals' wealth. Some portion of aggregate wealth consists of assets such as road and rail networks which contribute to the productive potential of the economy but are owned by no individual, rather by the state for common use. For these reasons the concept of income as that which may be consumed while leaving wealth intact is not easily related to the same concept at the individual level.

Keynes's Concepts of Income

The pursuit and disposal of income as perceived by individuals and firms motivates economic behaviour. Keynes's definitions of income — for there are two — are a curious and somewhat uneasy blend of the aggregate perspective with the perspective of the two sectors, Households and Firms. Although both are aggregate concepts, one, gross income, relates to firms' decisions to produce output, and the other, net income, determines what may be consumed. In Table 3.3 this is called the 'sectoral' approach.

In the *General Theory*, income is defined in *value* terms. This is not merely to recognise the insoluble difficulties of defining real income unambiguously in anything but a steady state, though this point is made; the more important point is that the advanced Western economies are *money* economies. Money not only serves as a unit of account and allows us to add the value of apples and oranges; more importantly, its acquisition is the proximate motivation of economic activity: workers sell their labour for a money wage, even though they only do so because of what they think the money will buy; firms produce goods in pursuit of money profit, and production is not profitable unless the goods are sold — for money.

Despite the emphasis on motivation, however, it was necessary to proceed beyond sectoral definitions of income to an aggregate, for income to households is a cost to firms, albeit a cost which provides the purchasing power on which firms' own profits depend. It was the failure of the economy to generate enough aggregate income to keep its people employed that required explanation. This failure is proximately due to firms' unwillingness to operate at a sufficiently high level of production; that unwillingness in turn is due to their estimate, fulfilled in the case of unemployment equilibrium, of inadequate demand for their output. The two sides — demand (by both consumers and firms) and supply (by firms) — interact to produce boom or slump.

This concentration on the motives behind supply and demand is responsible for another unnerving feature of Keynes's concept of income: its incorporation, through the concept of *user cost*, of expectations of the future value of the capital: it is the maintenance of value, derived not just from physical productivity but also from future demand conditions, with which firms are concerned when deciding whether to commit their machines to production or not.

To summarise, before going into more detail: Keynes linked the concept of income to its consequences for the behaviour of the two key sectors, stating it in money terms to conform with the realities of a profit-seeking, market economy.

Income Related to Production (Gross Income)

Keynes first defines income as it relates to production decisions: gross income. Firms are always making these decisions in the context of the short run, i.e. with a given plant and equipment available to them. Profit-maximising firms will choose that level of output which they think will maximise their gross profits, that is the proceeds of sales of final output less the variable (or prime) costs of producing it. Prime costs are factor payments less the cost of using capital to produce the goods from which the profit is derived.

To generalise this proposition to the aggregate level it is necessary to take account of the fact that prime costs to firm *A* include purchases of such things as raw materials or replacement parts from firm *B*. Since, as we shall explain later, all purchases between firms are called investment and are treated as changes in capital, the problem of deriving the aggregate measure embodying the appropriate treatment of interfirm transactions cannot be approached simply in terms of current output.

Production, Profit and the Capital Stock: Firms produce goods for sale and in the process capital wears out. Indeed 'working capital' — stocks of raw materials — is completely used up, in the sense that raw materials are transformed into something quite different. Capital also deteriorates with the sheer passage of time, even if not used, and through accidental damage. But in a money economy, an additional factor enters entrepreneurs' calculations: the 'value', in money terms, of capital. This value depends on the expected net revenue from the stream of output the capital is expected to produce in future. A fall in the demand for cloth reduces the value of looms (even though the firm has no intention of selling the looms), and so does the invention of superior equipment which will compete with the old looms. Because capital values are subject to fluctuations from shifts in demand or innovation, the physical maintenance of a machine may be a great concern one moment and of no interest the next.

Amongst all these considerations — deterioration through time and through use and the maintenance of value — there are many interesting balancing acts to be performed. First, there is a trade-off between maintenance expense and the life of a machine. An unused machine, scrupulously protected from the elements (oiled, painted, kept at a constant temperature, etc.), may be expected to last n years. If it is not maintained it attracts no expense but only lasts, say, $n-h$ years. However, there is no point in having it unless it is expected to be used, for if it is not even potentially productive, it has no value. When it *is* used, it will typically wear out faster, and the rate of wear will be a positive function of the level of output derived from it.

Not all the possible sources of changes in value are properly charged against income. There are losses due to natural disasters, over which entrepreneurs have no control and which are so unpredictable as to be uninsurable. Even forecasts made by other entrepreneurs will affect the value of a firm's capital in an unpredictable and uncontrollable manner. Changes due to unpredictable events outside the scope of the producer's decision, including unforeseen changes in the prospects of selling the output of a piece of capital equipment or the development of competitive equipment, are properly treated as windfalls and 'charged to capital account'. It is the deterioration due to time and use, both of which the entrepreneur can to some extent control, that are of importance in defining income.

User Cost: The depreciation which properly enters the definition of gross income is that due to use. It is called user cost. This cost is directly attributable to production and varies with the level of output and is thus part of prime or variable cost. It is necessarily incurred when it is decided to use capital to produce output. From the aggregate point of view, user cost is that part of current output which is used in the production of other output.

It is not an easy concept. The difficulty lies in disentangling this cost from other sources of change in the capital stock.

Some definitions are needed. Following the *General Theory:* let

Y = income
A = sales of finished output, of which
  A_1 = sales amongst entrepreneurs
G = actual value of capital equipment + stocks of raw materials + stocks of unsold finished goods + work in progress at end of period = value of these stocks at the beginning of the period + purchases (A_1) − exhaustion due to use
B' = optimum maintenance of capital if left unused
G' = value of capital equipment and stocks at the end of the period if B' had been undertaken
$G' - B'$ = the maximum net value which might have been conserved from the previous period, if it had not been used to produce A
F = factor cost of producing A
U = user cost of A
Π = gross profit = total revenue from sales less prime cost.

User cost is defined as

$$U = G' - B' - G + A_1. \tag{3.1}$$

G is the stock of capital (broadly interpreted) at the beginning of the period. Some of that stock will deteriorate even if it is not used, through the passage of time. There are other possible sources of change in the end value of capital — expected changes in demand, competing technology, etc. — but for the moment, ignore these. B' then measures the extent to which it pays to act against the ravages of time in maintaining the stock (e.g. by providing dry storage). If the maintenance or other action to preserve capital is actually taken, it is a cost borne out of current resources. (There is no presumption that the action actually *will* be taken.)

In use, capital deteriorates to an even greater extent. The loss of capital through both time and use can be mitigated by maintenance and reversed by replacement — at a cost. The firm may carry out these things with its own staff, in which case the maintenance of capital is reflected in the firm's labour cost but not in its output offered for sale. 'In-house maintenance' presents no aggregation problem. The difficulty arises when these things are supplied by other firms. A_1, which as noted earlier is capital purchases, measures the extent of this supply.

Think of A_1 as purchases of raw materials, spare parts, new or replacement equipment, and maintenance contracted out. These, unlike B', are actual expenditures, claims on currently produced output. The expenditures denoted by A_1 compensate, however, for time as well as use. There is no practical way to distinguish the *purpose* of a given investment expenditure. B' serves to separate the two by indicating what portion of A_1 is appropriately *charged* against use, whatever firms' managers may think they are doing.

It may help to take an extreme example. Suppose use were the only source of depreciation ($B' = 0$). Then if demand and costs are expected to remain unchanged in future, so that there is no benefit from increasing the capital stock, $U = A_1$: firms buy from each other just enough to replace what has been used in order to produce.

B' is the joker, for it is not obvious (nor does Keynes suggest) what constitutes optimum maintenance. That depends on the capital stock with which it is optimal to begin the next period. The optimum is not the absolute minimisation of that stock's loss of value, for that may entail undue expense.

Whether a given amount of maintenance expense is or is not 'undue' depends on the expectation of demand in future. Relax the assumption made earlier that future demand is not expected to change. At one extreme, suppose next year's demand is expected to be nil (as with fashion goods). Then the rational thing to do is run the machine flat out (if today's demand will absorb the output) and not maintain it. The future value of the machine, G', B' and U, are all zero. If, in contrast, demand next period is expected to improve on this period, so that the equipment gains in value, even more effort should be spent on conserving it than if demand were expected to be stable.

It can be seen that G' and B', and hence U, are not defined with reference solely to the current period and solely objectively. Expectations of the future are inescapably involved.

Gross Income: With user cost out of the way, the rest is easy. Recall that gross profit is the proceeds of sales of final output less the variable (prime) costs of production and that prime costs are factor payments (labour costs) plus user cost:

$$\Pi = A - (F + U). \tag{3.2}$$

Gross income is the sum of gross profits and factor costs and hence the value of output less user cost:

$$Y = F + \Pi = A - U. \tag{3.3}$$

There are three things to note about this definition. First, it is based on a concept of profit not much used in microeconomics; fixed costs are not subtracted before profit is calculated. Given that fixed costs have to be paid, this could be said not to be profit at all. However, since fixed costs do not affect the output decision, it is right to exclude them for the purpose at hand. Having maximised (or attempted to maximise) gross profit, fixed costs determine the first stage of the distribution of that profit.

Second, though user cost will not, for reasons of space, get the attention it deserves in the rest of this book, keep in mind that such things as changes in raw materials prices enter income through user cost.

Third, because of the incorporation of user cost, income is not self-contained within a single period, and not entirely amenable to objective measurement. To these awkward characteristics Keynes most of the time — but not always — turns a blind eye. Most of the time, regrettably, we shall have to do the same.

Income Available for Consumption (Net Income)

Not all of gross income could be consumed and still leave capital intact: a further subtraction must be made. Capital depreciates not only as a result of the deliberate choice to use it but also involuntarily. Some of this loss may be unexpected; these are the windfall losses referred to earlier. But other losses, although involuntary, are not entirely unexpected: most notably those due to the passage of time.[10] This type of depreciation Keynes designates:

$V =$ supplementary cost.

Profits net of both forms of foreseeable capital depreciation, U and V, are

$$\Pi' = A - (F + U) - V \tag{3.4}$$

and income available for consumption, net income, is

$$Y' = A - U - V. \tag{3.5}$$

Y' is 'available for consumption' in the sense that this is the amount which could be consumed and leave the value of the capital stock intact: both forms of depreciation, U and V, have been accounted for. The significance of the distinction between U and V — although it could be difficult to distinguish them with much precision in practice — is that V, being independent of output, does not affect the *generation* of income, but does affect its disposal.

The importance of the distinction between gross and net income arises from the fact that the retention of profit for capital replacement is unlikely to be synchronised with expenditure for replacement. When retentions are larger than expenditures, in effect firms are hoarding: this is deflationary. If the disparity is reversed, the effect is expansionary.

Accounting Concepts

Most textbook treatments of 'Keynesian economics' do not follow Keynes's definitions but adhere to accounting practices as reflected in income statements of the type given as Table 3.2, above. There are several differences. The accounting approach begins by defining gross income or Gross National Product as newly produced goods and services, allowing for changes in stocks of working capital (raw materials, work in progress, and stocks of finished goods), but not for changes in the value of more durable forms of capital. In other words, losses of raw materials are attributed entirely to user cost and additions to work in progress and finished goods are called investment. In dealing with durable machinery and buildings, a distinction is made not by cause, but by whether or not there has been actual expenditure on maintenance and replacement. Actual expenditures are counted as costs when reckoning *accounting* gross profit and 'depreciation' is not an expenditure at all, but an unspent sinking fund. User cost, in contrast, applies to both raw materials and more durable capital, and contains both actual expenditure and wear and tear for which there is no remedy short of full replacement in future. Supplementary cost is *largely*, but not necessarily exclusively, concerned with more durable capital (it would include, however, any deterioration in raw materials caused, say, by exposure to weather) and is expected therefore to be in large measure, but not exclusively, a sinking fund.

The accounting conventions are, by necessity, the framework in which firms operate: the practical difficulties of precise calculation of U and V are insuperable. Theory, however, can establish the salient distinctions. Accountants' figures are only a rough guide to the magnitudes which govern production; they are designed for another purpose — the monitoring and regulation of cash flows.

The position of two cash flows in Keynes's scheme is still unsettled: what has happened to fixed costs, and what is the relation between profits and dividend payments? Fixed costs are paid out of gross profits, after variable costs are dealt with (for the latter are essential to keeping the firm going). When paid out, they become either profits to another firm or (rent or interest) income to individuals. In the latter case they are obviously 'available for consumption'; in the former case they are available insofar as they in their turn are not retained as a sinking fund. In either case they remain part of aggregate income, just as labour costs do.

One could propose a third definition of profits, relevant to questions of industrial organisation, which was not central to Keynes's enquiry. This definition, Π'', would be net of fixed costs as well as all the factors already considered, and would conform to the accounting definition of profits net of depreciation but gross of direct taxes.

Shareholders have the last claim on profits — on Π'' *net* of taxes — and even then, within limits set by shareholders' unhappiness and its implications, payment of dividends is discretionary. Funds not distributed, 'retained earnings', are available for financing investment. (It will become clear in the next section that firms do not consume.) Dividends become household income and may finance consumption. ('Consumption out of profits', however, may include consumption out of entrepreneurs' salaries, rent, and interest income, if one wishes to define profits as everything other than labour income, as in the Cambridge tradition.)

Income: Summary

The distinguishing features of Keynes's treatment of income are (i) its definition in value terms, as befits a money economy, (ii) the sector basis for defining even a social aggregate, and (iii) the role of expectations in defining the borderline between income account and capital account. It follows from (iii) that the borderline can be unambiguously defined only when expectations are unchanged — i.e. in a state of 'tranquillity' or long-run equilibrium in the Marshallian sense. It also follows that the concepts developed here bear only a tenuous relationship to the National Income Accounts, which are backward-looking, and tell us what *has* happened, while these definitions are forward-looking, depending as they do on expectations. Only a forward-looking measure can serve as a guide to decision-making.

The Components of Income in the *General Theory*

In *(G.T.)* Chapter 6 everything seems straightforward. The components of income are distinguished by the buyer. Consumption (C) — more properly consumers' expenditure — is total sales, A, less sales amongst firms, A_1, i.e. the value of output sold to households:

$$C = A - A_1. \tag{3.6}$$

Gross investment (I) is sales amongst firms less user cost:

$$I = A_1 - U. \tag{3.7}$$

The character of the goods — their durability or productivity — is not really at issue. Consumer goods are investment as long as they are intended additions to stocks; they add to end-of-period capital and enter as negative user cost, unsold output against which factor payments have been made. They become consumption when they are sold.

Some Difficulties: I. The Chapter 7 Definitions

In Chapter 7, Keynes blurs the sharp distinction offered by the sectoral approach when he attempts to accommodate popular usage by defining investment as the purchase of *any* asset, real or financial (*G.T.* p. 75). Aggregate investment becomes identified with the purchase of newly produced real assets by the process of aggregation, in which the purchase of old assets — investment by one party — is cancelled by their sale by the previous owners (disinvestment). Financial assets are made to disappear by a similar process: every asset is someone else's liability.[11]

The result, his assertion (p. 75) notwithstanding, does *not* amount to the same thing as his definition of investment in Chapter 6, but differs in two respects: (i) the definition of Chapter 7 includes unintentional changes in inventories (see pp. 75–6), which in Chapter 6 are excluded; and (ii) in the Chapter 7 definition, investment may be done by households as well as firms, while in Chapter 6, investment is strictly an entrepreneurial activity.

The correct treatment of unsold goods is important, if only because textbook 'income-expenditure' analysis has placed so much weight on inventory changes as an adjustment mechanism. The textbooks have followed Chapter 7, where investment is robbed of its volitional character by the inclusion in that aggregate of the results of errors in forecasting demand (which is what unintended changes in stocks indicate). Compare the treatment of Chapter 6, where gross investment is defined as

$$I = A_1 - U = G - (G' + B'). \tag{3.8}$$

Since G' is the end-of-period value of capital stocks which firms *expect* to be optimal, and A_1 is voluntary, there is no room for involuntary changes in inventories due to unexpected variations in sales. Breaking down total sales into consumption, $A - A_1$, and investment as defined above we can rewrite the definition of gross profits as

$$\Pi = A - (F + U) = A - A_1 + A_1 - U - F = C + I - F. \tag{3.9}$$

Goods not sold do not appear in A. However, goods produced in the period entail prime costs, whether they are sold or not. If production for stock is planned, there must be a reason: firms must expect costs or demand to rise in future in comparison with today, thus affecting G', the optimal unused end-period capital stock (and its practical derivative, the optimal stock if used) and justifying incurring prime costs now rather than in future despite the lack of current revenue. It is accounted for as negative user cost, a deliberate decision.

An unexpected, unplanned accretion of inventories carries the same factor cost but there is no rise in G'. One concludes, in accordance with common sense, that unintended additions to stocks reduce profits below their expected value. Thus the Chapter 6 definition preserves both the volitional nature of investment and a sensible definition of profit. It also consistently defines aggregates by who buys them, where the Chapter 7 definitions include goods which the producing firm may simply unwillingly retain; they are not sold at all. It is difficult to reconcile this with the definition of I as $A - A_1$.

The Chapter 7 definitions are consistent not with plans and expectations but with the facts, *ex post*. Part of the appeal of the Chapter 7 definitions is that they bear a closer resemblance to the National Income statistics. There is, however, no doubt in my mind which definitions are, for analytical purposes, superior.

Some Difficulties: II. Saving

There remains the question of defining the aggregate called saving. The *General Theory* could have been written without this concept and would have been the better for its omission. It was needed only in order to speak against the Classical proposition that saving determines investment in the language of that proposition. The result of using the concept has been immense confusion, due entirely, in my view, to a lack of awareness of the disparity of meaning between individual and aggregate saving.

The question of the meaning of saving and its changes through time as the environment changed (the development of financial institutions being crucial) is discussed fully in Chapter 9. Here we have only to deal with its definition, which is rather straightforward.

Keynes begins from the proposition that it is incontrovertible that saving is that part of income which is not consumed. He has two definitions of income, gross and net, so, subtracting consumption from each he derives two corresponding definitions of saving. Gross saving, S, is,

$$S = A - U - (A - A_1) = A_1 - U \qquad (3.10)$$

and net saving, S', is

$$S' = A - U - V - (A - A_1) = A_1 - U - V. \qquad (3.11)$$

The first is obviously *identical* to gross investment,[12] defined at this juncture as 'the current addition to the value of the capital equipment which has resulted from the productive activity of the period' (*G. T.* p. 62). The second is *identical* to net investment: *gross investment* less loss of value from causes other than use (which is incorporated in *U*) or windfalls (which are charged to capital account).

Although defined in terms of *value*, the conception behind these definitions is real: the vision is of actual capital being produced and physically destroyed. There is no mention of the equipment actually being sold, or the profit expected from producing it actually being realised, or of changes in valuation due to altered expectations. The 'real' conception is even more striking in the case of net investment, where *V*, the financial provision for replacement, is now taken to be a measure of the actual need for physical replacement.

Correspondingly, the concept of saving is real (though also expressed in value terms). If one thinks about what saving in aggregate might mean, one can see that there can be no way for society as a whole to save other than by producing things which are not consumed — where consumption now carries the force of being destroyed (or transformed). Saving is thus the net addition to the things that *remain* at the end of the period to be carried over into the next. It is now clear that one of the two aggregates is redundant; they are conceptually, as well as technically, identical.

Saving and Decision: Notice that saving has not been defined as a positive act but as the absence of action: saving is 'not-consuming'. Consumption and investment are both positive acts, the first taken by households, the second by firms. Together they determine actual income. Saving, in contrast, is not known until income is determined. While an individual may know his income, at least in money terms, in advance, *aggregate* income cannot be known until the end of the period, after actual profits are determined. It follows that Keynes's aggregate 'saving' is an entirely *factual, ex post* concept which has no relationship to plans or decisions. It is entirely a residual: if saving is positive, the reason may be that in aggregate, households decided to buy less than they earned by producing, or equally, that actual aggregate income was higher than expected. Saving is definitely *not*, as Keynes asserts, the 'outcome of the collective behaviour of individual consumers ...' (p. 63); Keynes's concept of aggregate saving lacks any foundation in microeconomic behaviour.

The concept of aggregate saving obviously has nothing to do with the plans of households or what households actually *do* when they save. They do not (by assumption) buy productive capital goods, or decide the composition of production between consumer and capital goods, and they can hardly be expected to care about or even be conscious of the goods left on the shelf as a result of their failure to buy them. Introspection suggests that when households save they buy financial assets or keep money in the bank. This introspection accords with the scheme of sectoral aggregation earlier in this chapter. If, as assumed, only households consume, saving is income less consumption, and households do not invest, then the only way that households can save is by buying financial assets. If we allow firms to save, and wish to define saving in a manner different from investment,[13] then they too have no option but to buy financial assets. This is exactly what happens to sinking finds which are not currently spent on replacement of capital.

The reason for the disparity between individual and aggregate saving is now clear: financial assets 'consolidate out' for the economy as a whole.

Saving at the individual level is a proper *decision*. The decision is to acquire financial assets or to keep a larger bank balance than formerly. It may be subsidiary to the consumption decision particularly if consumption is at the level of basic need, where any saving is likely to be no more than an accident. And *ex post* it may be different from what is planned. But these aspects of individual saving do not make it a residual in the same sense that aggregate saving is a residual. Aggregate saving, because it depends, *inter alia*, on realised profits, involves elements over which the savers in the economy have no control. Since actual profits are a residual, so is aggregate saving.

This examination of saving at the individual level underscores the important proposition that saving and investment are not only activities undertaken by different groups of people, but involve different *things* — investment is the acquisition of machines and buildings, saving is the acquisition of paper assets and extra cash.

Units of Measurement

This entire discussion of income and its components has used only two concepts of measurement: the impractical one of a list of commodities and the obvious one of money values. The difficulty with using money values in the context of the motivation of decisions is the suggestion of 'money illusion' — the failure to recognise that a rise in money value has no counterpart in real goods. To obtain a measure of 'real' income, it has become customary to derive from the money value of income an index of 'real income', identified (none too accurately as we have seen) with real output, by deflating by a general price index. Measurements of this type were the units accepted by Marshall and Pigou in their theoretical work, they are presented in the national income statistics, and nearly all modern macroeconomic theory is based upon them. Keynes, however, did not accept them. He inveighs at some length against their vagueness and the difficulty of avoiding introducing notions of value by the back door (*G. T.* pp. 37–40). 'Real output' and 'the general price level' were not, in his view, useless concepts, but their

> proper place ... lies within the field of historical and statistical description ... for which perfect precision ... is neither usual nor necessary. To say that net output today is greater, but the price-level lower, than ten years ago or one year ago, is a proposition of a similar character to the statement that Queen Victoria was a better queen but not a happier woman than Queen Elizabeth — a proposition not without meaning and not without interest, but unsuitable as material for the differential calculus.
>
> (G.T. p. 40)

(Not that he employed much calculus, in the event.)

There may be an additional reason, implicit in the structure of the theory. The use of a general price level diminishes the importance of the distinction between consumption and investment. The division into the two aggregates is crucial to the explanation of the way the economy behaves. Consumption and investment together constitute aggregate demand, but they are determined by very different considerations. Consumption is designed to satisfy present wants; investment is provision for the production of goods to satisfy future wants. Investment goods are durable and their purchasers' equity in them extends far into the future. The expected stream of profits that makes their acquisition worthwhile does not even begin in the present, when the decision to invest is made, for there is a 'gestation period' before the product of the new machines or plant comes on to the market. Meanwhile, the purchase has to be financed; this commitment extends at least through part of the useful life of the investment. Thus the elements which determine investment demand pertain to a completely different time-frame from those which determine consumption. Most notably, the rate of interest, the relative price of money future in terms of money present, enters the determination of the expected value of investment assets and into investment demand; its role in determining consumption is by comparison trivial. Demand and hence the determinants of price are, therefore, fundamentally different for the two sorts of commodities. A general price index is not appropriate in the circumstances.

Furthermore, the price of consumers' goods enters the determination of the 'real' value of households' income, while the price of investment goods does not — except, if one wanted to stretch a point, in the most indirect manner, as a remote influence on future real income. Since it is most unlikely that expansion or contraction of production is balanced in such a way as to keep the relative price of consumers' goods and investment goods unchanged, the use of a general price index is a poor guide to the effects of such changes on households.

For certain other purposes Keynes used hours of labour as a numeraire, measuring income in 'wage-units'. (This device is explained in Chapter 4 below.) That is as close to the 'real income' of the 'Keynesian' textbook as we get in the General Theory.

Notes

1.   See Kregel (1971) Chs. 7–12, for a review and references.

2.   Rentiers, people whose income derives chiefly from interest income on debt instruments, are now an almost extinct breed. In the US, interest income, especially coupled with dividends from equity shares, is still important, though rentiers never formed a distinct social class as in England, and those who earned (and earn) substantial income by this means typically also took an active entrepreneurial role in the US. This was less usual in England. Now, financial institutions and the financial divisions of firms are the more important holders of debt instruments.

3.   This statement implicitly presumes the independence of individual decision — a standard assumption of most economic analysis (even where it recognises the essential interdependence of firms in the same industry). 'Group psychology' is particularly important in Keynes's theory of investment and of liquidity preference. There is a deeper question lurking here, to which I alert the reader but which I do not propose to settle, about individualism and group behaviour, and the validity of deriving aggregates from the responses of individuals who are members of a group.

4.   Keynes's own treatment of this problem is none too helpful for he seldom distinguishes clearly the level to which a statement pertains. Particularly, it is often difficult to discover whether he is referring to *plans* or to actual, observable magnitudes, or whether to the individual or the aggregate. Nor is it always clear whether 'plans' refer to a schedule or to a particular level. Illustrations of the importance of these distinctions will be plentiful enough, and nowhere are they more important than in the saving–investment controversy, as we shall see later.

5.   The commissions earned in marketing the assets count as income; the source of the income, however, is the provision of labour etc. by the broker or merchant banker; even if the commission is contingent on the successful sale of the security, that sale is not the source of the income.

6.   Interest may be contractual, as on bonds or debentures, or imputed, as with short-term assets that sell at a discount. A broader definition of interest as a rate of return would include dividends on equity shares, though there is no contractual obligation on firms to provide dividends.

7.   Some claims are not marketable (e.g. a deposit account).

8.   Not all interest-bearing claims do vary in value with the rate of interest (e.g., again, deposit accounts).

9.   See the essays in Parker and Harcourt (1969).

10. Keynes also lists changes in market value, obsolescence, and catastrophe. The predictable component of these increases as the span of time considered widens; over the short run I should have thought only some very broad provision is likely to be made, the rest being treated as windfalls.

11. Changes in the money stock present special aggregation problems; these cannot be dealt with as easily as Keynes suggests (p. 75).

12.   Keynes's 1934 draft is perfectly clear: 'for the community as a whole, investment and saving are necessarily, *and by definition*, equal.' (*C.W.* XIII, p. 476, emphasis added.)

13.   Once again Chapter 7 is a disaster. Individuals' purchases of financial assets are counted as investment. There doesn't seem to be any way left in which to save. Saving is thus revealed as having no meaning even for individuals on Chapter 7's definitions.

Part *II*
A STATIC MODEL OF A DYNAMIC PROCESS

Chapter 4

THE THEORY OF OUTPUT AND EMPLOYMENT

The Principle of Effective Demand

The primary purpose of the *General Theory* is to provide a theory of employment; the book's title is no accident or whim. And since the production decision is, with the rare exception of the moments when new capital is brought into use, made in the context of a given capital equipment, the determination of employment implies the determination of output.

Output and employment are determined by the Principle of Effective Demand. It is in the operation of this Principle that the characteristics of a production economy, organised on capitalist lines, play their role most clearly; the 'level of output' is determined by producers; thus the Principle of Effective Demand rests on a model of *firms'* behaviour.

In terms of the methodological distinctions of Chapter 2, the determination of output and employment is a problem in the production period. Investment is seen in this context as having been decided on the basis of long-term expectations which for present purposes are taken as given. If one wants to be more precise, one can assign unit length to the production period and take the relevant expectations to be those expected at $t = 0$ to obtain at $t = 1$ or towards the end of the period which begins at $t = 0$ and ends at $t = 1$ (period 0).

It is in the nature of the business of producing for sale on the market that the choice of what and how much to produce, and how to price things, must be made on the basis of estimates of costs and a forecast of demand. Because production takes time, the producer has *no choice* but to estimate the demand for his product and proceed according to this estimate, even though he is far from certain about it,[1] and even though he may be wrong about it.

Both costs and demand rise with the volume of output, but for a time, so do profits. Firms are assumed to choose to produce whatever volume of output they believe will maximise their profits, given their cost estimate and demand forecasts, and they will hire just enough labour to enable them to produce that output. The Principle of Effective Demand is the generalisation of this microeconomic proposition to the determination of output as a whole.

To explicate the Principle fully we shall have to appeal to the theory of the firm, but for now let us state it simply as a macroeconomic generalisation. The Principle states that the level of output as a whole and the overall level of employment are determined by the intersection of two functions of the level of employment, N: aggregate supply, $Z(N)$, and firms' estimates of aggregate demand, $D^e(N)$. The intersection point is called the point of effective demand.

Because its inclusion would create complications,[2] both functions are defined net of user cost. (We shall have more to say on this point.)

User cost having been omitted, prime cost consists entirely of labour. Thus the aggregate supply curve embodies estimates of the labour costs associated with each level of employment: it indicates the amount of revenue from the sale of the output associated with each level of employment which would give firms the incentive to push output and employment to that level.

The estimated revenue associated with each level of employment is given by the aggregate demand curve. Once the position of $D^e(N)$ is established, the appropriate point amongst all the profit-maximising possibilities given by $Z(N)$ is determined. Production plans are made and jobs offered on that basis.

Figure 4.1 portrays $Z(N)$ and $D^e(N)$. Employment is on the horizontal

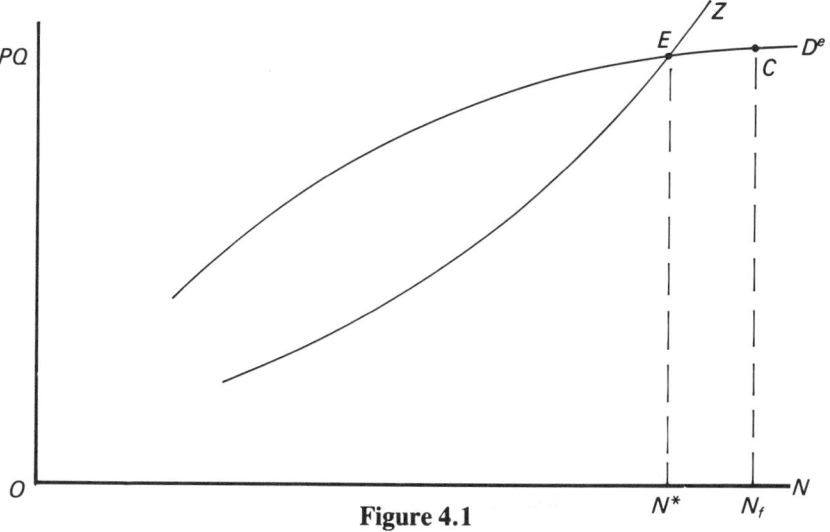

Figure 4.1

axis and the *value* of output on the vertical axis. Their slopes will be
explained presently. Point E is the point of effective demand. N^* is the
amount of employment determined by that point. It can be seen that this
proposition depends on the relative slopes of the two curves: the slope of
$D^e(N)$ must be less than the slope of $Z(N)$ in the neighbourhood of their
intersections, otherwise there is an incentive to expand further, as demand
to the right of N^* would more than cover the additional cost.

There is no presumption that N^* is a point of full employment; it can just
as well be a level of employment which will not fully satisfy the demands for
jobs. The mere existence of unemployment does not itself provide a reason
for firms to expand output further. If demand as estimated is not adequate to
compensate for the extra costs involved in producing more than the output
which N^* labour-hours can produce with the existing capital equipment and
employment, that is the end of the matter.

A Semantic Trap

Shortly, we shall discuss the shapes of the functions; in this chapter the
discussion will be brief and simplifying assumptions will be used, for the next
two chapters are devoted to the foundations of these two functions.

First, we must face a semantic problem which has led to much
misunderstanding. Keynes's choice of terms is most confusing, and he does
not use them consistently himself. There are two concepts with very similar
names: effective demand and aggregate demand. And aggregate demand
itself has two aspects, which Keynes did not make much fuss over. *Aggregate*
demand is a schedule, representing the volume of expenditure varying with
the level of income and economic activity associated with each level of
employment. It can refer either to the aggregate of consumers' and investing
firms' expenditure plans, or it can refer to the aggregate of *estimates* of
spending which *firms* make in determining the appropriate volume of ouput.
In determining actual levels of output and employment it is clearly the latter
concept that is important;[3] consumption and investment plans become
important only when the output, which must have been produced already,
comes to be sold. At that point, if sales show expectations to be incorrect,
firms' estimates may be revised, affecting *next* period's output.

Keynes did not elaborate on the process by which estimates were made;
there is little explicit theory of how firms perceive the likely level of demand.
Rather, Keynes proceeded to discuss, in his chapters on consumption and
investment behaviour, the determinants of aggregate demand as planned by
consumers and investing entrepreneurs rather than as estimated by the
producers of consumer and capital goods. This tactic follows from the
assumption, maintained throughout most of the first Book of the *General
Theory* (Chapter 5 is the exception), that firms' estimates of planned
aggregate demand are essentially correct.[4]

Effective demand, in contrast to aggregate demand, is not a schedule — it is the *point* on the schedule of firms' anticipation of aggregate demand which is 'made effective' by firms' production decisions. It is the volume of output they decide to produce, valued at their asking price; it is the *value of anticipated sales*. Effective demand is an unfortunate term, for it really refers to the output that will be *supplied;* in general there is no assurance that it will also be demanded. The only connection of effective demand with demand in the usual sense lies in the fact that by determining employment it determines household income and thus establishes which *point* on the function describing households' planned expenditure will 'be effective' in the market place.

As if the distinction just made were not subtle enough, confusion has been engendered in the literature by a transformation of the term 'effective demand' to mean 'a demand one can back up by purchasing power'. This meaning is usually contrasted with something called 'notional demand', which connotes 'what you would demand if you could sell all the labour you wished to sell' — i.e. demand at full employment. These terms refer to two points on the aggregate demand function, 'notional demand' corresponding to demand at full employment, N_{FE}, and 'effective demand' to the point of intersection with Z. The difficulty with defining effective demand in this way is that it *rules out absolutely* the possibility of a full employment solution within the *General Theory* framework; it confines the analysis to less-than-full employment in advance.

Furthermore, this usage obscures the distinction between firms' estimated demand and the curve representing planned expenditure. If the estimate of planned aggregate demand is accurate (as Keynes assumes), then what one might prefer to call the point of effective supply will indeed be a point of effective expenditure or demand, but accurate forecasts are not to be expected in general. So we should say that effective demand is that value of aggregate output, or that volume of sales, which firms, taken altogether, *believe* will yield maximum profits, given their expectation of the position of the aggregate demand function.

At this point, it will be sufficient to indicate the foundations of the aggregate supply and demand curves in broad outline. The many details, qualifications, and conceptual difficulties that attach to them are postponed to the following two chapters.

The Aggregate Supply Function

Briefly, the shape of the aggregate supply function depends upon the costs of production and the degree of monopoly, as well as the industrial composition of output, insofar as cost characteristics and the degree of concentration vary amongst industries. For present purposes, let us assume (i) atomistic firms; (ii) that labour is the only variable factor of production to be taken into account (recall the curve is net of user cost); and (iii) that the composition of output and demand does not change with the overall volume of output, Q.[5] Q then becomes a Hicksian composite commodity.

In the short run, output depends on the amount of labour employed with the given capital stock. Under the assumption just made, $Z(N)$ is derived from the aggregate production function

$$Q = Q(N). \tag{4.1}$$

This relation, and the theorem that the profit-maximising firm expands output until marginal cost equals price, determine aggregate supply. Since marginal cost is the wage divided by the marginal physical product of labour (Q') we have

$$w/Q' = P. \tag{4.2}$$

Multiplying both sides of this equation by Q gives

$$(w/Q')Q = PQ = Z. \tag{4.3}$$

To make Z an explicit function of N, write

$$\frac{wA}{Q'}N = Z, \tag{4.4}$$

where $A = Q/N$, the average product of labour.

At this point it is convenient to say that Z will be defined for a given wage. Thus there is a family of Z functions, Z_i, one for each particular wage, w_i. This simplification leaves the shape of any particular Z_i dependent on the relation beween the average and marginal products of labour, A/Q'.

For now we shall follow Keynes's assumption of diminishing returns. Thus the marginal product of labour is positive but declining at a constant or increasing rate: $Q' > 0$, $Q'' < 0$, $Q''' \geqslant 0$. When the production function has these properties, both A and Q' decline as Q increases. Therefore A lies above Q' and falls less rapidly than Q' and A/Q' increases as N increases, giving the shape indicated in Figure 4.1. If we had assumed constant returns $(A = Q')$, the function would be a straight line with the slope given by the wage rate.

Notice some similarities and differences with the treatment of the same ideas in microeconomics. There it is customary to determine the profit-maximising output for a given level of demand and structure of marginal costs. The marginal cost curve, like Z_i, is defined for a given wage. In microeconomics the implications for the demand for labour are left unstated, while in the case of Z it is the division between P and Q which is implicit. The relationship between firm-theoretic concepts and Z will be explored in the next chapter.

Aggregate Demand

The aggregate demand function is more difficult to discuss than aggregate supply, for two reasons. The first is that the relevant function is the firms' estimate, and neither Keynes nor anybody since has been very helpful on the question of how this estimate is made. Keynes's expedient was to assume that firms got the estimate right; this assumption allowed him to ignore the question of expectation-formation, for the curve is in effect determined by the spending plans of those who are actually going to spend. We shall follow the same procedure for present purposes. While that assumption is sustained, we are dealing with what Kregel[6] calls the static model.

The second difficulty is one of specification. It is appropriate to derive the aggregate supply function in money terms, because firms seek money profits. However, when it comes to aggregate demand, the object of expenditure is not to spend money but to obtain goods which yield real satisfaction. This means that the plans of consumers are properly specified in real terms: real consumption and the equivalent in goods of their money incomes. Entrepreneurs, too, want actual plant and equipment. This means that the behavioural basis of aggregate demand is properly specified in units different from those used to specify aggregate supply.

There is no getting around this problem: a behavioural function can be translated into other units of measurement in a mechanical way, but it must first be specified correctly in the terms which are relevant to it. The need to specify in 'real terms' gave rise to Keynes's device of the wage-unit, as we shall soon see.

The aggregate demand function is the sum of two major components, determined by the scheme of aggregation that has been adopted: the demands for consumption goods and investment goods. The unsurprising hypothesis is that aggregate demand varies directly with the level of employment.

It is chiefly the response of consumption expenditure to variations in employment which justifies this hypothesis. Although the proposition that investment also varies with the current level of economic activity, and thus with the current level of employment, has had some support,[7] Keynes's alternative view, that investment is chiefly sensitive to *future* expected demand and to current interest rates, is easier to accept, given the *purpose* of investment is to satisfy future demand. If investment is not a function of current levels of activity and employment and the rate of interest is excluded from the analysis (as it will be until Part III), then the assumption of given long-term expectations, mentioned earlier, means that investment is exogenous for present purposes. Thus the nature of the relationship between demand and employment is determined by consumption demand.

The 'true' determinant of consumption is, by hypothesis, real income. But to be comparable with aggregate supply, not only does one or other function have to be translated from real to money terms or *vice versa*, but consumption must be related to employment, not income. (Refer again to Figure 4.1.)

Real income is a measure denominated in goods: it represents the goods income will buy. Thus it is derived from money income by dividing money income by the rate of exchange of money for goods: the price level. In the same way, real income can be measured in terms of hours of labour by using the rate of exchange of labour for goods: the real wage. So it can be appreciated that variations in employment are a good proxy for variations in real income if the real wage is relatively stable. This holds even if the absolute variance of the real wage is not small: it is sufficient that it be small relatively to the variance of employment.

Such an assumption would solve the problem of using employment as a proxy for real income and in the depression conditions of the 1930s the assumption that employment is the most variable element in income is not implausible. In a period of wage or price upheaval, however, the assumption may not be serviceable. And in any case, this justification does not solve the problem of coherence of units between the *dependent* variables Z and D. Keynes's way round the whole problem was to translate all variables into a unit of measurement called the 'wage-unit', which, despite what he chooses to call it, measures things in terms of labour: it is really a kind of 'labour-unit'.

Wage-Units: In equations (4.1) to (4.4) above, labour was implicitly assumed to be homogeneous. Under that assumption, money-income could be measured in terms of labour (hours) simply by dividing by the wage (which is also homogeneous). However, labour is not in fact homogeneous and wages differ for different skills.

Compare, with heterogeneous labour, an increase in income (ΔY) due to the employment of, say, 10 hours of unskilled labour at a wage of unity (money-income rises by 10) with an increase due to hiring 10 units of skilled labour at a wage of 2 (money-income rises by 20). Converting to labour-units by dividing by w gives ΔY in terms of labour-units as 10 in each case. For the employed labour force as a whole, the average wage will have changed.

An alternative, the alternative Keynes adopted, is to take the wage of unskilled labour and hours of common labour-time as the basic units. Let us call these $\hat{w}$ and $\hat{N}$ respectively, to distinguish them from the average wage and actual man-hours. (When reading the *General Theory*, note that Keynes uses N to mean what we shall call $\hat{N}$.)

These units serve to convert labour into a homogeneous measure: an hour's work of a skilled worker whose wage is twice that of a common labourer is counted as two labour-units, for which he is paid two wage-units. In these units the problem given above would look like this. The rise in money-income from hiring 10 unskilled labour-hours is an increase in 'wage-units' (i.e. units of $\hat{N}$) of 10. The rise due to hiring 10 skilled labour-hours raises both income in 'wage-units' and money-income by 20. The 'wage-unit' is unchanged at unity; the change in the average *actual* wage does not count.

Wage-units are a satisfactory measure subject only to the condition that relativities amongst wage rates for different occupations are fairly stable (which in Keynes's observation they were); then variations in the basic wage are a reasonable measure of wage changes generally, and these variations do not upset the relative weights given to different types of labour.

The use of the wage-unit as a proxy for 'real' magnitudes allows the general level of wages to vary without shifting the function measured in these units. Consider a rise in money-income caused solely by a rise in the wage-unit (the basic wage). Since employment has not altered, 'income in wage-units' (i.e. in these specially-defined labour-units) does not alter either. The measure is thus independent of variations in money wages, which can be anything one likes. This is from time to time an enormous convenience for the exposition of Keynes's theory.

Consumption in Wage-Units: As an approximation to 'real' magnitudes, the function describing postulated consumption behaviour is specified entirely in wage-units (indicated throughout by a subscript w):

$$C_w = \chi(Y_w) \tag{4.5}$$

This formulation is at least 'real' enough to avoid the suggestion that wage changes give rise to money illusion on the part of households, and obviates the difficulties raised by measuring in units of heterogeneous output discussed in the previous chapter.

Equation (4.5) is the propensity to consume, and as (nearly) every schoolboy knows, it is maintained that the *marginal* propensity to consume, $C'_w(Y_w)$, takes a value between zero and one.

Equation (4.5) is an equation which with only minor qualification can be used to relate consumption to employment: Y_w is denominated in labour-units but may not be uniquely related to the volume of employment, insofar as the labour-input needs of different sorts of output vary and vary systematically (e.g. if expansion in capital-goods industries were more labour-intensive than in the consumption-goods industries, and income were to expand because of new investment, an increment of employment will overstate Y_w).

Aggregate Supply in Wage-Units: The approximation of a 'real' consumption function with C_w (Y_w) is imperfect, but not difficult to understand. The formulation of aggregate supply in terms of wage-units has, however, created some conceptual difficulties; there is now quite a literature concerning the interpretation of this function.[8] The essential problem arises from the fact that the theory of the firm is constructed in money terms, because the aim of the firm is the pursuit of money profits. It is necessary to rethink it in terms of $\hat{N}$, the unit of unskilled labour.

Aggregate supply in wage-units, Z_w (which is actually denominated in units of common labour), is $Z/\hat{w}$. Before we consider its properties, note the result of dividing Z by the *uniform* wage, w, which applied to the case of homogeneous labour. This would give $(A/Q')N$. The slope of Z/w (distinguish this from Z_w!) depends on the relationship between A and Q', as for Z in money terms, though unlike Z in money terms, Z_w does not shift with changes in wages.

Now consider what it means to convert Z into a function denominated in standard labour, $\hat{N}$, coupled with the proposition that each type of labour gets its marginal value product as its wage. Let us proceed by comparing the results of an increase in employment of skilled labour and unskilled labour. Suppose skilled labour is paid three times as much as unskilled labour. If one additional skilled worker is hired, employment in labour-units, $\hat{N}$, rises, not by one but by three, while the wage-unit, $\hat{w}$, the unskilled worker's wage, is unchanged.

If everyone is paid his marginal value product, the increment of employment, of whichever kind of labour, carries with it an equivalent increment in the value of output: $\Delta\hat{N} = \Delta PQ$. This implies, as Keynes states in the footnote *(G.T.* p. 55) which has caused such vexations, that the slope of Z_w is unity.[9]

This result does not conflict with the convex (from below) shape of Z or Z/w in any way. It is difficult, however, to relate Z_w $(\hat{N})$ to the theory of the firm,[10] because the variable input is defined in 'efficiency-units' — i.e. the resulting output — which begs all the interesting questions.

The Relation between Z_w and D_w

The discussion of wage units has been lengthy and somewhat tortured, but necessary. Now we come to the matter to which all this has been leading: the relationship between the slopes of Z_w and D_w. From this the relationship between the slopes of Z and D, which is what we really want, will follow.

The slope of Z_w is unity. The slope of D_w depends on the slope of the (wage-unit) consumption function C_w (Y_w) i.e. on the marginal propensity to consume, which is less than one. Therefore D_w cuts Z_w from above. This result is crucial to Keynes's entire argument, as we shall soon see.

The slope of C_w (Y_w) implies little about the slope of $C(N)$, the function in money terms, even if N and Y_w vary closely. The difference between the two functions depends on prices. As employment rises, prices will rise, so in money terms consumption will rise faster than it does in real terms if the price rise is anticipated. Thus $C(N)$ — and hence $D(N)$ — will have a greater slope than C_w (Y_w): it may even exceed unity and the second derivative could be positive. This would in no way violate the basic assumption of a fractional *mpc*, since that relates to the function in wage-units, where the dependent and independent variables are in the same units. We know, however, from that wage-unit analysis that the slope must be less than wA/Q', the slope of $Z(N)$.[11]

Say's Law

The result that D must cut Z from above is important, for it asserts that there is limit to the profitable expansion of output, and is the basis of the first step in Keynes's refutation of Say's Law. There are many versions of Say's Law,[12] and many interpretations,[13] but at its simplest, the idea was that production, by creating income, created simultaneously the power to purchase, and since the willingness to work was motivated by the desire to consume, there could be no impediment to the sale of *any* volume of output, and hence no reason for unemployment except a failure of nerve. General over- or underproduction except for short transition periods was inexplicable, if not impossible.[14]

If Say's Law holds, there is no obstacle to full employment: output can be increased until excess labour is absorbed, for a market for the additional output is created by the very income earned in producing it. Whether output was high or low, it was always the 'right' level of output, in the sense that the demand for it always equalled its supply. In such circumstances, equilibrium output is indeterminate; the system is one of 'neutral equilibrium' in which one level of activity is as good — that is to say, as profitable — as another.

Keynes asserted that the assumption on which this version of Say's Law rested was not in accordance with actual behaviour; workers could not be counted upon to spend all the proceeds of additional labour, and hence there was a limit to the profitable expansion of output, given by the intersection of the aggregate supply and demand functions. There was no reason, he asserted, for this limit to be reached only after full employment had been attained. It was equally possible that it should be reached while unemployment still existed.

Now it is easy to see that temporary unemployment could be caused by a pessimistic forecast of aggregate demand. But it was believed that inaccurate forecasts would eventually be corrected and full employment restored. It was, indeed, precisely for the purpose of shifting the argument away from this line of reasoning that Keynes adopted, in the early chapters, the *assumption that firms' forecasts of aggregate demand were broadly correct*:[15] Keynes wished to demonstrate the possibility of limits to the profitable expansion of output below full employment, *even when demand was correctly assessed*. Herein lies the significance, to Keynes, of the consumption function, for the first phase of this demonstration rests on the 'fundamental psychological law' of consumer behaviour: that the *mpc* is less than one. With the *mpc* less than one, the simple version of Say's Law is conclusively refuted.

For the full refutation of Say's Law the potential inequality of saving and investment had to be established. That was postponed by Keynes and we follow his tactics, in order to highlight the significance of the *mpc* and the assumption that expectations are met.

Involuntary Unemployment

The second major point to be grasped about the Principle of Effective Demand is that it gives meaning to the concept of involuntary unemployment — meaning which the then-prevailing theory denied. In basing their thinking on Say's Law, the 'Classics' had no room for a concept of involuntary unemployment that was anything more than a temporary disruption caused by changes in the composition of aggregate output. As economic theorists they were prepared to admit that finding a new job takes time, but not that the level of output could persist at a level too low to sustain full employment. In suggesting policies to deal with the unemployment which had been serious for ten years before the *General Theory* was published, adherents to neoclassical analysis made it plain through their policy prescriptions that they were not unaware of reality. Their many proposals of ways to deal with unemployment belied the notion that it would go away of its own accord — at least in an acceptable length of time. But their theory could not explain the reality that was all around them in interwar Britain nor provide a theoretical rationale for policies, such as government expenditure, which many were advocating. It was this lack of a suitable theoretical foundation which motivated Keynes. The first step was to assert the possibility of involuntary unemployment.

Keynes's definition of involuntary unemployment is as follows:

> Men are involuntarily unemployed if, in the event of a small rise in the price of wage-goods relatively to the money-wage, both the aggregate supply of labour willing to work for the current money-wage and the aggregate demand for it at that wage would be greater than the existing volume of employment.
>
> (*G.T.* p. 15)

This definition is couched in terms of demand for and supply of labour with reference to the real wage, and immediately conjures up Figure 4.2, in terms of which the definition at first reading appears paradoxical: how is it that *both* demand and supply will rise! But the reference is to quantity demanded and quantity supplied, not to the schedules. The conditions are fulfilled if employment is a point on the demand curve for labour, but not on the supply curve.

Consider a point such as *A* in Figure 4.2, which indicates a level of employment determined by Effective Demand. (The translation from Figure 4.1 to the present figure is not possible diagrammatically, though all the elements are present and we shall allude to them.) In the figure, N^D and

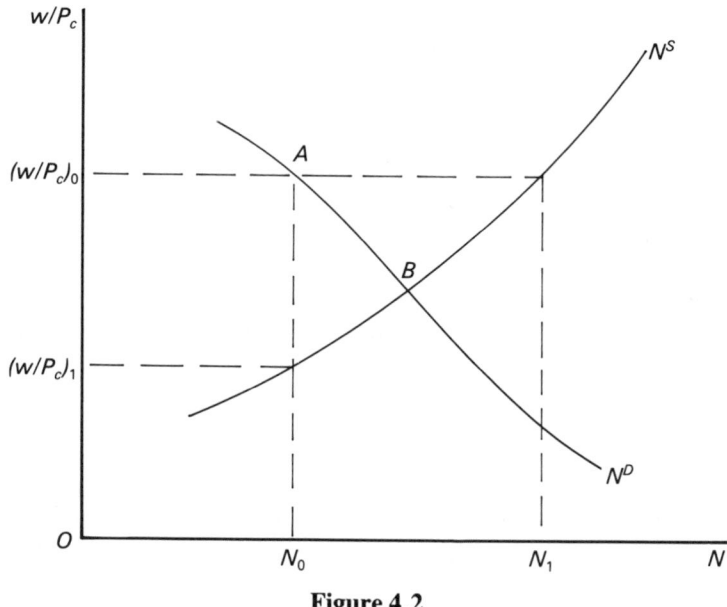

Figure 4.2

N^S are the demand for and supply of labour curves, w is 'the' money wage and P_c is 'the' price of wage goods or consumer goods.

The main trick is to understand that the labour supply curve gives the *maximum* amount of labour willingly supplied at each real wage.[16] To the left of N^S there is always labour willing to work, even if they would *prefer* still more employment. Thus a rise in the price of wage goods, the current money-wage remaining constant, results in a lower real wage, but labour willing to work at the real wage $(w/P_c)_0$, which obtained at A, would still be willing to work at any real wage above $(w/P_c)_1$; any fall in the real wage from $(w/P_c)_0$ to any wage above $(w/P_c)_1$ is consistent with a labour supply greater than N_0, the volume of actual employment, though of course the *maximum* amount of labour willingly supplied will fall as compared to N_1, the maximum available at wage $(w/P_c)_0$. It is not difficult to accept that firms' demand for labour will rise if at the going money wage there is a higher price for wage-goods. The rise in P_c, evidence of increased demand for output, enables firms to cover the higher costs which diminishing returns impose as a concomitant of profitable expansion.

So we have established that point A is a point of involuntary unemployment: it meets the definition. A point such as B would not meet it, for although the amount demanded would rise if P_c rose, the amount supplied would not rise. B is a point of full employment: everyone who wants work, at the relevant wage, has it.

Now there is no reason to expect that the point of effective demand will indicate an output sufficient to employ all those willing to work at the wage which firms expected to pay and on the basis of which they made their offers of employment. Effective demand determines the *point* on the schedule relating labour demand to real wages in Figure 4.2 at which the firms choose to operate. The determination of effective demand also asserts the existence of a unique profit-maximising price which is expected to clear the market for output. Thus if labour supply and demand are defined in terms of *money* wages, effective demand determines which of the family of demand-for-labour curves in that space, each defined for a given price level, is the relevant one, and it determines the operative point on that curve.

To anticipate the later argument, let us make a rather natural assumption, that in the absence of compelling reason to the contrary, firms expect wages today to be much the same as they were yesterday. As long as the volume of employment firms wish to offer at the going wage is no greater than the maximum willingly supplied, N^S, the analysis poses no problems: at points on N^S there is full employment, and should the level of effective demand imply a demand for less, only the amount demanded will actually be hired — there being no incentive for firms to take on labour they do not want.[17]

Unemployment Equilibrium

The above indicates the consistency of the principle of effective demand with unemployment. But it was Keynes's aim not just to demonstrate that involuntary unemployment was *possible*, but that there were circumstances in which it would persist. A hint of the theory which leads to this result is given in the following passage:

> ...[A] decline in employment, though necessarily associated with labour's *receiving* a wage equal in value to a larger quantity of wage-goods, is not necessarily due to labour's *demanding* a larger quantity of wage-goods ...
>
> (*G.T.* p. 18, emphasis in original)

A full discussion of the reasoning behind that statement is presented in Chapter 7, but a sketch of the argument is presented now.

The relative impotence of the household sector which Keynes alludes to results from the combination of the circumstances of prevailing unemployment, the absence of collective bargaining, and the sequential nature of decisions as they must be taken in a production economy. In a period of general unemployment, firms can reasonably expect to obtain as much labour as they wish at the wage they have been observing in the recent past. The labour supply curve indicates the *maximum* labour available at any given wage — to the left of the curve labour is always available. So there is no need to raise the wage to get more labour. The absence of collective bargaining which Keynes assumed means that households are in no position to make counter-offers if the wage/employment combination is not to their liking. Workers are rather in the position of buyers in fixed-price shops; the wage is set by firms, and those offered employment may take it or leave it. Indeed, the individual worker has no incentive to offer to work for less than the going wage, unless he has already had several job refusals. Furthermore, workers acting independently have no way to assess the implications of their individual actions for the overall level of employment and hence their own prospects.

For institutional reasons, it is also difficult for firms to lower wages. Although they observe an excess supply of labour, and this indicates that labour should be willing to work for less, the established convention of a uniform wage for the job implies that firms cannot hire new workers for less than they pay their present employees. And it is an extremely difficult negotiation to get one's work force to accept lower wages. The alternative — to fire one's existing work force and hire anew — has been known to occur, but is a fairly costly way of attempting ultimately to reduce wages. And if a significant number of firms succeed in lowering the money wage, this is likely to be counterproductive; that part of the story comes later (as does an elaboration of the points just made). What needs emphasising at this juncture is that wage-cutting is difficult both for firms and for labour, acting as decentralised decision units.

The sequential nature of decisions also operates against labour, for although labour can demand higher *money* wages if the level of activity warrants it, there is no assurance that firms will not raise prices in consequence, after the wage bargain has been struck. And it is these prices which labour must pay for its consumption. Even in propitious times labour cannot insist on an increase in its real wage. And if labour presses for higher money wages when firms are not optimistic, unemployment will result. Falling prices associated with a downturn will raise real wages, but they rise as a result of entrepreneurs' pricing decisions, not because workers demanded an improved real income for those lucky enough to remain employed.

These factors conspire to make it difficult for labour to have full power to determine the money wage for which they work and impossible for them to present entrepreneurs with enforceable demands for *real* wages which simultaneously accord with firms' expectations. If there is unemployment, and if the general expectation is one of overall price stability, with falling prices in the immediate future, as was the case in the 1930s, it is likely that firms expect to be able and will be able to obtain the amount of labour they wish at 'yesterday's' wage, even if a fall in real wages is implied. If in addition they have estimated aggregate demand correctly (and they need only do so in the neighbourhood of effective demand), their sales expectations, in aggregate, will also be met. Thus there is equilibrium of production and employment, for at the point of effective demand *all the expectations of firms regarding production plans at the aggregate level, are met;* whether the level of employment is full or not is of no consequence.

In terms of Figure 4.1, actual demand will equal effective demand at E. At full employment, given the wage implicit in Z, demand would have been say, C. Though a higher level of demand than at E, it would not have been high enough to cover the costs of employing all those who wanted work. Firms demand only N^* of labour, and at the level of income generated by that level of employment, demand falls to E. Thus firms' expectations are fulfilled. They therefore have no reason to revise their production plans or to increase employment. The economy is in underemployment equilibrium, and *it is not a mistake*.

This was the situation which Keynes perceived the British economy to be in by the early thirties. For nearly a decade employment and output had been declining. By the time the *General Theory* was published, the economy had got stuck; there was little prospect of spontaneous improvement. Low employment meant low income, low income meant low demand, and low demand hardly encourages increased employment.

Unemployment equilibrium is a somewhat curious concept when viewed against the *corpus* of economic theory, for there is no specified *mechanism* which would make it come about. It depends on firms' estimating aggregate demand roughly correctly in the neighbourhood of aggregate supply, so that their sales and labour-hiring expectations are met. But Keynes provides no theory of the process by which firms come to evaluate aggregate demand; the need for such a theory is obviated by Keynes's assumption — adopted, as indicated above, to highlight the importance of the law of consumption in the refutation of Say's Law — that firms' estimates are correct. There is also no detailed discussion of the dynamics of adjustment of those estimates when they prove to be incorrect. There is only mention of the fact that adjustments will indeed be made (*G.T.* pp. 47–48).

With the perspective of hindsight, it would appear that these features of Keynes's analysis did not serve him well. First, they served to reinforce the confusion between aggregate and effective demand, for the latter was always a point, the operative point, on the aggregate demand function, and, of course, movements in the function will displace the point. So will shifts in the aggregate supply function, but the similarity of the two 'demand' terms encourages using them interchangeably. So it came to be understood that unemployment is determined by *aggregate* demand: the role of supply is forgotten. The resulting damage to policy advice has been considerable; policy directed to aggregate demand was expected to have an immediate effect on effective demand, without much regard for supply conditions or allowance for different effects on firms' expectations at different times.

Second, underemployment equilibrium, as a concept, is a threat to neoclassical modes of thinking and has been almost universally dismissed as incorrect. There is no doubt that there is nothing in Keynes's system that drives the economy to that point; we have already mentioned the sparse references to adjustment. The circumstances which produce underemployment equilibrium may arise almost accidentally; all that is required is for anticipated demand for output to fall or for labour to become more eager to accept work at the going wage (a rightward shift in N^S) without first showing any increased eagerness to buy. Then the expectation that yesterday's wage will prevail is justified, and as long as aggregate demand is estimated more or less correctly, underemployment equilibrium prevails. A full-employment equilibrium would be no less accidental.

Because underemployment equilibrium is an aggregate concept, it is impossible to believe that it would be met precisely: the probability of hitting the relevant point on aggregate demand exactly must be insignificantly different from zero. *Some* firms will always be surprised. Theorists more concerned with purity than with relevance, who cannot accept approximations, would therefore argue that some force for adjustment, however weak, must always be present, and since Keynes provides no dynamic learning process by which estimates of demand are adjusted when they are falsified, he fails as a theorist in their eyes. In all these objections, the central point, that the marginal propensity to consume sets limits to profitable output in a given state of expectations, has been lost.

Underemployment Disequilibrium and Adjustment

In an ongoing economy, there is really little point in building a theory of how firms estimate demand *de novo*. But a general discussion of the behaviour of the system in disequilibrium (as opposed to the particular situation of the Great Depression) is useful, not least because it relieves the neoclassicist of any imagined belief (which I think is quite widespread) that Keynes claimed that *all* unemployment situations were situations of unemployment equilibrium. The existence of unemployment equilibrium does not, after all, preclude the existence of unemployment *dis*equilibrium.

Disequilibrium will manifest itself when actual production valued at the selling price decided upon or anticipated at the beginning of the period (effective demand) turns out to exceed or fall short of actual aggregate demand. In order to examine the latter possibility, let us suppose that for some reason, aggregate demand shifted upward, while firms are still operating on 'last period's' level of demand. Hence effective demand, A, is based on a general underestimate of aggregate demand, D^e in Figure 4.3. Z_0 is based on the wage w_0. For the moment, assume that demand is not materially affected by income redistribution caused by changes in the level of employment. The full employment point is somewhere to the right of the point of effective demand, A.

Firms will observe, when the planned output comes on to the market, that demand exceeds supply by the amount AC. Within the period governed by prior production commitments there are three possible responses to this

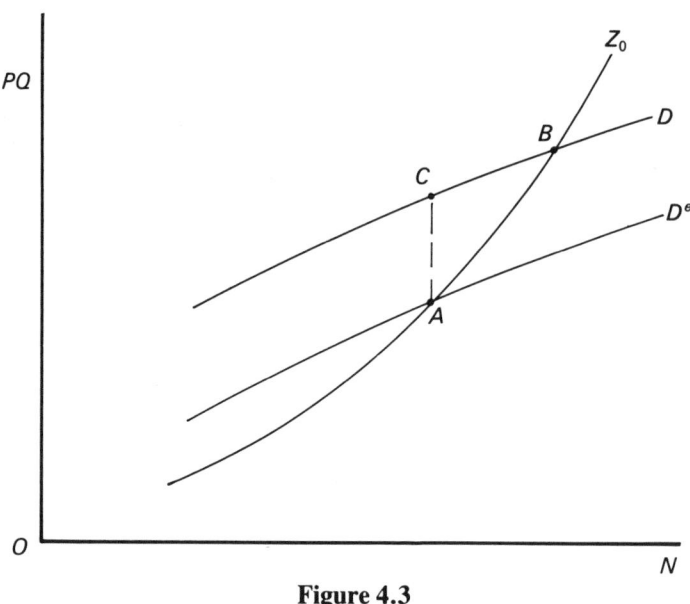

Figure 4.3

state of affairs: potential buyers may be disappointed; inventories may be depleted; or prices may rise. In practice, all of these responses are likely to occur in some degree.[18]

These adjustments to incorrect expectations occur at the end of the production period; it is obvious that any of these responses provide signals which should lead to revising D^e upward.[19] The system will move toward fuller employment, stopping at point B.[20] Whether *full* employment is achieved depends on the position of the labour supply curve (given w_0) at point B: if the full employment point lies to the right of B, it is unattainable: underemployment equilibrium is reached by an unexceptionable adjustment process. If full employment lies to the left of B, wages will begin to rise before equilibrium is reached. Wage changes cause great difficulty for the analysis, as Chapter 7 will demonstrate; the equilibrium will probably lie to the left of N_f in Figure 4.1 at a wage higher than w_0. (Price changes also cause analytical difficulties which we have ignored here.)

This adjustment process may also operate in the downward direction. If for some reason consumers decide to save more, so that the aggregate demand curve shifts downward, firms observe a fall in sales which causes them, when their expectations adjust, to cut back output and employment (and also prices). This downward adjustment takes place until the effective demand point coincides with the new aggregate demand function. Although a process of convergence to stable equilibrium, it has the unfortunate consequence of frustrating the attempt to save a larger money sum, for although the saving *schedule* has shifted *upward*, consumers find themselves further to the left on that new schedule, such that the *level* of saving has fallen. This phenomenon is known as the paradox of thrift, because the attempt to achieve a higher level of saving is self-defeating.

Being in the downward direction, the process just described could begin from a position of full employment; then the shift in savings plans creates a situation of full-employment disequilibrium — another 'contradiction in terms' which nevertheless can be very real. The disequilibrium is resolved by the adjustment process into underemployment equilibrium.

Indeed, the position of full-employment equilibrium would be just as fortuitous as our first example of unemployment equilibrium (which was achieved straightaway, not through adjustment). Full-employment equilibrium requires that aggregate demand (and entrepreneurs' estimates of it) intersect aggregate supply at exactly the maximum level of employment which labour will accept at the wage entrepreneurs expect and for which the relevant aggregate supply curve is defined.

To make the same point in the language of the textbooks; it is unlikely that the amount of desired saving at full employment would be matched by an equivalent volume of (expected) investment. This way of putting the point obscures the supply side of income determination, but it does highlight the adventitious character of equilibrium, for there is no connection which will make investment fill the expenditure-gap between consumption and income. This is equally true, however, whether one is talking about full-employment or underemployment equilibrium.

The long-run prospect for full employment is, in Keynes's view, no rosier than the short-run prospect. Long-run or 'full' equilibrium is characterised by stability of the capital stock. Thus in full equilibrium investment just covers replacement. Therefore the equilibrium level of output is that which induces no net saving. Keynes felt that the coincidence of these two conditions was unlikely unless unemployment (and thus low incomes) suppressed saving.

> The only alternative position ... would be given by a situation in which [the] stock of capital ... represents an amount of wealth sufficiently great to satiate to the full the desire on the part of the public to make provision for the future, even with full employment ... It would, however, be an unlikely coincidence ...
>
> (*G.T.* p. 218)

But that is getting ahead of the story.

Notes

1.   'An entrepreneur, who has to reach a practical decision as to his scale of production, does not, of course, entertain a single undoubting expectation of what the sale-proceeds of a given output will be, but several hypothetical expectations held with varying degrees of probability and definiteness. By his expectation of proceeds I mean, therefore, that expectation of proceeds which, if it were held with certainty, would lead to the same behaviour as does the bundle of vague and more various possibilities which actually makes up his state of expectation when he reaches his decision.' (*G.T.* p. 24, n. 3)

2.   These are outlined in *G.T.* p. 24, n. 2.

3.   '*Ex ante* decisions in their influence on effective demand relate solely to *entrepreneurs*' decisions.' (Notes for Keynes's 1937 lecture, *C.W.* XIV, pp. 182–183. The emphasis is Keynes's.)

4.   Kregel (1976) emphasises this point. It is a pity Keynes did not make more of it.

5.   This is a most extreme expedient, justified only by the complexities we face here. It must be relinquished later.

6.   See Chapter 2.

7.   The main argument is that investment is at least partly financed out of current profits, and profits vary positively with the current level of activity.

8.   Important articles for present purposes are those by Patinkin (1979), Casarosa (1981), Tarshis (1979) and Torr (1982).

9.   Keynes goes on in that footnote to state that the slope of the aggregate supply function, by which he means aggregate supply in money terms as a function of $\hat{N}$, is the reciprocal of the money wage. Patinkin (1976, p. 88, n. 8) has pointed out that the referent must be the Z axis instead of the $\hat{N}$ axis as one would expect. In addition 'the wage' should be interpreted as 'the wage-unit'. The student is advised that the whole matter of this footnote remains an open, and for present purposes not terribly important, question.

10.   It is this difficulty which has given rise to the problems raised in a series of articles in recent years of which those cited in note 8 are a part.

11.   The slope of Z is modified if the small firm assumption is not maintained. See the next chapter.

12.   See Sowell (1972), Baumol (1977).

13.   One of the most influential, that due to to Lange (1942), seems to me to miss the point of Say and those Classical writers who agreed with Say (e.g. Mill), nor does it seem to reflect the way Keynes thought of Say's Law.

14.   Just because something cannot be explained doesn't mean it doesn't exist or occur, though the temptation is to believe that it doesn't.

15.   The following justification is given:
'It will often be safe to omit express reference to *short-term* expectation (i.e. expectations of demand relevant to production decisions), in view of the fact that in practice the process of revision of short-term expectations is a gradual and continuous one, carried on largely in the light of realised results; so that

expected and realised results run into and overlap one another in their influence.' (*G.T.* p. 50)

16. The meaning of 'willing' is the same as when one says to the organiser of a sponsored walk that one is 'willing to walk ten miles'. It is understood that ten miles is the most you will walk, not that you will walk ten miles or not at all.

17. Things may be different under collective bargaining or with inflationary expectations, as we shall see in Chapter 8.

18. See *G.T.* pp. 123–4. Contrast this with the many expositions in which all adjustment falls on inventories; this results from the assumption of fixed prices so prominent in 'Keynesian' models.

19. See Keynes's discussion of the determination of these short-run expectations, *G.T.* pp. 50–51. Firms may need several observations, indicating that the shift is 'permanent', before deciding to change plans, but that is a side issue.

20. Any adverse effect on demand stemming from rising prices has been built in, as aggregate demand is specified in money terms.

Chapter 5

THE MICROFOUNDATIONS OF AGGREGATE SUPPLY

Despite the equal importance given to aggregate supply and aggregate demand in Chapter 3 of the *General Theory*, it is frequently alleged that Keynes's system ignores supply! There are many reasons for this. First, Keynes seems to have assumed that the supply side was easily understood. (How wrong he was!) Second, 'all the action' is on the demand side in Keynes — specifically, investment is the volatile element. There are good theoretical reasons for this, based on the specific assumptions Keynes's theory embodied. It is hoped to make these apparent in the course of this book, for the real-world conditions to which the assumptions approximate are not immutable, and there is a need to re-think the theory.[1]

A third reason stems from Keynes's anxiety to distinguish his theory as sharply as possible from the Ricardian tradition, in which costs (i.e. supply conditions) are of paramount importance and demand is afforded no significant role. On the face of it, ignoring demand seems absurd, but it arises from viewing the aggregate functions as originating or having validity at the aggregate level directly, instead of being derived from microeconomic behaviour. Patinkin (1976, p. 82) bears witness to

> how strange and difficult it was ... to think in terms of a demand for aggregate output as a whole — a demand that was in some way different from actual aggregate income ... How ... could one speak of a demand function for the aggregate of all goods taken together?

The difficulty Patinkin expresses is exactly that which gave rise to Say's Law in the form discussed in the previous chapter. Hawtrey (1955), also thinking directly at the aggregate level, likewise finds it impossible to consider aggregate demand and supply as functions which are not identical.

With such an orientation, one of the functions becomes redundant. It is then tempting to see Keynes as reversing, rather than refuting, Say's Law:

instead of 'Supply creates its own demand' we have 'Demand creates its own supply'. These slogans do justice to neither Say nor Keynes. Keynes's contribution on the 'real' side of his theory was precisely to give supply and demand the degree of independence required to break Say's Law. This is achieved by linking the aggregate functions to the motives and decisions of households and firms.

Throughout the *General Theory* Keynes was far from explicit about the link between the decisions of individual units and the behaviour of aggregate variables. We find this not only in the context of aggregate demand and supply; it arises also in defining both saving and investment. But it is perhaps in the context of aggregate supply that the link is most difficult to make, chiefly because of deficiencies in the treatment of the theory of the atomistic firm in microeconomics textbooks.

Firms produce in order to make profits. This is the central fact on which the aggregate supply curve is based:

> entrepreneurs will endeavour to fix the amount of employment at the level which they expect to maximise the excess of the proceeds (which the entrepreneurs expect to receive from the corresponding output) over the factor cost.
>
> (*G.T.* p. 25)

In other words, firms maximise expected profit. (Keynes says factor cost rather than prime or total variable cost because user cost has been omitted from both aggregate supply and aggregate demand.) Profits are reckoned in money terms: proceeds (or revenue, or sales) minus costs. Thus the relationship between aggregate supply and firms' behaviour is easier to see in the case of Z than of Z_w. The rudiments have already been presented in the last chapter.

One word in the above paragraph will strike anyone as anomalous for the atomistic firm: *expected* profit. Small firms are supposed to be assured of their market: they are 'price-takers' are they not?

That is where the trouble starts: the identification of the small firm with 'price-taking'. And so we must start there, elaborating what has been said in Chapters 2 and 4.

Market Forms and Price-Setting

The production and marketing of goods may take place in a variety of ways. Economic theory has treated these two processes rather as a unit, describing the resulting combination as 'the market' — for good X, for labour, even for things which have no market in the ordinary sense at all, e.g. 'the market for money'. 'Markets' (in the economist's sense) for commodities are described by two characteristics: how prices are set and the number and size of firms in the industry. This latter has been identified with the 'competitive structure' of the industry: many firms = 'competition', fewer firms = 'imperfect competition', and then 'competition' gives way to oligopoly, duopoly, monopoly, even though industries with few firms might be the most fiercely competitive of all. This identification is avoided by the term 'polypoly' which simply means 'many sellers'.

In economic theory there are two types of price-setting mechanisms: prices are said to be set by 'the market' or by firms when firms have 'some monopoly power'. With monopoly power identified with firm-size and the number of firms in the industry, price-setting is denied the small firm. Small firms are said to 'face' or 'take' prices established by 'impersonal market forces'. The nature and mode of operation of these 'forces' is quite unexplained. Price-setting is left to 'the market' because no firm is large enough to influence price by its own actions.

The price is said to be set by 'supply and demand'; let us examine what this means. In the usual textbook treatment, each firm 'takes' a series of possible market prices and, by profit-maximising, given its costs and these prices, determines its supply curve. The aggregate of the curves so derived, the 'market supply curve' is then confronted with the demand curve for the product and the price is determined with the aid of well-informed consumers and the self-interest of firms in some manner which is superficially intuitively appealing, but which has no basis in institutions or the knowledge available to market participants.

In the real world prices are always set by persons, not by impersonal market forces: by producers, retailers, jobbers, brokers. The question of the number of firms in the industry and how they interact is quite separate from the mechanism of price-setting. Even a stall-holder in a street market must set his prices — who else is going to do it? Of course the prices in the street market are not wildly dissimilar from one stall to another, but the market itself cannot set them. (Who sets his prices first? and how does he do it?) Large firms may have to 'take' prices from wholesalers or retailers or from brokers or jobbers on organised markets. These facts dissociate polypoly and 'price-taking'.

When the textbook version of price-taking is given a second thought, anomalies present themselves. The supply curve is said to be derived using prices 'given by the market'. These prices in turn depend on the sum of firms' supply curves. Critics of the model have offered several solutions to this paradox. (1) Everything is simultaneously determined. (This begs the question of what is meant by 'taking', as firms' supply decisions influence the outcome.) This solution restricts the analysis to single periods and really only determines one point on each firm's supply curve — the 'equilibrium' or market-clearing point. (2) The price (or level of demand) is regarded as predetermined (and thus 'takeable'). This permits extension of the analysis to more than one period — indeed the extension is required — but the price must not change. This is the model of 'tranquillity', a succession of periods whose characteristics are unaltered. As such, the tranquil economy partakes of the timelessness, certainty, and perfect information which characterise the simultaneous solution found by the Almighty Accountant or Auctioneer. (3) To allow for changed prices, it has been imagined by some that the idea of price-taking involves putting one's production on the market for whatever price it will fetch. The production plan must have been decided on some price prevailing in the past; the change in price occurs between that time and the fruition of the plan. In this view the firm is passive even to the point of not having a reservation price, which is pretty unlikely.

The whole paradox may be resolved, as it must if we are to make any sense of firms' behaviour under uncertainty, by distinguishing three stages in decision-making, based respectively on hypothetical, expected, and actual levels of demand.

The Derivation of a Firm's Supply Curve

The reader is asked to be patient if we begin with the obvious. A supply curve, a locus of optimal levels of production[2] intended for sale, depends on (i) the criterion of optimality, (ii) costs, and (iii) varying levels of potential demand facing the firm. (i) Profit maximisation will be taken as the criterion throughout; other criteria may be adopted by the reader to suit his taste. (ii) Apart from user cost, which will be ignored until the end of this chapter, costs are determined by input prices (wages) and technology. Technology is fixed throughout (the short-run assumption) and input prices by convention are fixed for any given supply curve.

It is the meaning of (iii) which has caused so much trouble, for it has come to be believed that only for the small, 'price-taking' firm can a supply curve be derived, because only for these firms is demand known and given independently ('by the market'). However, the market-determined price is quite unsuitable to the task of developing a supply strategy, for the reasons given above.

It is a misconception to think of the supply curve as a set of reactions to the market. It is a thought-experiment: a producer may pose questions of optimal supply for conditions of demand that he has not experienced but can imagine. For this he needs no price given by the market: indeed that would restrict him to past experience, unable to react to new situations. Demand possibilities, a range of hypothetical demand curves, are what is required.

Since the levels of demand which enter into the formation of the supply curve are purely hypothetical, the supply curve is entirely independent, conceptually, of either the level of demand expected[3] or the actual level of demand — though all three should have common properties of suitability to the institutional framework within which the firm operates. This is a point to which we return later.

The supply curve of a firm indicates the profit-maximising level of production and price given various hypothetical levels of demand, assuming no plan to accumulate or decumulate stocks of finished goods in a systematic manner in order to alter their average level. For each possible level of demand the profit-maximising price/quantity combination is found by equating marginal cost to the marginal revenue appropriate to each level of demand. The result is an overall strategy, ready for any specific expectation of demand. That strategy is the supply curve. The principle of its derivation is perfectly general, applicable to small and large firms alike.

Production and Pricing Decisions: Actual pricing and output decisions require a specific *expectation* of demand: one of the hypothetical demand curves must be chosen as the most likely. (This does not mean that the producer has a 'single, undoubted expectation', but that he must decide on the most likely outcome — that is the mathematical meaning of 'expectation' — and act on it.)

Once the producer has settled on an expected level of demand, the point on the supply curve which should be implemented is singled out. Thus hypothetical demands enter the supply curve, and that supply curve in conjunction with a *particular expectation* of demand determines the firm's output, pricing policy and offers of employment until that expectation, or some cost factor, changes.

These two stages of decision-making, the formation of a general strategy and the taking of a specific decision, do not involve the actual level of demand. Indeed they cannot, for the actual level of demand will not be manifest until long after the decision to produce and price is taken. In the terms developed in Chapter 2, we are still at the beginning of the production period. Thus it is unambiguous that both the supply curve and the amount supplied are independent of actual demand.

Naturally the producer hopes his expectation is correct, and when it is, the expected level of demand and the actual amount supplied are equal to actual demand. In that situation, which we can call equilibrium, there is no incentive to change, in subsequent periods, one's expected-demand level. If the level of demand expected when the output decision was taken does not turn out to be correct, then a third stage of decision-making may be entered into, in which the now past level of actual demand influences current expectations, causing the producer to choose another hypothetical level of demand as the basis for his decision. His supply response to that altered expectation has, however, already been formed: it is embodied in the supply curve.[4]

To fix ideas, consider Figure 5.1(a), which concerns a small firm. The demand-lines labelled d, d', etc. are hypothetical levels of demand. Their horizontal slope is determined only by the firm's size. The supply curve 'S' begins where variable costs are covered, i.e. at the minimum of AVC, the average variable cost curve, and is a bold line. D^e is the expected level of demand. P_0 and Q_0 are the profit-maximising price and quantity *given* that

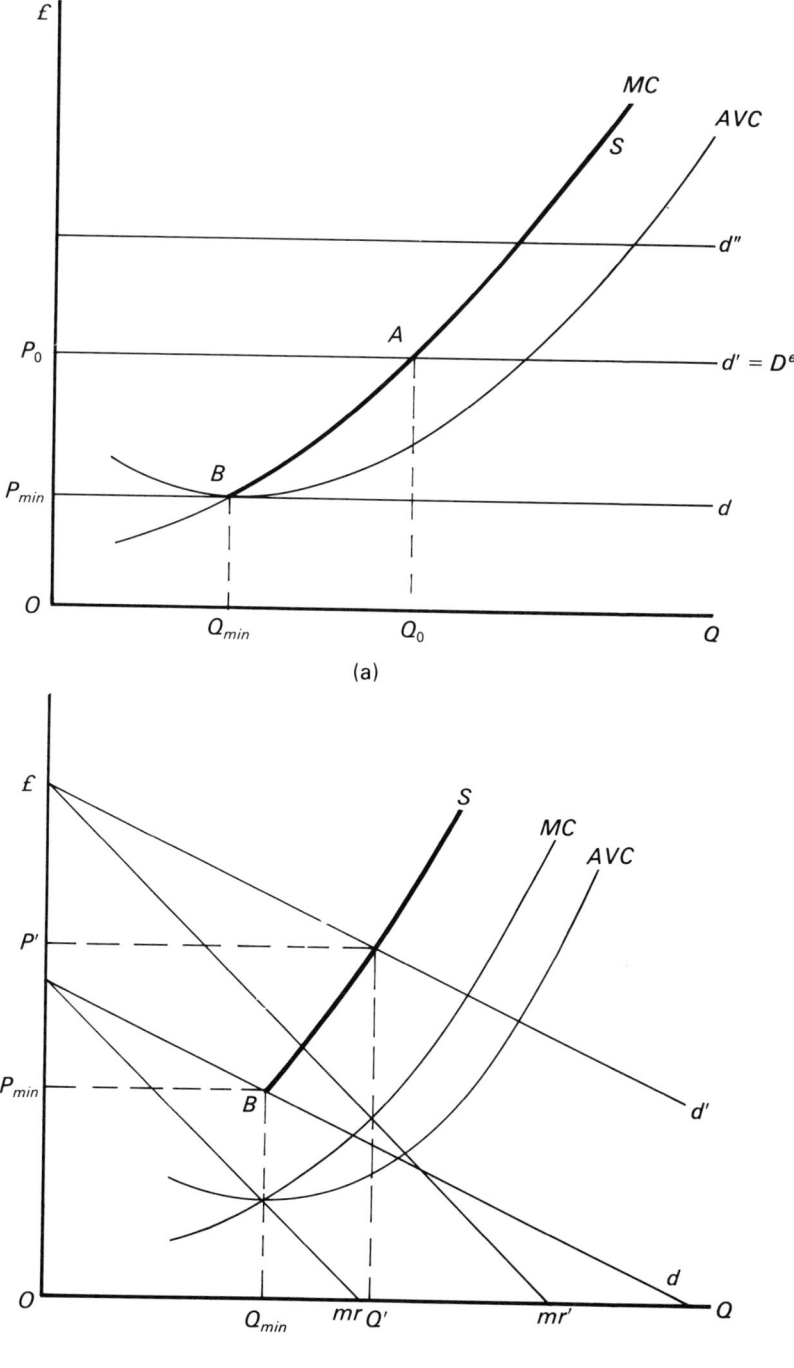

Figure 5.1

level of anticipated demand; point A corresponds to the point of effective demand in aggregate analysis. The actual level of demand may be anywhere; its position will only be known later.

Figure 5.1(b) concerns a not-so-small firm. (To avoid worrying about interfirm reactions, perhaps think of this firm as a monopolist.) The same procedure leads to a supply curve above MC. The relationship between price and MR (or MC) is given by:

$$P = \frac{|\eta|}{|\eta| - 1} MR,$$

where $|\eta|$ is the absolute value of the elasticity of the demand curve at the relevant point.[5]

Aggregation to the Industry Level

Aggregation may be discussed in two stages, to isolate the difficulties pertaining to each: aggregation to the industry level and to the economy as a whole. The first is true (at least in theory) for problems associated with heterogeneous output, but poses starkly the question of compatibility of firms' expectations or, alternatively, the relation between market demand and individual firms' demands, whether these be hypothetical, expected, or actual.

The problem is quickly understood by considering the relation between the individual small firm's perception of demand and the demand curve for the output of the industry as a whole: the former is horizontal, the latter downward-sloping. Aggregation of horizontal curves will not give a downward-sloping curve.

But why should one look at the problem that way round? Surely producers estimate the demand for their product and draw inferences for their firms, not the other way round. How *can* it be the other way round? The problem for the small firm, surely, is to infer the correct price from the market demand curve. To do it perfectly they must know other firms' supply responses, which is clearly impossible. So some assumptions are made about other firms' supply responses and price responses. These are hidden from view by the price-taking paradigm, which also disguises the fact that polypoly is no different in this respect from other market forms short of monopoly.

The horizontal demand curve is appropriate for a small firm not because it can sell absolutely any quantity at the designated price, but because if it prices low enough to sell anything, it can sell at least as much as it produces; the demand curve will become downward-sloping at some point determined by the market demand curve and by the single firm's share in the market (alternatively, the number of firms of a 'standard' size). This can be seen by imagining that all firms have identical cost curves; if they all estimate the level of demand correctly, they will exactly meet, and exhaust, market demand at that price. Their individual demand curves will slope downward just at the point of intersection with marginal cost.

At the other end of the spectrum, suppose one firm's estimate is out of line with the others. If it sets price too high, it loses all customers; if too low, its demand curve continues horizontal until the level of market demand at that price is reached.

The appropriate slope of a firm's demand curve is determined by the firm's relative size, nothing else. Relative size is partly a matter not only of the scale of operations but of other firms' price-setting behaviour.[6] (The effects of, say, undercutting would be obvious.)

The importance of other firms' price-setting behaviour is made explicit in monopolistic competition and oligopoly theory, but — and this is the important point — the principle is no different in the case of polypoly. This proposition justifies fully our freedom to draw supply curves for firms in all market forms[7] — which is just as well, since all firms must have a supply strategy. The information larger firms require may seem to be greater — they need to know demand elasticity as well as marginal cost — but in fact the problem of inferring the correct *level* of (horizontal) demand from a market forecast is at least as tricky for the managers of a small firm, when what is involved is truly understood.

The correct *shape* of an individual firm's demand curve, whether hypothetical or expected, does not depend on price-taking or price-making but on the firm's relative size, on the degree to which producers in the industry are likely to see market developments in the same way and the degree to which they price their output independently.

One cannot generally expect all producers to draw correct inferences for their firms, even if they all estimate market demand correctly. So there will be some 'coordination failures' no doubt. One can in fact expect such failures short of everyone knowing everything about other firms in the industry. Now, plainly, firms do not and cannot estimate the supply behaviour of all their competitors. The results of not doing so are well-known in, for example, agricultural production, where a high price provokes over-production and a lowering of price due to greater supply in the subsequent year. This sort of iteration plays a role in Keynes's discussion of wage cuts (Chapter 19), when firms believe their profit prospects to be greater than they turn out to be when other firms also expand. They learn from their mistakes and adapt their expectations. To construct an aggregate supply curve it is enough to postulate that producers make sensible inferences from expectations of market demand and their industrial structure, and correct their mistakes when other firms' behaviour is unexpected.

Aggregation over Industries

The most obvious problem in aggregating to the 'economy' level is that output is not homogeneous. In the previous chapter we used the trick of the Hicksian composite good, but trick it was.

Value is the obvious dimension to work in, and so it is that aggregate supply is specified in terms of the proceeds (or revenue) which would justify a given volume of employment. In the theory of the firm, one works in the dimensions P and Q, and the employment implications are left implicit. In aggregate, one works in the PQ and N dimensions and the division between P and Q is left implicit. (This has caused no end of trouble.) In microeconomics, the omitted function, the demand for labour, is treated separately but is derived from the same production function which generates the cost curves. In macroeconomics, the production function itself, which provides the link between Q and N and thus decides the division between P and Q, is omitted. That does not mean that the division is indeterminate; *most especially it does not mean that a change falls only on P or on Q at the whim of the theorist,* as is commonly believed.

(It is worth digressing to point out that the reason it has become widely believed that Keynes's theory is one exclusively of quantity-adjustments has to do with the complete omission of the aggregate supply curve in the *IS–LM* version of Keynesian theory.[8])

The translation from P, Q space to PQ, N space was demonstrated algebraically in the previous chapter, taking the small firm as representative in an economy producing a 'composite good'. Z-curves for firms which are not 'small' take the form

$$Z_i = \frac{|\eta_i|}{|\eta_i| - 1} \frac{wA_i}{Q_i'} N_i \qquad (5.1)$$

the subscript i indicating a single firm. This equation is, indeed, the general form, with $|\eta|/(|\eta| - 1)$ reducing to unity for the small firm.

It is immediately obvious that the economy comprises both small and large firms, that the extent to which a change in demand falls on price or quantity depends partly on the relative importance of the two sorts of firms, and that this in turn depends on the relative demands for the products of polypolistic and highly concentrated industries. From this it follows equally obviously that an aggregate supply curve must presume something about the composition of demand at different levels of activity.

Two assumptions occur to one: either that the composition of output does not vary substantially amongst industries or merely that the distribution of output is uniquely related to the level of output. The former permits the importance of each firm's supply to be weighted relatively to the aggregate, Z_i/Z, and the weights may remain constant along Z. This is the assumption made in the extremely important contribution by S. Weintraub (1958). In the *General Theory*, Chapter 20, however, Keynes made the latter assumption, supposing that all expansion took place in the investment-goods industries. Clearly that assumption suited his analytical purpose. There is no single 'right way'.

The composition of aggregate demand having been firmly linked to the level of the total, one could, it would seem, begin at the lowest level of (aggregate) demand at which some firms would be prepared to hire anyone at all, and add up all employment at that level, then make the same enquiry at a higher level of demand, and so on. The offers of employment are rooted in individual firms' supply decisions. This suggests that the general form of Z for the individual firm goes through in the aggregate:

$$Z = \frac{|\eta|}{|\eta| - 1} \frac{wA}{Q'} N \qquad (5.2)$$

where the absence of an index indicates aggregation.

User Cost: There is a qualification to this procedure, having to do with the fact that both aggregate demand and aggregate supply are net of user cost.

One tends to think of user cost in terms of wearing out capital equipment. The idea was more general, including that element of capital which gets most thoroughly used up in the process of production: raw materials. Insofar as these, and other elements of user cost such as replacement parts for machinery, are supplied out of the current output of other firms, they do not count in aggregate demand or supply. If nothing else, the mid-1970's rise in oil prices indicates that although user cost may be difficult to handle, it ought to be integrated into standard macroeconomics. As things stand, the whole supply side is ignored and almost nobody has ever heard of user cost.

From the exposition of Chapter 3 one can understand why it was ignored: it is a difficult concept. And proper treatment of it in terms of Z and D is more difficult yet:

> The essential point is that the aggregate proceeds and aggregate supply price net of user cost can be defined uniquely and unambiguously: whereas, since user cost is obviously dependent both on the degree of integration of industry and on the extent to which entrepreneurs buy from one another, there can be no definition of the aggregate sums paid by purchasers, *inclusive* of user cost, which is independent of these factors. There is a similar difficulty even in defining supply price in the ordinary sense for an individual producer: and in the case of the aggregate supply price of *output as a whole* serious difficulties of duplication are involved, which have not always been faced. If the term is to be interpreted gross of user cost, they can only be overcome by making special assumptions relating to the integration of entrepreneurs in groups according as they produce consumption-goods or capital-goods, which are obscure and complicated in themselves and do not correspond to the facts. If, however, aggregate supply price is defined as above *net* of user cost, these difficulties do not arise.
>
> (*G.T.* p. 24)

That is macroeconomic thinking: the whole input–output matrix is involved.

Netting out user cost prevents double-counting of output, putting aggregate supply on a value-added basis.[9]

The behaviour of user cost on the cost side may not be too difficult to intuit. There are two major components: physical wear and tear and the optimal end-of-period value of capital. Physical wear and tear should be positively related to output; this is obviously true of raw materials, and machinery also tends to wear out faster and be more difficult to maintain when run flat-out. On this count user cost adds little to Z at low levels of output and more at higher levels. Optimal future value may not follow output so closely: in a period of recovery, for example, one expects a sharp upward valuation of one's capital as expectations of future profits improve. In the slump, user cost on this count is almost nil: one's machinery is virtually a free good and de-stocking is beneficial to one's cash position. Similarly in a recovery the expectational aspect of user cost may be higher than it is at the crest of a boom as optimism fades.

In view of the difficulties and uncertainties surrounding user cost we will continue to define Z (and D) net of user cost unless otherwise stated, hoping that an input–output expert will take up macroeconomics and suggest a powerful simplification.

Properties of Z

Z and Wages

As in the case of the marginal cost curves basic to the construction of Z, 'the wage' is taken as given along any given Z. It will be clear, having discussed the wage-unit concept, that 'the wage' here stands for the wage *structure*, relativities between different skill levels being taken as roughly constant.

The level of wages determines the beginning- and end-points of each Z. The higher the wage, the greater the revenue necessary to justify producing at all. Recall that even in the short run (in the sense, here, of a short period of time during which a depressed level of demand is seen as temporary), no production will be undertaken which does not cover variable cost — i.e. to the left of point B in Figure 5.1(a) and (b). There is a corresponding point for the beginning of Z.[10]

If wages are given but employment and output can vary — i.e. if Z is a line, not a point — then it follows that the points on that line correspond to positions *behind* the labour supply curve. The point at which further output is impossible without bidding up the wage is the point where the labour supply frontier has been reached: full employment (at that wage). That is the end-point of a given Z.

Figure 5.2 illustrates these propositions. The top diagram portrays a labour supply curve. The bottom diagram draws Z curves for each of several

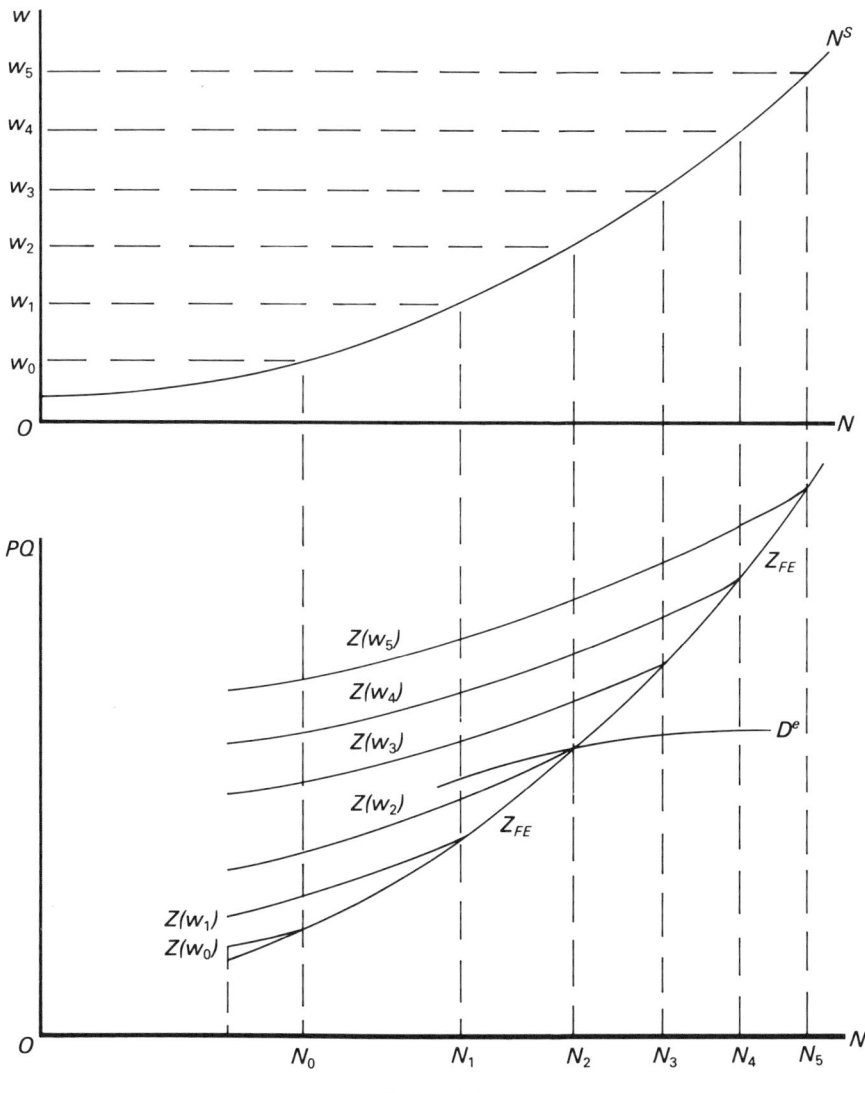

Figure 5.2

levels of wages, w_0, w_1, etc. beginning at the minimum-variable-cost point of
the most efficient firm. N_0, N_1, etc. are the end-points of Z corresponding to
these wage levels. An envelope curve, Z_{FE}, corresponding to full
employment and implying a variable wage, can be drawn. It can be seen that
full employment requires that expected aggregate demand, at the wage
firms expect to have to pay, say w_2, must intersect the final point of $Z(w_2)$, as
shown.

The Slope of Z

The slope of Z relates to the question of increasing or decreasing returns. The assertion of diminishing returns is an important feature of the *General Theory*. It provides the rationale for the acceptance of the first Classical postulate, for it is the necessity for prices to rise to cover increased costs as recovery from a slump proceeds that gives the inverse relationship between employment and real wages when money wages are sticky — indeed, even when they are fixed.

The assumption that prices rise with expansion of output has fallen out of favour based largely on scepticism concerning diminishing returns. There are at least two possible sources of this scepticism. First, there is the fact that the use of modern mass production techniques gives economies to large scale production. The efficient use of such techniques requires a high initial level of output; that is, increasing returns prevail over a substantial range. Second, there is empirical evidence. An early and influential study of cost conditions (Johnston, 1960) found that constant costs appeared to prevail over a broad range of output, and later studies have not contradicted this finding.

In the light of these points it is well to review the conditions under which profitable production in the range of increasing returns may take place. First notice that what we mean by increasing or decreasing returns is not always clear: the mass-production argument has to do with *average* costs (ATC or AVC) falling. The empirical evidence suggests that AVC is roughly constant and therefore MC is also constant.

Consult Figure 5.3, which portrays ATC, AVC and MC on the assumption that AVC eventually rises. Someone who defines increasing/decreasing returns on the basis of ATC will focus on point A, and say, perhaps, that over a range returns increase, then they decrease. But note: (i) if this firm is 'small', pricing at marginal cost, Range I is ruled out even for the short term, as it is better not to produce at all than to produce in that range. Range II is a loss-making range where production will continue for a limited time.

For the larger firm, however, part of Range I becomes feasible in the short run (Ib, Ic of Figure 5.4) and may even be feasible in the long run (Ic). Increasing returns may be a possibility.

As for constant AVC and MC, we have shown that there need be no incompatibility of the small firm with constant costs, for the demand facing a small firm does not extend indefinitely to the right, except for short-lived situations in which it underprices, but rather begins to slope downward when the market demand is shared out amongst firms in the industry.[11]

But those who argue the empirical case both for constant costs and for a degree of monopoly power must face the fact that if firms are profit-maximising, prices will rise with demand even though returns are constant — for the gap between MC and (expected) demand is continually rising.

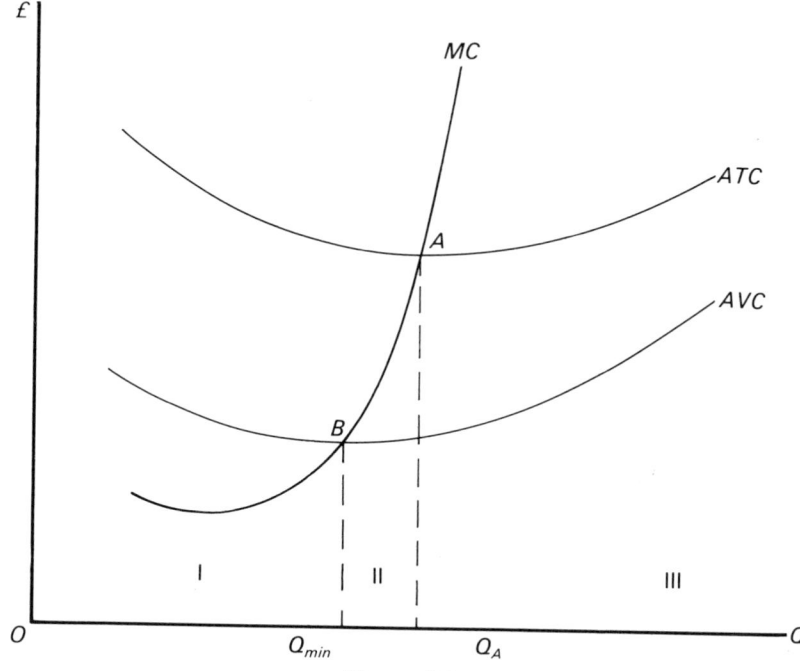

Figure 5.3

Figure 5.4

This makes the central point: the course of prices during expansion has nothing to do with *ATC* (for a profit-maximising firm) and has to do with *AVC* only as *AVC* determines *MC*. When *AVC* is not constant, no production is profitable where *MC* is not rising. The only possibility for prices to fall with expanding demand is for the elasticity of demand to fall sufficiently to offset rising *MC*. They may stay constant if the offset is exact. Prices may also stay constant in small firms with constant *AVC's*, if such there be.

The argument has been turned on its head a bit, as if the cost structure fully determined prices in all cases, forgetting that to 'move along a cost curve' expected demand has to be rising. And it is the *marginal* cost curve, not *ATC* or even *AVC*, which enters (and in the small-firm case determines) prices.

Z and Income Distribution

The wage is fixed for any given *Z*. Therefore we can superimpose on a *Z*-diagram a line representing the wage bill — a straight line through the origin with slope *w*. See Figure 5.5. *Z* begins at the point corresponding to Q_{min} in Figures 5.1(a) (b). The vertical distance between *Z* net of user cost and *wN* or prime cost net of user cost is of course gross profit.[12]

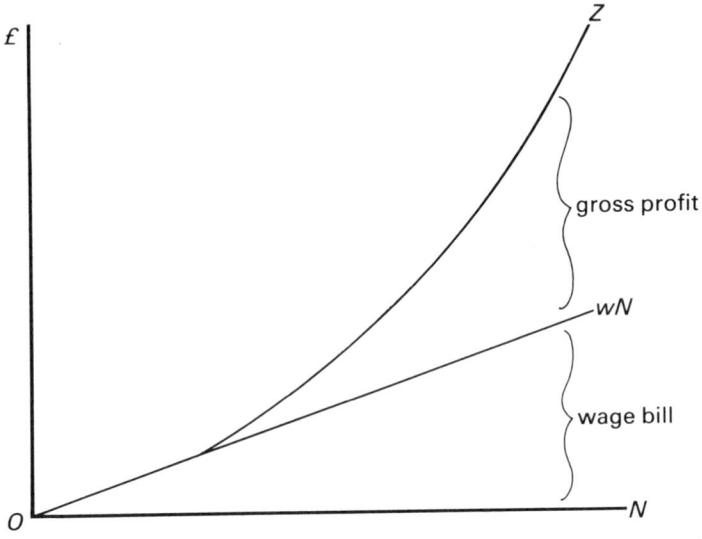

Figure 5.5

It can be seen from this figure that for every point on *Z*, and therefore every potential point of effective demand, there exists a unique income distribution. It can also be seen that while all points on *Z* are profit-maximising points, the *volume* of profit rises as output rises, in the short run and for a given wage. The distribution of income as between profits and wages clearly shifts in favour of profits in an expansion.

Notes

1. The emergence of 'supply-side economics' in the last few years is recognition of this point, even if what is meant by that term is a set of anti-Keynesian ideas.

2. This definition assumes a stable average inventory of finished goods and ignores transitory fluctuations in stocks. If the firm for a time adopts a policy of systematic inventory accumulation or decumulation this definition would have to be qualified.

3. Here the present treatment differs from that of Davidson and Smolensky (1964), who incorporate expected demand into Z and ignore the role of hypothetical demand.

4. To the literal-minded I must say that I do not suppose that actual producers consciously use precisely these constructs. In particular, supply responses may only be formulated in the producer's mind for a very limited range of variation of demand.

5.
$$MR = P + Q\,\frac{dP}{dQ}$$
$$= P + Q\,(\frac{1}{\eta}\,\frac{P}{Q}),$$

where η is defined as negative. Thus

$$MR = P\,(1 + \frac{1}{\eta})\text{, or}$$

$$P = \frac{1}{1 + (1/\eta)}\,MR = \frac{1}{1 - (1/|\eta|)}\,MR = \frac{|\eta|}{|\eta| - 1}\,MR.$$

6. Stigler (1966) Appendix B, gives a formal demonstration of the relation between the elasticity of a firm's demand curve and its relative size, in which the influence of the assumption of simultaneous changes in prices is also apparent. What a pity this treatment did not become part of the standard textbook treatment.

7. It is often alleged that this cannot be done. All that is required, however, is the assumption that the firm does not control or manipulate demand (this would reduce a range of hypothetical levels of demand to one demand curve and reduce supply to a point, rather than a schedule), and that the effect of interaction among firms in the oligopolistic industries can be accounted for in the firm's estimate of its own demand.

8. Something called the aggregate supply curve has found its way into textbooks in the last decade, but it has no foundation in firms' profit-seeking behaviour.

9.   Without Tarshis (1979) I would not have seen this point at all clearly.

10. Some authors believe Z should go through the origin. While it is true that there is no output if there is no employment, that reasoning is not sufficient.

11. Malinvaud (1977) has misleadingly called this 'rationing', but it is really to do with market shares.

12. The addition of fixed costs will indicate the point of long-run viability of the firm, but that point has no relevance to the Principle of Effective Demand.

Appendix to Chapter 5

DERIVATION OF THE DEMAND FOR LABOUR

In the body of this chapter we have shown that the end-points of Z are given by the labour supply curve and the rest of Z is given by technology and the assumed wage. In preparation for Chapter 7 it would be well to spell out the relationship between Z and the *demand* for labour, as well.

One may specify the demand for labour in either of two ways: as a function of the real wage or as a function of the money wage, expected prices being given. The principles involved in deriving the former are easier to explain, so we begin there. We restrict the analysis to a world of polypolistic firms.

For each Z the wage is fixed, so the demand for labour is, along any given Z, a function of the expected price, i.e. of the expected, or since we are dealing with the entire function, the hypothetical, level of demand. Movements rightward along Z imply rising prices, so offers of employment and prices are positively related; therefore the demand for labour (N^D) and the real wage are negatively related. The slope of the labour demand curve is determined by the extent to which a given rise in N is associated with a rise in P or a rise in Q. This division is given by the extent to which returns diminish: $P = w/Q'$. Hence along a given Z the real wage declines with N^D as $Q'(N)$ falls: $w/P = Q'(N)$: the basic neoclassical labour demand curve.

There is one vital difference with at least some neoclassical treatments: here, the dependence of N^D on Z is explicit. The demand for labour is *derived from* producers' expectations of demand for output which give the relevant point on Z; thus the full curve is derived from the range of output-demand possibilities that trace out Z. (For a contrasting, neoclassical treatment see the discussion of the extended *IS–LM* model in Chapter 13.)

We have shown how $N^D(w/P)$ may be derived from a single Z, but there is no need to restrict oneself to a given wage: w/P is only a ratio. It follows from the above however that N^D is fully determined by the factors that enter into the whole family of Z's derived for a given technology.

If one wishes to derive the relation between N^D and w, the money wage, one must indeed use more than one Z. Figure 5A.1 shows only two Z's but imagine the whole family. Now the microeconomic curve $N^D(w)$ assumes a level of demand, represented for an atomistic firm by a given price level. In aggregate, however, the

99

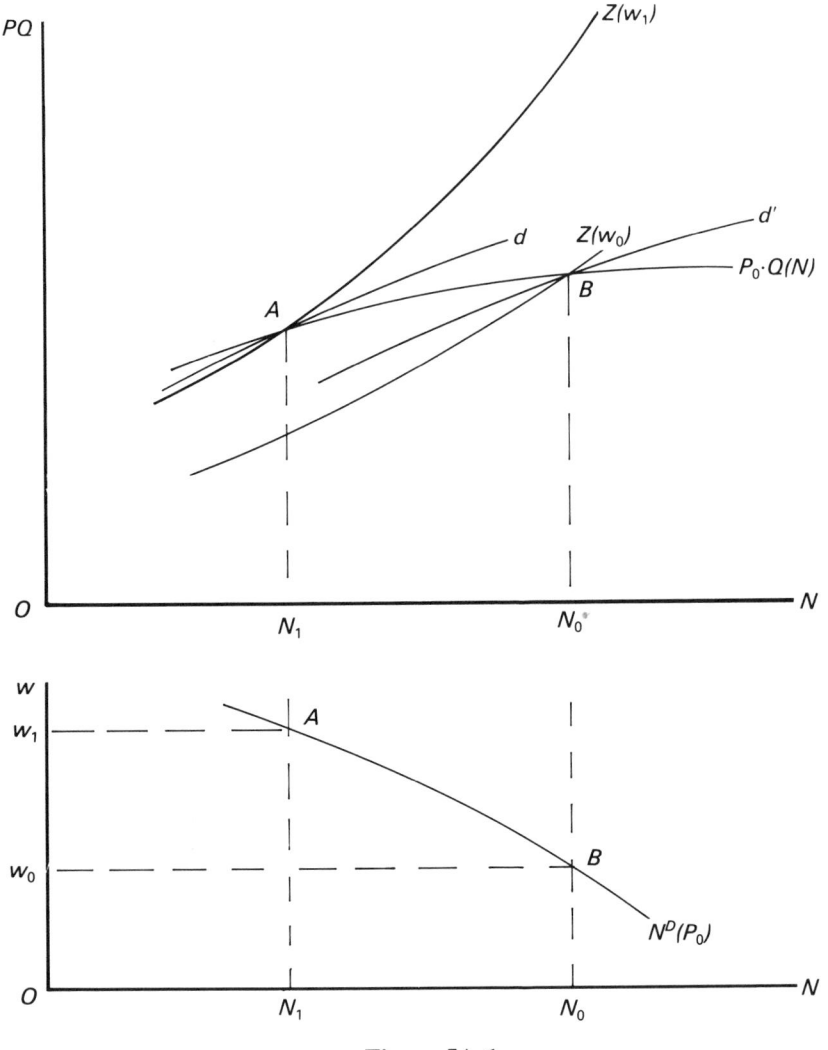

Figure 5A.1

level of output varies with N. So we superimpose on the Z's the production function, $Q(N)$, multiplied by an arbitrarily chosen price level P_0, to represent that level of output, with varying N, which firms could produce with a constant price. Then the Z's tell one the wage at which it would maximise profits to do so. Two points on $N^D(W)$ for P_0 are given by the points A and B: w_0N_0 and w_1N_1.

Hypothetical demand curves e.g. d and d' go through A and B of course (and every other point too). They are steeper than $P_0Q(N)$, for buyers are willing to pay higher prices, as well as to buy more output, when employment rises.

The importance of the three types of demand is well brought out by this exercise. Chapter 6 will show the links between the supply of labour and aggregate demand (planned expenditure). This chapter has shown that the supply of labour determines only the end-points of Z, and that the demand for labour is fully determined by Z, which is in turn derived from *hypothetical* levels of demand, and costs. A particular *level* of labour demand is thus a point on the demand curve for labour fixed by the producer's estimate of the wage (so selecting a particular Z) and the level of *expected* demand (which determines the relevant point on Z, the point of effective demand).

Labour supply and demand curves are essentially redundant: everything is embodied in the aggregate supply and demand curves. They are, however, convenient to use for certain purposes.

Chapter 6

AGGREGATE DEMAND

Expected and Actual Demand

The link between the aggregate demand consumers and producers intend to exercise (their plans) and demand as expected by producers is made only casually and tenuously in the *General Theory*. Those who complain that there is no theory of the formation of expectations of demand are entirely correct, and we shall not improve on the situation.

That does not mean that the expected-demand curve should be banished from theory, nor does it mean that the determinants of demand from the point of view of consumers and investing producers are not of interest. Purchasing plans will be manifest at whatever the level of activity and employment producers' expectations determine; and if the sales which result conflict with expectations, the latter will eventually be revised. In anything more than one production period, the plans of buyers and the expectations of producers are co-equal in the theory.

There is however a difference in the relationship between estimated and actual consumption on the one hand and estimated and actual investment on the other, a difference in the level of difficulty faced by a consumption-goods producer and a capital-goods producer in estimating demand. Consumption goods are bought fairly regularly (this is less true of durables of course, and these are now more important than they were in Keynes's time), so producers have a steady flow of information; their profit expectations being tested against the market almost continuously. And consumption is closely geared to current levels of activity. Capital-goods producers are rather in the position of second-guessing their customers' long-run expectations in order to form their own short-run expectations; recent experience may not be a good guide. The only thing that keeps this process on the rails, perhaps, is that major capital goods with long expected lives tend to be produced to order.

Those who complain that Keynes's aggregate demands, consumption and investment, are not rooted in microeconomic behaviour also have a point, for there are problems which Keynes by-passed in the urgency to create a genuine *macro*economics. The amount of work done subsequently on both the theoretical foundations of consumption and investment and empirical studies is truly staggering. It may seem perverse to the reader that we choose to ignore most of it, but there is a reason: almost all that work is entirely rooted in microeconomic behaviour (indeed plans and decisions must be formulated at that level), though in the case of investment in particular, not rooted in any sound microeconomic principles (for good reason), and not orientated toward re-integration with macroeconomics. Macroeconomics has become the *IS–LM* model plus the multiplier-accelerator; these models have not been materially affected by this mass of investigation. We wish to look at things slightly differently: necessarily at a fairly primitive level, but directed toward the general scheme of the theory. And so we pick up the subject where Keynes left it.

Consumption Demand

As we saw in Chapter 4, Keynes proposes the less-than-unitary marginal propensity to consume as a 'psychological law'. Postwar economics, with its urge to formalise economic propositions, has found this argument, or lack of it, unsatisfactory although ultimately such a proposition can only be a matter of judgement. In attempting to forge a stronger link to principles of choice, research on consumption theory has concentrated on individual motivation. Microeconomic specifications are generalised to the aggregate level without discussion or qualification, rather as they are in demand-for-money theory. This procedure is not always legitimate: the inclusion of financial wealth variables is the most obvious example.

One feels that Keynes's successors cannot be blamed: throughout the *General Theory*, Keynes slides between full aggregation, aggregation up to the relevant sector, and the completely disaggregated level. His discussion of consumption is no exception. There are major difficulties in aggregation; the choice of a representative consumer cannot be relied upon as an indication of aggregate consumption if the *distribution* of income changes materially. (The same point arose in Chapter 5 with changes in the composition of productive activity.)

It is illuminating, however, to use the theory of consumer choice to analyse the relation between consumption and income in a way which shows the link between the consumption relation and conditions in the labour market, taking the individual household as representative. This exercise occupies most of our attention. But let us begin by reminding ourselves how Keynes talked about consumption.

Subjective and Objective Factors

The method of choice theory is based on a system of preferences reflecting subjective tastes, which buyers use to make their best choices, subject to some objective constraint. The bland 'utility function' has its more colourful counterpart in Keynes's list of 'subjective factors' governing consumption: Enjoyment, Shortsightedness, Generosity, Miscalculation, Ostentation and Extravagance.[1] These factors can safely be assumed to be rooted in 'human nature' as shaped by a relatively stable social fabric. Thus it is the 'objective factors' — such as income — which are chiefly responsible for changes in consumption levels.

Amongst the objective factors, income is paramount. The rest are qualifications: (1) a change in the wage-unit, (2) a change in the difference between income and net income, (3) windfall changes in capital values, (4) changes in the rate of time-discounting: the relative preference for goods today over goods tomorrow, (5) changes in taxation and government debt-retirement policy, (6) changes in expected future income relative to present income.

Factors (4) and (6), though much-beloved by investigators of a neoclassical temperament, were included by Keynes more for completeness than their importance. Keynes regarded (6) as too uncertain and too variable across individuals to draw definite conclusions. In an era of inflationary expectations, the need to draw them, if not the ability, is perhaps more acute than it was in Keynes's time.[2]

Factor (4), approximated by the rate of interest, Keynes reckoned to have minimal effect purely through time preference, though he did allow importance to the effects on consumption of changes in the value of financial assets due to interest-rate changes. Clearly, here he is thinking at the microeconomic level, for security-holders as a body cannot realise capital gains and spend the proceeds: the effort to do so drives security prices down again. Even raising the level of consumption out of *income* when financial values are thus increased has only a microeconomic rationale. The same is true of factor (3).

Yet look at factor (2)! (A reminder here: net income does not mean, as it does in macroeconomics textbooks, personal income net of taxes; rather the distinction made in Chapter 3 is intended: gross income less supplementary cost.) Changes in supplementary cost are quite impossible for individuals to perceive except as they are reflected in individuals' dividend income. Similarly with factor (5): although an individual perceives changes in either taxes or subsidies, the aggregate net change in tax policy will be obscure to him. (Yet even aggregation over all consumers is not sufficient for those amongst us who maintain that consumption is affected by recognition of the *future* tax obligations following from government borrowing policy such as to render changes in that policy nugatory: they must aggregate over generations as well.)

The question of aggregative level applies most acutely to the primary determinant, income, itself. Thinking at the individual level one might propose (as did Robertson, Hicks and Samuelson) $C_t = f(Y_{t-1})$, for one can only spend what one has already earned. Thinking at the aggregate level, wage payment periods overlap and are more frequent than production periods (which also overlap); furthermore the wage/employment bargain is struck at the beginning of the period, so C and Y should be concurrent.

The tension between micro and macro also raises the question of the *role* of income; should we see it as a *constraint* on consumption or simply as a determinant? At the individual level it is only a constraint on the consumption of those who cannot borrow. At the aggregate level too, it is a constraint only if borrowing abroad is impossible. For a closed economy however, aggregate income sets limits on consumption in normal peacetime circumstances, when consumption out of wealth, through allowing wealth gradually to deteriorate, is rare except in deep depressions. Expected future income plays a strange role here: capital is allowed to deteriorate if (aggregate) expected income and demand fall, but individuals are able to consume more (by borrowing) when their expected future income rises.

It is pretty clear that Keynes's implicit assumption was that households did little borrowing, either individually or as a sector, and that was largely true. Consumer credit has become very much more important since, though still not so much as to convert the personal sector into a net borrowing sector.

Consumption, Income and Labour Supply

Whatever the role of income, on one point Keynes and subsequent writers agree: consumption 'is obviously much more a function of (in some sense) *real* income than of money-income' (*G.T.* p. 91, emphasis in original).

The standard textbook treatment shows no hesitation: 'real' means 'in terms of output'; money-income is converted to 'real terms' (i.e. output-units) by dividing by the price level, or possibly the consumer price index, and that is the end of the matter. Keynes's distrust of price and output indexes led him to the formulation which is so convenient on the production side: the use of the wage-unit (or labour-unit) as a proxy for output.

Keynes got what he wanted out of that: the proof that Z rose faster than D. But there is little doubt that the correct specification, from a conceptual point of view, is in output-units: consumers want goods, and the constraint on their command over goods is income in terms of goods. Anything else is either an approximation or a transformation of the original function. The transformation of a hypothesis in output-units to wage-units requires deflation by the rate of exchange between output and labour, namely the real wage. Thus if the relation between consumption and real income in ouput-units were supposed to be linear as in equation

$$C_O = a + bY_O \qquad\qquad (6.1)$$

(the subscripts O indicate output-units), the same function in wage-units would appear as

$$C_w = \frac{C_O}{w/P} = \frac{a}{w/P} + b\,\frac{Y_O}{w/P}\;. \qquad\qquad (6.2)$$

Equation (6.2) will only represent the 'true' hypothesis (6.1) faithfully if w/P is constant.

Keynes, in a fit of wish-fulfilment, assumes this constancy:

> ... [A] man's real income will rise and fall with the amount of his command over labour-units, i.e. with the amount of his income measured in wage-units; though when the aggregate volume of output changes, his real income will (owing to the operation of diminishing returns) rise less than in proportion to his income measured in wage-units. As a first approximation, therefore, we may reasonably assume that, if the wage-unit changes, the expenditure on consumption corresponding to a given level of employment will, like prices, change in the same proportion ...

(*G.T.* p. 91–2)

In the last three lines he proposes that PC_O/w, which (6.2) shows to be C_w, is invariant with respect to changes in the wage-unit. These lines appear to contradict the assumption of diminishing returns made just previously. In Chapter 19 he similarly assumes prices to follow wage changes leaving real wages unchanged.

The above makes clear the assumption necessary for $C_w(Y_w)$ to be a perfect proxy for $C_O(Y_O)$: fixed real wages. That assumption is too restrictive for analysis of the microfoundations of consumption demand. For that we revert to output units. The purpose of what follows is to demonstrate the exact character of the interaction between the determination of the labour supply and consumption plans. Since we are dealing with the formation of plans, 'income' is taken to mean household income, and the role of the distribution of aggregate income between households, as the wage bill, and firms, as profit, is ignored for the moment.

Consumption and Labour Supply: Let us now explore the process of choice by which households might determine consumption. Begin with a model in which the household is presumed to make plans for a number of hypothetical wage and price possibilities. At any particular time it may hold expectations about which wage and price levels are the most *likely*,[3] but these 'point estimates' do not enter the exposition, for the functions which we derive are to hold for all contingencies.

The willingness to work is assumed to be governed by the desire to consume, so that the consumption function and labour supply curves are simultaneously determined, as shown in Figure 6.1. Begin in the left quadrant, with the choice between income and leisure. Hours of work supplied are read leftward from the centre. N_{max} indicates some physical maximum amount of labour which it is possible to offer. The optimum amount of labour to supply depends on preferences and the expected real wage. Plans may be constructed for the entire range of hypothetical real wages, of which six are indicated by the slopes of the diagonal lines $OY_i^* : i =$ 1, ..., 6. (The height of each line at N_{max} gives the maximum income obtainable at each wage.) Tangencies with indifference curves indicate the household's optimum labour supply at each real wage. Their locus, the labour supply curve, is indicated by ON^s, and the level of real income given by that optimum at each real wage is marked on the central axis as Y_i ($i = 1$, ..., 6).

These income levels become a 135° budget restraint in the right-hand quadrant, where $C_O(Y_O)$ embodies the preferred disposition between consumption (vertical axis) and saving. This presentation ignores such things as whether a fluctuation in income is seen as temporary or permanent, with the attendant lags in adjustment; it is a purely static framework. Only those consumption choices relevant to the six optimal levels of income are shown. The consumption function is the locus of these choices.

This function has been drawn up in a thoroughly neoclassical manner, and with reference only to full employment states. After all, it is the purpose of the process of formulating plans to work out the optimum outcome given hypothetical parameters — in this case, prices and wages. The consumption function, however, has a wider applicability: it holds equally well in less-than-full employment states, to which unhappy topic we now turn.

Unemployment and Consumption: We explored the labour/consumption choice by the traditional procedure of varying hypothetical real wages. The other obvious way to vary income is to keep wages fixed and vary employment, the situation in which the households' optimal labour supply is not taken up. Indeed, one could argue that both Keynes's consumption relation and the Classical assertion of lack of impediment to full employment rests on the postulated response of consumption behaviour as employment increases: the classical position that employment will always justify itself in sales is not an assertion about the behaviour of workers as real wages change, but rather about their reaction to increased income from employment at *given* wages — that is, beginning at a position to the right of ON^s, where, as the disutility of work is less than the wage, labour is forthcoming as surely as it is on ON^s itself.

Households still must make consumption plans, whether or not the desired level of work is obtainable in full. The theory of consumer choice states that the consumption-saving decision depends on *income*

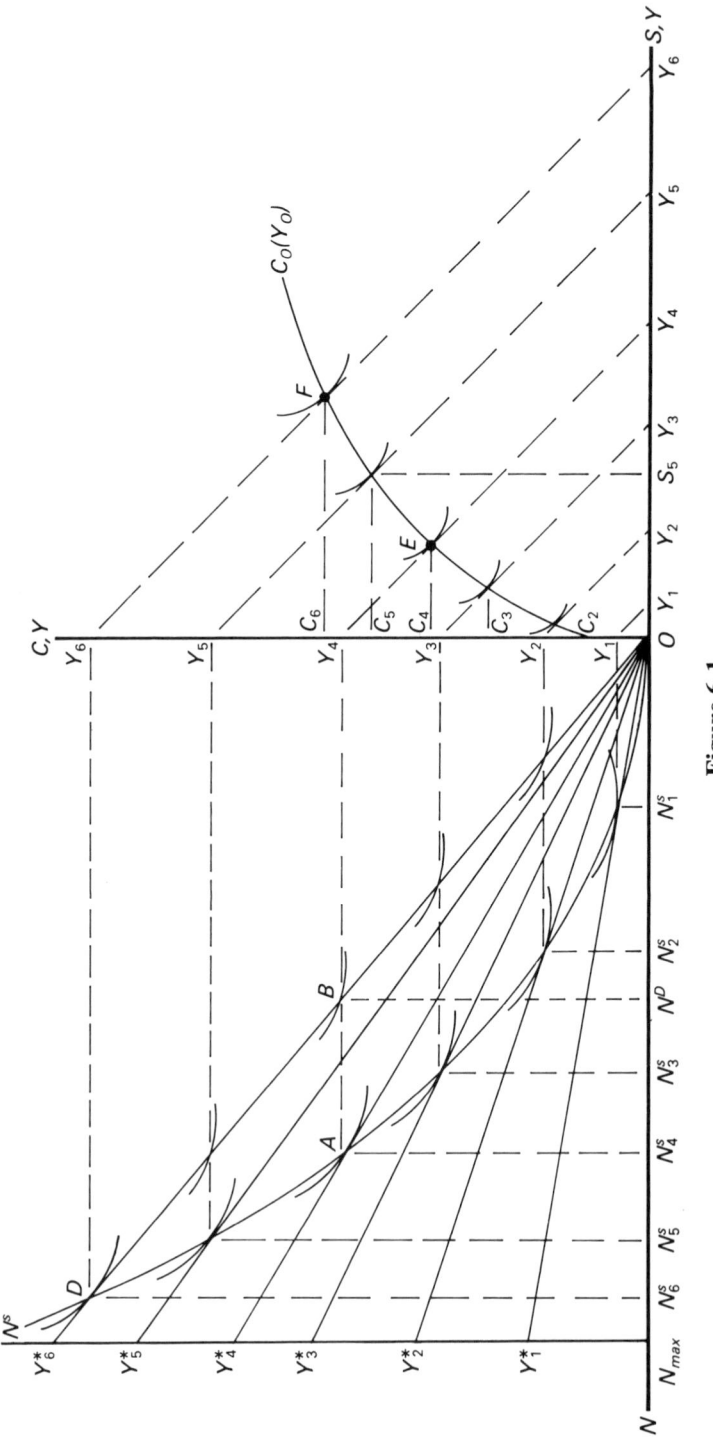

Figure 6.1

independently of its source in hours worked or the wage rate. Thus for the consumption decision, the fact that at the higher wage one might like to work more than one can, given the availability of employment, is neither here nor there. So $C_O(Y_O)$ holds for all points to the right of ON^s as well as for points on it.

This assertion can be seen very simply. Consider point A on wage line OY_4^*. The income generated by optimal labour supply at that wage, OY_4, can also be obtained from the combination at B: shorter hours at a higher wage. (There is another possibility on OY_5^*, not marked.)

The indifference curve at B *cuts* the income line. If the marginal disutility of work is less than the wage, the slope of the indifference curve is less than the slope of the wage line, as drawn. Only at D are they equal. D is a full-employment point. Other indifference curves along OY_6^* exist at income levels at first found for full-employment combinations of wages and hours. (They can be drawn along all the income lines, of course, but this would clutter the diagram.)

Each of the intersections drawn represents an income derived from working the number of hours offered by firms: working ON^D hours generates the income Y_4, just as Y_4 was also generated by working N_4^s hours when the wage was lower. Notice also that for those in employment, the position B is preferred to the full-employment position A: the same income is obtained for less work. (At the wage indicated by OY_6^* the position at the top of the diagram, D, would be preferred to either of these, to be sure.)

Consider consumption when employment and wages are as at B. Income will be Y_4, though Y_6 is preferred. Consumption is given by income and tastes at point E and is C_4, as when Y was generated by N_4^s hours of work. The same is true of all the other underemployment positions drawn — and not drawn. Full employment at OY_6^* gives consumption-position F, a point further along a function which is unaltered by the fall from full to less-than-full employment.

Say's Law Again

The importance of the result just demonstrated — that the position of the consumption *function* is invariant with respect to the level of employment — can be seen most easily if we ignore investment. (This merely simplifies the exposition; the reader can allow for it with ease.) The implication is that production costs must be covered by sales to consumers/workers, who now are to the full both firms' prime cost and the market for their output. The inherent contradiction is obvious: producers want cheap labour but rich consumers. The balance is struck at the point of effective demand.

Let us suppose that the aggregate supply curve goes through point E (Figure 6.2(a)). We know it rises more rapidly than $C_O(Y_O)$ thereafter. So the mere fact that full-employment consumption would be greater in

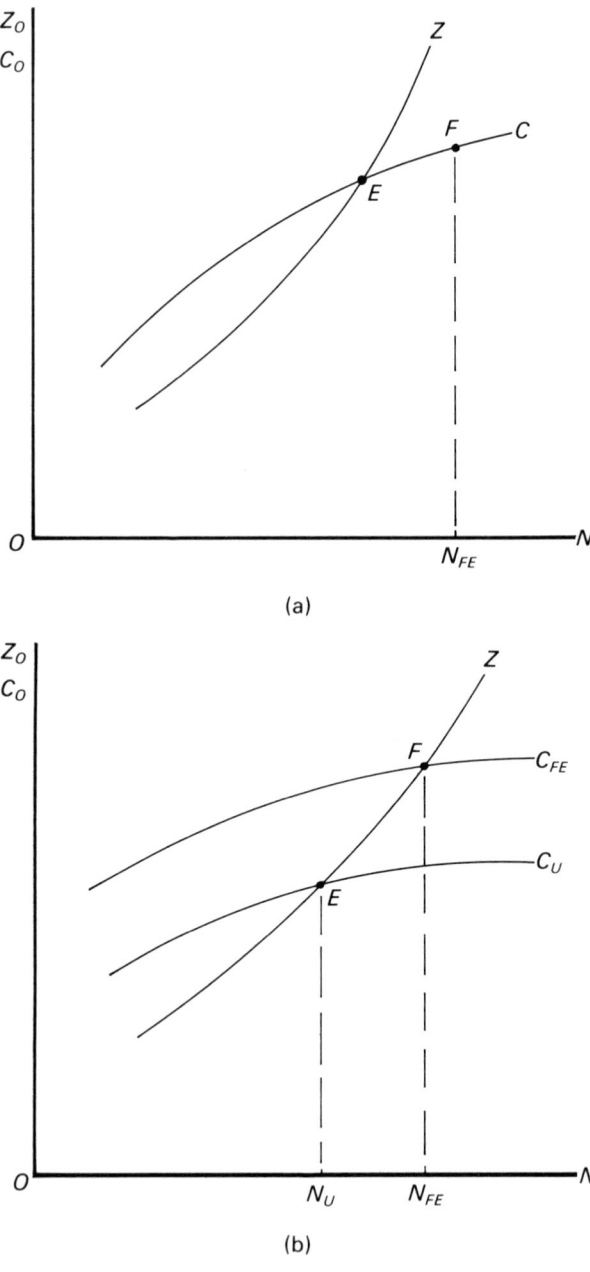

(a)

(b)

Figure 6.2

absolute amount (compare F with E) does *not* justify expanding employment so as to reach F. It is not, as it were, greater enough.

This result contrasts with a widespread interpretation: that if only producers knew that consumption would rise if they offered more jobs, the full-employment position could be reached. This view (associated notably with Leijonhufvud, 1968) regards the presence of unemployment to be due to lack of information, based on uncertainty about consumers' intentions. This was not Keynes's contention.

It may be that the first intuition I had, which turned out to be false, is one which many would find appealing: I thought that there should be two consumption functions, the full-employment one lying above that representing demand with unemployment. Such an image gives scope for the incorrect interpretation. In Figure 6.2(b), C_{FE} and C_U represent such functions, it being postulated without proof that Z goes through C_{FE} at the point N_{FE} indicating the full employment of labour. If employment is stuck at N_U, it is only out of ignorance of the possibility F. This interpretation is inconsistent with the assumption that consumption depends on income irrespective of its source: on wN rather than w and N separately.

Note that in the 'imperfect information' story the existence of a full-employment solution was assumed without proof. The rest of the discussion in this section bears on that issue.

The derivation of $C_w(Y_w)$ from $C_O(Y_O)$ highlights one point which Keynes, in the passage cited, discounted or perhaps overrode as too complicated. It concerns the role of prices. Anticipating the next chapter slightly, consider the proposition which Keynes was attacking — Say's Law — again. According to Keynes, the Law (in its simple form relating only to consumption) holds only if the functions Z and D (or Z_w and D_w) coincide (not intersect, coincide).

Certainly the way Classical theorists talked about production providing the income which allows the production to be taken up would suggest the interpretation Keynes put on it. But to impose his framework was a mistake. His framework cuts across their perspective in saying that, yes, income provides the wherewithal, but the wish to spend it must also be present: demand is composed of preferences (or propensities) as well as a budget restraint — and the propensity to consume does not rise *pari passu* with the ability to consume. That is sufficient to despatch 'the Classics'.

It is doubtful whether anyone today would express the pre-Keynesian bafflement of Harrod or Patinkin (see Chapter 5) over the non-identity of aggregate demand and supply. We have been differently schooled. And the argument has shifted: a proposition not unlike Say's Law, but based on demand rather than simply ability to spend, has become a widely-accepted axiom, that if only prices and wages were flexible, full-employment would be established as the equilibrium solution. According to this view it is only wage or price rigidity or market imperfections of some kind which are responsible for Keynes's result. It is the existence of this modern (neoclassical) version which makes the Say's Law controversy still worth discussing. The essential flaw in the Classical argument, a faulty notion of demand, has been corrected, but that does not deal with the neoclassical idea that only price and wage rigidities can keep the economy from full employment.

Let us just note what is required for full-employment equilibrum. First, labour must be willing to produce a profit-maximising output at a real wage which exactly exhausts its willingness to work, and second, consumers and investing producers must be willing to purchase the output at the prices firms had expected that output to fetch.

Figure 5.2 portrayed a position of full-employment equilibrium in terms of Z and D. They must intersect at exactly the point at which Z ceases to be defined. Now, we know from Chapters 4 and 5 that every point on Z implies a different real wage, and we know from this chapter that the consumption function *shifts* when real wages alter. Hence the equilibrium given by these conditions is a unique point, not the neutral equilibrium obtained by ignoring the preference side of demand. And since, furthermore, the income distribution implied at that end-point of Z must correspond to that inherent in the level of demand, it becomes abundantly clear that conditions required for full-employment equilibrium are very stringent. There can be no question of Z and D coinciding throughout their length: one will be lucky to find one full-employment solution.

The solution is as improbable as the assumptions which give rise to it: perfect flexibility of prices and wages. What this apparently harmless assumption means is not just that prices and wages are able to move, but that they move before any *commitments* are made on the basis of 'wrong' prices and wages.

This assumption was made by Walras, the founder of general equilibrium theory, by means of (quite an elaborate) system of 'recontracting', so that if the price — or the wage — is not 'right' (that is, will not clear the market) it can be changed before any output is actually produced. The effect of this assumption is to abolish the uncertainty inherent in the producer's world and to ensure that the full-employment real wage obtains. In the neoclassical, or Walrasian, world, instantaneously-flexible prices and wages may achieve full employment. But in the *real* world, where prices and wages alter not instantaneously but through time, production is based on expectation rather than certainty of demand, and expectations are based to some extent on history, there is no such guarantee. That is partly the subject of the next chapter.

Consumption and Non-Labour Income

Important classes of non-labour income are interest, rent and profits. These sources of income pose two questions: (i) the appropriate level of aggregation (again), and (ii) the effects of income distribution on consumption, which was treated rather casually above.

The second of these issues has had greater exposure in the literature. The first relates to the sectoral treatment of aggregation favoured in Chapter 3. It can be dealt with simply.

If consumption is defined as what households spend, then firms cannot consume. Only households earn labour income, and only firms make profits. Interest income and rent can accrue to members of either sector, but it would do no harm to regard these as mainly household income. The important division is between profits and the rest, and the reason it is important is that firms control the distribution of profits to households, and only to distributed profits does any idea of a marginal propensity to consume apply.

Profits retained by firms may be used to finance investment or to provide a sinking fund, held in financial assets, to cover replacement investment. Insofar as supplementary cost is accounted for but not matched by equivalent orders for replacement investment, there exists an indirect deflationary influence on consumption, as the gap between gross and net income is not matched by the income from investment. (Keynes's second objective factor.)

Thus the effects of the share of profit on consumption have to do with more than differences in the marginal propensities to consume out of different sorts of income. Though the net effect can be portrayed by such a device, it implies consumer sovereignty over the disposition of funds which consumers do not in fact control. The same is true, in lesser degree, of interest and rent accruing to firms.

Income Distribution

There are two ways of looking at income distribution: by type of income ('functional distribution') and by size ('personal distribution'). As hinted at the end of the last section they are not independent. The average income of households whose income consists mainly of interest, rent or distributed profits is higher than the average of households earning almost entirely labour income.

There are reasons for supposing that high-income families have a lower marginal propensity to consume than low-income families, and there is cross-section evidence to support this view. Thus it can be argued that a redistribution of income away from labour income toward, say, rent is likely to lower the average *mpc* at that level of income. *A fortiori* a shift toward profit has this effect, as to some part of profit (that which is retained), a zero *mpc* applies.

If the *mpc* is different in different income groups, income redistribution

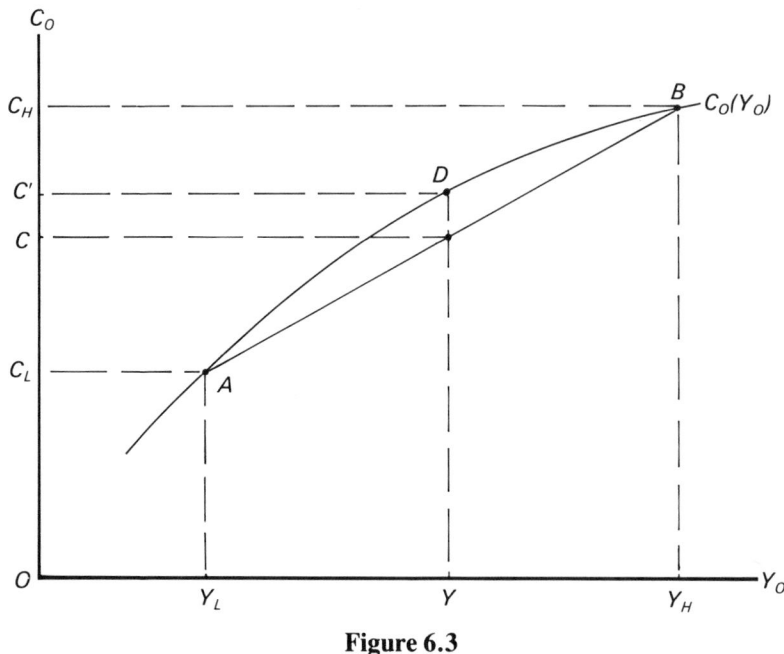

Figure 6.3

shifts the consumption function. This can be seen in Figure 6.3. The consumption function represents the behaviour of two groups of individuals with different incomes. Observe that those with a low income, Y_L, have a higher *mpc* than those with a high income, Y_H. If aggregate income is equally distributed between the two groups, average aggregate income lies midway between Y_L and Y_H at Y. Average aggregate consumption, C, lies halfway between C_L and C_H, in other words at a point on a straight line between A and B, at Y. Contrast this level with the amount of average consumption we would observe if Y were equally distributed. Keeping overall income unchanged, average income remains at Y, but average consumption, C', is now represented by the point on $C_0(Y_0)$ at Y: point D. Average (and aggregate) consumption rises because the low-paid raise consumption by more than the high-paid lower theirs.

Almost any change, in prices, wages or employment, will have some effect on income distribution, if only because these changes never occur in all markets (for goods or for labour) simultaneously. But it seems safe to suggest that changes in income due to changes in employment, which take people off the dole to substantially higher levels of income, are likely to have a far greater redistributive effect amongst wage earners than will changes in wages or prices. Indeed Keynes assumed that relative wages were kept fairly constant, because of labour's sensitivity to them; the importance of relativities as a bargaining issue is amply apparent.

Even if significant changes in relative real wages occur, it is still an empirical question whether or not the consumption function has enough curvature to make income distribution a major issue — or indeed whether the extent of redistribution is large enough to preclude approximating the consumption function with a straight line (constant *mpc*). It is likely that the distribution between broad classes of incomes, inevitable during expansion in the short run, is of greater significance, but if it is of too much significance, shifts in $C(N)$ will undermine the exposition of the Principle of Effective Demand in Chapter 4. Clearly Keynes thought the consumption function was stable enough.

Consumption in the Longer Run

Perhaps one reason for playing down the short-run changes in income distribution consequent on expansion was an implicit belief in the longer-term stability of the propensity to consume — a belief not borne out in post-war empirical studies — based in turn on an expectation of a stable population and social structure, in which income and consumption might gradually rise to a comfortable level and be maintained there.

The assumption of a stable population would have been influenced by experience of relatively low rates of population growth — an annual average of 0.51 per cent in the 18th century and 1.31 per cent in the 19th, falling to 0.47 per cent for the 1920s and 30s; not much stimulus to consumption from extra mouths to feed and bodies to clothe and house!

A sense of social stability informed Keynes's world, the 1914–18 war notwithstanding, including a sense of a stable pattern of consumption. This pattern was largely class-determined and working-class consumption was pretty closely tied to current income. Durable goods, postponable in the timing of their purchase and often requiring credit, played a distinctly less-important role.

After the 1939–45 war the development of 'Keynesian' theory largely translated to America, with its greater population growth (annual rates of growth in the 19th century ranged from 2 per cent to over $3\frac{1}{2}$ per cent and the average for 1945–75 was more than twice the UK rate). These rates of growth might have been sufficient in themselves to challenge the stability of the consumption-income relation even without the additional factors of the deliberately-stimulated consumption demand noted by Galbraith (amongst others) and a social structure involving much 'keeping up with the Joneses' (emphasised by Duesenberry).

Early Empirical Work on Consumption: The upward drift of the propensity to consume was an empirical, not a theoretical, discovery. Empirical estimates began to be made almost as soon as the *General Theory* was published. These estimates became a matter of urgent policy interest during the Second World War, for there was fear that demand would fall due to demobilisation. The predicted level of consumption was far lower than the level of demand which actually emerged. The policy-makers were not unhappy about this, of course, but the economists hardly had reason to be pleased: their estimates on interwar data failed spectacularly to predict postwar consumption, and this cast doubt on the usefulness of a simple relation between consumption and income. Variables were added and 'new' hypotheses proposed, some of which are very clearly foreshadowed in the *General Theory* itself.

The first variables to be given a place were wealth and liquid assets: it was argued that the accumulation of financial assets during a period when incomes were fairly high but consumer goods were not available, was financing the pent-up demand which wartime restrictions had left. (It was entirely reasonable to include financial assets in an aggregate consumption function as long as rates of interest were stabilised as a matter of policy, for capital losses do not in those circumstances attend large-scale sales.)

It was also pointed out that the estimates covering a short span of years, which implied a positive level of consumption at zero income, could not possibly be sustained in the long run. The possibility of a difference between short-run and long-run adjustments of consumption behaviour to variations in income was foreshadowed in this passage in the *General Theory* (p. 97):

> [A] man's habitual standard of life usually has the first claim on his income, and he is apt to save the difference which discovers itself between his actual income and the expense of his habitual standard; or, if he does adjust his expenditure to changes in his income, he will over short periods do so imperfectly. Thus a rising income will often be accompanied by increased saving, and a falling income by decreased saving, on a greater scale at first than subsequently.

The supposition that the long-run consumption function differed from the short-run was borne out empirically. Kuznets, in his celebrated study (1946), used ten-year moving averages of data from 1869 to 1938 and found a long-run consumption function of the form

$$C_O^L = bY_O$$

a function with no significant intercept and a steeper slope than had been found for functions fitted to annual data.

It was thus conceived that a short-run function of the textbook form

$$C_O^S = a + bY_O$$

had been shifting upward over time. And, of course, the range of observations moves to the right as secular growth proceeds, so that the regression for the period as a whole would indeed be 'tilted upward' as Figure 6.4 shows. It was proposed that the shifts were due to such things as the decline of the rural sector, secular income redistribution, and the introduction of new products, but the quantitative significance of these factors proved inadequate. The 'alternative hypothesis' proposed by

Duesenberry was, in effect, precisely the protection of consumption standards proposed by Keynes. Formally Duesenberry proposed that consumption was a function of current and previous peak income, so that his consumers adjust downward by less than the amount suggested by any fall in current income (consumption being held up, as it were, by the observation of a previously higher level and the hope of returning to it), but they adjust upwards to the full when current income attains and surpasses its previous peak. Thus the relevant parts of Figure 6.4 are the long-run function, which applies when the previous peak is being exceeded, and the short-run functions to the left of C_O^L when the current income falls.

There is a connection here with the role of wealth, at least for the individual, for pursuit of the short-term protection of consumption requires temporary adjustment of planned accumulation of wealth, and may even require dissaving.

Friedman's permanent income hypothesis (1957) is also designed to resolve the disparity between short-run and long-run consumption behaviour.[4] The hypothesis at its simplest is that one takes a view as to one's long-term income profile based on past experience and the general pattern of others in one's occupation and on the basis of that profile establish a long-term consumption plan. Short-run deviations of income from its permanent level, called transitory income, are assumed to be random and not to affect consumption, which also has a random component. Since people whose

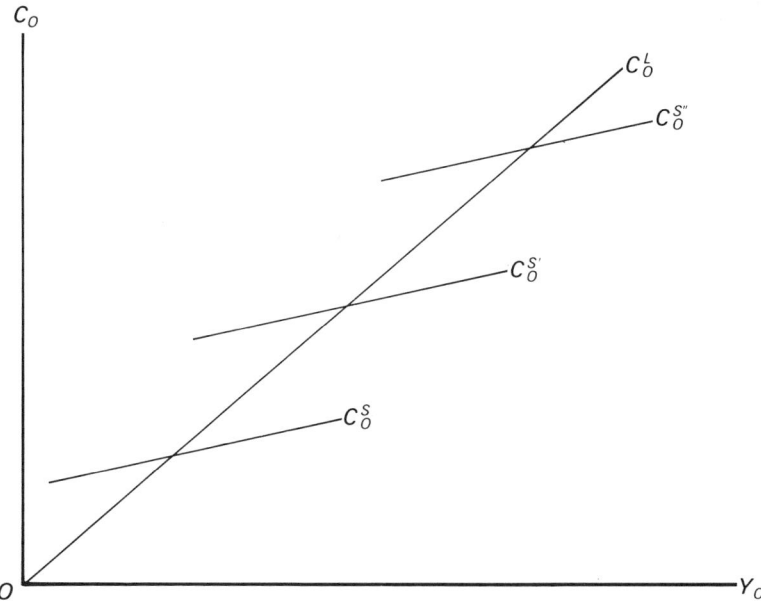

Figure 6.4

transitory income is negative will be found displaced to the left on the income scale while their consumption varies randomly around its permanent level, and those with positive transitory income are similarly displaced to the right, also without a systematic displacement of their consumption, the relationship between actual income and consumption has a lesser slope than that between the permanent components of both, which is the long-run relationship.

The chief value of the empirical work has been to illustrate the lack of stability of the simple consumption-income relation over substantial periods of time. It would be acceptable in many quarters to reply that the long run was not what Keynes had in mind. That comment both confuses the technical meaning of 'long run' with 'a long run of years' and ignores the fact that Keynes does concern himself at several points with the implications of his postulated consumption function in the long run in both senses. A detailed discussion of that must wait until Chapter 17. Suffice it to say here that the theoretical and empirical work held out hope against the deep pessimism to which a projection of a short-run function far into the future leads — for the implication of that projection is long-run stagnation.

An aspect of consumption theory which has never to my knowledge been explored empirically and which, in the light of the above discussion would prove of considerable interest, is whether systematic differences in consumption behaviour arise according to whether changes in income arise from changes in employment, money wages or prices. The work at the beginning of this chapter predicts that the results may not be invariant to the source of change.[5]

Investment

Investment constitutes the second component of the aggregate demand function.

The treatment of the demand for investment in the *General Theory* has come in for much criticism, not all of which I find is well taken. The theory Keynes presents is one which can be simply handled but is I think quite rich. It depends on distinguishing between the valuation of existing capital and the price at which new capital can profitably be produced, and between the rate of return on capital equipment and the rate of interest — things neoclassical theory often confuses.

The Producer's Decision: Why should a producer want to invest? Consider for a moment the familiar diagram of successive short-run average cost curves, e.g. Figure 6.5(a) or (b). The movement from *SRAC* to *SRAC'*, achieved by investment, represents in the first case a prime cost reduction, in the second a cost reduction involving a rise in output. So, one thinks, if

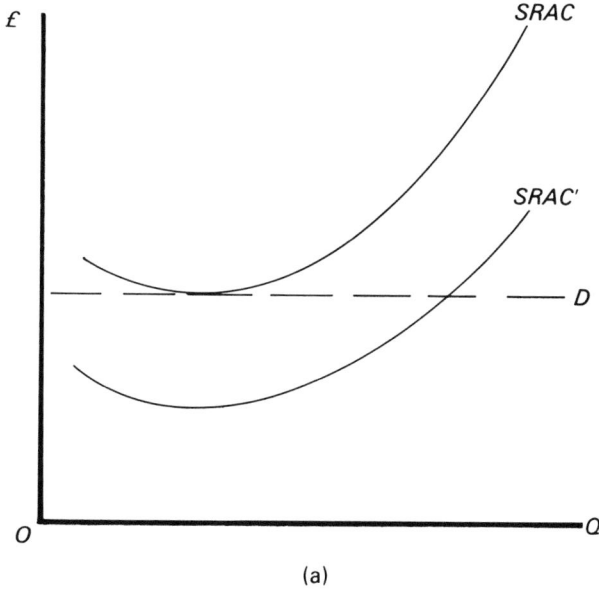

(a)

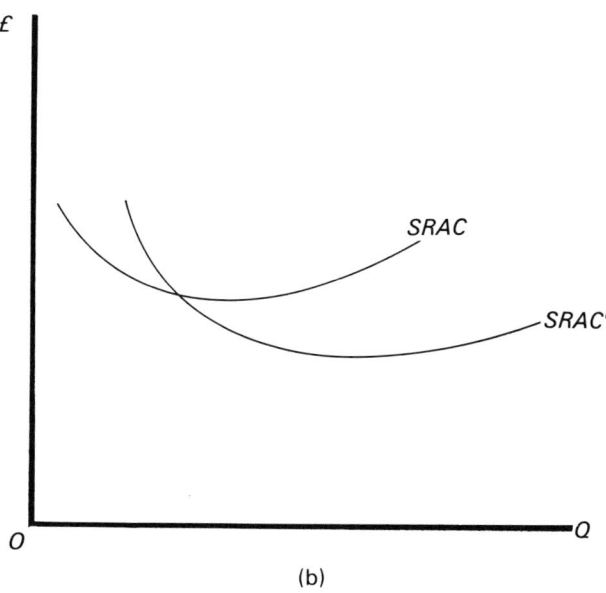

(b)

Figure 6.5

demand were at the level D, why does the producer not invest; his profit would increase. The answer is that investment involves costs not shown in the diagram, which will only be recouped if demand stays at D for some length of time also not shown in the diagram. This length of time necessarily involves several production periods (those covered by the capital's expected life), and begins in some future period when the investment comes on-stream. This is the sense in which investment depends on long-term expectations and is therefore independent of current levels of income.

The benefits of investment are the future profits directly attributable to the investment; these are to be set against the current cost of the capital equipment, and then the net result compared to the alternative of lending one's money out at interest, or to the cost of borrowing if finance must be sought.

The profit accrues in the future; the cost is borne in the present. Sums of money can however never be compared over time even in periods of price stability: money today is worth more than money tomorrow, because of the alternative uses to which it can be put if you have it today. In particular it can be used to purchase interest-earning financial assets. If £100 today could be worth £105 in a year's time through earning 5 per cent interest, then £105 of profits could in a year's time have a *present* value of £105/1.05 = £100: the sum is discounted by $1+r$, r being the rate of interest. If the interest as well as principal is reinvested, the £100 would be worth £100 $(1.05)^2$ in two years' time; thus the discount factor for money obtained two years hence is $(1+r)^2$, and so on. If we assume that profits accrue at the end of each year, then the present value of the stream of expected profits during the life of a machine (n years) which begins earning at time j is:

$$\sum_{i=j}^{n} \frac{\pi_i}{(1+r)^i}$$

where π is profit. Scrap value, if any, is added, discounted by $(1+r)'$ to obtain the value of the machine, to be compared with its price.

The evaluation could be made by another method, which, if the rate of interest is expected to be constant, is equivalent. Begin as before with the expected profit stream and the price of new equipment, P_k; but instead of discounting the profit stream by the market rate of interest, find that rate of discount, d, which will equate P_k with the present value of the profit stream; that is, *solve* the following *for d*:[6]

$$P_k = \sum_{i=j}^{n} \frac{\pi_i}{(1+d)^i}.$$

Keynes calls d the marginal efficiency of capital (*mec*).[7] It measures the *rate of return* on an expenditure of the amount P_k and has the same dimension as the rate of interest. If it is greater than the rate of interest, the return from investing in the machine is greater than the return from lending out an equivalent sum at the current rate of interest, so the producer decides in favour of the machine.

All this is very precise, and of course the investment decision is based on a high degree of uncertainty. It is very doubtful that any firm would go on investing right up to the margin at which $d = r$, though that is what the theory suggests. In the first place, it is doubtful that many firms have so many projects in prospect that one of them is marginal. And it would be rational to make a considerable allowance for risk. However, if only prudent projects were undertaken, it is likely that the volume of investment would be slight indeed; the gambling instinct provides a counterweight to prudence. Indeed, it was Keynes's view that 'animal spirits' substantially dominated the investment decision. What we have exposited above is merely that *part* of the decision which is amenable to economic analysis.

Finance: One aspect glossed over just now was the question of finance. Indeed, in suggesting that the alternative to investment was lending the money out, it was implicitly assumed that the firm possessed enough money to make that choice. Retained earnings have become important in the finance of investment: if retentions are to be used, the rate of interest measures the opportunity cost involved in selling-off enough of the financial assets in which these funds have been placed to undertake the investment, or at least initiate it, future profits being relied on for the rest of the necessary finance. At the end of the life of a machine whose *mec* is at least equal to r, sufficient funds will have been generated to replace the equipment (if replacement is desired) and to provide profit on the shareholders' equity (equal to P_k) at the market rate of interest.

It is, however, typical of the business sector as a whole that it is a net borrower. If the firm proposes to finance its investment by borrowing, the interest rate represents the cost of funds. The return on the investment must (at least just) exceed r in order to generate enough funds to pay off the loan and put the firm in a position to borrow again if it is desired to replace the equipment.

It is worth pointing out that neither depreciation nor borrowing costs are included in the calculation of *mec*. Only the costs directly associated with buying and operating the equipment are included. The need to provide for replacement or repayment is implicit in the comparison of *mec* with r. Also implicit is the assumption that as profits accrue they are either invested in financial assets (at the current interest rate) until they are required, at time n, to finance replacement, or they are used to amortise the loan. The former applies to the use of internal funds, the latter to borrowing.

To fix ideas, consider some numerical examples. Consider a machine with a life of four years, paying £100 per year starting at the end of Year 1. Its present value at 10 per cent is £316. Assume the project is marginal — that is, the price of the equipment is also £316. If the firm uses retained earnings for the purchase it can reinvest the proceeds (profits) as they accrue, getting £100 $(1 + r)^3$ for the first year's proceeds, £100 $(1 + r)^2$ for the second, and £100 $(1 + r)$ for the third, as shown in Table 6.1. The difference between total receipts and the original outlay, £148, is available for distribution to shareholders. Ten per cent interest on £316 cumulated over four years is £146.80, which demonstrates that (rounding errors apart) the potential distribution is equivalent to the rate of interest which shareholders could obtain on the £316 on the open market. The firm is then left with just enough money to replace the machine and repeat the process.

It is equally just-profitable to borrow £316 from the bank or elsewhere if the contract permits paying back both principal and all interest at the end of the life of the machine. The firm must invest the profits as they accrue if the repayment is to be met.

Alternatively, a more realistic contract may be struck with the bank, in which the loan is amortised continuously. Table 6.2 illustrates this scheme. All profits are paid to the bank. Interest is 10 per cent of the outstanding balance. The rest is available for repayment of principal. In the last period, the remaining interest and principal can be repaid, leaving a small residual arising from the approximate nature of the calculation.

Table 6.1

Year	0	1	2	3	4	Total
Profits (Π)		£100	£100	£100	£100	£400.00
Interest on Π_1			10	11	12.1	33.10
Interest on Π_2				10	11	21.00
Interest on Π_3					10	10.00
						£464.10
Outlay	£316					316.00
						£148.10

Table 6.2

Year	0	1	2	3	4	Residual
Profits		£100.00	£100.00	£100.00	£100.00	
Interest		31.60	24.76	17.24	8.96	
Repayment of Principal		68.40	75.24	82.76	89.60	
Outstanding Principal	£316.00	247.60	172.36	89.60		£1.44

Aggregation

Having established the general principles guiding the analysable part of individual investment decisions, we need to proceed to determine *aggregate* investment. The transition is not simple. There are two problems; heterogeneity of capital and the calculation of the supply price of capital.

Heterogeneity causes no serious difficulty. The *mec* calculated for every project and every entrepreneur (for there is no reason to suppose that all entrepreneurs will take the same view of a project's prospects) can be ranked in descending order; an amount of investment expenditure associated with each value of *mec* may then be determined and arranged in order of the value of the *mec*. So, in Figure 6.6, projects valued at £OA have an expected return of 25 per cent, projects worth £AB have an expected return of 15 per cent, and so on. If the rate of interest is 12 per cent, all projects included in OB will be profitable to implement. The rest will not. So equality of *mec* and r determines investment demand.

For the individual entrepreneur the projects were valued at market price. At the microeconomic level it could be assumed that the price of new equipment was something easily ascertained, and a firm's demand would not typically affect the price materially. At the aggregate level this is plainly not true: the price of capital equipment will be affected by the pressure placed on capital-goods suppliers, whose supply price, naturally, rises with the volume of orders placed.

Or think of it this way. A great deal of capital equipment for the individual firm can be supplied out of stocks. But for the economy as a whole this cannot be. On average, over time, orders must be met out of new production. If one were only concerned with equilibrium, there would be no harm in using the market price of capital equipment as a measure of value; but for a general function, designed to hold in transition states as well, the relevant measure is not market price but supply price — what demanders of investment goods must offer the producers of these goods in order to get the goods produced.

The supply price of capital goods is (if we stick to diminishing returns) an upward-sloping function, whether for a firm or in aggregate. Therefore the supply price of capital depends on how much capital is being demanded (in aggregate), and the aggregate curve must take this into account, even though individual firms do not — indeed cannot. The logical gap opened up by this fact is inescapable and cannot be closed by anything short of full disclosure of plans on both sides of the market. We saw this problem in the last chapter and propose to deal with it here in the same way: by merely noting exactly what is involved and stating that it is the aggregate function which is wanted. Firms may misestimate the cost of their investment plans whenever the supply or demand for capital goods changes.[8]

The discomfort of some readers at this point might be mollified by considering the quite reasonable supposition that the suppliers of capital

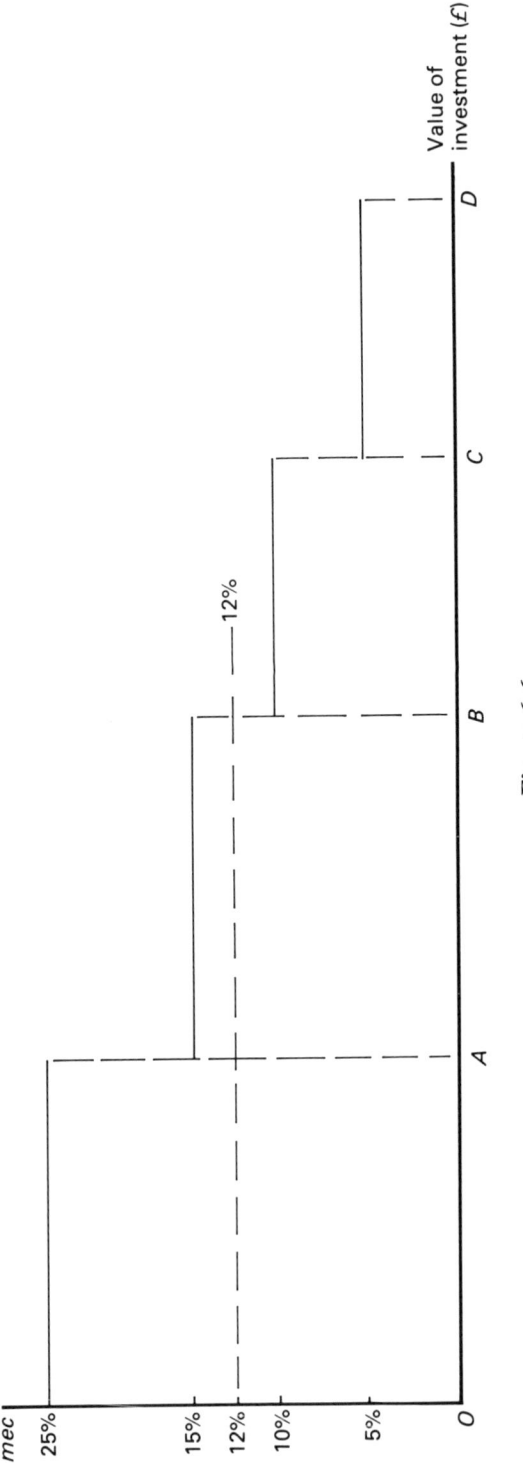

Figure 6.6

goods have a fair idea of the likely level of demand and set their quotations to firms accordingly, in which case quoted prices and supply prices of capital are not incongruous. Suppliers of capital goods must, after all, take a forward-looking view on the demand for their output. Indeed if the assumption of accurate demand forecasts, made in Keynes's Chapter 3, is applied, this assumption follows naturally, though such extremes are necessary only for an absolute logical consistency no-one has any right to expect in macroeconomics.

When the capital-goods producers do estimate investment demand correctly, the embodiment of their supply conditions into the aggregate investment demand schedule means that the intersection of *mec* with *r* determines *actual* investment.

It is to be noted that expansion of a *given* kind of capital equipment may be expected to lower the *mec* of that equipment for two reasons at the macroeconomic level: (i) more equipment implies greater output, but the output can only be sold at lower prices; (ii) the supply price of capital rises.

Objections

The theory of investment just exposited has been subject to many criticisms, three of which are worth raising: (i) that it does not model expectations, (ii) that it assumes a constant interest rate, and (iii) (by far the most serious point) that it determines only the demand for a change in the capital stock, not a rate of change over time.

The objection concerning expectations is, of course, perfectly correct, and quite consistent with the method of the *General Theory*: in the early chapters long-run profit expectations are taken as given and later (in *G.T.* Chapter 17) they take the course predicted for them as capital accumulates, and fall. But how, at any time, producers formulate them is not explained. It was enough to show their *consequences*.

Subsequently, of course, the accelerator principle was grafted on to Keynes's system — but without exploring the possibility that the principle can be viewed as a model of producers' adjustments of their expectations in response to an unexpected variation in demand.

The second objection is also correct, as applied to the *mec* calculation. Clearly, if one is going to compare the *mec* to the current interest rate, one is ignoring the possibility of future variations in that rate — at first blush an odd juxtaposition with the expectational character of the profits stream. The present value method avoids the need to restrict the interest rate to a constant value: a time series of expected future interest rates, r_{t+i}, $i = 1, \ldots n$, may be used to discount the profits stream. This has been claimed an advantage of the present value approach over that used in the *General Theory*.

It is not, however, a matter of *absolute* importance to allow for variable interest rates. Whether one wishes to do so depends not only on whether interest rates are expected to vary significantly over the relevant time horizon, but also on the mode of finance chosen.

Keynes's calculation applies ideally to investment financed by a fixed-interest loan entered into at the outset and running for the life of the machine. In that case the fixed-interest assumption does no harm at all. It is not the most apt calculation in the present environment: new fixed-interest security issues over the last ten years have been of trivial magnitude. Firms have been unwilling to commit themselves to borrowing at rates pushed up by inflation and have turned to the banks for loans.

Future variations in interest rates are obviously important if the investment is to be financed by credit of shorter term than the life of the machine, for the cost of 'rolling over' the initial loan is unknown at the outset. They are also important, though less so, if the firm is using retained earnings to finance the project, for profits retained as a sinking fund for the equipment's replacement must be reinvested, and the returns forecast. The same is true of finance by sale of new equity, though in practice dividends are fairly easily varied to make up any shortfall of interest earnings.

The third objection is the most interesting. It was first made by Haavelmo (1960) and taken up by Witte (1963), Minsky (1975) and Wells (1965), among others. The argument is that the *mec* calculation establishes a desired *level* of capital stock — and, given the existing level, also the desired change in capital — but investment has the dimension of a flow: the rate of change *per year*. If the marginal efficiency exceeds r, the *change* will be positive but the *rate* of change is undefined.

This argument ignores both the timing of the profits stream and the time dimension inherent in supply price. The latter is particularly pertinent at the aggregate level. Because of the rise of the discount factor as time extends further into the future, a project just worth undertaking now will not be worthwhile if delayed. Compare the present value of four periods' profits of £100 each, beginning at the ends of periods 1, 2, 3, 4 and 5, as shown in Table 6.3.

Table 6.3

Profit from period	Present value
1 to 4	£316
2 to 5	£288
3 to 6	£262
4 to 7	£238
5 to 8	£217

If the price of capital is fixed, it is obvious that if the investment is worth doing it should be entered into immediately, in order to begin the profit stream as early as possible, preferably immediately.

The price of newly-supplied capital is not fixed, however, and even ignoring installation and running-in time, immediate investment is only possible if the equipment is available out of stocks. At the macroeconomic level, therefore, instantaneous investment is impossible; some investment demand will be met from current production, where the price is positively related to the volume supplied *per period*. If a very short delivery date is chosen, the equipment may only be supplied at a substantially higher price than if the producer is given a larger time until delivery, because of the necessity to pay overtime. As the delivery date lengthens, it is possible for the supplier to hire more labour, but even then costs will rise, because of short-run diminishing returns. In a still longer run, as factors become increasingly variable and the potential for increasing efficiency improves, supply price may fall. Thus there may be a trade-off between the desirability of early profit and the benefit of lower cost.

Figure 6.7 illustrates this point for the short run. The left-hand diagram portrays the supply curve of the capital-producing industry. The first portion is elastic, indicating that on average the amount S_0 of the capital good is available each period out of stocks. After that, orders must be met out of current production, at a rising supply price. The total amount of investment contemplated is I_1^d. It is impossible to supply this amount out of stocks. If the whole of I_1^d must be delivered at the end of one period, the supplier quotes P_1 as his price. The right-hand diagram indicates the present value of I_1^d delivered at progressively distant dates, up to the end of four periods. At the end of period 1, $PV > P_1$ and the entrepreneur will accept the supplier's terms. The investment ceases to be worthwhile if delivery is postponed longer than the end of the second period, for then the asking price is higher than the present value. The supplier's quotations for delivery at the end of the ith period are derived on the assumption that production of the order is spread evenly over the relevant number of periods. Thus I_2^d lies halfway between O and I_1^d; I_3^d lies a third of the way along, and I_4^d a quarter.

It can be seen that if the supply curve rose more steeply, so that SP_k cuts PV from above, the quotations for *early* delivery would be refused.

If a positive gap between PV and SP_k emerges and the entrepreneurs are on their toes, the volume of investment will increase until that gap is eliminated. If SP_k cuts PV from above (and cuts only once), entrepreneurs will take the earliest opportunity to invest profitably despite the fact that PV progressively exceeds SP_k to the right of their intersection, because of fear of competition from other entrepreneurs. Thus, as long as investment is pushed to the point at which the *mec* equals r (or $PV = SP_k$), there is a determinate *rate* of aggregate investment.[9]

If, on the other hand, the total volume of investment is I_4^d, only purchase out of inventories is profitable. Such investment as takes place then does so

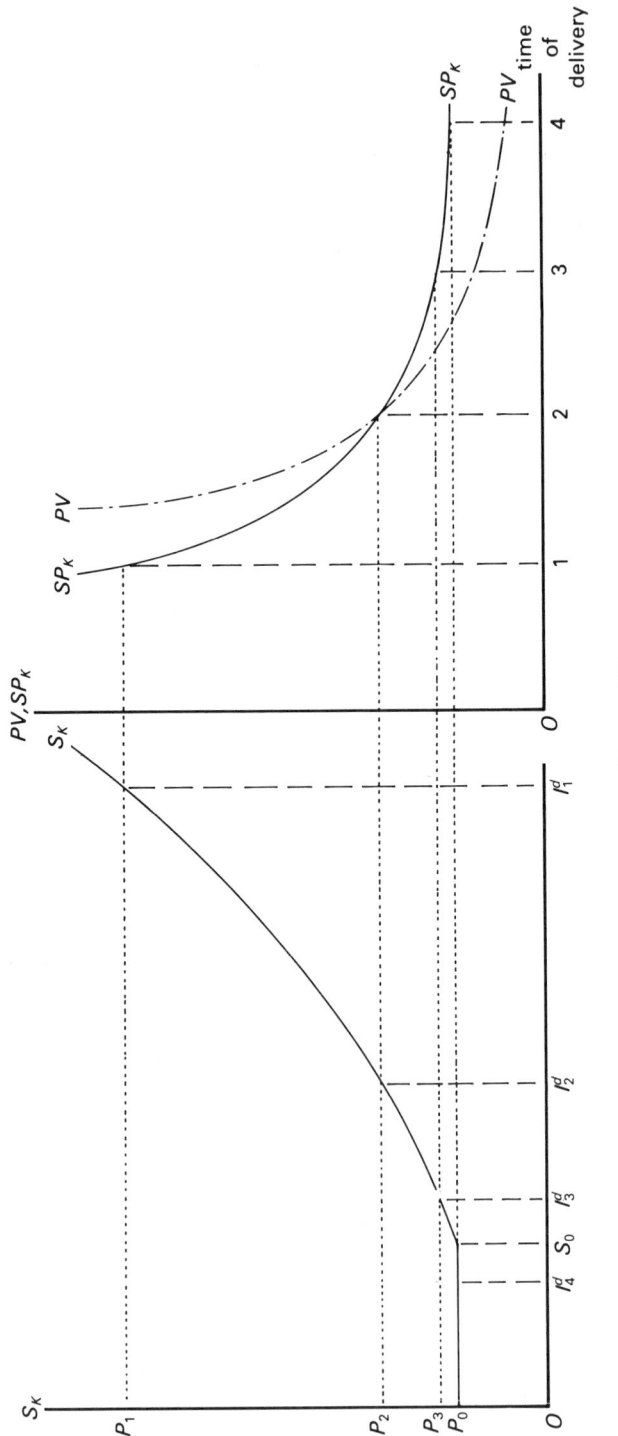

Figure 6.7

at an 'infinite' rate, thus validating Haavelmo's objection, but this case is irrelevant at the macroeconomic level.

Expectations

The marginal efficiency schedule relates investment to the interest rate — *given* expectations of future profits. But what, then, determines expectations? Keynes was impressed with the subjective nature of their formation, and the need for 'animal spirits' and a gambling instinct for investment to take place at all. Surveys of investment intentions[10] are some indication of the general state of optimism or pessimism, but no one actually knows what causes fluctuations in businessmen's perceptions of the future. These fluctuations of expectations are crucial to Keynes's explanation of cyclical fluctuations in the economy at large: a collapse of confidence (a leftward shift of the investment demand function) precipitates recession, and policies to restore confidence, we shall see, are the key to restoring activity and employment.

These expectations cannot be as closely related to *fact* as can the expectations of demand on which production plans are based. Output is sold continuously, whereas the profitability of a machine cannot be known in full until the life of the machine is over. Clearly interim assessments may be made, but that does not alter the basic proposition that considerable time must elapse before firms have some idea of the wisdom or folly of their undertakings. It is this time lag that gives such force to subjective changes of mood and opinion in the determination of investment. Producers of consumer goods constantly put their expectations to the market test in a way that capital-goods producers cannot.

The horizon of investors' expectations allows for considerable independence from the confirmation or falsification of short-term expectations. If one is building a nuclear power plant, year-to-year variations in electricity demand do not cause one to abandon and re-start the project. For this reason Keynes was able to discuss the determination of output and employment on the assumption that long-term expectations were given and independent of short-term results.

Empirical Evidence: It is widely believed that the rate of interest is irrelevant to investment. The first studies, by Henderson (1938) and Sayers (1940) came early. In answers to their questionnaire, businessmen averred that the rate of interest had little if any influence on their investment decisions. Later econometric evidence has not been any more encouraging. But before writing off the idea, consider how difficult such an influence is to capture. Asking a businessman what influence the rate of interest might have *other things being equal*, when those 'other things' are deeply uncertain profit estimates, is problematic enough. In addition to the fact that the expected return must include a substantial risk premium over the rate of interest even to be marginal, most investments will *not* be marginal.

The econometric investigator is no better off. He investigates this problem over cyclical fluctuations when both the *mec* and the supply of funds (or the interest rate) are shifting. Consider what he might observe. First, it is reasonable to suppose that internal funds will be valued at less than external funds, so there is a discontinuity when firms must seek outside finance. Assume that the supply of both internal and external funds is upward-sloping and that firms use internal finance whenever they can.

Now consider four phases of a cycle: (1) upturn, (2) boom, (3) downturn, (4) recession. One would expect investment to be positive but small in the upturn, to increase as excess capacity is used up in the upturn and to diminish as the level of activity declines, perhaps becoming negative in phase (4) of the cycle. The *mec*, measured at the midpoint of each cycle phase, might shift as in Figure 6.8. (The relationship between these levels is only intended to be impressionistic.) Meanwhile the supply-of-funds function *SF* is almost certainly shifting. A rough description of the cyclical behaviour of this function indicates the following: in phase (1), stocks of liquid assets are ample and increasing, due to rapid accumulation of internal funds. Dividend payments are low, profit margins are high, and profits are rising. All this would indicate that internal funds alone are sufficient to finance investment and that the external funds portion of the curve was irrelevant. In phase (2), retained earnings have levelled off and liquid asset balances are declining. (Internal funds are being used faster than they are being replaced.) The

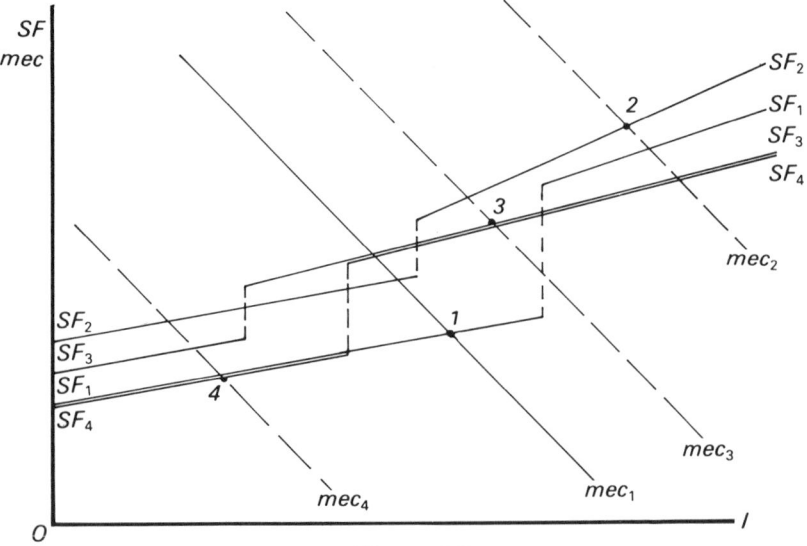

Figure 6.8

internal funds portion of the curve is shrinking in absolute length. The slope of the external portion of *SF* is steeper as lenders become less liquid, and the cost of internal funds is also reckoned dearer. Internal funds shrink still further in the downturn and may recover slightly in phase (4) as stocks are run down and labour laid off. External funds become cheaper.

The net result is an absence of any systematic relation between observed investment and interest rates: observed levels and rates in Figure 6.8 are given by the points 1, 2, 3, 4.

Notes

1. The need to consume for survival does not seem to have crossed Keynes's mind.

2. The surprise over the behaviour of the savings ratio in the (UK) inflation of the 1970s illustrates my point(s). See Bulkley (1981) and the references cited therein.

3. For example, in a period of stability, they may expect tomorrow's prices and wages to be the same as today's.

4. His definition of consumption follows the 'durability' scheme (Table 3.1), but this contrast to Keynes's definition is not important for *present* purposes. (It is important in other ways.)

5. This question simmers under my critique of the Clower–Leijonhufvud reinterpretation of Keynes. See Chick (1978), Clower (1965) and Leijonhufvud (1968).

6. There are multiple solutions, which can be a bore. See Johnson (1971, pp. 38–9) for an uncomplicated discussion.

7. This name is perhaps unfortunate, for it encouraged confusion between two concepts, the marginal efficiency of the capital stock (which can in principle be measured for any level of the capital stock) and the efficiency of an increment to the existing capital stock. One wonders how the confusion arose: the context, additions at the margin to a historically-given capital stock, is crystal clear. In Chapter 17, where the short-run assumption is relaxed, and capital accumulation allowed, the first concept comes into play, but only at the margin where the two concepts give the same result.

8. Asimakopulos (1971) regards the supply price of capital as the introduction of some *ex post* information into the investment function. That is perhaps easier to take at one level but it pulls the theory toward a simultaneous-equation framework.

9. A rising supply curve of finance would have the same effect.

10. For example, by the *Financial Times*.

Chapter 7

THE LABOUR MARKET: KEYNES VERSUS THE CLASSICS

Study of the microfoundations of aggregate demand and supply in Chapters 5 and 6 has demonstrated the technical convenience of assuming a given level of money wages. However, the use of this assumption is dangerous, for it may lead the reader to accept the widely-held belief that the persistence, and even the *existence*, of unemployment is due to an assumed rigidity of wages. The idea that the *General Theory* is based on fixed wages is blatantly incorrect. If this point is not obvious from the title of Chapter 19, 'Changes in Money Wages', consider: there would be no need to go through all the business of using the wage-unit as a deflator if wages were fixed. Wages are, in Keynes's analysis, completely free to move wherever economic forces shall take them. It is the central purpose of this chapter and that which follows to demonstrate that the proposition that wages are 'sticky' — that is, loath to move although perfectly free to do so — is not an assumption but a *prediction* of Keynes's theory, the same theory that rejects the Classical theory of the labour market and its denial of sustained involuntary unemployment.

Keynes's objection to the Classical theory of the determination of wages and employment amounts to a denial of a fundamental tenet of price theory — that price and quantity sold are determined by the intersection of supply and demand — as applied to the market for labour. Harrod warned Keynes against this step:

> The effectiveness of your work … is diminished if you try to eradicate very deep-rooted habits of thought *unnecessarily*. One of these is the supply and demand analysis. I am not merely thinking of the aged and fossilised, but of the younger generation who have been thinking perhaps only for a few years but very hard about these topics. It is doing great violence to their fundamental groundwork of thought, if you tell them that two independent demand and supply functions won't jointly determine price and quantity. Tell them that there may be more than

one solution. Tell them that we don't know the supply function. Tell them that the *ceteris paribus* clause is inadmissible and that we can discover more important functional relationships governing price and quantity in this case which render the s. and d. analysis nugatory. But don't impugn that analysis itself.

(*C.W.* XIII, pp. 533–4)

Harrod's letter was remarkably prescient, not only foretelling the general consequence but also the exact forms into which Keynes's argument would be twisted if Keynes did not oblige by taking one of the suggested evasions himself. Neither established macroeconomics nor microeconomics has ever managed to grasp the analytical basis of Keynes's insistence that the supply curve of labour may have no influence on the observed volume of employment or the wage. Instead, those who do not take the easiest route of the assumed fixed wage follow one of Harrod's three suggestions. 'Tell them we don't know the supply function' comes out in two forms: either that unions are responsible for the downward stickiness of wages or that labour is subject to money illusion, not taking the value of their wage into account. Others argue that the microeconomics of labour is simply irrelevant, either because in the real world the assumption of atomistic units, fundamental to the Classical analysis, does not hold, or because it is the interdependence of supply and demand at the macroeconomic level which is responsible for Keynes's result. (The latter is a form of 'tell them that the *ceteris paribus* clause is inadmissible'.) This latter point justified the possibility of non-uniqueness (Harrod's first suggestion) and gave rise to the notion of a choice between a high-wage and a low-wage economy, each of which was possible,[1] the high wage not prejudicing employment, because the high-wage economy was supposed to have higher demand.

There is truth in all these points, but to concentrate on any of them as central to Keynes's argument is, exactly as Harrod suggested, a way of avoiding confrontation with Keynes's fundamental point. To put unemployment down entirely to money illusion or monopoly power allows one to accept neoclassical microeconomics and Keynesian macroeconomics simultaneously. Problems associated with aggregation and the existence of interdependence at the macroeconomic level forestall any feeling of inconsistency between neoclassical microeconomics and acceptance of Keynesian conclusions in macroeconomics. Others may generalise their microeconomics to the macroeconomic level and come into conflict with the first group on that basis.[2] The macroeconomic interdependence point cannot, however, be crucial to the argument with Classical theory, or it could not have been delayed to Chapter 19.

Those who emphasise the modifications to Classical theory necessary to allow for large firms or for unions are for present purposes also counterproductive. Though the empirical relevance of these modifications cannot be doubted, they must stand as *additional* reasons why the Classical model does not hold, for Keynes fully accepted, for theoretical purposes, the atomistic firm and household, precisely in order to meet Classical theory on its own terms. Not to take on a theory on its own terms is simply evasive.

So, uncomfortable though it may be, the point must be insisted upon, for the whole structure of the *General Theory* depends upon it: the disturbance of established habits of thought is *not* unnecessary.

The attribution of Keynes's conclusions to the points mentioned is not only an instinctive reaction to a threat to established modes of thought. A good deal of the fault lies with Keynes's own exposition. The argument in the *General Theory* comprises both inferences about behaviour based on empirical observation and theoretical propositions which are not adequately argued. Furthermore, it is not always clear whether Keynes is talking of actual observations or schedules representing plans.

The structure of his argument, in effect, is the following:

   (i)   The labour supply curve of Classical theory is open to challenge.
   (ii) Even if we accept the supply curve and the partial-equilibrium framework of Classical theory, wages are sticky downward and employment is not always full because the adjustment mechanism presumed in Classical theory is not in fact present in modern industry.
   (iii) The partial equilibrium framework, in any case, is inappropriate.

Perversely, however, he presented (ii) after (i), and (iii) does not appear until Chapter 19. (iii), if valid, would make discussion of (i) and (ii) unnecessary, were it not for the fact that the behaviour of small firms cannot be expected to take account of the macroeconomic effects of their actions: this is not a model of perfect information or foresight. It is here that the unnecessary disturbance to deep-rooted habits of thought has created so much difficulty.

In what follows, (ii) is discussed first, then (i) and finally as much of (iii) as can be presented without first discussing monetary aspects of the theory. We shall be departing substantially from Keynes's exposition in order to remedy the deficiencies mentioned, though in this chapter we shall not go outside his frame of reference. In the next chapter the argument will be extended beyond Keynes's treatment, in an attempt to account for important features of the present-day labour market.

The Classical Theory of Employment

It is best to begin by describing the theory of wages and employment to which Keynes took exception and to which he provided an alternative. This may seem an unnecessarily roundabout way to approach the matter. The immediate recognisability of the model will, however, demonstrate that it is not obsolete, but is current teaching: it is the model of a perfectly-competitive labour market. Expositions of the model are usually followed by modifications which take account of less-than-perfect competition in the labour market due to the existence of large firms and unions; the labour market has even been portrayed as a problem in duopoly theory; but as in other areas of analysis, the perfectly-competitive model is still the starting-point of microeconomic analysis, and models first-learnt tend to dominate one's thinking. It is the model on which is based the idea that pressing for higher wages is futile, as it can only create unemployment. In what follows, 'Classical theory' must be understood to encompass its contemporary equivalent.

The Classical theory says that wages and employment are determined by the supply and demand for labour. In the *General Theory* (Chapter 2) the theory is described as consisting of two Postulates:

1. *The wage is equal to the marginal product of labour.*
    That is to say, the wage of an employed person is equal to the value which would be lost if employment were to be reduced by one unit (after deducting any other costs which this reduction of output would avoid); subject, however, to the qualification that the equality may be disturbed, in accordance with certain principles, if competition and markets are imperfect.
2. *The utility of the wage when a given volume of labour is employed is equal to the marginal disutility of that amount of employment.*
    That is to say, the real wage of an employed person is that which is just sufficient (in the estimation of the employed persons themselves) to induce the volume of labour actually employed to be forthcoming; subject to the qualification that the equality for each individual unit of labour may be disturbed by combination between employable units analogous to the imperfections of competition which qualify the first postulate. Disutility must be here understood to cover every kind of reason which might lead a man, or a body of men, to withhold their labour rather than accept a wage which had to them a utility below a certain minimum.

(*G.T.* pp. 5–6)

The language in which the Postulates are expressed is ambiguous as between planned and actual magnitudes: Keynes speaks of '*the wage*', not 'the demand price' or the 'supply price' of labour, and of 'employment' and 'the volume of labour actually employed' rather than 'offers of employment' or 'the supply of effort'. These words suggest actual magnitudes. Further down the page however we have:

The first [postulate] gives us the demand schedule for employment, the second gives us the supply schedule; and the *amount of employment* [in Classical theory] is fixed at the point where the utility of the marginal product balances the disutility of the marginal employment.

(*G.T.* p. 6, emphasis added)

In the Classical theory there is no conflict: the theory is that the actual observed wage and level of employment conform to both the amount demanded and the maximum amount willingly supplied: both Postulates are satisfied in practice. If no more labour is willingly supplied at a given wage than the amount indicated by the supply curve, it follows that Classical theory says that all who want a job will have one — there is full employment. (We return to the concept of full employment in a moment.)

The fact that unemployment was observed in the real world from time to time was accounted for by appealing to 'market imperfections', including the 'imperfection' that it sometimes takes time to find a job. This latter attribute of the real world gives rise to frictional unemployment, which is by its nature transitory. And people are free of their own volition to cut back their hours or to render themselves unemployed.

> Subject to these qualifications, the volume of employed resources is duly determined ... by the two postulates. ... The amount of employment is fixed at the point where the utility of the marginal product balances the disutility of marginal employment.
>
> (*G.T.* p. 6)

Any *enduring* involuntary unemployment was held to be impossible, so long as real wages were free to move. This idea presupposed that 'there are forces' tending to push the wage toward a level which will give full employment and profit-maximisation — i.e. toward the level which satisfies both Postulates.

The Demand for Labour: Let us be clear about what is entailed in satisfying both Postulates. First, notice that the expected outcome (with transitory aberrations) satisfies 'the amount' demanded and 'the maximum amount' supplied. There is an asymmetry. Points on the demand curve for labour represent the profit-maximising strategy of firms at each possible level of wages, given the demand (and hence the price) they expect. Thus for any given wage they want, ideally, neither more nor less than the amount given by the demand curve.

The Supply of Labour: The supply curve, on the other hand, indicates the *maximum* total hours willingly devoted to work at each wage (given expected price). To the left of the curve, the utility of the wage exceeds the disutility of work. There is an unsatisfied demand for work but those who have jobs work willingly — indeed they would work for much less. In Figure 7.1, N_0 of labour, though paid w_1, would work for as little as w_0. So the labour supply curve can be thought of as a frontier: all positions to the left of it are acceptable to workers lucky enough to get a job, while positions to the right are unacceptable. Willing supply of labour at each wage is indicated by the horizontal lines, in principle infinitely dense, ceasing at N^s.

Classical 'Forces': The Classical theory asserts that where the wage and the employment level do not conform to both Postulates, there will be forces leading toward the observation which does so conform. The supply-and-demand diagram is often supplemented by arrows indicating these forces, as in Figure 7.2. Interestingly, they are always vertical, indicating wage adjustment without saying much about the adjustment of employment, which is supposed to follow. That is because the characteristics of observed levels of employment other than the 'equilibrium' level are rarely discussed. We shall return to this point.

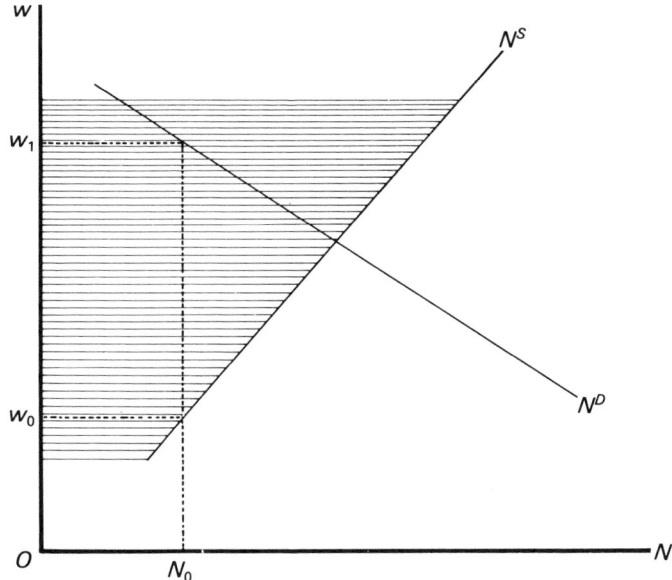

Figure 7.1

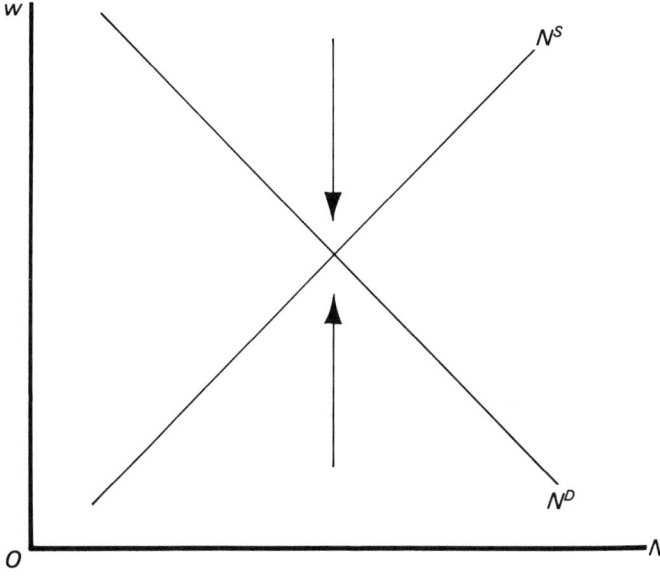

Figure 7.2

Full Employment, and Full-Employment Output

If we define full employment as the state in which everyone who wants a job has one (temporary dislocations aside), then full employment is a point on the supply curve — any point, the level of full employment depending on the wage. In contrast, full employment is often spoken of as a unique level of employment. Since full employment is the benchmark from which unemployment is measured, and since more than one measurement exists, the concept deserves some discussion.

The idea that full employment is a unique volume of employment probably originates from thinking implicitly in terms of the Classical model, in which the only relevant level of full employment is that point on the labour supply curve which intersects with labour demand. The labour demand curve is derived from the (expected) demand for output. Thus 'full employment' becomes associated with a unique level of output as well as a unique number of labour-hours.

Where the curves are related to the real wage, as they should be in Classical analysis, the way to a determinate quantity of full-employment output and labour-hours is more devious. Specifying in terms of the real wage leaves both the wage and the price level free to vary. Thus any point on the demand curve is consistent either with a high price level deriving from buoyant demand for the product and willingness to pay high wages, or with lower levels of these variables: the demand curve is not immediately associated with a given level of product demand, as it is when related to the money wage. However, the curve is derived from product market supply and demand, which determine profit-maximising output and price. Thus the intersection point indicates the volume of employment which is consistent with all planned output being sold at the intended price level; the wage is that which will induce labour both to produce the output and to buy it. If full-employment labour-hours (in this sense) are determinate, then in a given state of technique so is full-employment output.

The intersection point is, however, far more specific than full employment in the sense that everyone who wants a job has one; that concept is indicated by the labour supply curve *alone*, where clearly the amount of employment needed to satisfy workers varies with the wage, real or monetary. The intersection point is the only *sustainable* full-employment level given profit-maximisation and a given capital stock, not the only position of full employment from the employees' point of view.

The idea that full-employment output and full employment are single values is reinforced by the notion of a labour force defined by social custom — say, all able-bodied men between the ages of 18 (give or take a couple of years depending on educational opportunity) and 65 or so, plus some less easily defined proportion of women in roughly the same age bracket, working 35 to 48 hours a week, depending on conventional practice. On this definition[3] the number of labour-hours constituting aggregate full employment could be calculated fairly precisely, as could the output associated with it, in a given state of technique.

This notion is valuable for policy-making, for it gives a target to aim at: raise income to such and such and we shall have full employment. As a policy tool the idea may seem reasonable as a rule of thumb, but there are difficulties. Undeniably, both the numbers of workers in the labour force and the maximum number of hours they would like to work are variable. Statistics on both employment and unemployment exist; if the labour force were a measurable single value, one of these would be redundant. In practice, the labour force varies in size, the level of participation depending, *inter alia*, on the level and structure of wage rates: an upward-sloping supply curve indicates that higher wages will draw people into the labour force or encourage them to offer longer hours. Higher wages may, however, have the opposite effect: they may encourage the taking of a greater amount of leisure, either shorter hours for those remaining employed (and thus enjoying the income effect of higher wages), or withdrawal of secondary workers when primary workers receive the higher wage. If these effects occur, the labour supply curve is backward-bending.

The point of inflection of the curve, if it were to be measured, is a measure of the maximum labour force obtainable, and this figure could be taken as 'full employment'; it is in fact the satiety level of employment: nothing, at least nothing pecuniary, will persuade anyone to work any additional hours. Few would suggest that the economy be geared to satisfying the desire to work to this extent; a less utopian goal is full employment in the sense of a point on the upward-sloping supply curve.

Full employment at a level below satiety is the sensible concept: and it is contingent on the wage. For a start, the notion of voluntary unemployment depends on sensitivity to the wage, and without a clear idea of this concept it is difficult to make much sense of Keynes's idea of involuntary employment, or even why he went to considerable effort to insist upon its existence.

An Excess Supply of Labour

Observed unemployment could be transitory. But the observed existence of people willing to work longer or enter the work force at the current wage was a serious problem for the theory, for it implies that the disutility of work at the margin is less than the wage. Keynes's comment on the Classical rationale for this phenomenon is interesting:

> The classical school ... [argue] that ... this situation is due to an open or tacit agreement among workers not to work for less [money-wages] ... [Such] unemployment, though apparently involuntary, is not strictly so, and ought to be included under the above category of 'voluntary' unemployment due to the effects of collective bargaining, etc.
>
> (*G.T.* p. 8)

for ironically, the 'imperfection' of a monopoly element in the bargaining power, due to collective bargaining, is perhaps the most common rationale offered by 'Keynesians' for both sticky wages and persistent unemployment. Keynes is said to have supplanted the Classical upward-sloping supply curve with a curve having a horizontal portion at or above the wage which would clear the 'Classical' market, as portrayed in Figure 7.3. Unemployment is thus seen to result from an inadequacy of demand insofar as demand falls short of the upward-sloping part of the curve, but simultaneously the rigidity of the wage is at fault; in the figure, unemployment is the distance AB. Such a supply curve, with a fixed-wage portion, is, according to Keynes, still consistent with the two postulates, as long as the utility of workers is understood to encompass whatever made them agree to establish a floor wage as well as the usual pecuniary returns from work.

Some would argue (and I would concur) that this is to stretch the notion of utility too far. It also challenges the definition of the supply curve as the *maximum* labour-hours available at each wage. These points are not the central issue, however; the point is to note that both Keynes and 'the Classics' regarded this effect of unionisation as consistent with the Classical theory, so that one must look elsewhere for his differences with them.

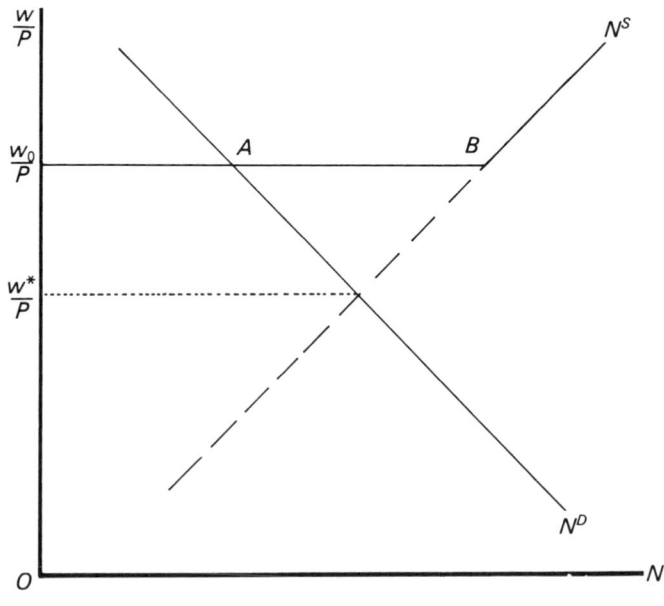

Figure 7.3

Keynes's Fundamental Objection to the Classical Theory

Classical theory asserts that except for transitory aberrations, the real wage is equal to the marginal product of labour and the marginal disutility of work. Keynes accepted the first Postulate — that employment is determined by the demand for labour — and rejected the second — that it is also determined by supply. His rejection of the second Postulate has two components. The first 'relates to the actual attitude of workers towards real wages and money-wages respectively and is *not theoretically fundamental*' (*G.T.* p. 8, emphasis added), though it involves rejecting the classical supply curve. The second objection rejects the presumption that labour is in a position to decide the real wage for which it works or the amount of work it undertakes. Without these possibilities there is no guarantee that the wage will equal the marginal disutility of work.

It can be seen that this second argument is perfectly consistent with the proposition that labour determines how much it would *like* to work on the basis of the real wage (i.e. one can accept the supply curve as an expression of preferences). If, however, labour lacks the power to *implement* its plans or preferences in its negotiations with firms, *actual* wages and employment can be a point off the supply curve, and that observation may be more than transitory. It is this point which *is* fundamental, which 'impugns supply and demand analysis itself' and which should be dealt with first.

A plausible argument can be constructed. Regrettably, Keynes only offers two assertions: first, that the real wage is not, contrary to Classical presumption, settled and agreed between firms and workers in the wage bargain; second, that labour has not the power to insist on the real wage for which it will work. The first assertion, which has been interpreted as evidence of money illusion on the part of workers and thus dismissed as irrational, has to do with an aspect of the first stage of a full argument: namely, why we might ever observe unemployment in the first place. The second assertion suggests a challenge to the assumption that there exist 'forces' leading to that wage which equates supply and demand.

The Wage Bargain

There is no doubt that as a matter of *fact*, the wage bargain settles the money wage, not the real wage. It is impossible to settle the real wage. This fact is not peculiar to a money economy. One's employer's output is not bundles of goods conforming in their composition to one's desired consumption. Typically the output is some subset of this bundle or, in the case of producers of capital goods, a product outside the consumption set. Therefore even if one is paid in one's own output, say wheat, at least some portion of this wage will be exchanged for other goods, at prices not settled in the wage bargain. These prices depend on the production decisions and productive performance of others and on external factors such as the weather or demand by others. Prices, i.e. the real value of one's wage, only emerge *after* the contract to work and be paid, in some commodity or in money, has been made. Furthermore, the real value of the wage to the *employer* may depend on an entirely different bundle of goods (the whole idea of 'real profits' is so nebulous it is rarely discussed). So the real-wage bargain must both straddle time and reconcile disparate aims.

This was achieved in Walras's analysis (1926) by a clever device of 'tickets' for potential output, written up by entrepreneurs in response to a vector of wages and output-prices suggested by a central information-gathering body or 'auctioneer'. The workers are then asked if they would buy the goods represented by the 'tickets' at the prices stated, given the wages offered, and if they would be willing to work the number of hours necessary to produce the stipulated outputs. Until the answer is 'yes', no production takes place.

In terms of the time-structure of production, therefore, the 'tickets' are a device to prevent prior commitment of resources and a contract to pay wages until sales are assured. Thus the beginning and end-points of a production-period are brought together, and profits expected at the beginning can be confirmed before work is begun. *Time* has collapsed to a single point. That is what is necessary for a contract to settle real wages. The meaning of money illusion attached to not bargaining for a real wage also becomes clear: one has 'money illusion' if one does not know the outcome at the end of the production period. Money illusion is, in that sense, anything less than perfect foresight.

Effective Demand and Offers of Employment

Keynes does not assume perfect foresight on the part of everyone in the economy. In his theory foresight is partial: firms are assumed to estimate the general level of demand correctly.[4] But this assumption was made for a tactical reason only, as explained. It is not meant to be a realistic description of the environment within which firms attempt to function. The procedure is one of forming estimates at the beginning of the period, entering into cost and production commitments, and discovering one's profit at the end. The demand for labour for any given money wage, for a profit-maximising competitive firm (which Keynes assumed) is given by labour's marginal product (a 'real' concept) valued at the price at which the output of that labour is expected to be sold — the 'marginal value product'.

The actual number of jobs offered is given by the point of Effective Demand, but that point is itself contingent on the wage. Therefore some estimate of the wage must be made by firms; the most plausible assumption, if their demand for labour was met last period, is that yesterday's wage will continue. Say that price expectations of firms and workers agree, so that there is no difficulty in thinking in real terms while speaking of the money wage. So long as the aggregate of jobs offered does not exceed the maximum supply of labour, actual wages and employment are consistent with demand. The first Postulate holds. But, as has been seen earlier, there is simply no reason for these levels to be consistent with the maximum workers wish to supply. The second Postulate need not hold, and does not for a point like A in Figure 7.4.

Suppose, however, that firms overestimate the availability of labour at yesterday's wage, and their demand exceeds supply: that is, the wage is now below the intersection of supply and demand. The argument one expects is that firms cannot force workers to work more hours than they wish: thus we might expect to observe that below the market-clearing wage actual employment was always a point on the *supply* curve, but *not* on the demand curve. (This pattern of observation at prices other than those consistent with both schedules is described by the phrase 'the short side of the market dominates'.) Such an observation would be inconsistent with acceptance of the first Postulate.

Consider the fact that firms, at any rate those not bound by long-term wage contracts, are free to offer increased wages when they find they cannot obtain sufficient labour at the old wage. If one assumes that wages are bid up quickly to the full extent necessary to satisfy demand, points below the market-clearing wage w^*/P *are not observed* (except temporarily). For a given technology and set of expectations about product demand, then,

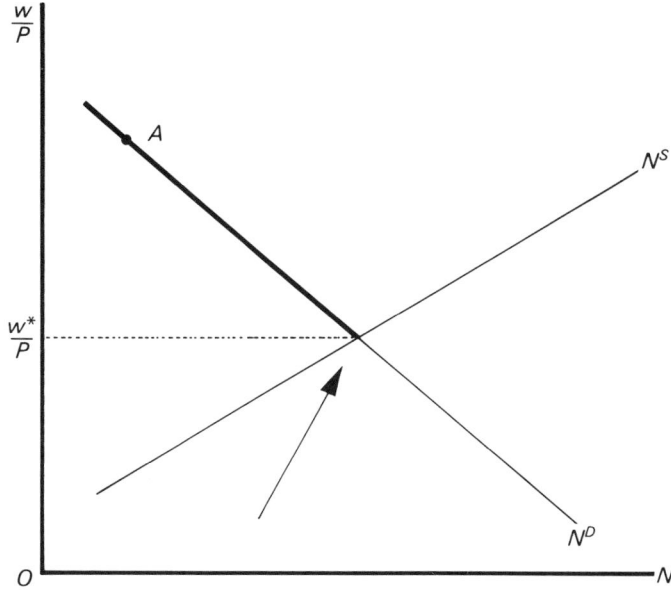

Figure 7.4

potential positions of observed employment are those depicted by the bold line in Figure 7.4 truncated at w^*/P.

Those 'Forces'

To say that the observed wage–employment combination must lie on the demand curve does not settle the determination of wages and employment: it merely establishes a range of possibilities, some of which may be only transitory. In contrast, Classical theory concludes that there is a unique, determinate wage and employment level at w^*/P. *All* other observations are transitory, in the presence not only of the upward forces which we infer Keynes accepted, but also of a downward force on wages acting above w^*/P to bring wages down and thus to increase employment. This force is supposed to come from the side of labour:

> [The] Classical theory assumes that it is always open to labour to reduce its real wage by accepting a reduction in its money wage ... [bringing], if they wish, ... their real wages into conformity with the marginal disutility of the amount of employment offered ...
>
> (*G.T.* p. 11)

It is this proposition which Keynes rejects, though he does not elaborate on his reasons.

One possibility is simply that it contravenes the principle that offers of work are made by firms and labour accepts or rejects them. While true (and important), resting a refutation of established orthodoxy on this argument would be a bit cavalier even for Keynes. Better to ask why, indeed, it would be in labour's interests to exercise a downward pressure on wages. It is not adequate to answer 'to get itself employed'. Some of 'it' is, one must not forget, already employed. The employed and the unemployed constitute two groups of workers whose interests are not the same.

Those who have or get jobs at a wage exceeding their marginal disutility of work are quite happy thank you; they are getting something akin to consumers' surplus. It would be asking a great deal of 'solidarity' to suggest, particularly in the atomistic market of Classical theory, that the employed would accept lower wages for the benefit of the unemployed, so long as workers do not act collectively.

Three considerations bear on the position of the unemployed:

  (i)   whether it is rational for them to wish to lower the wage;
  (ii) if yes, whether they have the power to exert downward pressure; and
  (iii) whether, if they are successful, they will achieve their objective of gaining employment.

Clearly if they do not wish to lower the wage there is no point in discussing (ii), and if there is no mechanism by which it can be done (iii) is irrelevant.

  (i) Many of the unemployed are willing to work for less than the going wage. So, for that matter, are the employed. (Utility theory predicts that quits occur only when the wage falls below w_0.) But they might resist the suggestion of working at a lower wage (a) because it damages their self-image, knowing the currently-employed are getting more, (b) because it would diminish their human capital (i.e. damage their future earning potential as well as their psychological image) if the new wage became established, (c) because willingness to work for less may be taken by the employer as evidence of these particular workers' inferiority. Furthermore, (d) they are competing with the other unemployed, not with the employed. If there is reason to suppose that the probability of getting a job is random, and therefore chances of a job would not be improved materially by a lower wage-offer, they might as well hold out for the going wage. (This is not a strong argument and is likely not to hold as unemployment persists.)

(ii) If, in spite of the above, the strategy of offering to work at a lower wage is accepted, there is no institutional mechanism in modern industry by which to make this offer. Either job offers are made by firms at wages they set or bargains are struck, usually with their existing work force or with a union.[5] In a union at least the unemployed may have a voice, though it is notably weak. Outside the union framework they are simply not in direct competition with those already employed. Therefore the individual's prospects of employment depend on demand for labour increasing; then an offer to work for less might favour him over his fellow-unemployed, but if employment is limited by demand, there is little force behind his *willingness* to work for less.

So the forces from the side of labour are absent or weak. But, you ask, why don't *firms* take advantage of the existence of unemployed workers to lower the wage? Recall first that firms are 'on their demand curves' — they have on the payroll all the labour they want at the going wage. Only if demand for output is expected to rise would producers consider hiring *additional* people, even at a lower wage.

Suppose an employer reckons to lower prices and expand demand if he can get cheaper labour. If a producer employs an additional worker at less than the wage received by others, he violates the principle of a uniform rate for the job and creates unrest among his existing workers. The fear of retaliation must make him hesitate. The potential worker will feel a similar hesitation to accept, knowing he will not be treated well by his fellow-workers, who rightly see him as a threat to their own wages.

The alternative is for the employer to bring the wages of his entire work force into line with the proposed lower wage. Two possibilities suggest themselves. The employer may achieve a cut in wages throughout his firm by agreement with existing workers before hiring anyone else. This stratagem has indeed been attempted in the past, with minor successes and major disruptions. Alternatively, firms may seek out workers with lower reservation wages than their present work force, fire their existing workers and replace them. This stratagem, while logically sound and in the past even attempted, has been made impractical by the existence of costs of hiring, firing and training workers.

It can be seen that there is little justification for expecting wages to fall in periods of unemployment, at least not until the unemployment and the low profits associated with the low level of demand for output have persisted for quite a time.

Ironically unions, if they were to act on behalf of all their members, unemployed and employed alike, would be more likely to produce Classical downward forces than the atomistic market! A congress of unions could take a social (national) view of the wage bargain and negotiate industry-wide or skill-wide reductions in money wages where necessary. In practice, however, unions are not much more likely than individuals to benefit the unemployed by reducing wages, because of the anticipated reaction of their employed members, who hold greater power than the unemployed.

The results of this investigation justify the assertion that observations are consistent with the second Postulate only coincidentally, when it happens that firms want the maximum labour willingly supplied at a particular wage. The implications are disturbing, for the supply curve — that is, the desires and decisions of households — may have no influence in the determination of wages or employment. Below w^*/P, supply factors determine the extent to which wages must be bid up, given demand. Above w^*/P, the supply curve is quite redundant, serving only as a measure of the extent of discontent, a discontent unemployed workers are powerless to alleviate.

Classical theory, in contrast, presumed that workers both would, and could, lower their wages in response to unemployment, and that this action would improve employment: they expected a positive outcome to consideration (iii) above. Since modern neoclassical economists hold a similar belief, it is worth exploring that belief's foundation.

(iii) The above argument relied on certain institutional factors, such as atomistic competition, a uniform wage for the job, the fact that firms usually stipulate the wage, the absence of counter-offers from workers even in the unlikely event that they wished to make them, and the presence of any already employed work force. It is worth examining the Classical theory to determine the precise source of difference with Keynes.

Classical theory is known to be based on atomistic competition; there are assumed to be many buyers and sellers of labour. The supply curve of labour is an aggregate derived from individuals' choices between the disutility of labour and the utility of income over a range of hypothetical wages. The choices are made in the context of the following hypothetical question: if the going wage were so much, what is the most you would work? And if it were some other amount? And so on for each possible wage. In offering work, the supplier of labour is concerned only with seeking the best terms for himself; whether his actions indirectly cause another person to be unemployed is of no concern. The willingness to supply labour is also based either on the

supposition that work is available in unlimited quantities to the individual —
he is 'small' in the market — or that unemployment is distributed randomly
so that the probability of employment is not influenced by any individual's
strategy or tactics, nor are his decisions influenced by the probability of
unemployment. There is no difference from Keynes in any of this.

The demand curve is based on a similar hypothetical question asked to
each firm: 'given your existing capital equipment, how much labour would
you hire if the wage were so, or so, or so?' for each possible wage (output, of
course, is a variable). This implies the uniform wage for the job.

The uniform rate in Classical theory does not, however, create the
impediments for wage cutting that it did in the theory which supports
Keynes. To see why, consider again the conceptual experiment behind the
demand curve: the question assumes the same wage applies to all, in each
case; the answer gives firms' responses to different wages in otherwise
equivalent situations. It is not a question about a response to *changes* in
wages or a response to the opportunity to change the wage offered, where
some arrangement must be made to deal with existing workers; in effect
there *are* no existing workers — the firm always begins afresh, with no
workers on hand.

It is important to realise that the demand curve derived from the above
conceptual experiment applies most closely in the real world to situations in
which the work force is hired anew each day, as in industries where casual
labour is the rule. Industries where casual labour prevails, where employers
go every day to the hiring hall for the labour they want, used to be not
uncommon. They are very uncommon now.[6] Yet this is the institutional
framework to which the Classical model pertains. Comparative static
analysis pertains to comparisons, and the only institutional framework to
which the hypothetical question is relevant is one in which the pre-existing
situation (a given labour force being paid some given wage) has no
influence.

The labour supply curve is built up from thought-experiments of
individuals acting in isolation, with no presumed knowledge (or at least
taking no heed) of the recent history of wages. Workers, who are assumed to
be entirely concerned with their subjective evaluations of leisure, have no
reason to *insist* on earning a wage above their marginal disutility, although
they would be pleased to receive it. The wage that the existing work force
has been getting does not enter into their calculations. In these
circumstances, it is an easy matter for an employer to come to the hiring hall
offering lower wages and find workers who accept them. Alternatively, the
instigation could come from workers offering to undercut others when they
find they are not being hired. (The hiring hall puts all workers in direct
competition with each other in a way that the unemployed are not in direct
competition with the employed in the modern setting.) Some firms may
receive enough of these counter-offers to satisfy all their labour demand.

A world with no commitments to an existing work force and no connection with even the recent history of the market, and where search or training costs and non-wage hiring and firing costs are absent, is one in which the profit motive would always see to it that firms employed labour at the lowest possible price.

These are the preconditions for the 'perfect wage flexibility' of Classical theory. They are not met in the world as we know it. The world in which this perfect flexibility is to be found is not one of marginal adjustments, but of all-or-nothing changes where the history of prices and wages and existing arrangements count for nothing. The phrase 'comparative statics cannot analyse change' has become a shibboleth, not the warning and guide to analysis that it should be. Whether it disturbs established habits of thought or not, the need to analyse how labour will behave if wages are *cut* or how firms will behave if they find they must *raise* the wage to get the workers they want are the important questions and a theory which cannot analyse change must be seen as at best irrelevant and very likely misleading.

Employment and Shifts in Demand: Once it is accepted that observed employment need not conform to the maximum amount labour would like to supply, the other piece of the Classical puzzle is easily solved. There is simply no inconsistency between additional labour coming forward at a lower real wage when the marginal disutility of work is still well below that real wage, and this is what being off the supply curve to the left implies. With the Classical presumption that one begins *on* the supply curve, such behaviour is of course impossible.

It is easier to analyse this question with money wages on the vertical axis. The supply and demand functions are then each contingent on expected prices of goods.[7] Begin in Figure 7.5 at point A, with unemployment, given price expectations consistent with N_0^D and N_0^S. Now suppose that producers expect demand for their output to rise, implying that they wish to expand output and may charge a higher price. The higher price shifts the demand curve for labour to, say, N_1^D. There is no reason to insist that workers also anticipate this rise in demand and price. If they do not, N_0^S remains the relevant supply curve,[8] and producers, who in turn had no reason to suppose that the wage would change, attempt to hire $N_1 - N_0$ additional workers at the old wage and are successful.

Note that between A and B money wages do not rise as employment increases (wages are sticky upward) and that, consistent with the first Postulate, all observations are on demand curves. Not until point C is the observation also consistent with the second Postulate as well as the first. After C, wages must rise. (Wages are not fixed; upward forces do exist.)

Classical theory would not have predicted the successful retention of old workers and hiring of new ones at a lower real wage. That is due to the assumption, inherent in the theory, that one begins from a position on the

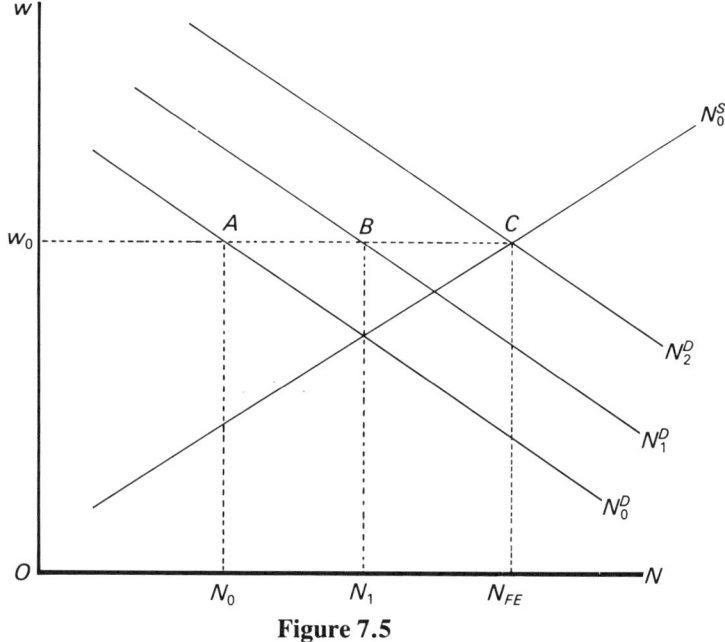

Figure 7.5

supply curve. It is not entirely surprising that workers do not immediately withdraw their labour when prices rise. This is entirely explained when there is unemployment to begin with, even if the Classical supply function is accepted. Their marginal disutility of work is still a long way short of the real wage they receive, and if unemployment is widespread they may count themselves lucky. What *does* need to be explained, however, is their willingness to accept an erosion of real wages caused by a rise in prices while resisting a similar fall caused by a cut in money wages. This is where Keynes's doubts about the Classical supply function come in.

The Classical Labour Supply Function: By making the *ratio* of wages and 'the price level' the determinant of labour supply, Classical theory asserts that it is a matter of indifference whether the money wage falls or the price level rises by an equivalent amount. Keynes's hypothesis is that although both wages and prices enter into the decision to supply labour, their influence may not be symmetrical.

Of the many reasons it is possible to offer in favour of this hypothesis, Keynes chose to argue from his observation of collective bargaining. As he saw it, the aim of the unions was to protect or enhance the relative position of the group of workers whose contract is being negotiated. A change in the money wage for a particular skill or other subgroup of workers is easily interpreted: it represents an obvious change in the position of that group relative to other workers. A change in product prices, on the other hand, affects everyone, whether they work to produce the affected commodities or not.[9] So workers who would resist a wage cut may be more likely to acquiesce in a reduction of their real wages when caused by a change in consumer-goods prices, because the price change affects not only all workers, but all consumers, whatever their source of income, equally.[10]

Keynes could have gone on to point out that the only remedy for the erosion of the real wage was a rise in the money wage, since the firm one works for bears no responsibility for, and cannot directly affect, the general level of consumer goods prices. A rise would be difficult to negotiate in a period of unemployment, so even if the fall in the real wage was deplored, it was likely to be accepted.

The asymmetry in response to wage and price changes which Keynes proposed is, of course, more likely to hold when price changes are small (as Keynes pointed out) and when prices are observed to fall as well as rise. It is difficult, with our own experience, of prices rising continually (though at varying rates) to appreciate this latter point. If we are to make sense of Keynes and alter his theory appropriately, we must try. Recall from Chapter 1 (Table 1.1) that prices in the 1920s were made to *fall* quite sharply for the sake (ostensibly) of a sound £, and prices continued to fall as the depression deepened. So the expectation projected from immediate experience would not be something to which labour was likely to object.

Let us consider also a slightly longer-run perspective — the sort of experience which might be more deeply embedded in a society's collective expectation than that which experience of a decade or so is likely to forge.

Table 7.1 presents price data from the Napoleonic Wars up to the First World War, averaged over cycles. The influence of the wars can be seen and so can cyclical fluctuations, but the outstanding feature of the long years of peace in between is that prices go up and down in longish waves. There

Table 7.1
UK Prices: Cycle Averages
Wholesale Price Index
1913 = 100

1811–18	176	1875–83	103
1819–25	129	1884–89	83
1826–36	111	1890–99	77
1837–46	109	1900–07	85
1847–53	96	1908–13	93
1854–60	116	1914–20	193
1861–65	119	1921–29	154
1866–74	108	1930–37	102

Source: W. Arthur Lewis, *Economic Survey, 1919–39*, p. 202.

would have been nothing in the sort of expectations founded on one's own experience and that of the two previous generations — the usual span of direct communication — which would suggest any secular trend of prices in either direction. So unless one's place in a cyclical swing was obvious, it would not be reasonable to expect prices to be relatively stable over the period for which a wage was agreed.

In the 1980s, we have a rather different perception of things. Predictably wage negotiations during the 1970s, a period of significant inflation, exhibited little acquiescence to the erosion of real wages through price changes, even with the high level of unemployment prevailing. Protection of one's relative position in a period of sustained inflation necessarily involves taking price expectations into account in wage bargaining. More of this, and the related issue of money illusion, in the next chapter.

So far, two of the arguments against Classical labour-market theory have been presented. They can be put in perspective with the aid of Figure 7.6. The argument has been that if there is unemployment, as at A, the downward force indicated by the arrow labelled 1 is lacking, because a fall in the real wage is not, in general, in labour's interest nor, given the difficulties, is it in firms' interests; and those who might have an interest in seeing wages fall (the unemployed) have no power to encourage them to do so. There does however exist a force leading towards full employment, indicated by arrow 2, *provided* the demand for labour rises. The argument of this section is that this force will not be impeded by an adverse reaction on the part of

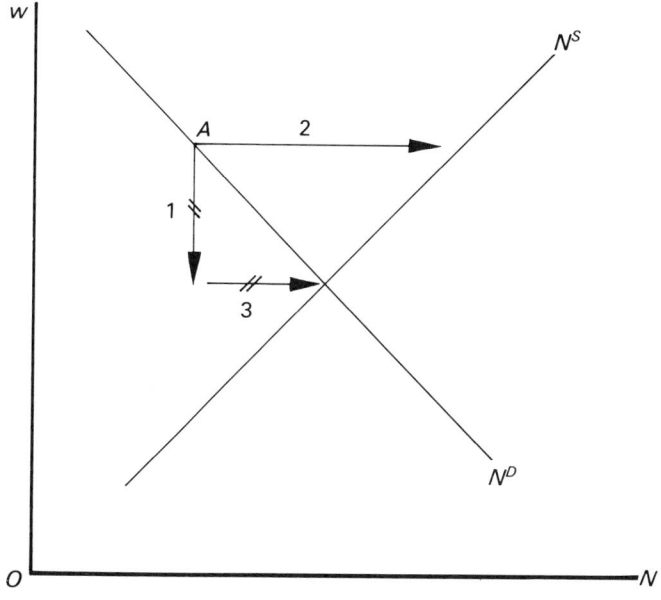

Figure 7.6

labour to the fall in the real wage which is entailed. Its presence, however, does not follow from the existence of unemployment, so it does not constitute an automatic corrective mechanism.

The third part of Keynes's argument, to which we now turn, relates to arrow 3. In Classical theory, a fall in wages would encourage employment, because labour was now relatively cheap, etc. Arrow 3 therefore is contingent on arrow 1. Despite Keynes's denial of the force indicated by arrow 1, the existence of the employment-creating potential of a wage change is also denied, on the grounds that the wage change will not leave the aggregate demand function unaffected.

When Money Wages Do Fall

It is sometimes argued that Keynes's concern with the downward-stickiness of wages was policy-prescriptive rather than theoretical or descriptive. It is said that Keynes showed that money wage cuts could be inimical to the desired end of increased employment and that the objective could be achieved more successfully by allowing prices to rise instead and that therefore wages should be *encouraged* to be sticky. Keynes did indeed say all those things, but saying them does not vitiate the theoretical-descriptive character of the discussion we have just rehearsed and elaborated, nor should the theoretical nature of Keynes's objections to a microeconomic analysis of a wage change be discounted. The words 'rather than' in the first sentence of this section are at fault; the only reason for the 'either-or' thinking that they represent is to dismiss the importance of the theoretical dispute and contribution.

The conclusion that sticky wages may be *desirable* derives from exploring the feedback effects on demand of a cut in money wages. The results contrast with Classical theory, which saw only the cost aspect of a wage cut. Analysis of the effects of reducing wages may seem paradoxical, for if wages *are* sticky, if the adjusting 'forces' do not exist or are weak, this would appear to obviate the need for such a discussion. However, it was useful in heading off both the possibility of encouraging wage cuts by policy and forestalling the hoary argument that 'if only wages were flexible everything would be alright'. This argument has by no means disappeared.

The Classical Argument: One argument proposing that lower wages will increase employment is very simple: reduced costs will encourage each firm to expand production and employment. It fails, however, to examine the result of these firms' expansion. The *market* supply curve has also shifted rightward, creating a downward pressure on prices, if, as assumed, demand conditions are unaffected. The price falls and the result for individual firms is that their expansion does not pay the profits anticipated. In Figure 7.7, D_0 is the original level of demand facing a single firm. *MC* and *AC* are marginal

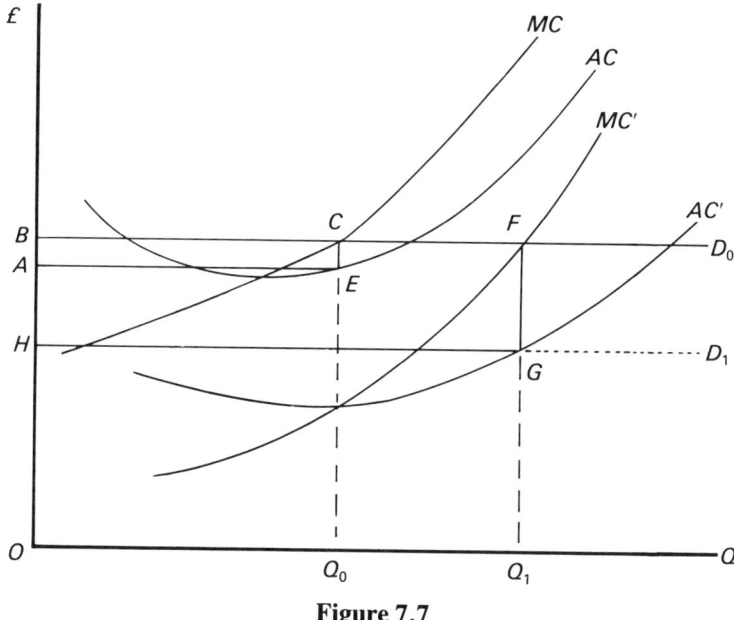

Figure 7.7

and average costs. Production is at Q_0 and profits are $ABCE$. Now costs are lowered to MC' and AC', and production expands to Q_1, on the expectation of unchanged demand. Expected profits are $HBFG$. But realised demand is less than D_0 by some undetermined amount. If it falls below D_1, not even normal profits are made on Q_1. It is therefore easy to see that the expansion can even make this firm worse off than before the wage cuts, though, of course it may not. The outcome is quite uncertain. What is certain, however, is that profits will be less than expected ($HBFG$), and that a retreat from Q_1 will follow.

The Direct Effect of a Wage Cut on Aggregate and Effective Demand: The above analysis was entirely about supply. The demand schedule was assumed unaffected. However, 'the precise question at issue is whether the reduction in money-wages will or will not be accompanied by the same aggregate demand as before ...' (*G.T.* p. 259).

The correct answer is 'probably not', although an unequivocal 'no' is usually given. The repercussions of a wage cut on the level of demand have come to be analysed very simply (while in the *General Theory* the analysis is predictably complex); the usual argument is that the fall in the wage reduces workers' incomes and thus consumption demand, which, other things being equal, will reduce employment. This argument has two major flaws. First, though wage income falls, profits rise. It does not *follow* (though later we shall argue that it is *likely*) that aggregate expenditure will fall. Second, costs are ignored. A fall in demand only leads to a fall in income if it falls further than costs.

The relevant question is the extent of the fall in each. If the point of effective demand were vertically displaced (Figure 7.8, point *A* to point *B*) employment would be completely neutral with respect to wages. Sometimes it is even suggested that the wage cut might make matters *worse*, reducing demand more than supply. If the latter were true, a policy of *raising* wages to cure unemployment ought perhaps to be entertained; indeed it has been urged by trade union leaders.

Keynes analyses the question in terms of wage-units: briefly,

> ... the volume of employment is uniquely correlated with the volume of effective demand measured in wage units, and that the effective [*sic*: aggregate] demand, being the sum of the expected consumption and the expected investment, cannot change if the propensity to consume, the schedule of the marginal efficiency of capital and the rate of interest are all unchanged.
>
> (*G.T.* p. 260)

Looking at the microeconomic sequence of events he asserts that entrepreneurs, disappointed by the effects of their initial expansion, will cut back exactly to previous levels of output unless the *mpc* is equal to unity or investment rises to fill the gap.

This result has an air of magic about it: specifying *Z* and *D* in wage-units has produced this result like a rabbit out of the hat, for the very subject of

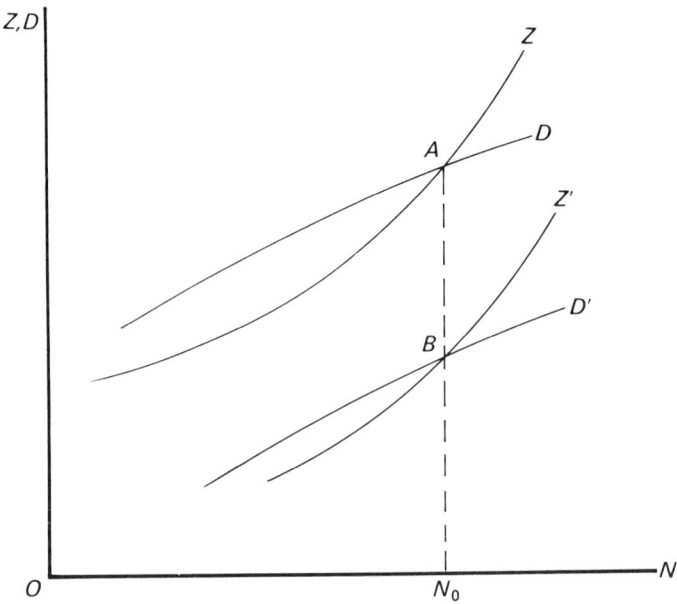

Figure 7.8

discussion, a change in wages, is not visible: the curves have been defined as stable with respect to wage changes. Along each, wages may vary freely. What this magic allows us to see is that for there to be a net effect on employment, the wage changes must affect the *position* of the consumption function (i.e. the consumption function in wage-units is *not* stable) or the volume of investment. These we call indirect effects; they are discussed below.

Let us be clear what this result tells us. Aggregate analysis is the opposite extreme from that which begins with what the individual firm perceives. It predicts what firms would do if they could foresee all the repercussions both of other firms' actions in increasing supply and of households' demand responses. Full knowledge, it says, would give the Classical long-run result: employment and output are, in the end, unchanged. From this we infer that prices fall as much as wages, and real wages are unchanged. The actual path, and perhaps even the outcome, when the process unfolds through time (as it does in fact), depends very much on rates of adjustment, for example, how fast the demand effects of changes in employment come through and how quickly firms react to their initial disappointment. The outcome of such a process is not captured by any of the comparative statics exercises in which we have been engaging here.

Indirect Effects of Wage Cuts on Aggregate Demand: If a wage cut is going to affect employment one way or another, one must look for indirect effects on aggregate demand — effects which shift the propensity to consume or alter investment plans. Keynes suggests several such influences, the net effect of which is ambiguous. These will now be mentioned briefly.[11]

The first influence to be analysed is that of the redistribution of income on consumption. Keynes begins rather oddly, by stating that 'the reduction in wages will somewhat reduce prices', then looking at the effects not of the wage change itself but the price change. One can, however, safely conclude that the wage share has fallen in money terms: the increase due to paying the newly-employed will be outweighed by lower payment to the much larger number of those already employed, i.e. the elasticity of demand is less than one. Payments to other factors entering prime cost, e.g. to raw materials suppliers, have not been reduced per unit and so will at least maintain this share. Gross profits may rise (depending on how much adjustment is assumed to have taken place),[12] and fixed factor payments are of course fixed, though they will be smaller as a relative share in the expansion phase of adjustment. On the other hand, the real value of those fixed incomes has risen, as have the incomes of non-wage prime factors. *A fortiori* the wage share in real terms has dropped and the share of the latter two groups increased. In money terms the effect on the aggregate profit share is somewhat mixed. The net profits of final-goods producers most likely have fallen, while profits of raw materials producers have risen. Keynes simply assumes that the price effect dominates, transferring real income from entrepreneurs to rentiers (and landlords, one should add).

It is reasonable to assume that wage-earners' marginal propensity to consume is the highest amongst types of income earners. The relative position of entrepreneurs, landlords and rentiers is more ambiguous. As remarked earlier, the rentier has been largely displaced by financial institutions, which pay dividends to households to whom these payments are secondary to their labour income. These households will typically be from the higher income brackets, with, consequently, a lower *mpc* than wage-earners. Entrepreneurs are also no longer an easily identifiable class about whose consumption behavioural generalisations may easily be made. So the effect of the redistribution between these three groups is in doubt. The chief identifiable influence, then, is the redistribution of incomes away from high-*mpc* wage-earners toward the lower-*mpc* groups as a whole. This will shift the consumption function downward, in addition to the effect of the wage cut itself, discussed earlier.

Another influence on consumption is expectations of *future* wage changes. If the current reduction is viewed as temporary, there will be a greater willingness to sustain consumption standards than if it be thought permanent or, worse, if further cuts are anticipated. The prospect of a return to higher wages in future is also alleged to be favourable to investment, raising the marginal efficiency of capital (presumably on the grounds that a substitution of capital for labour would be desirable in the circumstances).

These responses, which are favourable to demand, are of course reversed if the wage cut is thought to be insufficient, thus raising the expectation of further cuts. Thus 'the most unfavourable contingency is that in which money-wages are slowly sagging downwards and each reduction serves to diminish confidence ...' (*G.T.* p. 265). Confidence may also be disturbed, and demand adversely affected, if the wage cut causes labour unrest, and if falling prices make the debt burden oppressive.

On the other hand, the lower wage cost relative to costs abroad will stimulate exports.

Enough has been said to illustrate the proposition that the indirect effects of a wage cut on demand are ambiguous. There remains the possibility of an effect on investment through the interest rate, which indeed is sometimes called the 'Keynes effect'. Since monetary aspects of the *General Theory* have not yet been discussed, it can only be mentioned briefly at this point, to be referred to again later. If wages and prices fall, less money is required for the payment of wages and the purchase of goods. If the overall supply of money is unchanged, some money may be released from this sphere of circulation and will find its way into securities markets. This will lower the rate of interest, which is favourable to investment if the expectation is that the new wage level is likely to persist for a fair time. If wages and prices are expected to rebound, the Keynes effect is likely to be adverse to investment (working in the opposite direction to the effect of expectations on the *mec*) because the effect will be to encourage short-term lending at the expense of long-term, which is what matters most to investment because the expected price rise erodes the real value of long-term lending.

The general conclusion to which this last section leads is that in view of the ambiguous indirect effects, and the impossibility of achieving a rise in employment through the wage cut alone, it is not a wise policy to engineer a wage cut even if it were politically feasible, and it is not sensible either to rely on 'the market' for an automatic mechanism by which higher levels of employment (much less *full* employment) can easily be regained.

In the present institutional setting, the problem takes on a somewhat different cast. Both firms and unions have become accustomed to the use of government 'stabilisation policy', be it fiscal or monetary, to expand demand when unemployment threatens. In such a climate, it is not cuts in money wages that are at issue, but the relative rate of rise of wages and prices. The elements needed to recast the theory in these terms are, however, all present in the material of this chapter.

Notes

1. This idea was associated with Fabian socialism in the late 1950s and early 1960s and occasionally crops up in speeches by trade union leaders.

2. These two groups are, roughly, represented by the neoclassical Keynesians and their thoroughly neoclassical opponents.

3. Taylor (1976, p. 14) calls it the 'capacity view'. He adopts it, and seems to feel no qualms in doing so.

4. The precise composition of demand may be open to error, in contrast to Walrasian theory, where every firm's profit expectation is met.

5. It will be understood that this and some other factual descriptions do not apply to jobs where individual skills are highly differentiated and bargaining is individual.

6. Dock workers were the last major example, apart from the rather irregular arrangements which still exist to some extent in the construction industry.

7. Neither the expectations nor the bundle of goods need be the same for producers as they are for workers, but we abstract from that consideration here.

8. It is reasonable to suppose that workers take the price rise as temporary, and therefore do not adjust their expectations, in a world in which prices rise and fall irregularly and the inflationary trend that has marked the postwar period was not in evidence. Alternatively, we could assume that the price rise is anticipated or quickly incorporated into expectations after having been observed. This would shift the supply curve to the left, perhaps even far enough to necessitate raising the money wage. We return to that latter possibility in the next chapter. For present purposes we require that it *not* shift

so far as to create an excess demand for labour, but that is sufficient; it need not be fixed, as assumed in the text.

9.   In modern language, the two changes convey different 'information'.

10. If the price rise is thought to be temporary and turns out to be permanent, then in terms of the Classical model, where such a conflict of interpretation is absent, workers may even be 'off the supply curve' — the curve that embodies true prices — to the right. In terms of the real-wage Figure 7.4, observed employment may lie on the demand curve *below* w^*/P. This extends the relevant range of the first Postulate.

11. One of these (point (e), *G.T.* p. 263) seems to refer to a movement along a stable consumption function rather than a reason for it to shift. It will therefore not be discussed.

12. Keynes does not discuss this. (One can see why.)

Chapter 8

THE DEMAND FOR LABOUR FURTHER CONSIDERED

The First Postulate

The previous chapter gave reasons for rejecting the second Classical Postulate and for supporting Keynes's acceptance of the proposition that wages and employment are determined by demand — that is, by firms. Careful readers will have noticed, however, an unwillingness to give support to the first Postulate as specified: 'the wage is equal to the marginal product of labour'. This is due not so much to the existence of a degree of monopoly — it is an easy matter to qualify the Postulate to read 'marginal revenue product' — but to the general weakness of the theory from which even the altered Postulate derives in dealing with change, once there is an existing work force to think about. Wage cuts become difficult to arrange, as we have seen, but that causes no difficulty to the first Postulate. However, when demand expands, a divergence between the average and the marginal cost of labour emerges whenever additional labour if not freely available at the wage already received by the existing work force. This fact invalidates the first Postulate, as a general principle.

The supply curve of labour is upward-sloping. Thus if the demand for labour expands from a position in which there is no involuntary unemployment at the going wage, the wage must rise. But the additional labour firms want cannot be obtained at the cost of that additional labour alone: the higher wage necessary to attract more labour must be paid to everyone. If the previously-prevailing wage is x and the wage necessary to get one more unit of new labour is $x + h$, the marginal cost of hiring an additional worker is $mh + (x + h)$, where m is the existing labour force. This fact would suggest invoking the analysis developed to analyse monopsony in the labour market,[1] which draws a marginal-cost-of-hiring curve (MCH)

above the supply curve. This divergence of *MCH* and supply applies, however, every bit as much to 'small' firms in an industry which has 'reached its supply of labour curve' as it does to a firm large enough to have an individual impact on the wage.[2]

In the 'monopsony' analysis, profits are maximised where the labour is hired up to the point at which marginal revenue product of labour (*MRP*) equals the marginal cost of hiring labour, which lies above the supply curve. The supply curve indicates the wage which must be paid.

Consider now the dynamic behaviour of money wages and employment. Begin at a position of unemployment *A* in Figure 8.1, which relates employment to the *money* wage. Firms are paying the wage prevailing before the drop in demand represented by MRP_0. Provided firms' sales expectations are met, there will be no change (*A* is an underemployment equilibrium). If expectations of demand for output should rise, the *MRP* curve shifts to the right; employment rises while wages remain fixed (since firms have no incentive to raise them) until full employment is reached at *B*, after which further shifts in labour demand will necessitate raising money wages:[3] then the *MCH* comes into play. Employment and wages remain at *B* until *MRP* rises above MRP_3, when the profit-maximising volume of employment is given by equating *MRP* and *MCH* (e.g. points *E*, *F*). The wage necessary to get the labour is indicated by the supply curve. As demand shifts upward, wages and employment rise along the supply curve as indicated by the bold line to *C* (the portion *CD* will be discussed in a

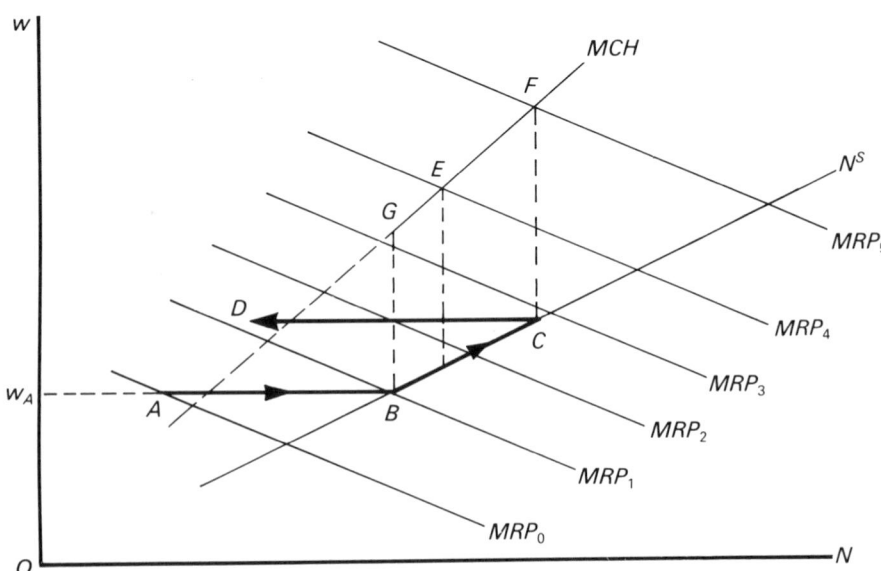

Figure 8.1

moment).

The *MRP* curve determines offers of employment for a profit-maximising firm, but *not* the wage, except during unemployment. The wage but not the volume of employment is determined by the supply curve, once full employment is reached. *Thus the first Postulate does not hold in general.* With an excess supply of labour, the *MRP* curve *does* indicate profit-maximising behaviour and the Postulate holds in this, but only in this, circumstance.

It will be noticed that no reference has been made in the above analysis to a labour demand curve. Once *MCH* comes into play it is, indeed, difficult to construct one, for demand is completely insensitive to a falling real wage implied between points *B* and *G* in Figure 8.1, and the level of employment at which that inelastic portion occurs depends on the volume of labour already employed (whose existence is ignored in neoclassical analysis).

The Determination of Wages and Employment

Keynes's refutation of the second Postulate implies that there is no unique relationship between *N* and *w*; once one goes behind the frontier of the supply curve, many levels of wages are in principle consistent with a given level of employment, and many levels of employment are consistent with a given wage. And now it has been argued that the demand curve based on marginal productivity is not really much help either. What, then, determines *w* and *N*?

The bold line *ABC* of Figure 8.1 gives the levels of *N* and *w* which will be observed as demand for output rises, *given* that the demand-rise begins when there is unemployment and the wage is w_A.

The locus *ABCD* may be called an *employment function*. This is not a behavioural function in the usual sense, but a locus relating *actual* levels of employment to the real wage in the case of expansion beginning with unemployment.[4] Prices rise for each shift in *MRP;* thus the real wage is progressively falling between *A* and *B* and rising, perhaps less rapidly than the money wage, to the right of *B*.

It is plain that the employment function is not reversible, since, as it has been argued, it is difficult not only for labour but also for firms to reduce money wages. The expected path in the face of shrinking demand is a horizontal movement to the left. If demand falls, say from the level that created MRP_5, firms will shed labour — they would do so immediately if there were no marginal costs of firing, but there are. This factor is too awkward to take account of in the figure. At some unspecified point, therefore, observed employment moves back along the bold line towards *D*. If demand picks up again, employment will expand along the same line back toward *C*.

The examination of the behaviour of the labour market in this and the previous chapter has revealed some uncomfortable features. (1) Wages and the level of employment are not uniquely related; a given level of employment is consistent with any level of wages on or above the supply curve. (2) The employment function is not reversible. (3) The location of the horizontal segments of the employment function *is a historical accident.* Indeed, the whole employment function is given by the interaction of demand and supply forces with history: it matters whether demand is expanding or contracting — it matters where one has been. It matters, too, how much labour is already employed when employment expands. Neither of these things can be included in the method of comparative statics; in terms of that method, w and N are indeterminate. But that is an indictment of the method, not an indictment of the present conclusions: w and N *are* determined, partly by demand and supply broadly interpreted and partly, as anyone with common sense would expect, by history.

Sticky Wages

The above discussion demonstrates the difference between wages which are arbitrarily fixed, by assumption, for analytical convenience, and wages which are *sticky,* that is, loath to move. Sticky wages emerge as a consequence of an analysis of the interests of all parties in *changes* in wages, in a setting which conforms to the institutional characteristics of the labour market. Some strong disincentives for change have been adduced in favour of downward stickiness: a fall in wages during unemployment is really only in the interests of the unemployed (though firms may imagine it to be to their benefit if they do not take demand effects into account). And no-one expects firms to raise wages if unemployed labour is available. What emerges in this chapter is a case for complete[5] upward stickiness, for a time, even at full employment and in the face of rising demand, and even after wages begin to move, greater stickiness than the Classical model suggests: the *MCH* curve is steeper than the supply curve.

It is, of course, difficult for individual workers to raise either wages or hours of work; in the absence of collective bargaining this action is up to firms, and even in the presence of bargaining success depends on the existence of excess profits or the expectation of a rise in demand.

However, to say that wages are sticky does not rule out their eventual change. (In what follows, I assume a relatively stable price level.) At the onset of a recession, firms will expect to pay the going wage, for although each individual firm may have adopted a pessimistic view of the future, there is little reason for them to expect that this opinion would be widely shared. Thus they place themselves in the position of price-takers, an accurate position even if the pessimism were indeed shared, as long as it is not expected to be shared. Later, as a downturn becomes general, staff turnover or job re-classification may permit some substitution of cheaper labour;

wages may begin to fall. If the situation persists long enough, wages will certainly fall, though not necessarily as far as the market-clearing wage. The practical procedures paving the way for a fall in wages are of a type that could take a considerable time.

It also takes time for labour to accept a revised estimate of its worth. Once it does so its 'reservation price' — the price below which it elects to continue to seek work rather than accept less — will change.[6] But it will be resisted. For all these reasons, wages, while not *rigid,* in practice are sticky downward.

In the upward direction the same mechanism operates. The source of stickiness, the existing labour force, is not itself fixed. Workers will move, eventually, to those firms which are, for one reason or another, able to raise wages earlier than other firms; this lowers the *MCH* for those remaining, and wages will drift upwards.

Collective Bargaining

The above analysis applies to the hiring of additional labour on an individual basis: the wage is raised when it is necessary to attract extra workers and profitable to have them on the new terms, which then apply to everybody. It violates the first Classical Postulate in the sense that labour demand is no longer determined exclusively by marginal product but does not touch the propositions that the volume of employment is determined by firms and that labour controls the wage only at full employment. These latter propositions are challenged by the existence of collective bargaining: if confronted with coalitions of workers, is it not possible, not only for firms to be 'off their demand curves', but off them to the right? This would violate the assumption that in a disequilibrium situation it is the short side of the market which dominates the actual outcome, so it perhaps deserves more than a cursory examination.

Neoclassical analysis holds that in the absence of productivity increases the attempt to raise wages is self-defeating, resulting in unemployment. An attempt by a union to better the wages of its members is portrayed either as misguided or worse, a wilful sacrifice of employment for some of their members to the benefit of those who remain employed. As unions see it, they are protecting their members against undue exploitation. When they bargain for higher wages, they do so in the expectation that the rise in costs can be absorbed without prejudice to employment. Who is right?

The neoclassical argument is based, usually only implicitly, on the whole range of assumptions of the model of perfect competition. Now it is surely correct that in an economy of atomistic firms, with every industry in equilibrium (where all firms are earning just-normal profits), the unions could only succeed if there were indeed productivity gains to share — unless their claim were validated by an expansion of demand. This last qualification is important, and we shall return to it.

But first let us consider a more realistic set of conditions than those which support the neoclassical view: we suppose that in at least some firms and industries there exist excess profits, whether because of a degree of monopoly power, incomplete adjustment to industry equilibrium, or recent technological innovation. Moreover we do not rule out increases in demand for final products. These departures from full-industry perfectly-competitive equilibrium leave open the possibility of raising wages without necessarily damaging employment: the higher wage bill diminishes excess profits but does not push the firm into making losses. The unions are, of course, uncertain as to the ability of any given firm or industry to pay a higher wage in the future: excess profits in the recent past are only a guide to future excess profits, which are the basis of the union's claim. Firms are also uncertain: that is what makes a wage bargain interesting.

Modelling Supply and Demand

Simplifying heroically, the essence of supply in a unionised industry is that labour is only obtained at union rates, is freely available at those rates until it runs out and is simply not available after that, since wages are controlled upwards as well as downwards by contract. Further labour can be obtained by upgrading job classification or extending overtime so as to raise the effective wage, but the supply curve with respect to the actual wage has only two vertical portions,[7] e.g. OW_A and AN^S in Figure 8.2.

The process of wage negotiation consists in 'trying out' supply curves based on different wages to see what firms say their implications for employment might be. Thus the nature of the wage negotiation has something of the quality of wiping clean the slate of history that is inherent in neoclassical theory. Although one would be foolish to say that the wage agreed or the process of agreeing it was entirely independent of the recent history of wages in the industry, the question being posed in presenting the union's demands to the producer is an all-or-nothing choice between N units of labour at wage x, or no labour at wage $x - h$: will the firm be willing to employ N_x or not? This is similar to the question on which the demand for labour is based. The similarity is limited by the fact that the length of time for which withdrawal of all labour is threatened has no place in neoclassical analysis, but it is not so dissimilar as to prevent the re-introduction of labour demand curves in this context.

Let us consider the union's claim for a higher wage with no loss of employment. Assume the firm or industry was in a profit-maximising position previously; therefore the wage and level of employment were on its demand curve, say at point A in Figure 8.2. Then the union attempts to move to a point such as B. It is readily conceded even by neoclassical theorists that if firms expected demand for output to rise sufficiently to cover this new wage by higher prices, (i.e. to N^D or above), the claim could be successful (although of course it will be resisted). At the aggregate level, without a change in the propensity to consume, this rise in aggregate demand could be effected by a rise in the money supply, which, while not disturbing the relation between real income and consumption, permits expenditure and prices to rise. The demand for labour curve will, accordingly, shift upwards; a shift to $N^{D'}$ will assure the success of the claim, in money terms. Whether the claim succeeds in raising aggregate *real* wages depends on prices in the consumer-goods industries rising less than capital-goods prices.

Excess Profits: The more interesting case is that in which demand is not expected to rise, either for monetary reasons or by virtue of a change in tastes, and yet some excess profits are expected; for while the neoclassicist would flatly deny the possibility of successfully raising wages without increasing unemployment in this case, it can be shown that a rational firm may agree to hire more than the 'maximum' indicated by their demand curve.

To see this we develop the concept of isoprofit lines. All positions on the demand for labour curve represent profit-maximising solutions, given a fixed quantity of capital equipment, but each point on the curve represents a different *level* of profits. For a given level of product demand, the price of

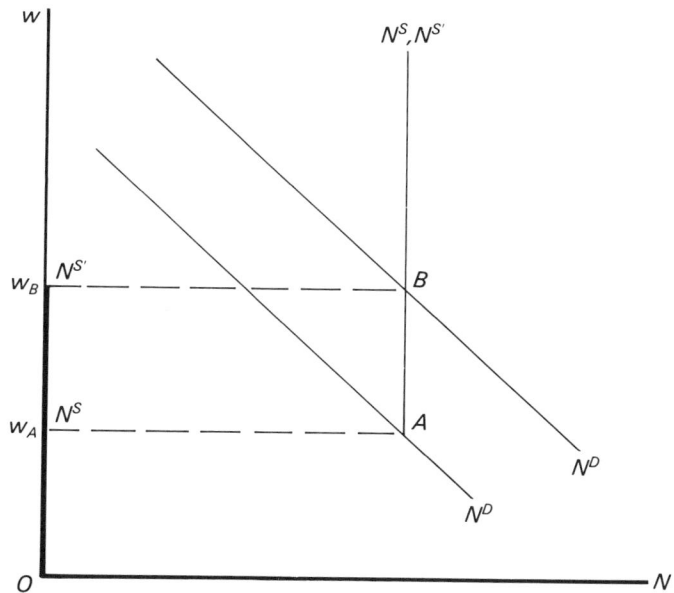

Figure 8.2

the product is given; thus output and profits rise as labour becomes cheaper, moving downward along the curve.

Now choose a point on the demand curve in Figure 8.3, say A. The maximum profit given the wage at A, w_0, is Π_0. The same level of profit can, however, also be obtained by other combinations of N and w. If less labour than N_0 is employed, output and hence revenue will be less, so to keep profits the same, costs must also be less. Since we know that points along the line w_0A to the left of A entail lower profits than at A itself, we also know that the isoprofit line must lie below w_0A : costs must be reduced by more than the reduction in employment; wages must fall also.

Follow the same reasoning to the right of A. More employment means more output and more revenue. Costs rise because N is larger, and if the wage w_0 is maintained, profits will fall. The isoprofit line lies below w_0.

Since the level of profits varies continuously along the N^D curve, there is a family of isoprofit curves, one for each level of profits. Two curves are shown in the figure (Π_0 and Π_1).

Let us return to the problem at hand: can the union obtain a contract which implies a position to the right of the demand curve — say a move from E to point B, raising wages from w_E to w_B, with no loss of jobs. In the absence of any anticipated improvement in demand, this claim must imply a reduction of profit, but note that although this bargain is not *optimal* for the firm or industry, it is certainly feasible over most of the range of the labour

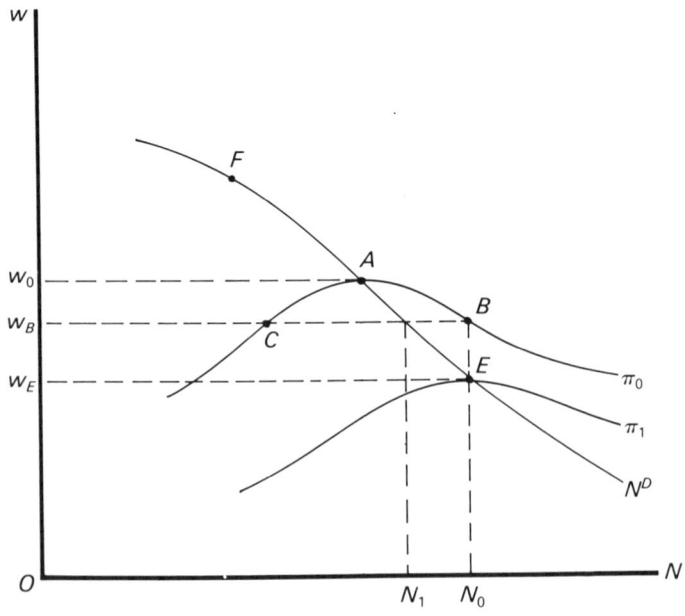

Figure 8.3

demand curve. At some point, say F, total costs including normal profits are just covered. Unions would be unwise to play this game at or above that point. But below it there are excess profits which the firm can be coerced into giving up.

So point B is feasible. Now notice that although the firm would prefer, at wage w_B, to cut employment to N_1, it is a matter of indifference whether they accept the bargain represented by point B or by point C: the level of profit retained after wage payments is the same. Thus there is no case for saying that points to the left of the labour demand curve are any more feasible than those to the right. The only question is whether firms can be shaken off their demand curves at all. Common observation suggests that they can; the asymmetry of power which characterises firms' bargains with individuals, even when the firms are themselves 'small', is at least partly removed when labour bargains collectively. The result for macroeconomic theory is to offer another challenge to the first Classical Postulate.

Price Expectations

The whole argument up to now has assumed a non-inflationary climate. As pointed out in the previous chapter that was a reasonable assumption in the 1930s, but conditions have changed. By the early 1960s in Britain, later in the US, the expectation that prices are generally rising, only more or less rapidly, had taken hold. The theory must be re-examined with that in mind.

First let us reconsider the labour supply function and re-open the question of money illusion, which has been used to reduce Keynes's dispute with Classical theory to the issue of workers' rationality and to discredit Keynes's theory generally. Evidence of money illusion is found, by those eager to find it, in Keynes's emphasis on the fact that the wage bargain is struck in money terms and in his assertion that workers are not observed to withdraw their labour when prices rise by a small amount.

The latter point has to do, as we have shown, with progress towards full employment from a position to the left of the supply curve and therefore need have no implications for the supply curve itself. In actual fact the supply curve may shift;[8] the point of specifying a small price change is that it will not shift far enough to affect the result. We shall return to this point after considering the supply curve itself.

The simple fact that wage bargains are made in money terms does not imply money illusion as a corollary. In deciding how much labour to offer, households consider a range of hypothetical incomes based on different money wages; that does not preclude their taking into account the expected purchasing power of the money wage. Is there any doubt that union bargaining positions are established on the basis of expected inflation rates and that their acceptance of offers takes the expected price level into account? No, nothing inherent in the wage-setting process rules out a concern for real purchasing power.

Mere *concern*, however, is not enough to satisfy Classical theory. The Classical model (and its modern equivalent) assumes that it is a matter of indifference to both firms and workers whether the money wage rises or 'the' price falls by an equivalent amount. There are several reasons why this assumption is untrustworthy. The first and most obvious point, bypassed in the previous chapter, is that firms and labour are concerned with differnt prices. Even if prices were brought into bargaining explicitly, so long as bargaining takes place industry by industry, only in a few cases would any bargain relate directly to enough wage-goods to be significant, and only if the bargaining were economy-wide would an agreement about prices guarantee the controllable elements of real wage. (Import prices are assumed to be beyond the control of the bargaining parties.)

In the absence of a mechanism for bargaining over prices as well as wages, any notion of the real wage involves a *forecast* of prices, for it is prices obtaining *after* the receipt of wages that determine wages' real value. In Classical theory, forecasting presents no problem: the theory applies to a world of 'tranquillity' where prices have been what they are for some time and may be expected, with some confidence, to remain there.[9] Expected and actual prices are effectively the same, so fixing the money wage establishes the real wage. In the *General Theory*, in contrast, the future is uncertain. Thus while the willingness to supply labour is necessarily predicated on an *expected* real wage, in Keynes's framework the *actual* price level which emerges may surprise workers (favourably or unfavourably). The money wage bargain does not fix the real wage.

Thus there is no inconsistency between accepting Keynes's attack on the Classical assertion that the interaction between entrepreneurs and workers could determine the real wage and denying that the attack depends on money illusion in the labour supply function. Subject to the qualification of inadequate foresight there is no need to reject the theory that the willingness to supply labour is determined by the disutility of work, though workers' estimates of the consumption possibilities afforded by a given amount of work may not be accurate and may result, in the first instance, in *actual* employment's being off the supply curve to either side.

If the actual level of prices turns out to have risen less than labour expected, some would wish they had offered more labour than they did, to capture the higher real wage. This phenomenon is more likely to arise in a downturn, when prices would tend to be lower than expected. The actual real wage will be above expectations if workers take 'yesterday's' prices as their forecast. When the true real wage becomes known (or if it is anticipated) the labour supply curve will shift to the right, exacerbating unemployment, for while it is easy enough to withdraw one's labour if the real wage disappoints, workers are not, individually or in aggregate, in a position to insist on longer hours. An unpleasant surprise should make the labour supply curve shift leftward, but again this need not have any effect. If it does, it will be in the *next* round of wage negotiations. Time moves only in one direction; the wage bargain is struck and employment arranged *before* the goods whose prices determine the real wage come onto the market.

Time plays an important role in Keynes's theory of the labour market. During an expansion beginning with unemployment, producers are assumed to base their labour requirements on the expectations of 'yesterday's' wage and 'tomorrow's' demand. Until full employment is reached nothing falisfies their expectation about the wage: it remains where it was. Workers' expectations are, however, passive: they are assumed to expect yesterday's prices, and though their expectations are continually falsified during this process, their willingness to supply labour does not change significantly. Their passivity is part of the reason that the level of employment is entirely demand-determined.

Passive price expectations are reasonable in a background of cyclical movements in prices but not in a period of sustained inflation. To make money wages reflect real wages even approximately, it becomes necessary for labour to forecast prices actively. Thus if they perceive a shift (rightward) in demand, there will be a leftward shift in supply. The higher the expected price rise, the further to the left the supply curve will shift. This hastens the day when producers discover that they cannot get all the labour they want at the going wage — and at that point, as we have seen, the willingness to supply labour is equally important with demand in settling w and N. In effect, active expectation of price changes by labour reduces the asymmetry of Keynes's argument, though it does not eliminate it. That would require eliminating involuntary unemployment altogether.

Even if workers get their estimate of forthcoming prices right, it does not follow that any observed unemployment is voluntary. This is so firstly because workers and firms are concerned with different prices: the marginal revenue product depends on producers' prices and the real wage depends on the prices of consumer goods. And even if all firms produced 'representative bundles' of consumer goods and workers correctly estimate what firms will in fact charge, there still is no guarantee that at the real wage so determined workers will actually buy what firms think they will buy or that firms will produce the volume of output which workers expect. Only a recontracting arrangement such as Walras's system of 'tickets'[10] can ensure the Classical result.

Thus important asymmetries remain between workers and firms; the best that the most active and accurate forecasting can assure for labour is that no one is involuntarily *over*employed — i.e. off the supply curve to the right. Furthermore, firms have greater information at the time of bargaining. Firms, basing their offers of employment (and the wage) on anticipated product demand, have already determined what prices they plan to charge.

Thus firms know the 'real' implications to them of the wage they are offering, while workers come to bargain over money wages without this knowledge (and at the microeconomic level it is not usually their own firm's pricing policy which is relevant anyway).

Not only do producers come to the wage bargain knowing their pricing policy; they are also in a position to change that policy after the bargain has been struck,[11] if firms find they have agreed to pay higher wages than they planned. The practical scope for doing this depends, of course, on demand conditions.

The atomistic firm has no scope to raise prices unless demand turns out to be greater than anticipated. Firms which face downward-sloping demands for their products will however, if they are profit-maximisers, always raise prices when costs rise, for whatever reason.

When the reason is wage costs, another interesting possibility presents itself. Suppose that an important number of unions manage to achieve a wage increase not justified by expected demand. The Classical result is a reduction in employment. Suppose in constrast that the unions have managed to obtain commitments to maintain the existing work force. Thus output does not decline, but labour income expands at the expense of profits. The argument of the previous chapter concerning a cut in money wages now comes into operation in reverse: aggregate demand is likely to rise because of the income redistribution (though as before there may also be influences working in the opposite direction). There is some possibility that the wage rise itself may present firms with the possibility of recouping some loss of profits by raising prices.[12]

The likelihood of firms being able to recapture profits lost in wage increases is greatly enhanced by government commitments to a full-employment or high-employment policy. When government enters the picture, there is systematic bias toward raising demand by government measures to protect employment — that is, to cushion firms against adverse effects of wage increases. If both unions and firms predict that demand will be supported by government expenditure, they may well agree to wage increases which would otherwise be unacceptable.

Notes

1. Rothschild (1947).

2. One is reminded also of Arrow's (1959) treatment of disequilibrium in atomistic markets as similar to firms' having a 'degree of monopoly' as long as the price is not 'given by the market'. I would argue against this terminology as it reinforces the quite unnecessary, and stultifying, identification of perfect competition with price-taking.

3. In practice, wages will start to rise before full employment is reached, because of bottlenecks in particular labour markets.

4.   Its resemblance to the supply curve in Figure 7.3, the curve put forward as Keynes's supply function by those who believe that Keynes *assumed* fixed wages below full employment (e.g. Patinkin 1965), is only in form. The conceptual basis is quite different.

5.   As before, we abstract from bottlenecks, which are likely to be of substantial practical importance.

6.   By including a point made in search theory, I do not accept that theory as sufficient.

7.   The horizontal portion is broken to preserve the concept of the supply curve as a maximum.

8.   Whether it does shift depends on whether the price change is seen as permanent or not.

9.   In modern, ultrarigorous analysis, perfect foresight is assumed.

10. See the previous chapter.

11. This possibility is denied them within the theoretical method of the main argument of this book, where the requirement that price and output policy must be established at the beginning of the production period is imposed in order to highlight the expectational character of those decisions. In practice, these decisions may be revised at any time in the light of results.

12. Where firms do not agree to maintain employment at the old level but react 'classically' by laying some workers off, the probability of this outcome is, of course, much reduced — indeed, aggregate demand may even fall and exacerbate the original effect on employment in subsequent periods.

Part III
FINANCE

Chapter 9

SAVING, INVESTMENT, INTEREST AND FINANCE

It will have been noticed that the determination of aggregate demand is incomplete, for the rate of interest remains a mystery, and without it the level of investment is not determined. Investment will still not be fully explained, for it depends also on long-term expectations of profit, which are even more problematical than short-term expectations. But the rate of interest is amenable — perhaps all too amenable — to discussion.

What is Interest?

Interest is the return for lending a sum of money for a specified period of time. From the lender's point of view, interest provides an incentive to part with cash and hold a debt instrument instead. It compensates him for both the financial risk and loss of flexibility involved in giving up money now in exchange for a promise of money later. The risks are those of default and of capital loss if the principal should be needed before the debt matures. Uncertainty about both future interest rates and expenditures are involved in the latter kind of risk.

For the borrower, interest may be thought of as the cost of bringing forward some expenditure.[1] The borrower gains liquidity now at the expense of committing himself to relinquish it later. He must be persuaded that the expenditure he proposes is sufficiently worthwhile, in terms of profit or satisfaction, to justify both the interest and the future illiquidity.

Keynes argued that his theory of interest follows naturally from what interest *is*: the price of having money now instead of later; the price of being liquid. It would seem, however, equally plausible to describe interest as the price of borrowed funds and to approach the theory of its determination by looking at the demand for and supply of credit or loanable funds, rather than the demand for and supply of money. It might even seem, since money is either retained or loaned out, that the two approaches are equivalent. These are interesting issues to be explored a bit later.

What rate of interest do we need to determine? The one that affects investment, if we knew what that rate was: the rate on bank credit? on long-term securities? Both of these sources of finance are feasible choices for firms, particularly when we remember that working capital is part of investment. What is the relationship between these sources and other interest-bearing assets, such as govenment securities, or assets that yield a return similar to interest, like equity shares?

Interest and the Finance of Investment

Implicitly, we have linked the interest rate to the financing of investment. Curiously, in the *General Theory* Keynes makes almost nothing of this connection:

> The schedule of the marginal efficiency of capital may be said to govern the terms on which loanable funds are demanded for the purpose of new investment; whilst the rate of interest governs the terms on which funds are being currently supplied.
> *(G.T.* p. 165)

That is all. Funds are available from unspecified sources at the going rate of interest.

Keynes seems to take for granted the financing of investment, and if it enters 'Keynesian' analysis at all, one is given to understand that at the end of the multiplier process, *saving* finances investment. This is obviously odd, since one cannot finance something after it has happened if one needs finance to make it happen in the first place. It is even odder to the reader who was convinced by Chapter 3 above that saving and investment are on Keynes's definitions identical. Therefore the one cannot finance the other.

Therein hangs a good bit of the tale, and much of the rest will not come out until Chapter 14. But we can begin with some simple points about 'finance'. Income is a source of finance; it was implicit in earlier chapters that income was adequate to finance consumption — not for everybody, but on average and in aggregate. Indeed, there would usually be some money left over. (That is the natural way to put it: some *money* left over.)

Investment, on the other hand, was portrayed as interest-sensitive precisely because current income did not finance it: either previously-accumulated financial assets had to be sold, or the money had to be found from outside the firm. It is easy to see how the rate of interest (the terms on which money may be borrowed) become bound up with saving (income not consumed) and investment.

It is useful to think of economic decision-units — e.g. households, firms or government departments — being either in financial surplus or deficit insofar as they spend within their incomes or not. The surplus units are creditors of the deficit units. Financial intermediaries, including the banks for the moment though often we shall speak of the banks separately, complicate the picture precisely because they intermediate; they stand between final debtors and final creditors.

It is useful to define *direct* borrowing and lending as that between deficit and surplus units and indirect lending as that involving a financial intermediary: thus a mortgage is indirect, a rights issue direct. One can also speak of the sources and uses of funds.

What possible sources are there? Income has already been mentioned. Current expenditures are financed out of current income, fitting into the macroeconomic picture as the 'circular flow of income': the regular payments of wages and the regular purchases of goods. The finance is generated by the spender. The subject of this chapter is the financial connections *between* potential spenders — potential because they wish to spend in excess of income but their ability to do so is not guaranteed — and possible lenders.

In this context consider 'internal funds'. This term can mean two things which have very different implications for theory: firms' cash flow from sales, or their liquid asset holdings. Some investment may be financed out of current cash flow, but current sales cannot be, for the economy as a whole, a major source of finance for investment. Financial asset holdings, on the other hand, could play a substantial role from time to time.

Assets accumulated for the finance of investment constitute the financial provision for expected outpayments to replace worn equipment and may even be sufficient to finance some net new investment. The accumulation of assets over and above what is spent constitutes a diminution of net income for a given gross income, even when set aside for new investment as well as on supplementary cost account, for it is profit not distributed. As the funds are spent, the gap between the two measures of income lessens. Hence consumption, which is governed by net income, is affected by alterations in timing of the accumulation and disbursement of these funds.

From another point of view, firms' financial assets could be seen as 'business saving'. The aggregation scheme of Chapter 3 has rather ruled that out, but if the terminology were admitted, this component of saving would be closely linked, in terms of motive, to intended investment. The two actions are only separated in time. That separation may be, from time to time, important, but perhaps from the point of view of highlighting the disjunction between saving and investment Keynes was wiser than subsequent theorists in treating this source of finance as the difference between gross and net income.

This approach is also useful in preserving the sectoral approach. Borrowing and lending and more certainly sales of financial assets amongst firms and amongst households occur. These transactions may even be numerous, but it is doubtful that they are as significant for understanding the important forces in the economy as are intersectoral transactions. A single household may be a surplus or a deficit unit, but the household sector as a whole is typically a net creditor. The business and government sectors are net debtors. Households save, firms invest, and investment is financed by borrowing. That is the basic framework.

Although there exists a rich variety of financial assets, it is useful to describe direct borrowing as taking two basic forms: fixed-interest contracts of fixed maturity (bonds, or debentures) and ownership (equity) shares carrying the prospect of disbursements related to profits (dividends). Rights issues to equity holders are not in the strict sense borrowing.

We shall be concerned mostly with the former, while keeping in the back of our minds the fact that the two instruments are alternatives to savers, to be evaluated in terms of their relative attractiveness, which has several dimensions: certain interest *versus* uncertain dividends, prospects of capital gain for different reasons, differential taxation of income and capital gains, etc. These matters are the subject of the theory of finance or portfolio theory, which is highly pertinent, but better to exclude.

There remains the possibility of financial intermediaries as a source of funds for entrepreneurs and a repository for the savings of houseolds. Banks are of premier importance, both quantitative importance in the real world and in the break which Keynes made with Classical and neoclassical interest theory. To that subject we now turn. It will occupy us, one way or another, for the rest of the chapter. We do this not for doctrinal reasons, but because an examination of that dispute will uncover much of the structure of Keynes's system and demonstrate the interplay of institutional change and theoretical development.

Classical and Neoclassical Interest Theory

Keynes's attack on the interest theory he inherited and which was current in his own day will not be easy either to describe or to analyse for several reasons. First, non-Keynesian theories were not always stated with great explicitness. Second, Keynes's attack is sometimes directed to the assumptions and sometimes to the conclusions or implications of the other theories and it is difficult to see what he is doing. Indeed, he may not have known in full himself. Kaldor (1981) cites Keynes's (1924) comment on Marshall as prophetic of Keynes's own work:

> Those individuals who are endowed with a special genius for the subject and have a powerful economic intuition will often be more right in their conclusions and implicit presumptions than in their explanations and explicit statements.

As for the Classics, Keynes remarked that although he and his contemporaries had all been brought up on it, he found it difficult to state precisely or to discover an explicit account of it in the leading treatises of the modern classical school.

It is fairly clear, however, that this tradition has regarded the rate of interest as the factor which brings the demand for investment and the willingness to save into equilibrium with one another.

(*G.T.* p. 175)

As for neoclassical theory, it has

led to the worst muddles of all. For [the neoclassical theorists] have inferred that there must be *two* sources of supply to meet the investment demand-schedule; namely, savings proper, which are the savings dealt with by the classical school, *plus* the sum made available by any increase in the quantity of money .... .

(*G.T.* p. 183)

It sounds like a bit of a muddle all round.

At the risk of being unfair, the Classical theory could be seen thus. Interest was a reward for 'waiting', for delaying consumption — in other words, for saving. How much 'reward' entrepreneurs were prepared to pay depended on the prospective return to capital or to production by roundabout means during which some consumption was necessarily delayed.

The Classical theory was, therefore, that aggregate saving and investment were kept in equality by means of the rate of interest.

Indeed most members of the classical school carried this belief [in $S = I$] much too far; since they held that every act of increased saving by an individual necessarily brings into existence a corresponding act of increased investment.

(*G.T.* p. 178)

Insofar as that theorem could be supported, the Classical theory of interest supported Say's Law with a different rationale from that offered earlier. It is no longer necessary to argue that no one would work who did not wish to consume the full proceeds of his labour. Instead, the desire to save is admitted but it is argued that there exists a mechanism whereby saving is automatically matched by investment: viz., variations in the interest rate. As long as this mechanism works, it does not matter whether income is saved or spent: what is produced is sold, if not for consumption then for investment.

One of Keynes's objections to the Classical theory was that it dealt with the theory of interest in an entirely non-monetary way, yet interest is paid for borrowing *money*. At least the neoclassical theory brought money into the picture. However, the theory was so designed that the conclusions or implications of Classical theory still held.

In particular, saving was still *prior* to investment. Investment could however be financed out of dishoarding or from new money as well as from 'saving proper' — i.e. saving in the Classical sense. Sources and uses of funds are fundamental to this theory, hence its designation as Loanable-Funds Theory. Sources and uses may be indicated by an equation:

$$I + H = S + \Delta M \tag{9.1}$$

where the new symbol, H, is net hoarding (i.e. the accumulation of cash balances by surplus units less dishoarding by others). This equation looks alright: 'saving' can go into hoards as well as into investment, and investment can be financed by dishoarding or new money as well as by 'saving'. So indeed investment can, but this school argued that price changes would result from finance involving H or ΔM which would be absent if investment were financed by 'savings proper'. These price changes gave rise to what they called 'forced saving'. It was to this latter concept that Keynes had violent objections in the *General Theory* (see *G.T.* p. 183 for the tone of the writing), although he supported the idea in the *Treatise* — and although (ironically) it is possible to interpret at least one version of the multiplier (as he presents it) as involving forced saving. (This is discussed in Chapters 12 and 14.)

It is also the case that Say's Law is given support, though not unqualified support, by this theory, and the priority of saving was not challenged (though it could have been) by its advocates.

It is probably best to view loanable-funds theory as an attempt to preserve a Classical outlook on interest, saving and investment while adapting the theory to a monetary economy. The significance of this remark cannot be made clear at this stage; it is made at this point to give something to watch for as we trace our way through three interrelated issues:

    (i)   the question of the equality of saving and investment, and the determinants of saving and investment;

    (ii) the priority of saving versus the perturbing influence of autonomous investment; and

    (iii) the relevance of these matters to Say's Law.

With the exception of the first, these issues will be handled here in an incomplete way, for the complete story requires Chapters 10 to 14. The overriding purpose of this chapter is to establish that the frameworks within which Keynes's and the earlier theories are formulated are dissimilar. If this is successful, the implicit assumptions of much of monetary theory after Keynes are easier to see.

The Saving-Investment Controversy

> Unlike the neoclassical school, who believe that saving and investment can be actually unequal, the classical school proper has accepted the view that they are equal.
>
>   (*G.T.* p. 177)

There is no doubt whose side Keynes was on here: he insisted that it always *turns out* that saving and investment are equal, but he was equally (and rightly) adamant in insisting on the importance of the fact that the *decisions* to save and invest are made by different people in advanced Western economies. The *point* of this latter insistence was to prepare the ground for demonstrating that the Classical economists had perpetrated a *non sequitur* in suggesting that 'saving' flows *automatically* into investment. Neither is it a *precondition* for investment. Miraculously his argument prevailed, despite the massive confusion (the debate over this issue continued in the journals for ten years!) caused by his insistence that saving and investment were separate but equal. What he was driving at was not helped by his definitions of saving and investment.

The resolution achieved by those ten years of argument is well known: whatever savers' and investors' intentions, the two magnitudes will *in fact* be equal *ex post* (rather the way that purchases and sales are equal), though the planned (*ex ante*) magnitudes are not equal except by accident.[2] There remains the question (equivalent to the problem of whether the amount actually sold is the amount demanded or the amount supplied) of which quantity the *ex post* magnitude conforms to: *ex ante* saving or *ex ante* investment. The accepted answer is that conflicts between *ex ante* magnitudes are resolved in the immediate run by changes in inventories, so that the outcome is decided by the desired amount of saving: an excess of saving over investment is identified with an excess of production of consumer goods over planned purchases of that class of goods, so that unplanned investment in the forms of stocks of finished consumer goods takes place. A deficiency of saving results in unplanned decumulation of stocks to reduce investment to the level of 'saving'.

This standard resolution of Keynes's puzzle should have made it difficult to sustain the vision of investment as the engine of change against the background of a stable consumption function, for then it is investment which adjusts to saving (non-consumption). The inventory changes on which the story relies are clearly more pertinent to variations in consumption demand than investment: it is unlikely that capital-goods suppliers keep stocks of capital equipment, much less buildings, on hand to satisfy an 'excess of investment'. The contradiction with Keynes's postulate of a leading role for investment was not seen.

The other problem with the agreed resolution of Keynes's conundrum is that it fails to face the question of real and money values; with any disparity of plans falling on inventories, prices need not change. (This resolution has reinforced the belief that Keynes's model follows the 'fixprice' method.[3]) As remarked in Chapter 4, Keynes made no such assumption, even for the very short run. If prices may alter to resolve a conflict of plans, the question of how consumers react to changed prices is as important as firms' reactions to changes in sales. An expected rise in planned consumption, given planned investment (not quite the same as a deficiency of saving) may raise consumer-goods prices. Then it is likely that the volume of consumer goods purchased will be less than planned, and it is not obvious what the effect will be on the money value of consumers' expenditure. Thus there is no guarantee that plans to save a given money sum will be fulfilled.

Proponents of the accepted solution to the saving-investment problem might counter by saying that price changes are not an issue: it is *real* saving (or real consumption) that motivates consumers. The latter point is surely correct, but what *is* real saving?

'Real saving' is usually just 'defined' as S/P — money saving deflated by the price level, both in current values — and there the matter rests. The use of the current price level indicates clearly that S/P indicates the goods which could have been consumed but weren't — an aggregate idea which, as shown in (our) Chapter 3 is *identical* to investment and cannot account for any divergence of saving and investment.

Furthermore, this concept bears no relationship to the positive action of saving. This is hardly surprising since in a decentralised economy plans and decisions are microeconomic in character. The idea of real saving when applied to what people actually *do* when they save is quite awkward. In the mind of the saver the object of saving is to be able to consume in the future out of income earned now. Thus the real value of saving from his perspective is not the goods forgone now, but the goods he expects to buy later.

Clearly, if prices are assumed to be fixed, use of the current price deflator provides a reasonable proxy. But where prices are allowed to vary, as they must be if the theory is to apply to a world of uncertainty, it can be seen immediately that real saving to the saver depends upon (i) the expected composition of his future expenditure, (ii) the expected timing of future expenditure, and (iii) the expected prices of the relevant commodities at the expected date of purchase. The possible inaccuracy of these expectations and their variance amongst individuals would make it difficult enough to make any use of such a concept of real saving.[4] It is certainly not possible to form on this basis an aggregate with which to compare investment — which itself can only be thought of in real terms as a vector of heterogeneous things.

Micro-Macro: In a decentralised economy, plans can only be made by individuals; *ex ante* saving therefore is a microeconomic concept. The excess of income over consumption is represented to an individual as a sum of money which — given that the definition of consumption rules out saving in the form of consumer durables — must find its way into some financial investment, including bank deposits and cash. This is the process of saving we all understand (because we do it), and which may be defined by what it *is* rather than what it is not; it is the acquisition of financial assets.

It is certainly easier to think of this saving in money terms; and in principle it should not be difficult to aggregate — or is it? Saving has been positively defined as the acquisition of financial assets including money. So, you might think, it should be possible to measure aggregate saving: the sum of individual acquisitions of financial assets. However, individuals can only acquire what is available, and the stock of securities outstanding is determined at least in the first instance by *suppliers* of these instruments (borrowers) not demanders (the savers). Nothing savers can do can force ICI to float debentures (though ICI's timing may depend on its estimate of demand). Banks will always take deposits, but the aggregate amount of deposits is determined at least as much by borrowers' requests as by the extent to which people entrust cash to the banks. Nor do all deposits of cash indicate saving.

And how should we treat revaluations of securities in measuring saving? If savers place funds in securities when the aggregate supply of these instruments is fixed, the rise in security prices indicates saving in the sense defined, but if the rate of saving is steady while new issues are made and capital values fall, one should not infer that dissaving, even unplanned dissaving, is taking place. Dissaving may take place as a result if people had planned to spend their acquired wealth and find that its value had fallen, but there may be no dissaving of any kind, as paper losses do not *have* to be realised.

Fluctuations in interest rates, whatever their origin, cause variation in market values of many types of financial assets, but not all of them: most notably, bank deposits which bear no interest, even deposit accounts, which do, retain their value when interest rates change. Thus the problem goes deeper than the measurement problem posed in the previous paragraph. Saving is the sum of demands for financial assets, but this aggregate fails the test of the composite good:[5] that the relative prices among the components be invariant, and the value of saving so measured may alter without any action on the part of savers.

It will be clear that aggregating this financial notion of saving up to the level of a closed economy produces exactly the result obtained in Chapter 3 by a different route. The assets of one economic unit are the liabilities of another, and saving disappears, leaving only investment. Consolidating a balance sheet of financial assets poses problems fundamentally dissimilar to those encountered in adding up units of goods produced. We knew that all along.

It must be concluded that there are severe, perhaps insuperable, difficulties in defining aggregate saving, even for a sector, which has any direct connection with the process of saving as planned and conducted by the household or firm. It does, indeed, seem impossible to find an aggregate concept which has the positive quality desired. Perhaps it is only possible to say what aggregate saving is *not*, after all.

Once the absence of a connection is acknowledged, puzzles arising from Keynes's exposition fall into place, especially the idea that saving is a residual. If this statement is interpreted as relating to individual actions, based, for example, on the assertion that 'consumption has first claim on a man's income', while saving adjusts to temporary or unexpected variations in income, then it is possible to say that saving is only a residual during adjustment and that genuinely *planned* saving is not a residual but is every bit as deliberate a decision as planned consumption. Interpreted at the aggregate level, where, as we have seen, the positive concept of the sum of individual saving plans is untenable, saving is most certainly a residual. It is *defined* as a residual. It is presumably aggregate saving that Keynes had in mind when he wrote: 'As for the concept of *ex ante* saving, I can attach no sound sense to it' (*C.W.* XIV, p. 210).

The Determinants of Saving and Investment: According to Keynes's understanding, the Classical theory postulated that the rate of interest was determined by saving, which was positively related to it and by investment, which was negatively related to it. Keynes accepted the latter relationship with a sense of certainty now lost,[6] and as we saw in Chapter 6, there is no serious impediment to developing an aggregate investment-demand schedule from microeconomic behaviour.

Saving as a function of the rate of interest, however, he did not accept. He had two arguments against it, or perhaps three: he sometimes seemed to argue as if a function could only contain one determinant, and since income, he had decided, was the crucial determinant of saving, interest could not have any effect.

The two slightly more serious arguments were the following. (i) A change in the rate of interest has both a 'price' or 'substitution' effect, altering the relative incentive to consume now and in future, and a wealth effect as the capital value of most financial assets changes with interest rates. The effects on saving operate in opposite directions and the outcome is unclear. Therefore the interest rate effect is probably not important. (ii) He pointed out the fact — obvious at a superficial level but requiring the whole edifice of his liquidity preference theory to support is as a fact with important theoretical implications — that people just as truly save when they add to their idle cash as when they lend it out at interest. This was enough to break any *necessary* connection between interest and saving, though it is surely not enough to justify the unimportance of the rate of interest in the saving function.

However weak his reasons for excluding the rate of interest — and however unnecessary, for it was enough just to assert the importance of income — he was then in a position to argue, as he did, that the rate of interest could not be determined by saving and investment alone.

Excluding the rate of interest from the saving (or consumption) decision did serve to increase the dramatic impact of his theory: S and I now were brought into equality by income; gone was the theory that S and I were equated by the rate of interest. No one could fail to spot the difference. It also had the advantage of greatly supporting his assertion that investment *caused* saving and not the other way about.

Before we turn to that point, however, it is to be noted that the Classical economists were, in Keynes's view, less than clear what they *meant* by the rate of interest. They tended to equate it with the rate of return on capital or the marginal efficiency of capital. Keynes distinguished sharply between these concepts and the rate of interest; they have the same dimension, that is all. Interest is a monetary phenomenon; the rate of return on capital has to do with costs and revenues from productive activity. It is not difficult to find works today in which these two concepts are treated as identical.

The Priority of Saving in Classical Theory

Although Classical theorists had acknowledged the influence of income on saving, they had ignored the role of investment in determining income and treated income as predetermined in the theory of interest. This was, according to Keynes, their big mistake.

The causal ordering implicit in the Classical scheme (as portrayed by Keynes) is clear enough: insofar as saving is determined by income it is predetermined, leaving only the interest rate's influence. The supply of funds is adjusted, more or less at the margin, by the willingness to pay interest, and the amount of investment that actually gets done is determined by the volume of savings.

In reversing the causal ordering, it was convenient for Keynes to be able to argue that the rate of interest was determined independently of saving and investment. For then we have, in order, (i) the formation of the *mec* schedule independently of r, (ii) the confrontation of *mec* with r to determine actual investment, (iii) the impact of I on Y and *hence* on actual S.

Keynes's theory *presumes* that sufficient funds are forthcoming at r to support all investment projects whose *mec* is greater than r. Thus one way of looking at the dispute is that it concerns the elasticity of the supply of funds.

That view, however, is more suitable to the conflict between Keynes and neoclassical or loanable-funds theory than with Classical theory. There is, I believe, a simple resolution to 'Keynes versus the Classics' on interest-rate theory which separates that debate from the conflict with loanable-funds.

'Saving' is a concept whch has been defined in such an open-ended way that its form can change over time while retaining the same label. Classical theory had its beginning in the setting of an agricultural economy, where the archetypal form of saving was the seed-corn: production not consumed, a *real* resource. (Being real, there is no problem with aggregation.) Income, the harvest, *is* predetermined. When corn is held back from consumption it is saving, when sown, investment. The saving is done (slightly) prior to the investment in the nature of things and it is only done for the purpose of investment, which in turn is closely allied to both the time-preference of consumption and the expected return from investment.

In such a society, borrowing and lending would as often take the form of promises of labour time or produce, as of loans of money, and the latter would be seen, if undertaken purely for economic gain, as a way of participating in a venture, rather than as saving. One can understand both why saving and investment were not sharply distinguished and the validity of equating interest with the return on capital.

The industrial revolution changed all that, gradually. In the sole proprietorship or partnership, which was the early common form of business, much saving was still done by those who were investing — and for the *purpose* of investing. Once the entrepreneur needed outside funds however, it became possible for the saver and investor to diverge.

Only then does it become reasonable to argue about the priority of investment or saving. And only with the emergence of borrowing and lending chiefly in the form of money is it *possible* to divorce the rate of interest as we now know it from the rate of return expected from devoting real resources to a project designed to enhance future income.

The priority of saving of Classical theory carries over well to the beginnings of industrial society, when sole proprietors and partners saved in order to invest in their businesses and outside funds were typically borrowed direct from lenders through the issue of debt obligations. The owners or lenders had to have saved in order to have money to invest or lend. The separation of the act of saving from the act of investing is therefore not sufficient to reverse Classical causality. It is indirect borrowing which creates the possibility of a reversal.

Keynes Versus Loanable-Funds Theory[7]:   Recall from equation (9.1) that loanable-funds theory (LFT) admitted the possibility, emphasised by Keynes also, of holding idle balances to serve as a potential source of funds for investment. The divergence he points to concerns the treatment of saving. LFT counts hoarding as separate from 'saving proper'; for Keynes one may save by holding either money or an interest-bearing asset: hoarding is a *form* of saving for Keynes.

The LFT concept of hoarding was more subtle than perhaps Keynes was prepared to admit, but to go into that here would take us further into the realms of history of thought than we need to go. It is the conflict between the implicit framework of loanable-funds thinking and Keynes's theoretical structure that is illuminating.

LF theory is concerned with flows of funds. Investment and hoarding are demands for funds, to spend and to hold, respectively; newly-created money and previously-accumulated idle balances now dishoarded were sources of supply. It is clear that LFT sees all saving as available for investment, i.e. it is identified with *lending*. When net hoarding is zero and the money supply unchanged, saving and investment determine the rate of interest. Add to this the fact that LF theory thinks of hoarding as an unusual and temporary phenomenon and LFT approximates Classical theory so long as the money supply is fixed.

Keynes, too, took the money supply as fixed in developing his theory (though not, naturally, when discussing monetary policy), so this assumption was not at issue. (However, it emerges in Chapter 14 below that it should have been.) What was at issue was the underlying assumption of LFT that money which did not circulate in the payment of wages and consumers' purchases went — the aberration of hoarding apart — into saving and almost automatically into investment. The only matter to be settled was the rate of interest. Although a bit of a hybrid, interest remains a reward for saving.

The whole vision is essentially microeconomic or at most sectoral in character. This must be so whenever money is envisaged as circulating from hand to hand or being borrowed and lent.

Keynes's vision is an unresolved, or at least implicit, mixture of macro- and microeconomic perspectives. Aggregate saving in the *General Theory* is not a financial variable at all. It is 'non-consumption', and non-consumption cannot finance anything. At the microeconomic level, the saving decision may be thought of as taken jointly with the consumption decision; then a further decision must be made; how to dispose of the income not spent on goods. If one is 'thinking macro', not until the stage of disposing of 'saving' does *decision* come into the picture. Thus in the *General Theory* there is an important separation; the level of income determines the (residual) amount of income not consumed, and the rate of interest determines where it is placed. If 'saving' is not a decision, the theory of the rate of interest can be developed entirely in terms of the demands for financial assets.

The interest rate, however, influences not only the placement of current savings, but of previously-accumulated savings ('wealth') as well: the stock of pre-existing wealth of households (who do not own instrumental capital) and firms' retained earnings must also be held in financial assets. Since saving — marginal additions to financial wealth — is fairly small in relation to the stock of wealth over a shortish period of time, and since the whole of the stock of wealth must be allocated, saving is trivial by comparison. So the demands for financial assets are independent of saving in yet another way.

There was a similar separation of investment from the flows of funds that might finance it, though achieved more by lack of discussion — rectified later in his debates with Robertson — than a series of identifiable and defensible assumptions.

The schemes of Figure 9.1 indicate the two views. Notice the absence of investment in the scheme representing the structure in the *General Theory*. ΔB^D stands for acquisition of 'bonds', an archetypal interest-bearing asset. The dotted line from C to ΔM^D represents the transactions demand for money and W stands for financial wealth. Figure 9.1(b) shows the grafting-on of hoarding (ΔH) and changes in the money supply (ΔM^s) to an essentially Classical scheme, though 'saving' is no longer real (e.g. seed-corn) but financial. r^* is the 'neutral' or 'natural' rate of interest on which this theory concentrates. r in Figure 9.1(a) is the actual (nominal) rate of

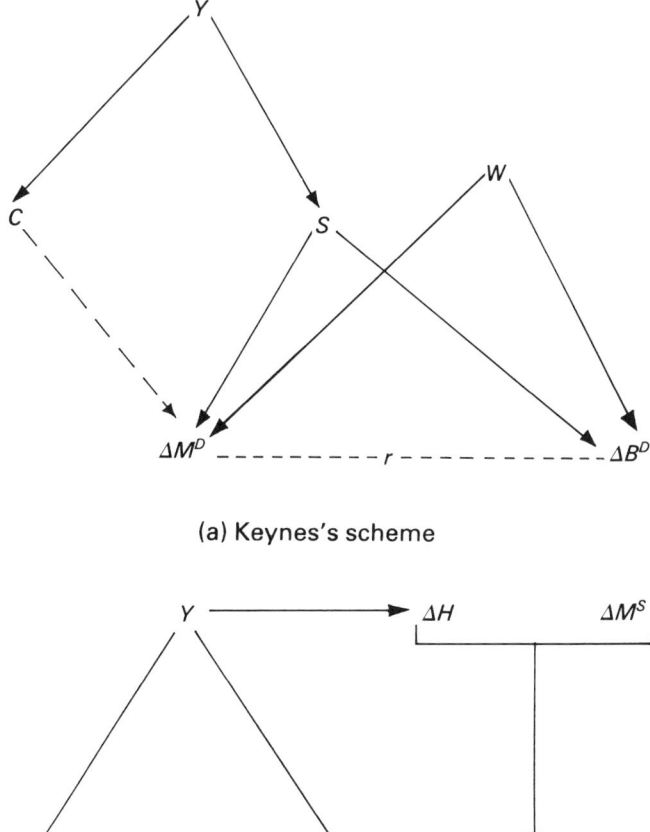

(a) Keynes's scheme

(b) Loanable-funds theory

Figure 9.1

interest.

Although LFT's vision is essentially microeconomic there is one macroeconomic element: exogenous changes in the money supply. Full analysis of this will be left until Chapter 14: for the moment LFT will be regarded as not in direct conflict (or congruence) with any of Keynes's (or the Classical economists') macroeconomic propositions about saving and investment. Yet macroeconomics has microeconomic foundations, however difficult it sometimes is to make connections. So the dispute between Keynes and the LFT is worth pursuing.

There are really two areas of dispute, apart from the role of the money supply, between Keynes and LFT. One is the identification of saving with lending in LFT and the other is the temporariness of hoarding. The second point cannot be discussed without the material of the next chapter, so we turn to the first.

The argument will be conducted in terms of three assets, cash, bank deposits and 'bonds', the latter an archetypal interest-bearing borrowing instrument.[8]

Saving, Lending and Existing Assets: The observation that one can save by holding idle cash as well as by lending at interest points up a crucial difference between Keynes and loanable-funds theory, but leaves Keynes in a weak position. For insofar as the 'idle cash' is not *literally* cash (notes and coin) but bank deposits — a far more plausible way to save — one immediately thinks that the banks' advances will rise, so there is lending at one remove.

The following, it seems to me, would have been a more robust argument. Financial assets being, within each class of asset, homogeneous, a market in secondhand ('seasoned') securities has grown up and flourished. A saver is quite indifferent between getting a given return from an existing security he buys off its former holder, or from a newly-issued security.[9] However, only sales of new issues represent borrowing and lending; the rest is transactions amongst current savers and existing security-holders.

Now suppose we accept the loanable-funds view of the world insofar as we go along with the identification of investment with borrowing (no financing from internal funds) and of saving with buying securities — which is not quite the same thing as lending. And suppose that from a situation of equality of saving and investment, entrepreneurs' expectations become pessimistic while saving is not affected, the supply of new financial instruments falls, savers compete for the existing supply and the rate of interest falls, but not all of the saved funds go to finance investment — only those which were used to buy *newly*-issued securities. The rest drain into capital gains for holders of existing securities.

Only if those who make capital gains go and spend those gains on consumption (in the current period) will the demand for goods and services be unaffected. Otherwise, the effect is exactly the same as if cash were withdrawn from circulation. And the likelihood that some of those gains, perhaps most, will be reinvested in financial assets seems quite high.[10]

This is the sense in which I meant my earlier remark about Keynes's two-asset simplification. One asset would have been enough; so long as there are existing as well as new assets, the direct link between saving and lending is broken. They are semi-independent at least. (Keynes made them *completely* independent, which was probably an overreaction.)

Existing Securities, the Rate of Interest and Say's Law

The implications of my example for Say's Law are rather interesting. Savers were able to fulfil their saving plans in the sense that they were able to place the money they intended to place in securities, but there is no automatic guarantee of investment, or consumption out of capital gains, of similar magnitude.

If one defines 'real saving' as 'intended future real consumption', then one can confidently predict that not enough investment will have taken place to produce the extra consumption goods which were expected when the saving was undertaken.[11] Keynes's proposition that saving is not a successful signal of intended future consumption holds, even without saving taking the form of idle balances.

If saving falls below investment, interest rates rise and the market value of securities falls. There will be inadequate funds to carry out all investment projects this period, but original consumption plans, which might have filled the gap, are unlikely to be carried out in full, now that the value of (financial) wealth has fallen. Saving and investment still determine interest, but Say's Law need not hold.

The chief reason that saving and investment do still determine interest, in this model, is that asset-holders are given no alternative asset to hold. If there is an alternative, non-interest-bearing asset (cash) a decision to vary the composition of one's wealth would change interest rates entirely independently of the rate of saving. A theory based on this consideration has more powerful results, as we shall see by the end of the next three chapters, but variations in the timing of saving and investment where there is a market in existing financial assets, or equivalently, establishing lending as only a subset of saving behaviour, is enough to break Say's Law. The option of holding idle balances gives a *further* reason.

The Priority of Saving, Again: At one level, Keynes's reversal of the Classical priority is easy to accept. Saving, like consumption, depends on current income, so although it will rise if income rises, it cannot *initiate* a change in income as long as the propensity to consume is stable. Investment is independent of current income, reacting to long-term expectations which are independent of short-run expectations or results and is therefore free to move, to shift. Expectations being quite fluid, perhaps even volatile, investment may move about quite suddenly. A change in income, and with it saving, will result.

But, asks the sceptical LF theorist (DHR), surely if the investment is not financed, it will not take place. Willing it does not make it so; one needs to back demand with purchasing power.

Quite so, and Keynes never talked about that in the *General Theory*. Robertson (1940) showed that if a rise in investment over the previous level was actually to take place, that investment had to be financed by new money. (His demonstration is discussed in Chapter 14.) Investment in excess of 'saving' in the LF sense (i.e. direct lending) had to be financed by the banks.

Indeed, if one thinks about it, where else could the money come from *in excess* of direct lending. (Now the LF theorist is thinking in aggregate terms.)

Let us return to the historical perspective. We have shown that saving must precede investment when saving is seed-corn or takes the form of direct lending. (In the latter case saving must precede investment but not all saving need go to finance investment as long as there is a market for seasoned securities.) A new issue might draw idle funds into securities markets, but still saving has preceded investment.

That leaves the possibility of bank finance.

The point that needs making will be discussed further in Chapter 12, but it can be put succinctly here. In early stages of their development, when there are many banks and the use of bank-notes or cheques for payment is not widespread, banks' ability to expand credit is severely limited, so much so that each bank is very nearly restricted to lending out no more than was deposited with it. Thus it was said that banks were merely channels, passing the money from primary lenders to ultimate borrowers. Investment financed by bank-created money was therefore financed by saving at one remove.

For as long as that description was reasonably close to the facts, the existence of banks did not affect substantially the propositions that saving financed investment and must precede it. Once the banks were able to 'create credit in excess of savings' to a significant extent, the reversal was possible.

The accuracy of the proposition that investment precedes saving thus *depends on the stage of development reached by the banks.*

Oddly, LF theory has scope for money-financed investment, yet conveys the impression of supporting the priority of saving. This it does through its imagery of money-flows from surplus to deficit units. Projection of the economist's personal experience (which is a useless guide in macroeconomics) of borrowing and lending does the rest. Money-financed investment is said to entail 'forced saving' (see Chapter 12), but it is simply not the case that the forced saving precedes the investment.

Despite this, the causal reversal was resisted by those of an LF turn of mind and it is still being resisted.[12] There were good reasons for this resistance, though they are psychological and ideological rather than intellectual.

The ideological significance of this view of investment *resulting* directly from saving is clear enough: savers determine the rate of capital accumulation. The choices of households control the firms: consumer sovereignty determines current output and saving determines future output.[13] And ignoring the lags implicit in the 'prior saving' argument, whether households decide to spend ('consume') or save, *total* expenditure will be unaffected, for 'saving' is only undertaken in order to finance investment. Therefore there will not be a sustained period of unemployment due to insufficient demand.

To this convenient ideology was added the power of a morality which, although it had outlived its social usefulness by the 1930s, was embodied in the antagonists to this new idea. The Victorian virtue of thrift was undermined by Keynes's theory. But surely that Victorian principle was urged in that subliminal way that societies find their way to, because its basic aim was industrialisation, and the banks, in their 19th century stage of development, were not adequate to cope with the needs of rapidly-expanding industry. Most borrowing had to be direct, and that meant prior saving.

With the development of the banks the facts that theory should capture had changed. The banks of the 1930s could finance investment independently of saving. 'Right' theory is decided by history as well as logic.

Contrary Visions — A Summary: To summarise, let us contrast the LFT perspective with both Keynes and textbook Keynesianism, as far as we can do at this point.

LFT imagines people receiving income in the form of a sum of money. The money is then used to buy goods or it is saved. (LFT would specify $C_t = f(Y_{t-1})$ for the consumption function to reflect this flow-of-funds approach: one spends money previously acquired.) If it is saved the sensible thing is not to put the money in a biscuit tin but to lend it — even holding a bank deposit is lending to a bank. Borrowers borrow to spend, and so the money returns to the circular flow of income.

(One can see that introducing saving and investment does nothing to disturb Say's Law from this perspective. Saving is just a roundabout way of spending; no funds are idle.)

The perspective of textbook Keynesianism is the diametric opposite: all saving is a leakage. Nothing is said about where it goes. If it *happens* to be matched by investment, all is well; if not, income adjusts until the two are equal. This story, using *ex ante* saving and, implicitly, money-flows, is more in keeping with LFT's perspective than JMK's. As for investment, its independence from current income suggests it is financed by borrowing, though the vital question of whether that borrowing results in an increase in the money supply or a rise in its velocity is not addressed. The student concludes that all saving, to be a leakage, must go into idle balances yet he is told later, in the multiplier story, that saving finances investment!

Keynes's perspective involved a strange admixture of a concept of saving which was aggregative and, though in value terms, defined in terms of sales, or rather non-sales, of real output. Therefore the main importance of saving was the deflationary impact of consumers' 'not-spending'. There was also in the *General Theory* a concept of individual saving which did have to do with money-flows, but only to separate saving from investment. At the aggregate level, savings as money-flows were swamped in their effect on the rate of interest by transactions amongst existing wealth-holders.

The net effect of this construction was to *isolate* happenings in financial markets from the circulation of money in the payment for goods to a very great extent, but not completely. They connect, not by money-flows, but through the rate of interest.

The Rate of Interest — A Look Ahead

The rate of interest, in an economy where saving in the form of non-interest-bearing money was possible, could not be the 'reward for waiting', rather it was the reward for parting with liquidity — for holding non-money assets. Interest is determined by liquidity preference and the supply of money.

One would have thought that it was natural to approach the determination of the rate of interest from the side of bonds or that it was a matter of neutrality whether to analyse from the standpoint of money or bonds. Perhaps Keynes had an instinct to shy away from a theory which could (if existing assets were forgotten) be interpreted in LF terms. Whatever the reason, analysing from the side of money permitted a full influence from the level of activity on interest rates while not taking an explicit money-flow approach.

Those with strong instincts to see things in money-flow terms may miss the money-flow aspect of the *General Theory* if it is not explicitly pointed out that when money circulates in the payment for goods and labour, Keynes calls it *income*. Failure to see that has led to analysing money *entirely* in a wealth-holding portfolio framework appropriate only to the speculative demand for money and the speculative and asset-holding demands for other financial assets.

Notes

1. Interest is not always actually *paid*. Short-term debt instruments are sold at less than their maturity (or par) value. The selling price constitutes the proceeds to the borrower and interest is implicit in the difference between the selling price and the par value. This arrangement is used when the term of the loan is too short to make actual interest payments, given the administrative cost involved. On long-term debt there is a contractual interest payment (coupon yield), which is paid at regular intervals. The actual interest rate differs from the coupon yield for anyone who buys the debt instrument for less or more than its par value, as the market price is the actual principal on which the interest rate is reckoned.

2. The terms *ex post* and *ex ante* were devised by Swedish economists to distinguish outcomes from the plans which precede (and shape) those outcomes. My general preference for the words 'planned' and 'actual' derives

from the different understanding of 'plans' in the Swedish and English traditions, of which it is helpful to be aware in reading original material on the saving-investment controversy. The English tradition is to think of plans in the sense of *schedules* and the Swedish in terms of particular magnitudes. The discussion of this section is implicitly in terms of magnitudes, so the Swedish concepts apply.

3. The method is discussed in Hicks (1965). See also Hicks (1974) and Malinvaud (1977).

4. Added to these difficulties is the fact, on which much of Keynes's argument depends, that neither the composition nor the timing of much of future expenditure is commonly well-formulated in the saver's mind.

5. Hicks (1939).

6. '... *no one doubts* that the investment demand-schedule falls with a rising rate of interest' (*G.T.* p. 182, emphasis added).

7. Further discussion of the issues raised here may be found in Chick (1981).

8. Keynes has been criticised for the limited scope of the assets he considered, but, as we shall see, for theoretical, as opposed to descriptive, purposes, these can be quite adequate to make some important propositions.

9. I have tried to phrase this sentence to rule out 'stagging', which arises from underpricing new issues.

10. If all participants realised the situation of excess demand and/or if all security prices went up simultaneously, then one would expect that those who sold their existing assets did intend to use the gains for consumption. The ability of stock market prices to inflate substantially suggests that the mechanism I postulate is not far-fetched.

11. This point is nicely demonstrated in Lipsey (1972).

12. See Leijonhufvud (1981) for a reassertion of loanable-funds theory.

13. For an elegant 'modern' (i.e. postwar) statement of this principle see Hirshleifer (1958), where investment is determined by time preference. The restricted applicability of the earlier model is made explicit in Hirshleifer (1980).

Chapter 10

INCENTIVES TO LIQUIDITY

Money has no *intrinsic* use — it cannot be eaten, nor will it keep one warm. Its usefulness derives from what it will buy, and the flexibility it affords over the timing of payments. Financial assets, similarly, have no intrinsic use; they are held only for the interest they yield. Both are 'temporary abodes of purchasing power', ways of holding over income which is not to be spent immediately. Ready money may burn a hole in one's pocket, financial assets may lie undisturbed in one's passbook or deposit box, but all will be spent eventually, or bequeathed.

When deciding which abode one's purchasing power shall occupy, the relevant question is *how long* it is expected not to be wanted for the purchase of goods. There must be time enough to earn some interest and make the bother of buying and selling bonds worthwhile, if the unspent income is not to be held in cash.

To a large extent, the question of time is related to the type of expenditure envisaged. Keynes is not very explicit about this connection; the analysis can gain in precision if the matter is gone into in some detail.

Transactions Demand, Consumption, and the Wage Bill

Some expenditures are made on a very regular basis. Of these regular payments, some are contractual, such as the firm's payments of wages, interest and rent, and the household's rent or mortgage. Other expenditures are regular because of the nature of the goods bought: food and household supplies are usually bought on a regular weekly basis. These expenditures may vary in their frequency, but the overall pattern is highly predictable. Certain elements of income are also highly predictable, both in amount and frequency, whether this income be wages and salaries for the household, or certain kinds of sales which produce a cash flow to firms.

The typical pattern for the household is a frequency of payments greater than that of the incoming cash flow. Because income is predictable, expenditures can safely be planned to be paid for out of that cash flow. This is the model for the simplest kind of transactions demand. For a given individual one may define an 'income period', the interval between receipts. If out-payments are regular and all transactions balances are held as money, then the *average* transactions-money balance over the income period is proportional to income:

$$M_T^D = kY. \tag{10.1}$$

The size of k depends on the pattern of payments within the income period; the more payments occur soon after income is received, the lower the average amount of cash on hand, as compared to cash holdings of households whose payments are closer to the next income date.

For firms the pattern may be reversed, exhibiting a steady build-up of cash from daily sales to be paid out in weekly wages. The result for average balances is the same, with a payments period as the base.

Devising a satisfactory expresssion for the *aggregate* demand for transactions balances is not a simple matter unless the payments pattern is very stable indeed,[1] but it does no serious harm to assume a stable pattern, in which case the general form of (10.1) applies.

Additional assumptions, namely (i) that the income period is too short or the rate of interest net of brokerage charges is too low to justify transactions balances in bonds, and (ii) that the transactions exhaust income, produce the familiar 'quantity theory' result that the total demand for money is wanted to conduct transactions; then M^D as a whole is a constant fraction of income.

If one is taking the income or payments period as one's base, and I feel one must,[2] one should make it clear that these are *not* the same as the production period, but typically shorter (refer back to Figure 2.1) and of course overlapping continuously for the economy as a whole. The size of k for aggregate transactions balances has to do with the relationship of the income and payments periods to the production period.

The Precautionary Motive

There were two elements of certainty in the above description: the amount and timing of both incoming cash flow and cash outflows were assumed known. That is why the household could be described as willing to run its transactions balances down to zero by the end of the income period. That level of certainty does not, however, generally apply. Even if income is certain (for households with labour contracts) expenditures are not, nor can firms count on steady sales. It is to have enough cash to cope with unpredictable expenditures or receipts that *precautionary* balances are held by those whose incomes more than barely cover their expenditures.

Interestingly, the textbook version of precautionary demand typically gives as examples of unexpected expenditures such things as hospital bills, while Keynes stressed the desirability of having extra money to take advantage of unexpected bargains. This is more than a reflection of a rather more positive approach to life on Keynes's part; it is related to the possibility of holding liquid assets instead of money for precautionary purposes. Many unexpected outpayments can be met, with a day's notice, out of liquid assets.

Keynes reasoned that the average amount of unpredictable expenditure (and, he might perhaps have added, the range of income fluctuations) was correlated with income; therefore precautionary balances could be lumped together with transactions balances. Their sum, which he called M_1 — *not to be confused* with the collection of monetary assets later christened *M1* — was related to income, as before by a constant factor k:

$$M_1 = kY. \tag{10.2}$$

The constant, k, might differ for the two types of balances, but as long as the average was relatively stable, applying (10.1) to both sorts of balances would, he reasoned, create no difficulty, and it had the advantage of simplicity for his purpose, which was to highlight the speculative demand.

This simplicity is bought at the expense of glossing over a fundamental problem in monetary theory: what constitutes 'active' and 'idle' money. There is no doubt about the transactions balances: the way they have been defined, all balances held for the transactions motive are spent within the income period and can therefore be counted as being in active circulation, even though they are held idle briefly. As such they do not count as 'saving', that is, money-income withheld from consumption, even for the short time they are held. Transactions balances and consumption are intimately linked, but the relevant *periods* differ.

If the links were perfect, the velocity of circulation of money with respect to consumption could be expected to be constant. Precautionary balances intervene; they represent money which sometimes, but not always, is spent, and it is their essential feature that they are *not* spent in the same income period in which they are accumulated, while exactly the opposite is true of transactions balances. These balances, therefore, could be counted as 'saving' when accumulated and 'dissaving' when spent; they are 'idle' balances by general intention, only becoming 'active' when the contingency for which they were acquired arises.

The income period is thus seen to be crucial; the above distinctions are made on the basis of interperiod *versus* intraperiod changes in money balances. Treating money held for the two motives as additive thus poses the additional problem of the relevant dimension of measurement. Transactions balances are in the nature of what accountants call a 'suspense account', accumulated only to be run down; any notion of a demand for these balances must refer to their *average* over the income period. The intention to accumulate money balances for the precautionary motive, on the other hand, is an intention to *carry over* money from one income period to the next; precautionary balances — if they could be separated from monies held for other purposes — could be measured as an average of *stocks* held at the end of several income periods, whereas the end-of-period stock of transactions balances ought always to be zero, regardless of Y.

Keynes's device of lumping transactions and precautionary demands together poses problems from the technical point of view. But in any case Keynes paid little attention to the precautionary motive. One might think this odd, considering the level of uncertainty which attaches to income in a period of high and variable rates of unemployment. However, precautionary *money* balances are unlikely to be held against *major* contingencies, such as a prolonged spell of unemployment, where highly liquid assets bearing interest are available instead. Saving against unemployment is much more likely to be done in non-money forms, particularly by lending to financial intermediaries, and then whether these balances are withdrawn from the spending stream depends on what the intermediaries do with them.

Transactions and Precautionary Demands and the Interest Rate

The implication of the availability of interest-bearing assets as an alternative to cash is, plainly, that the choice between holding money or such assets for transactions and precautionary purposes is likely to be interest-sensitive. The fundamental work on the interest-elasticity of transactions balances[3] demonstrates what common sense would predict — that for a given income period, the larger is income (or the volume of transactions), the more likely it is that a given interest rate is sufficient to compensate for the brokerage and nuisance costs of moving into non-money assets and out again when cash is required. And for a given volume of transactions, the longer the income period the more attractive is a given rate of interest, because there is a longer time in which to earn it.[4] The same points have been shown to hold for uncertain payments streams,[5] i.e. for precautionary balances.

The significance of an interest-elasticity of transactions and precautionary balances lies in its challenge to the quantity theory as expressed in equation (10.1). If the speculative demand for money is accepted,[6] there is no particular need to attack the quantity theory in this way.

Though the proposition is clearly an interesting one, it should not be allowed to distract us. It gives a reason for having the rate of interest appear in the demand for money function which is entirely different from the speculative motive. That is not to say that it is 'wrong': its relevance is illustrated both by the behaviour of business firms and their bankers, who have developed a variety of ways in which firms may economise on their barren cash-holdings, even for such frequent payments as wages, and by households, who in periods of high interest rates are said to economise on non-interest-bearing deposits (though I do not know of any direct evidence). It does, however, apply *only* to money which is not interest-bearing.

This is particularly unfortunate in the British context, where arrangements for automatic transfer in and out of deposit accounts lower 'brokerage costs' to a minimum. It also divides money from other assets on the basis of the non-interest-bearing attribute of money rather than the capital-safety of a wide range of assets which for certain purposes one may call 'money' because their value is realisable without (substantial) loss. The speculative demand is made to look ridiculous because it seems to imply that speculators occasionally hold a totally barren asset when obvious alternatives are available.

The Finance Motive

In response to comment on the *General Theory* by Bertil Ohlin (1937), Keynes (also 1937) developed a third expenditure-related motive for desiring cash: the 'finance motive'. Ohlin had argued that the rate of interest depends on the supply and demand for new credit arising from *ex ante* saving and investment. While not accepting the 'Classical' implications of this formulation, Keynes did agree that he had not allowed for a demand for money as a precondition for investment (*C.W.* XIV, pp. 201–23).

Keynes and Ohlin did not, however, have the same thing in mind. Ohlin meant the demand for *credit*, while Keynes, being consistent with his earlier definitions, meant only the demand to *hold money* — this time to finance expenditures which are both *not routine* (and therefore not appropriately financed out of current income) and *large* (too large to be financed from precautionary cash balances).

The most obvious type of large, non-routine expenditure is investment in capital equipment. The link between the finance motive and investment is not perfect, however: certain sorts of household expenditures would also come into this category, while investment in working capital would be excluded as being routine. It is a useful approximation, however, to connect the finance motive with intended investment as long as the two are not regarded as identical.

The finance motive does not refer to the funds required to support an investment project until the end of its life, but only to the amount of money needed to get the project started: 'e.g. when a new railway is undertaken it is not usual to borrow the *whole* of what it will cost before the first sod is cut'

(*C.W.* XIV, p. 216, n.2).

This sense of 'finance' — cash required between the decision to invest and the beginning of construction — is *neither* finance in the cash flow sense (being able to pay for a project) or in the sense of being able to pay the fixed cost of a given capital stock. The need does not last for long for any individual firm: only for the interval between the decision to invest and its implementation. It may be satisfied by the sale of liquid assets — a transformation of precautionary holdings of bonds to 'finance-motive' holdings of cash — or (and this is the channel Keynes emphasised) the cash may be borrowed from banks. Thus this motive is different from the others, in that it is not a motive for retaining income and holding it in the form of cash (which if held for more than an income period is a kind of 'saving') but for money to hold temporarily in anticipation of exceptional spending.

A rise in the desired level of precautionary balances would be satisfied by holding off both consumption and lending to hold money idle (until needed, of course). This action will have a deflationary impact on producers and (*cet. par.*) will put pressure on interest rates, as the supply of funds is reduced. A need for 'finance' satisfied by internal funds will raise the rate of interest because of the increased supply of liquid assets to the market from the investing firms. A rise in the desired amount of borrowed 'finance' will also raise the rate of interest, but from the demand side. In neither case is the demand for 'finance' deflationary, for no funds have been diverted from expenditure on goods; any deflationary impact the finance motive has arises only from its interest rate effect.

It can be seen that the withdrawal of funds is very temporary for the individual firm: the money returns to the income stream as soon as the equipment is bought or the construction workers are paid, and much of it will return to the banks (almost all of that used to finance consumption and some of the remainder). The funds are to be borrowed or liquid assets sold as close to the time of expenditure as possible, in order to minimise interest cost (actual or forgone). In the case of using bank overdrafts to satisfy this motive, no cash is actually held by the borrowing firm at all; there is no interruption of the flow of spending in that case.[7]

The finance motive's importance at the aggregate level arises out of the *variability* of investment, for it is only when plans to increase (or decrease) investment are made that the finance motive has its effect. If the volume of investment is steady overall, the pressure on sources of finance arising from one project will be counterbalanced by expenditure of finance balances as other projects get underway.[8] Thus it is a motive whose importance is based on *change* in the economy. The transactions motive, on the other hand, is most cogent when based upon stability: a recurring pattern. The precautionary demand is also based on stability: the pattern of payments is irregular and unpredictable in a single income period, but broadly predictable over several income periods and thus (probably) over the production period.

Keynes makes another distinction between the finance motive and the others:

> I allowed [in the transactions and precautionary demands] for the effect of an increase in *actual* activity on the demand for money. But I did not allow for the effect of an increase in *planned* activity, which is superimposed on the former ...
> (*C.W.* XIV, p. 220)

This passage has caused much controversy. The indisputable fact is that planned expenditure requires financial planning and actual expenditure implies that the need to finance it is over. This has led Davidson (1965) to reformulate the demand for money in terms of planned consumption and investment and to propose that the finance motive, thus interpreted, be taken as the model for the demand for money to spend, encompassing the transactions demand. Compare Shackle (1968, p. 138): 'Of course, the transactions motive is an *ex ante* motive. Whoever said it was not? Only the proponents of a mechanical quantity theory of money.'

The interpretation offered in this chapter mediates between these views. Transactions balances are held in anticipation of payments, and so are related to planned expenditure, every bit as much as 'finance' balances are. The difference is that no special effort is taken to acquire them: they arise out of income or from sales. The market for funds, and therefore the interest rate, is not affected. The expenditures against which they are held are expected to be undertaken within the income period: they are planned but one can think of them either as not being planned very far in advance (if one thinks *within* the income period), or as planned in general terms for a fair run of income periods; it does not matter, for the income and payment flows are assumed stable. The analytical basis of transactions demand is the 'tranquillity' of the Classical tradition, in which the distinction between *ex post* and *ex ante*, planned and actual, is not important.[9] The relative importance of the finance and transactions motives can thus be seen to depend on the extent to which plans are *changing*.

The Speculative Motive

Money held for the transactions, precautionary and finance motives satisfies relatively immediate needs — certain and uncertain — for purchasing power. Money for the first two of these motives is retained out of the cash flow which represents income. Income not required for current or near-future purchases must also find an 'abode' which is also temporary, albeit less so. With a longer time horizon between the receipt of income and the intention (however vaguely formulated) to make purchases, the pursuit of interest income becomes more worthwhile. On the face of it, it is difficult to justify the holding of money for long periods of time: it would seem that however low the rate of interest is, it is better than nothing.

The suggestion that the level of the interest rate might influence the amount of cash held for precautionary purposes is persuasive, but the reasoning is much less compelling in the case of assets designed to be held for a long time. Indeed, if one knew the time horizon to which one was working with any exactness, one could arrange to hold securities which matured just before cash was wanted.[10] Given the existence of government securities, even the risk of default is minimal. (This might be an ideal world in which to apply the Classical theory of interest, for 'saving' is always loaned out.)

However, even if expenditure plans were either certain or of long horizon, there are always some assets which by their nature have *no* secure capital value: equity shares and consols[11] are perpetuities; their value fluctuates with changes in demand and supply. Wealth held in the form of these assets is *always* of uncertain value and uncertain return, for the return involves not only dividends or interest but also the difference between realised capital value and original purchase price. Holders of these assets risk not getting the returns they expected. Interest on consols is contractual and certain, dividends are not contractual but in practice are kept fairly stable; the major uncertainty is the variation in capital value.

This uncertainty need not be particularly worrying if the expected date of realisation of the capital value is flexible. It may be acutely uncomfortable if purchasing plans are in any way rigid and not postponable, as the need for cash may force the sale of securities at a particularly disadvantageous time.

The risk of realised capital losses is also less the further into the future is the expected expenditure relatively to the maturity date of fixed-term assets. To the extent that there is a chance that money will be wanted before the asset matures, the holder is concerned with market fluctuations in the value of the asset. And the longer the term of the asset, the more a given change in interest rates will affect its capital value.

The risk of a disadvantageous sale is, however, no reason for holding *money* in an economy with short-term assets. These one may hope to hold in sufficient volume to allow the optimal timing of sales of perpetuities and longer-term assets. In that role they serve as a kind of precautionary demand — for liquid assets — as uncertainty over the timing of expenditure provides the incentive to hold them.

Keynes does not discuss this issue. He is content to leave it to the reader or analyst to decide what to include in 'money' to suit the purpose at hand:

> Without disturbance to this definition, we can draw the line between 'money' and 'debts' at whatever point is most convenient for handling a particular problem. For example, we can treat as *money* any command over general purchasing power which the owner has not parted with for a period in excess of three months, and as *debt* what cannot be recovered for a longer period than this; or we can substitute for 'three months' one month or three days or three hours or any other period; or we can exclude from *money* whatever is not legal tender on the spot. It is often convenient in practice to include in *money* time-deposits with banks and,

occasionally, even such instruments as (e.g.) treasury bills. As a rule, I shall, as in my *Treatise on Money*, assume that money is co-extensive with bank deposits.

(*G.T.* p. 167, n.1, emphasis in original)

Not everyone can tolerate this degree of flexibility. The theory of liquidity preference, which is so well-equipped to encompass something like portfolio diversification for precautionary purposes — the problem just mentioned — has been robbed of much of its value by a search for concreteness, in the belief, presumably, that therein lies precision.[12] The passage just cited is *important*.

The Speculative Motive and Asset-Holding Contrasted

People construct theories that reflect themselves and their times. Keynes played the financial markets, both for himself and for his College. In America in the 1920s it became a popular sport, before the stock market crash in 1929. The personal experience, I dare say, led to the development of the theory; the historic event showed its importance.

The speculator is distinguished from the ordinary saver or wealth-holder by the *purpose* of his market dealings. While the 'ordinary wealth-holder' earns his main income by the sale of his labour and 'stores his wealth' in the form of financial assets for some rather distant future purpose, the speculator commits funds to the active pursuit, derived from buying and selling assets, of an income based on 'knowing better than the market what the future will bring forth' (*G.T.* p. 170) so that — subject to the inevitable mistakes — he captures capital gains and avoids capital losses by predicting the future course of security prices.

The borderline between these two types is fuzzy: even the most lackadaisical wealth-holder may be spurred to active forecasting and decision-making by news of a take-over bid. He may move funds about in an attempt to avoid capital losses, but not with the same rapidity as the speculator, nor will he give the matter the same attention. The speculator may do little else, and of course the professional portfolio manager's *job* is to do nothing else. It follows that to a great extent the latter's decisions will be based on the same principles as the speculator's. In what follows, the term 'speculator' can be interpreted to include him.

The speculator's time horizon is short; he does not leave his portfolio to generate interest quietly, for interest, relatively to what can be made on capital gains, is small beer. It is by constantly seeking to sell at the peak and buy cheaply that his income is to be made. Not only are the long-term forecasts, suitable to a stable portfolio position, difficult to make, but price changes in the intervening time will be missed. In contrast, the 'ordinary investor', who doesn't want to spend as much time as the speculator in managing his portfolio, may take the long view, and let some potential gains go.[13]

Consider the effect of a change in the interest rate on the value of financial assets over time. Let us suppose that all interest payments are reinvested in the interest-bearing security, so that 'wealth' — the value of a portfolio of securities — grows at the rate of interest, the slope of the line AB in Figure 10.1. Now suppose the rate of interest rises at time t_1. The value of the portfolio falls at that time and then grows, at the higher interest rate (the slope of CD), more rapidly than before. It can be seen by extending AB (the dashed line BE) that in time the higher interest rate recoups the loss made at t_1. If the wealth-holder's horizon is longer than t_2, the (unrealised) capital loss at t_1 has done no harm.

On the other hand, if he had forecast the change just before t_1, say at t_{1-k}, he would sell his shares and buy them back at the lower price, holding idle cash in the interval. Then the growth path of his wealth would follow the line FG, clearly a superior result. (F is slightly below B to allow for brokerage costs and interest lost in the interval between t_{1-k} and t_1.) There are two reasons, however, why the wealth-holder may not take action, settling for growth along CD instead. One is the lack of time to devote to the necessary forecasting and the other is the risk of getting it wrong. If he thinks his change of forecasting correctly is no better than 50–50, and his time horizon is quite long, it is better to take the long view and let the portfolio rest. (Indeed, his chances must be quite a bit better than 50–50 to compensate for his time and transactions costs.) The speculator has a more optimistic view of his chances.

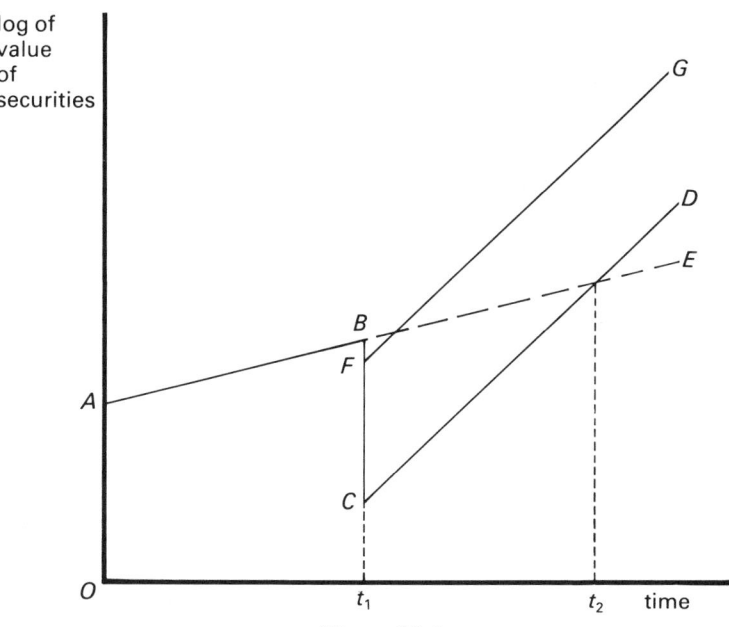

Figure 10.1

The Speculator's Behaviour

We will give the speculator two assets to play with: money, which is capital-safe, and bonds, which are not. He moves into bonds when he expects their price to rise (interest to fall) and sells out, holding money instead, when he expects the price to fall (interest to rise). The speculator's decisions are thus based not on levels of interest rates, but on forecasts of changes in the interest rate. There are many hypotheses one could entertain as to how these forecasts are made, but we shall simply retail Keynes's.

The concept of a normal rate of interest is central to Keynes's theory of how speculators form their expectations. Each speculator, i, has an expectation of a 'normal' rate of interest, r_{iN}, toward which the actual rate of interest, r_t, tends to return. Keynes did not discuss how the normal rate was estimated; this failure has been a cause of the theory's rejection, most notably by Dennis Robertson.[14] However it is derived, one feature is crucial: it is a subjective assessment. Once that assessment is made, the speculator is in a position to make the forecast on which he will base his portfolio decision. If at time t the actual market rate of interest, r_t, is higher than r_{iN}, speculator i expects the rate in the near future, r^e_{t+1}, to be lower than r_t, and if r_t is below r_{iN}, he expects the rate to rise; that is, rates are expected to regress toward r_{iN}. Formally, Keynes's theory of expectation-formation may be written:

$$r^e_{i,t+1} - r_t = f(r_{iN} - r_t), \qquad f > 0. \tag{10.3}$$

When $r^e_{i,t+1} - r_t < 0$, speculator i expects capital gains on bonds and hence purchases bonds in t, holding no speculative balances in money. In the opposite situation he moves out of bonds into money to protect against the realisation of a capital loss. Money is reinvested in bonds once the fall in price has occurred.

It should be obvious that if an individual is going to speculate, he does not hedge his bets. If he expects capital gains he must commit all his *speculative* funds[15] to the pursuit of those gains, even though he has doubts. To do otherwise is to risk losing potential profit. If he expects losses he would be irrational to hold any quantity of the assets whose prices are expected to fall.[16] His behaviour results in the discontinuous demand function of Figure 10.2.[17]

The length of the horizontal axis of Figure 10.2 is given by the total quantity of speculative funds. The demand for money to satisfy the speculative motive of individual i is measured rightward from the origin O_{iM}; the demand for bonds for speculative purposes is measured leftward from the origin O_{iB}. At current rates of interest above r_{iN} the demand for money is zero; all speculative balances are held in bonds to capture the expected capital gains. At rates below r_{iN}, no bonds are held.

Divergent estimates of the normal rate give an aggregate speculative

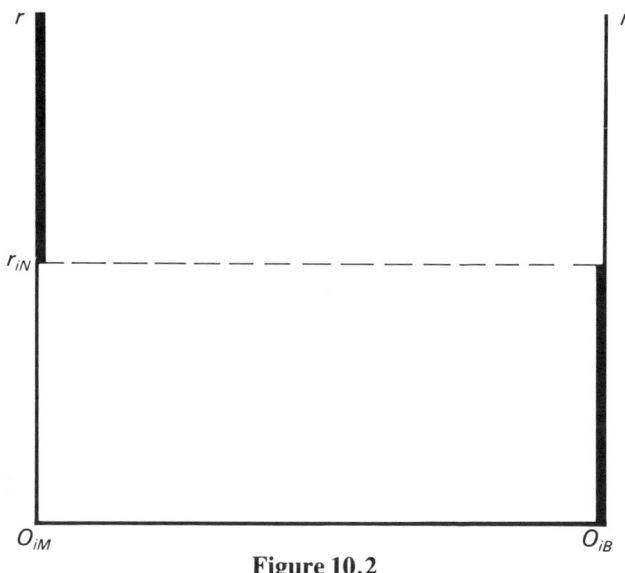

Figure 10.2

demand function which for a number of transactors is a series of vertical lines, as shown in Figure 10.3. Above r_1, everyone (everyone who speculates) believes the rate is too high to be sustained, and no one wishes to hold money rather than bonds. r_1 is the normal rate of some individual, for below that rate he switches his speculative funds, the extent of which is indicated by the distance between the axis and the first vertical segment, into money. At r_4, no one expects the rate to fall further, and all speculators switch out of bonds.

The importance of differences of opinion concerning the normal rate is obvious enough. If all speculators held the same view, r_N, the aggregate speculative demand function would be two discontinuous segments. According to whether the rate of interest lay above or below the common normal rate, all would be trying to sell or buy bonds. At best, speculators would be buying from or selling to non-speculating investors. Assuming there is enough speculative activity to make the subject worth discussing, the price of bonds would fluctuate substantially. If *everyone* were a speculator, bond prices would rise to infinity when $r_t > r_N$ (there being no sellers) and fall to zero if $r_t < r_N$ (there being no takers). While the limiting case is a practical impossibility, it illustrates the role of a divergence of opinion in maintaining the stability of security prices:

> ... opinion about the future of the rate of interest may be so unanimous that a small change in present rates may cause a mass movement into cash. It is interesting that the stability of the system ... should be so dependent on the existence of a *variety* of opinion about what is uncertain.

(*G.T.* p. 172)

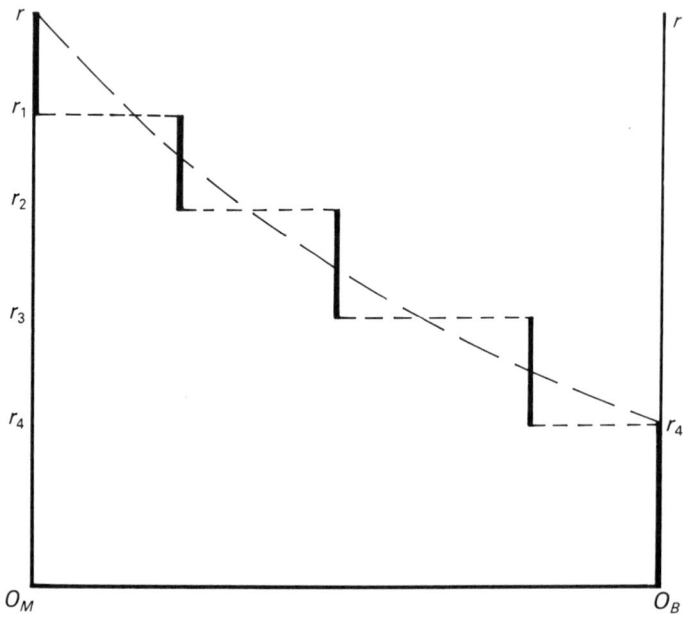

Figure 10.3

At the extremes of high and low rates of interest, opinions coalesce; there comes to be substantial agreement that rates cannot rise any further, or fall any further. This is enough to give the speculative demand function its concave shape. Added to this is the fact that the considerations affecting speculators might also affect long-term wealth-holders at low rates of interest:

> Unless reasons are believed to exist why future experience will be very different from past experience, a long-term rate of interest of (say) 2 per cent leaves more to fear than to hope, and offers, at the same time, a running yield which is only sufficient to offset a very small measure of fear.

(*G.T.* p. 202)

The expectations hypothesis proposed by Keynes permits the current level of the interest rate to be used as a proxy for expected *changes* in the rate as long as feelings about the normal rate are unchanged. Thus one may write

$$M_2 = f(r) \tag{10.4}$$

where M_2 is money held for the speculative motive — again not to be confused with a money definition. The speculative demand for money is added to the M_1 demand to give

$$M^D = M_1(Y) + M_2(r) \tag{10.5}$$

or in general form

$$M^D = L(Y, r). \qquad\qquad\qquad\qquad\qquad\qquad\qquad (10.6)$$

All the factors determining a preference for liquidity have now been brought together.

To return to the speculative demand: the assumed stability of the normal rate necessary to formulating the demand for speculative balances is a parallel to the analytical strategy of not permitting short-run fluctuations to influence long-term expectations on the production side. Just as entrepreneurs' expectations of long-run profit, which govern investment, need not react to short-run variations in income, or may change when current demand is quite stable, so may the evaluation of what is a normal rate of interest remain stable as rates fluctuate daily, or, conversely, shift unpredictably in a period of quiet trading.

A change in the normal rate will, of course, shift the function. A rise in the normal rate means that some interest rates which were above the old normal rate, and hence indicated potential capital gains, are now below the new normal rate. The demand for money will have increased, because at a given current rate the belief in capital losses on bonds is now held more widely. On the same reasoning, a fall in the normal rate reduces the demand for speculative balances, shifting the curve to the left.

Since the normal rate is subjective, the speculative demand for money is potentially volatile. And given that capital gains and losses affect the whole of one's holdings of financial assets, the possible disturbance to securities markets from this source far outweighs the effect of any flow from current saving.[18] It is also able to outweigh the impact on market transactions of the more quiescent long-term investor seeking long-term returns with a minimum of fuss.

The Classical theory regarded interest as a reward for 'waiting', for putting-off consumption, and the rate was determined by the potential productivity of investment, which determined the demand for funds, and the thriftiness of the population, which determined their supply. On this view, buyers of financial assets took no heed of market psychology but were governed only by prospective 'real' returns. Thus funds would go to finance the most profitable, and in that sense the 'right', projects or firms. The overall level of the interest rate then conforms to the rate of profit and investment is undertaken at the pace which is justified by the willingness of 'the public' to lend for the purpose and (as reflected in profits) to buy the resulting output.

A speculative approach to the placement of funds is significant because it cuts the link between long-run profitability and the supply of funds. To demonstrate this fully one should bring the return to equity shares into the argument. Suffice it to say here that since equities and bonds compete for 'savings', the rate of interest and the rate of return on equities are closely related. Speculation occurs both in bonds and equities, and not only speculators narrowly defined, but professional investors generally

> ... are mainly occupied, not with making superior long-term forecasts of the probable yield of an investment over its whole life, but with foreseeing changes in the conventional basis of valuation a short time ahead of the general public. ...
>
> [It] is, so to speak, a game of Snap, of Old Maid, of Musical Chairs — a pastime in which he is victor who says *Snap* neither too soon nor too late, who passes the Old Maid to his neighbour before the game is over, who secures a chair for himself when the music stops. These games can be played with zest and enjoyment, though all the players know that it is the Old Maid which is circulating, or that when the music stops some of the players will find themselves unseated.
>
> (*G.T.* pp. 154–6)

A financial market dominated by speculation may exhibit an interest rate which owes more to mass psychology than to the long-run profitability of production and spend its energy trading in existing financial instruments rather than channelling funds into investment.[19]

There are two undesirable results of speculation. One is that the cost of borrowing, when influenced by speculative considerations, does not reflect the social utility of investment: it may be either 'too high' or 'too low' at various times. The other effect, which particularly concerned Keynes, is that the existence of a capital-safe asset, money, sets a floor to the rate of interest by offering a safe haven when the rate of return offered on bonds is thought inadequate compensation for the risk of loss. Once that point is reached, investment can only be stimulated by improving expectations: the rate of interest can fall no further.

How important is speculation, you may ask? One cannot say definitely, of course, for speculators and long-term investors cannot be distinguished by the colour of their eyes or any other objective criterion. Any active portfolio management must have an element of speculation in it, and there are always some whose behaviour is dictated by considerations of long-term profits of the firm issuing the security, even given the uncertainty of such distant prospects. The relative importance of these two groups will of course vary according to circumstances. History offers many examples of speculative 'fevers' which stand out against a background of more normal temperatures. The fever of the late 1920s undoubtedly prompted this imagery:

> Speculators may do no harm as bubbles on a steady stream of enterprise. But the position is serious when enterprise becomes the bubble on a whirlpool of speculation.
>
> (*G.T.* p. 159)

Just because the stock market has not behaved quite so spectacularly since the 1920s we should not conclude that the speculative demand is not important. The rise in importance of financial intermediaries as a vehicle for saving and the increasing importance of corporate retained earnings have both enhanced the role of the professional investor, who, given the size of the fund he has to deal with, is unlikely to forgo the attempt to capture intramaturity capital gains, and if these are won by outguessing the market, market opinion will influence him.

Other Speculative Margins

The speculative demand for money in the *General Theory* was related to a particular *kind* of speculation: in bonds. There is, however, no reason to limit one's speculation to this kind of asset. In a broad sense, anyone holding an asset with any thought of future re-sale is speculating, taking an open position in something which may gain or lose capital value — as money itself does, in terms of purchasing power, when the price level varies. Speculation needs only two things: a lively market and sufficient variation in prices to make the game worth playing.

Two areas in which speculation has in recent years been prominent spring immediately to mind: real property[20] and foreign exchange. The emergence of inflation as a serious and continuous problem for the last fifteen years or so (people differ in what they regard as 'serious') has shifted the *margin* of both speculation and long-term investment away from money-denominated, interest-bearing assets toward assets offering more protection to the real value of wealth.

Purchases of real property for speculative purposes, or with a speculative element, are likely to occur when inflation is anticipated (as in the UK in 1972, fuelled by a great relaxation of credit, and again in 1977–8). The effect is to divert funds away from both currently-produced goods and finance for productive investment, into capital gains on the existing stock of houses or land. Prices will continue to rise as long as they do not exceed what buyers *believe* to be the price which the house could reasonably realise in a subsequent sale. Obviously this has little to do with the general rate of inflation for someone intending to sell out rather quickly, for there isn't time for the inflation to take place. But at the end of the chain there is always someone who wants the property for a longer period, and it is their beliefs toward which the price is driven. If a belief in ever-accelerating prices takes hold, the rise in house and land prices will eventually exceed the expected short-term rise in the general price level by enough to make property difficult to re-sell, and the speculative boom abates.

Getting ahead of our story slightly, the theoretical importance of speculation in the *General Theory* was that it provided a theory of the general level of interest rates. Speculation in land is speculation on future property prices, not interest rates. Yet interest rates are affected, in two ways. One is specific: the mortgage rate is pushed up by the buoyant demand. (In 1972 this was not noticeable, for the property boom was fed by a great increase in the supply of mortgage funds.) Keynes mentions instances of the interest on farm mortgages exceeding any reasonable expectation of return from working the land. And in general the loan market is being starved of funds it would otherwise be getting, thus affecting all interest rates to some degree.

Even in a period of inflation it may not be rational for a particular individual to speculate in land. Transactions costs are high and so is the minimum volume of funds committed. Speculation in financial markets will, therefore, be likely to co-exist with land speculation.

Equity shares were once thought to be a hedge against inflation. Indeed Keynes treats them (Chapter 12) as if they were indistinguishable from real capital equipment — except for the ease with which they can be bought and sold. The experience of inflation in the 1970s showed, however, that though they may be a good hedge against demand inflation, which is good for business, they are likely to be a poor hedge against cost inflation, which is not.

With the freeing of exchange rates, speculation on exchange rate changes is a further attractive possibility for those not subject to exchange controls. Transactions costs are low, markets are active, and the potential gains in recent years have been large. If this margin of speculation plays an important part in the demand for money, the expected exchange rate becomes an argument of that function, just as expected property and other prices did in the previous case. The differential in interest rates between countries also enters, for funds are placed in interest-earning assets, and a large differential may compensate for interest rate risk.

Exchange rates have varied with (among other things) relative rates of inflation in different countries. When all currencies look a poor bet, as at the moment, when lengthy recession threatens and governments are tempted to buy their way out, the desire to protect wealth is turned to purchases of durable real assets which will withstand a currency debasement. The money that supports that price rise is held off the loan market and away from productive use just as it was in Keynes's model when speculators held 'money' idle.

Insofar as bonds are the vehicle for speculation, the entire operation is conducted with regard to maximising the *money value* of one's assets. One does this, of course, in order to maximise real value — real purchasing power — but as long as one is choosing between two money assets the rate of inflation is not relevant: the demands for those assets are properly specified in money terms. There is little justification for the specification in real terms that one finds in most textbooks. The appropriate action, if one feels inflation threatening, is not to increase one's speculative holdings of money-denominated assets, but to find a real commodity or asset in which to speculate.

Notes

1.   See Ellis (1938) and Fleming (1964). The more usual approach is to assume that the micro results hold, but that is not justifiable.

2.   If one does not set this standard, one begins to argue that all money is 'idle',

non-transactions money except for the instant before it is spent. Hicks (1967) and Sayers (1960) have puzzled at length over this problem. Tsiang (1966) argues, correctly in my view, that holdings at any particular time are not to do with intent, but the accident of the timing of payments and receipts.

3.   See Tobin (1956) and Baumol (1952).

4.   Barro (1970) investigates the optimal payment period; we have assumed it and the time-shape of payments to be exogenously determined.

5.   See Miller and Orr (1966), Patinkin/Dvoretsky (1965) and Niehans (1978).

6.   It is *not* widely accepted, more I think because it has disagreeable implications both for the functioning of markets and for the equilibrium method dear to economists, than for anything to do with 'truth' or relevance.

7.   Provided, as Keynes pointed out (*C.W.* XIV, p. 223), that bank decisions are not altered by the existence of unused overdrafts.

8.   This is Keynes's 'revolving fund' of finance. His debate with Robertson about this 'fund' founders on a confusion between the demand for liquidity being extinguished and the loan being repaid; Robertson seems to suggest that until the loan is repaid the bank will not lend again, while Keynes sees the return of deposits to the banks as sufficient. The argument is incomplete without specifying the banks' reserve position (see *C.W.* XIV, pp. 226–234 and Robertson (1938)).

9.   The theory is 'mechanical' in that it is ill-equipped to deal with variations in expenditure, for then the expenditures are no longer routine.

10.   Many financial intermediaries, notably life assurance companies and Euro-banks, have made a fine art of this procedure of 'maturity-matching'.

11.   Keynes treated equities quite separately from fixed-interest securities.

12.   Criticism of liquidity preference theory on the grounds that speculators would not hold cash when they could hold Treasury bills reveals that a combination of careful reading and common sense did not prevail.

13.   This behaviour is not irrational, as some seem to think. (Cf. Hicks, 1967, p. 44, who argues as if there were only one mode of rational behaviour, and that everyone would speculate if transaction costs (e.g. brokerage fees) were low enough.)

14.   The suggestion that the normal rate is generated by some adaptive learning mechanism based on past interest rates would, I think, be rejected by Keynes. Of course speculators learn from the past, and a long history of low rates is bound to lower the normal rate; but speculators undoubtedly use more than past history to derive r_N.

15.   Note he will still hold money to satisfy non-speculative motives. The allegation (Tobin, 1958) that Keynes's theory precludes portfolio diversification is *simpliste*. If it were not for such interpretations, indeed, one needn't go on at such length.

16.   In behaving in the way described, the speculator is *not* ignoring uncertainty or taking risks for the sheer enjoyment of the risk itself. (Tobin (1958) has alleged that the speculator is either indifferent to risk or positively enjoys it.) It is simply a consequence of the decision to attempt to make money by speculating that he must act on his best guess, *as if* he were certain, even though he is not.

17. With one qualification, the exposition of this and the next paragaph follows Tobin (1958). The qualification is the rejection of Tobin's 'critical rate' in favour of Keynes's 'normal rate'. Tobin's critical rate, the rate at which the portfolio will shift, allows for the fact that expected capital losses are partly compensated by interest earnings. But this allowance is very tricky. The critical rate is not independent of time: if a capital loss is expected, there is always *some* length of time over which the capital loss can be recouped. The critical rate thus depends on the expected holding period. Tobin's period is an arbitrary unit period with no correspondence to calendar time. Interest can only be earned over calendar time. Furthermore, we have argued above that the holding period is not an arbitrary matter; rather it reflects a substantive difference in the intentions of savers and speculators. Speculators have, by hypothesis, a time horizon so short that the possibility of compensation may be ignored. As the rate falls to very low levels, however, the lack of compensation becomes more important to ordinary wealth-holders. As the risk of loss also increases at low rates (see text, below), they may come to behave like speculators.

18. Note that it is not the size of speculative holdings that matters, but the size of offers to or demand on the market arising from this source, relatively to both the flow of current saving directed to securities and offers and demands from long-term portfolio holders.

19. This statement in no way conflicts with the proposition for which Friedman (1953) is well known, that *speculation* must be profitable for the activity to survive. It is precisely the possibility of private financial gain which could result in 'wrong' signals about social costs and benefits of investment which concerned Keynes. Entrepreneurs cannot act in the social interest if the signal for *their* private profit is subject to 'interference' from speculators.

20. See *G.T.*, pp. 241–2 for discussion of land as a speculative medium.

Appendix to Chapter *10*

LIQUIDITY PREFERENCE AS BEHAVIOUR TOWARD RISK OR UNCERTAINTY

The ambition of this Appendix* is to make clear once and for all that the portfolio-theoretic approach to the demand for money is not, as its author claimed and as is widely believed, a development of or an advance upon Keynes's justification for the interest-elasticity of the demand for money but an entirely *different* theory, relating to the behaviour of a quite different set of transactors, motivated by a desire to invest, rather than to speculate. In principle, therefore, portfolio theory need not displace Keynes's analysis of the speculative demand for money; it could instead be treated as complementary to it. In practice, it will be shown, portfolio theory is an unsatisfactory analysis even of investor behaviour.

Although portfolio theory has been much refined and extended since the seminal articles of Markowitz (1952) and Tobin (1958),[1] we shall have little to say about these developments. We shall be concerned with fundamentals, for which an examination of Tobin's article will suffice.

In many respects portfolio theory and the speculative aspect of liquidity preference theory are compatible. The former deals exclusively with microeconomic behaviour while the latter is interested in the aggregate, but there is a microfoundation to liquidity preference. They both assume that the pool of resources available for placement in one or other asset is, for purposes of the analysis, fixed. They both deal with the question of choosing between assets, one of which is capital-safe and the other of which is not,[2] so the potential return on the latter asset includes the possibility of capital gain or loss.

The differences between portfolio theory and Keynes's liquidity preference theory derive, fundamentally, from the comparative-static nature of the former. The comparative-static method requires analysis within a confined period of abstract 'time' (it is not actual time), the 'unit period' during which certain features of the model are not allowed to alter. In the case of portfolio theory it is the *probability distribution* of returns from the risky asset which is taken as given. Keynes's speculators are operating in time and forecasting specific future values of interest rates.

---

*   I am deeply indebted to J.J. Thomas of the London School of Economics for discussions which have shaped significantly the argument of this Appendix.

Tobin's Framework

The basic framework of Tobin's article is easy to summarise. Returns on the variable-price asset are given by the interest rate and capital gain or loss over the unit period. The distribution of probable returns is given and is symmetrical around the mean, which is the interest rate, such that it can be described completely in terms of the mean μ and variance σ, which are mutually independent. 'Money' is assumed to have a zero mean and variance. Various proportions of money and bonds can be chosen, giving different levels of return and risk (variance) for the 'portfolio'. Choices are made according to the preferences of the holder for return and risk.

The risk-averse person is taken as the norm. He will only accept greater risk in return for greater returns. While corner solutions are possible they are not thought likely; the article's central purpose is to explain the observed phenomenon of diversification.

Risk and Uncertainty

Tobin entitled his celebrated and influential article 'Liquidity Preference as Behaviour Toward Risk'. 'Risk' was accurate, and the word immediately indicates that he will not be analysing speculative behaviour. The distinction between risk and uncertainty is one which it has become fashionable to claim does not exist or even that one does not understand(!). It is not difficult to understand.

We live in time and are aware that the future is unknown: we are uncertain. Because we cannot know with certainty our future environment or the outcome of our actions, we realise that life is risky. These are accepted usages. We speak, however, of a 'calculated risk' and of 'insuring against risk' (e.g. of loss by fire). Implicit in these ideas is *probability*. One distinction, in the technical use of these two words, is that risk pertains to what is in principle insurable — it can be described by a probability distribution — and uncertainty is whatever falls outside such a description.[3]

Even within the realm of insurable or calculable risk, however, uncertainty lurks. Uncertainty attaches to the *time* of the insured event occurring. One insures against fire risk but one is uncertain whether when one returns home on a particular day one will find a fire or not. An actuary will tell you the probability of death within any time period you specify, but the time of death is still uncertain.

These examples have been taken from the realm of time, for that is where the confusion about these terms is deepest. But the comparative-static framework of portfolio theory is timeless. In a static framework, uncertainty arises from the fact that the outcome of a random draw from a given distribution is unknown. The distribution itself is generated by repeated sampling from a fixed population of observations, existing independently of time.

Actual draws must be taken successively, for we live in time, but conceptually the order of the draws is of no consequence if outcomes are sequentially independent. Here a better analogy for the risk-uncertainty distinction is the difference between a doctor conducting a drug trial and one prescribing a drug in clinical practice. The first takes his 'population' as homogeneous from the point of view of the likely effects of the drug and determines the mean response and its standard deviation. The doctor dealing with an individual patient, if he is a good doctor, attempts to assess where on that probability distribution that patient is likely to be. He is dealing with uncertainty; the drug trial indicates the risk.

The Unit Period

To return to portfolio theory, the probability distribution is fixed for the unit period. One may compare the effects of different hypothetical probability distributions, different risk-return configurations, on asset-holders' choices.

For every combination of (μ, σ) parameters, portfolio theory determines the optimal portfolio to be held for the unit period. Thus it is a theory determining a one-period choice, where the period can be any length, so long as conditions do not change. Since there is no mechanism within the model to generate change, it is in fact implicit that the portfolio is held forever, once it has been chosen.[4]

This conclusion is difficult to reconcile with the role played by capital gains and losses as the source of risk in portfolio theory. Capital gains or losses are said to occur when the asset's price differs from the expected value. But capital gains can only be relevant if there is a plan to sell assets at some future date before the asset's maturity date T ($T = \infty$ for perpetuities).

If a portfolio is chosen once and for all, variations in the market price of the assets generate only paper gains and losses. They are never realised. Hence they are irrelevant to the portfolio decision. The rate of return is given by the stream of contractual interest payments appropriately discounted, divided by the current purchase price. Rational choice depends on the coupon yield and current asset prices only: there is no risk in holding default-free securities forever.

Capital-loss risk is consistent with the single-period interpretation if (and only if) we impose the condition that portfolios *must* be encashed, and gains and losses realised, at the end of the period. If the investor has the option of not realising losses by refusing to sell his assets at some predetermined date, and of realising capital gains whenever he observes a price rise, then he can always do better than the expected rate of return as given by the distribution simply by waiting for a favourable price. The mean is then not his expected return and the standard deviation of asset price is no measure of his true risk.

The logic of the situation suggests that we must impose encashment at the end of the unit period and forbid it before the end. The asset-holder is now interested in the price at only one date: P_n, the price at the close of the unit period. The course of the price during the unit interval is of no interest. Its variance serves only one purpose: to permit the calculations of the risk that P_n will be other than *the* expected value.

This is an insurance problem. Indeed, in the portfolio model the risk-averse investor could arrange insurance. Properly calculated insurance would on average compensate those who had to take capital losses out of the capital gains of others (plus a premium for doing the work). Investors would earn a return equal to the rate of interest (less insurance).

It should be plain by now that this model does not describe speculative behaviour. Speculators were defined as a class of people seeking to make profit from capital gains, not an income from interest payments. Portfolio theory describes the behaviour of the long-term investor. There is *no reason* for such a person to hold cash as an asset, until the rate of return falls so low that he in effect becomes a speculator.

Equally, there is no reason for a speculator to deal with insurable risks for the above has shown that *insurable* capital gains and losses cancel out. They cancel out because they are random. If they are random, they cannot be forecast, and speculation is based on forecasting.

By mentioning forecasting we have reintroduced time. To move the analysis into the time domain requires that the asset-price distribution functions be interpreted as giving either the relative frequencies with which given prices will occur over time or the probability that an asset's price will take any given value on any particular date chosen at random. If either such dynamic intepretation were intended, one would expect portfolio theory models to specify the process by which the time series of each asset's price is generated from its static distributions, and they do not. There is a fundamental ambivalence in the portfolio choice literature between the static method and a dynamic interpretation.[5] There is no doubt, however, that we must choose the dynamic approach if portfolio theory is to have any relevance.

To do this we make some hypothesis about the dynamic process by which the probability distribution is generated.

A Random Generating Process

Suppose the price of a security with a given coupon yield is a random variable, generated by the following demand and supply relations:

$$Q_t^D = a + bP_t + w_t ,$$ (10.A1)

$$Q_t^S = m + nP_t + v_t .$$ (10.A2)

On the assumption of market clearing we have by substitution

$$P_t = \frac{m - a}{b - n} + \frac{v_t - w_t}{b - n}$$ (10.A3)

where w_t and v_t are normally distributed with zero means and standard deviations σ_w and σ_v respectively. For simplicity, define

$$K = \frac{m - a}{b - n}$$

and

$$u_t = \frac{v_t - w_t}{b - n}$$

so that we can write (10.A3) as

$$P_t = K + u_t$$ (10.A4)

which is normally distributed with mean K and standard deviation σ_u. Thus we have a distribution completely described by its mean and variance.

There is a certainty in the sense that it is assumed that all investors know the mean and standard deviation of (10.A4) with certainty. But it is obvious that having perfect knowledge of the parameters of the distribution (and all other distributions, for other assets) does *not* imply full and perfect certainty about the future.

Future prices are given by

$$P_{t+i} = K + u_{t+i}, \qquad i = 1, \dots, n.$$

The i's are days (or hours) within the unit period of length n. Perfect certainty implies knowledge of the true values of u_{t+i} for all i. By the nature of a random variable, knowledge of the u's is held to be impossible.

What is the speculator's best forecast of prices on any date $t+i$ covered by this distribution? K, the expected value, is a constant. To do better than that he must forecast individual u_i's, which is impossible. A two-parameter distribution independent of time *rules out* any possibility of profitable speculation. Some may try it for a time, but the game would soon pall.

An Autoregressive Scheme

Consider, alternatively, a time-dependent generating process such as the autoregressive scheme

$$P_t = K + u_t, \text{ where } u_t = \rho u_{t-1} + \epsilon_t .$$

The ϵ_t are normally and independently distributed, with zero mean and standard deviation σ_ϵ. Assume $|\rho| < 1$.[6]

If such a scheme generates price observations it is no longer true that one day is like another. It is possible to 'beat the market' if ρ is known and u_t has been discerned at least once. But this would mean that three parameters, not two, enter decisions. Ignoring ρ is of course safe if ρ is small, but it is obvious that the smaller it is, the closer one approximates the random generating process.

It is also interesting in the light of the discussion in the main text of Chapter 10 on holding period horizons that ρ is less important the further into the future one is forecasting. The autoregressive structure implies a high covariance of adjacent and nearby observations, but observations widely spaced in time approach randomness. Thus the long-term investor could well ignore ρ: thus the two-parameter assumption does little damage. The speculator, however, must take it into account.

In the real world, of course, information other than the past behaviour of prices may play a major role. This is not explicitly allowed for in Keynes's forecasting model, but at least he does have a forecasting model. Tobin does not.

It should be clear that Tobin's model does not refer to speculation. Altered to impose encashment, Tobin's model could be used to explain long-term investment. With its applicability thus restricted, it is clear that only when running yields are too low to compensate for expected loss within some well-defined calendar period — or when the expected yield will not cover an insurance premium — does it make any sense for the long-term investor to which this model applies to hold any cash. The long-term investor *will* hold money, but on transactions and precautionary account, not asset account. (This conclusion is modified when there exists a 'money' — i.e. deposit accounts and NOW accounts — paying interest.)

Notes to Appendix

1.   For a thorough treatment of the subject see, e.g. Mossin (1973) or Sharpe (1970).

2.   Portfolio theory has been extended to include several assets of variable capital value. The Tobin article simplifies, as does Keynes, to the choice between 'money' (a capital-safe asset which in Tobin is also non-interest-bearing) and 'bonds'.

3.   This distinction is due to Knight (1937).

4.   Rousseas (1972, p. 268) has also made this point.

5.   This ambivalence runs through all comparative statics exercises. For example, we speak of price *rising* to a new equilibrium after a shift in demand — clearly a dynamic process of adjustment. Tobin, in another context, protests:
     'As is usual in comparative analysis, the purpose is to describe the difference it makes whether a parameter — in this case demand debt — is smaller or larger. The analysis is timeless, even though it would be

impossibly puristic to try to explain it without chronological language.'

Impossibly puristic or not, only the timeless explanation is strictly legitimate.

6.   This ρ has nothing to do with the ρ of Chapter 11. It is merely a fractional constant.

Chapter 11

THE DETERMINATION OF
THE RATE OF INTEREST

The rate of interest determines how much investment demand there will be. What, in turn, determines the rate of interest? Keynes's answer is at least apparently straightforward: the rate of interest is that which brings into equality the desire to hold wealth in liquid form with the available supply of money. A simple enough proposition, one might think, but it is made on two very different levels: that of static equilibrium and that of dynamics. Chapter 13 of the *General Theory* is concerned with the static equilibrium, yet the determination of interest turns out to involve the entire structure of Keynes's theory. We shall present that first, although it is less interesting than the dynamic stories one can tell with the same theoretical structure, and which are merely hinted at, *passim*, in the *General Theory*.

Much of the energy in Keynes's presentation of his theory of interest is devoted to refuting what he conceives to be[1] Classical and neoclassical theories. Although one does not want to perpetuate old disputes, the contrast between Keynes's theory and 'the' Classical theory helps one to see the *causal* structure of Keynes's theory. In this chapter we see that a dynamic approach to liquidity preference theory also tells us something about causality.

The Static Theory

Assume the stock of money is given. This need imply nothing about the behaviour of banks or the monetary authorities, only that in the static equilibrium whose characteristics we are about to explore, the stock of money in the economy is whatever it is: it is not a variable determined by the equilibrium solution. This stock must in equilibrium be willingly held by the

219

economy's individuals and organisations: money being, by its very nature, exchangeable for all marketed commodities and assets, the existing stock must satisfy, and no more than satisfy, the motives for holding money. Since the existing stock must be held somewhere in the economy, while each individual holder may dispose of money freely, the variables determining the demand for money will assume, in equilibrium, values which bring the demand into equality with whatever the supply might be. By this mechanism the rate of interest is determined.

The motives for holding money will be taken, following the *General Theory*, to exclude the finance motive. We can repair that omission later. According to our Chapter 10 (or Keynes's Chapter 15), the transactions and precautionary demands depend on income and the speculative demand on the interest rate. It is easiest to take these motives as separable, for the moment, and to begin with a subterfuge: because income takes time to be generated, it is at any given moment fixed, say at $\bar{Y}$. Now assuming that the supply of money, $\bar{M}$, exceeds the quantity demanded as M_1 balances at that level of income, the difference, $\bar{M} - M_1(\bar{Y})$, must be held as speculative balances in equilibrium. The speculative demand function, $M_2(r)$, indicates what rate of interest would engender sufficient fear of capital loss on lending instruments for all the excess of $\bar{M} - M_1(\bar{Y})$ to be held willingly as idle balances. This method of interest-determination is portrayed in Figure 11.1.

From the point of view of a dynamic story, the assumption of income fixed for lack of time to change it is a useful device, and we shall return to it. But in Keynes's *static* model it will not quite do, for it omits the feedback through investment to income. Take the interest rate as approximately determined above. This will fix the point on the *mec* curve of actual investment demand, I^*.

I^* is a component of aggregate demand, which, together with the propensity to consume, determines income and hence M_1. Income cannot be fixed arbitrarily in the static model; the system is seen to be fully interdependent.[2]

Keynes chose a different method of making the same point, a method which caused much confusion in subsequent literature. On (*G.T.*) p. 171 he abandons the formulation of the demand for money as two separate components and states a downward-sloping relationship between the rate of interest and *liquidity preference as a whole*. The reason for the inverse relationship is now not just speculative behaviour, but includes an increase in transactions demand due to the fact that as r falls, I and hence Y increase and also acknowledges that the opportunity cost of holding transactions balances diminishes as the rate of interest falls. The latter consideration is a departure from or qualification of the original transactions-motive hypotheses: M_1 is now a function of both Y and r. But that is a minor consideration compared to the embodiment in a single function of the outcome of a complex set of macroeconomic interactions. It is heroically *mutatis mutandis*. No wonder it has caused such confusion, for all of us have been thoroughly schooled in construction of models based on behavioural relations embodying the *ceteris paribus* principle, where simultaneity is expressed by the manner of solution, not the construction of the functions. The usual response has been puzzlement over why Keynes said 'liquidity preference' when he should have said the narrower 'speculative demand'. But he *meant* the broader concept. Keynes's conclusion that the rate of interest is determined by the quantity of money and the state of liquidity preference can now be understood to encompass the state of aggregate supply and demand as well. The static model is fully interdependent.

The static solution is not, intrinsically, very interesting: it is too contrived. The mixture of highly volatile speculative demand with the full repercussions of the resulting interest rate on aggregate demand and output involves the quite disparate time horizons of speculators, producers of current output and demanders of long-lived capital equipment. The existence of the equilibrium depends crucially on not permitting the flow of funds generated by saving, or the demand for them generated by the desire to invest, to alter the volume and composition of financial wealth and thus spill over to the liquidity-preference side of the argument.[3] It is clear that for this separation to hold over repeated periods, one must make some assumption, either that these elements are small relatively to the bulk of existing money and debt, or that the wealth elasticity of demand for each asset is unity and that this accumulation does not affect expectations. 'Smallness' is reasonable to assume for temporally short periods, but fits uneasily with the timeless construct of the Marshallian short run. And the use of the term 'equilibrium' for something which will become invalid with the sheer passage of time is not very helpful. The second suggestion is that adopted by the Yale School.[4]

Keynes appears to have ignored these problems, perhaps because he saw them as insoluble — or perhaps he was concentrating on another issue, his dispute with the Classical theory of interest. Of that, more later. Let us turn instead to the dynamic stories one can tell with liquidity preference theory, even if they belong to Part IV. They are important both for assessing the likely responses to *change*, especially the effects of policy, and for establishing the causal structure of Keynes's model.

An Open-Market Operation

Let us first look at the response to an increase in the money supply by some means that does not alter income, e.g. by open-market operations. In the short interval during which the government broker is in the market, income is surely fixed, and in the nature of open-market operations the value of money and bonds taken together also varies little.[5] This is very convenient, as the assumption made in the last chapter of a fixed total of financial wealth

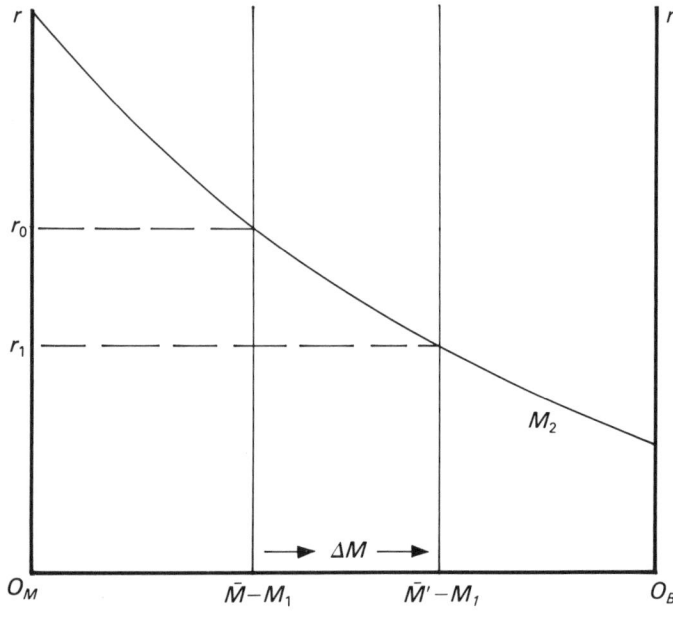

Figure 11.1

is then approximately correct. In terms of Figure 11.1, $\bar{M} - M_1$ moves to the right by the amount of the purchase and the slope of M_2 over the relevant range indicates the extent to which the interest rate must change. The new money is held, in the first instance, by those for whom the new rate is below their normal rate and thus expected (by them) to rise again in the near future. If the fall in r stimulates investment, entrepreneurs may try to recapture these idle balances by floating new securities at an attractive rate — perhaps exactly that rate which the bear speculators expected! And as investment rises, income will rise and with it M_1. This leaves less for M_2 and the initial fall in r will be partly reversed: the initial setting of the rate of interest is only provisional.

Note that the only source of an effect on income is through the rate of interest on investment. The increase in money does not stimulate spending directly. This may seem counterintuitive, as it is easy to imagine that bond-holders will spend the proceeds of their sales. Keynes's theory, however, assumes that the bond-holders who sold to the government broker were speculators, in the broad sense; therefore when they sell bonds they hold the *proceeds* of bond sales idle. Since the volume of aggregate wealth has only increased by the capital gain, and that is held idle, there is no excess of funds available to be devoted to speculation (the sum of bonds and M_2 balances) which might spill over into purchases of goods.

A direct effect on spending, while ignored by Keynes, could be envisaged if we allow explicitly for changes in the timing of expenditure as a result of capital gains, thus breaching the wall between M_1, which, if solely a function of income, will not have changed, and M_2. It is particularly likely that firms, which hold sinking funds as liquid assets, would bring some investment projects forward after realising capital gains. However, while some firms and individuals might spend the entire proceeds, for the economy as a whole, the effect on spending is probably limited to the capital gains achieved rather than the size of the entire bond purchase. Any attempt to spend more than the capital gains would constitute a net dissaving out of wealth, and at the aggregate level such behaviour is unlikely. Should it occur, prices must rise, for 'real' expenditure is limited to the amount of output produced.

A Government Deficit

The sequence following an open-market operation is repeated in modified form for any act of money creation, so long as the income elasticity of M_1 is less than one. Suppose, for example, the government expands its expenditure without increasing taxes or interest-bearing debt. The finance must come from new money. Money and income thus rise, initially, by the same amount, but ΔM_1 will be less than $\Delta \bar{M}$. (If you feel queasy about stocks and flows at this point, your condition indicates that you are not used to thinking dynamically.[6]) Before income has time to change further, the excess must either be held as idle balances, or be used to purchase securities. The purchase of securities — this time by the public rather than the government broker — drives the interest rate down until M_2 expands sufficiently to absorb the new money.

This sequence is more difficult to represent diagrammatically, for the stock of total assets available has risen: the overall length of the horizontal axis on which M_2 is plotted is extended by the amount $\Delta \bar{M} - \Delta M_1$, or, if $M_1 = kY$, by $(1 - k)\Delta M$. In Figure 11.2, $\bar{M} - M_1$ represents the original asset supplies measured from the origins O_M and O_B. After the government expenditure takes place the figure is extended to the left (because money increases while the stock of bonds is unchanged) by $(1 - k)\Delta M$. Now $\bar{M} - M_1$ also measures the new asset supplies, from the origins O'_M and O_B. The M_2 function now has a new reference point and must also be shifted to the left by some amount which depends on the wealth elasticities of demand for bonds and money. The intersection of the new function, M'_2, with $\bar{M} - M_1$ gives the rate of interest immediately after the government expenditure and before any further repercussions. The rate of interest thus determined, r_1, sets the new level of investment. The rise in investment, however, will raise income and M_1; $\bar{M} - M_1$ will shift back to the left — how far depends on how much time has elapsed and how rapidly the multiplier process is working. The original fall in the interest rate is partly reversed, investment may be[7]

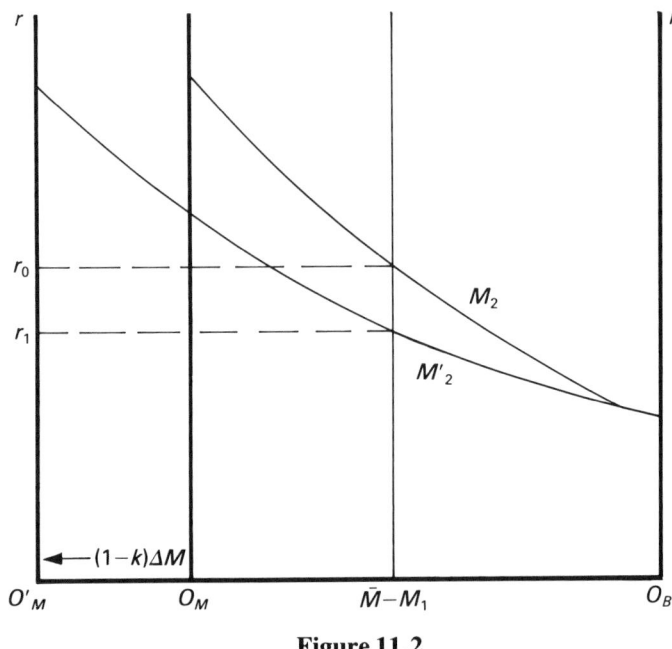

Figure 11.2

reduced, and we end up — somewhere. (This dynamic story is told in slightly more condensed fashion in *G.T.* p. 200.)

A Rise in Investment

A rise in investment expenditure may be financed either by bank credit, which results in a rise in the money supply, or by the activation of idle balances. Bank credit will be treated in the next chapter. A rise in investment to be financed by direct borrowing by the investing firm from the public involves issuing securities, but in contrast to the case of open market operations, the supply of securities rises while the money supply is unchanged. This increases the total value of assets, expanding the limits of $M_2 + B$ in Figure 11.3 (as in Figure 11.2 but with the extension, ΔB on the right). The M_2 function shifts to the right, again in a manner determined by the wealth elasticities. Meanwhile, demand for funds to satisfy the finance motive appears as a rise in money demand equal to the proposed investment, independent of current income. Despite its independence of Y we shall add it to M_1, for convenience. $\bar{M}$ is unchanged, so $\bar{M} - M_1$ shifts to the left. The net effect is the rise in the rate of interest from r_0 to r_1.

To make the story coherent one must assume that firms anticipated the rise in the cost of borrowed funds that would result from their increased demand for them. The moral of the story is clear enough: investment can

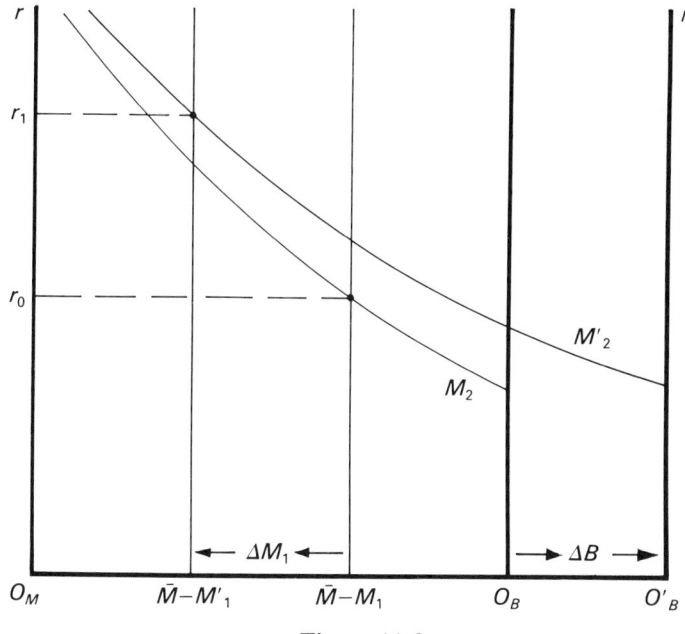

Figure 11.3

take place with no alteration in the rate of saving, as long as there are idle balances to be tapped.

With internal funds playing such a much larger role in the finance of investment now than in the 1930s, the existence of idle assets is assured. The process of financing by selling off interest-bearing financial assets is similar to the previous case but not identical. The total of assets available to the public as a whole is unchanged, and $\bar{M} - M_1$ moves to the left because of the finance motive. The rate of interest rises to the extent indicated by M_2 over that interval. Once again a transfer of assets is sufficient to enable investment to take place.

Shifts in Liquidity Preference

The variables which have acted as the sources of disturbance in the dynamic stories we have been telling are the quantity of money and the desire to invest. The quantity of money in the case of policy actions has been treated as a purely exogenous variable; investment plays that role when expectations change, for this may occur independently of all current variables. Speculative demand also is liable to shift unpredictably: its stability with respect to r depends only on the stability of the set of opinions concerning the normal rate; if, for whatever reason — a change in government economic policy, broader political events, new discoveries — a significant number of speculators change their view of what is 'normal', the function will shift.

A rise in the average normal rate, say from r_N to r'_N, will shift M_2 to M'_2 in Figure 11.4(a).

A high rate of interest such as r_1, will still be expected to fall, though fewer will hold this view, but a rate such as r_2, which was formerly expected, on the balance of opinion, to fall, is now interpreted by the majority as a rate which is likely to rise. Capital losses, in other words, are more likely than before; demand will shift away from bonds toward money. Conversely, if the normal rate falls, more asset-holders will feel safe holding bonds at lower rates than formerly: the function shifts leftward. With unchanged asset supplies, the rate of interest changes entirely independently of either saving or investment.

General optimism or pessimism may also shift the function: an improved economic outlook lessens the threat of default and enhances the willingness to hold securities; improved dividend prospects encourage equity-holding; the demand for liquidity should fall. At the bottom of a recession, when rates of interest have perhaps been low for long enough to lower the normal rate, some promising change in the economy could shift the curve still further leftward just as that same promising change is having a favourable effect on the marginal efficiency of capital. One can see from Figure 11.4(a) and (b) that the simultaneous leftward shift of M_2 and rightward shift of *mec* will have a most favourable effect on investment. Had M_2 stayed fixed in the higher position, with the rate of interest at r_3, investment would only have risen from I_0 to I_1. With the fall in liquidity preference, bringing the interest rate down to r_4, investment rises to I_2.

One can see that as optimism and pessimism are 'catching', such a simultaneous shift is as likely in the downward direction, with less happy consequences. The movements in investment are exaggerated by this effect as compared to movements of *mec* not synchronous with shifts in M_2.

An 'Inherently Restless Variable'?

The position of the speculative demand function depends on opinion. That is most distressing, for it means that the rate of interest may vary for purely subjective reasons. How, then, is this opinion formed? If it were based on the long-run profitability of investment, it becomes attractive to argue as follows: if the long-run profit persisted at a given rate long enough for both bulls and bears to adjust to it as 'normal', the rate of interest would establish itself at a level in relation to the rate of profit with an allowance for the greater commitment involved in running a business. This level could then be stable; repeated observation of the absence of fluctuations would lead to an increased confidence in the capital safety of securities and the speculative

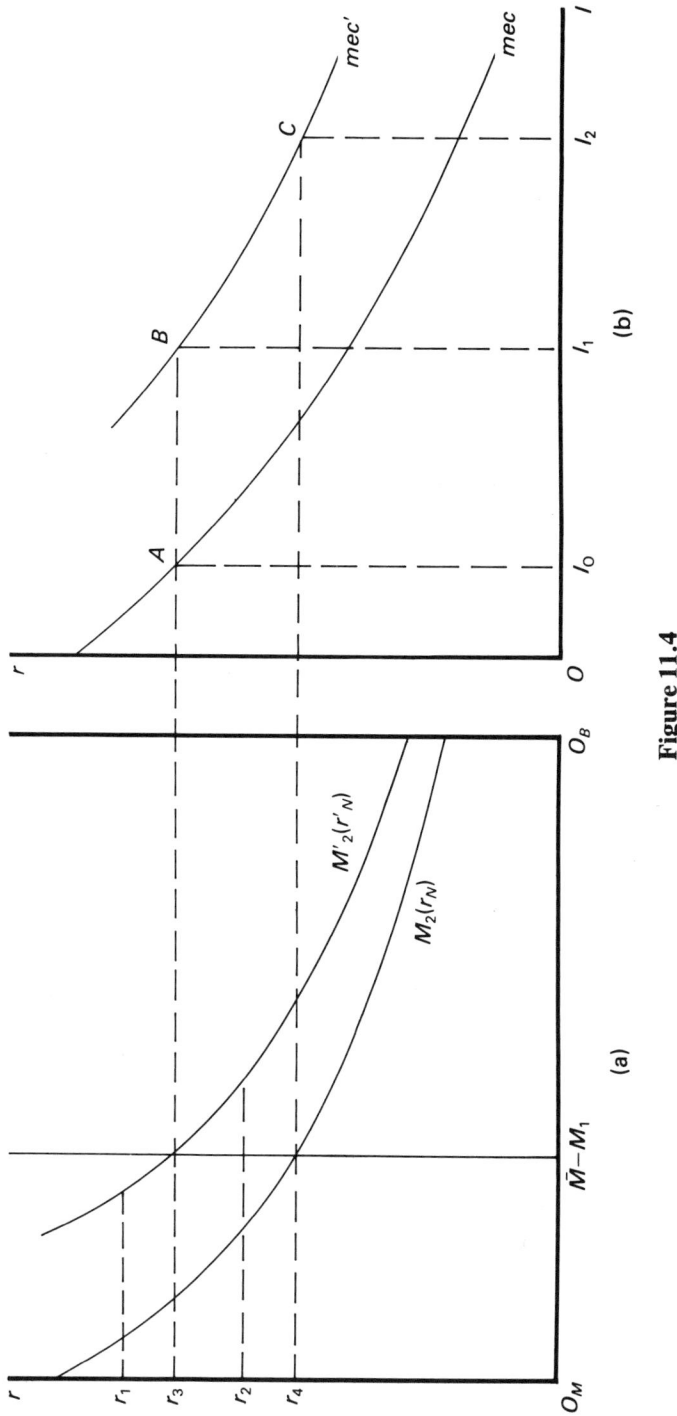

Figure 11.4

demand for money would then collapse to zero. Money would be held for transactions and precautionary motives only. Idle funds would all be held in interest-bearing assets. We are back to the neoclassical perception.

Shackle (1968) has pointed out, however, that the process of convergence on some 'long-term', 'equilibrium' rate of interest would not leave the rate itself unaffected, as implicitly assumed in the previous paragraph. For although both bulls and bears vanish, in the sense that speculative activity ceases once the equilibrium rate is established, when it is *believed* that the interest rate *will* be steady, bears try to buy bonds and bulls retain theirs. Thus the interest rate is forced down, falsifying expectations. The process of moving toward equilibrium destroys it. It is for this reason that Shackle calls interest 'an inherently restless variable'.

Shackles's reason concerns the inherent instability of the $M_2(r)$ function due to a feedback between observations of actual interest rates and the normal rate. The dynamic stories told in this chapter reveal additional reasons which justify his description of inherent restlessness: the initial movement of interest rates is reversed through the effects of change in r on income. It cannot, therefore, be overemphasised that while as a matter of theory there may exist a static equilibrium of the sort presented at the beginning of this chapter, its empirical *and theoretical* relevance is slight: its main purpose was to meet Classical theory on its own ground in terms of method. The establishment of an alternative is better done in terms of dynamics.

Inflation and the Rate of Interest

The liquidity-preference theory has been called a 'bootstrap' theory or likened to the disembodied grin of the Cheshire cat (the latter image, predictably, was Dennis Robertson's). The objection was to the total absence of any theory of the *'normal'* rate, on which everything else depends. 'The normal rate' was not even a single rate, but the collection of entirely subjectively-determined, personal normal rates. What was normal? 3 per cent on long term? For long runs of peacetime years that would not have been a bad guess, though it sounds ludicrous now. The test is whether at that rate there is a continuous willingness to hold securities as investments, not as speculations.

The Radcliffe Report (1959, para. 442ff.) also grappled with this problem. At various times in history, rates were generally in 'low gear', 'middle gear' or 'high gear'. They did not foresee that we would go into overdrive.

Radcliffe did not *explain* the gear shifts any more than Keynes did, but perhaps the reader is beginning to sense that there is a certain truth about the bootstrap theory. What Keynes was supposing was that there was very little to tie the 'normal' rate of interest to anything objective: as long as opinion believes its proper level to be 3 per cent, strong forces are set up to drive it toward 3 per cent. If 17 per cent, well, so be it.

There is a point where objective fact takes over. The burden of interest payments can only be supported if future income rises adequately to cover them, and unless one has invested in the most amazingly clever projects, 17 per cent is not possible without inflation. So beliefs about interest rates are bound up with beliefs about inflation or price stability.

Modern monetarists have popularised the approach of Irving Fisher to this problem. He argued that if the rate of inflation was expected to be, say, 5 per cent, no one would lend at less than 5 per cent plus some acceptable real rate of return. And borrowers with similar beliefs would be prepared to pay this rate, expecting to be able to raise the price of output (or of their labour) in line with inflation.

The level of the rate of interest (it is customary to say 'the nominal rate of interest' but in the real world the rate of interest can only be nominal) is, if this theory is correct, the sum of some 'real' rate of return, ρ, and the expected rate of inflation, $\dot{P}$:

$$r = \rho + \dot{P}. \tag{11.1}$$

The next step, a crucial step, is to suppose that investment (and also saving, if one is thoroughgoing) is a function not of r but of ρ. There is a case to be made for that: it is the same as that made above, that the inflation will cover higher nominal rates and the 'real' return on the investment will cover ρ.

Profit on investment is not the easiest variable to define at the best of times, and anyone who followed the debate on inflation accounting in the mid-1970s will know what a slippery concept profit becomes when prices are not stable. The substitution of ρ in the investment equation begs a good many questions in this connection.

Furthermore, whether inflation will cover interest costs depends rather on what sort of inflation one is having. If only the price of output rises, one may safely assume the Fisher theory will hold. But there are also wages, raw materials and provision for a higher replacement cost of capital equipment to worry about. None of these problems are addressed, and it is not at all obvious that the demand for borrowed money will be indifferent to the nominal rate as the theory supposes. One should perhaps say that it is unlikely that the *mec* will rise *pari passu* with the expected rate of inflation.

Lastly, and most relevant to British experience in the 1970s, the theory assumes that expectations of inflation are shared by borrowers and lenders and that their time horizons are the same. There is no particular reason to assume shared expectations — though there is no *a priori* reason either to assume that lenders expect higher inflation than do borrowers or *vice versa*. On the question of time horizon however there is a systematic bias.

The existence of something called 'normal backwardation' used to be an accepted feature of financial life: borrowers wished to borrow long in order to know where they stood in terms of their commitments and their cash flow, and lenders wished to lend as short as possible consistent with a reasonable return. Individual lenders can get out of their commitments to securities and into cash at any time, whereas borrowers requiring finance of a lengthy project do not want the risk of having to re-borrow while the project is still going on.

One expects to observe, therefore, long-term rates of interest exceeding short rates, and so one typically does during a period of price stability. When prices are not stable, however, the difference of time horizon means that borrowers must estimate the rate of inflation over the life of the loan, whereas a lender buying a ten-year bond, say, need only estimate the rate of inflation for the first few years. (Exactly how long is not clear, for although changes in expected inflation will influence the capital value of the bond, how many years' expectations the market will discount to the present is unknown.) It is unlikely, for Keynesian-speculative sorts of reasons, that the expectations over the whole life of the security will be fully reflected in the present price.

British experience in the 1970s,[8] with long rates falling below short rates, suggests that firms did not believe interest rates would continue at their present high rates and therefore did not wish to commit themselves to long borrowing and that lenders feared that present rates would not cover inflation over a long period. It is also true that the inflation was not, after say 1972, of the helpful sort (i.e. demand-pull).

No one, I think, would deny that inflation-expectations influence interest rates. What is slightly more in doubt is what influence they are likely to have.

To return to Fisher and Keynes for a moment. Fisher's theory requires not only that expectations of inflation be shared, but also that some long-term rate of return be regarded as acceptable and 'normal' by both sides, as was 3 per cent in much of the 18th and 19th centuries.

The 'real rate of interest' in theory was a kind of norm from which interest rates departed over cyclical fluctuations marked by rising and falling prices. The Fisher framework belongs to the stable universe of Classical and neoclassical theory. Keynes's subjective normal rate allows most extraordinary freedom for departure from that universe. That is why it was and is such a discomfiting concept. But it may be the right one for our times.

Notes

1.   'What is the Classical Theory of the Rate of Interest? ... I find it difficult to state it precisely or to discover an explicit account of it in the leading treatises of the modern classical school' (*G.T.* p. 175).

2.   Hansen (1953) complained that Keynes ignored this interdependence, but see *G.T.* Ch. 14 and the formulation on pp. 171—2.

3.   When the flow-of-funds effect is permitted, all the stock-flow problems arise, as we shall see in Chapter 14. See also Chick (1973a).

4.   So called because it has been developed chiefly by J. Tobin and his associates at Yale.

5.   There will be some change due to revaluation of the bonds remaining in private hands.

6.   Bernard Schmitt, of the University of Dijon, suggested in an LSE seminar that we should think as physicists do, of quanta. This brilliant approach to the multiplier-velocity problem (or expenditure–asset transfer problem) was not well received at the time.

7.   See Chapter 14, below.

8.   Documented in the Wilson Report (1980) and in Bain (1981).

Chapter *12*

THE BANKING SYSTEM

The banking system has come to occupy a most curious role in macroeconomics. The textbook version based on *IS–LM* analysis treats money as exogenous, implicitly assuming either that 'money' is entirely supplied by government or that banks are ruled entirely by the supply of high-powered money. This assumption is sometimes modified to allow the supply of money to respond to interest rates, though this modification is really only of a trivial technical kind and is justified by the barest mention of bank or central bank behaviour. Another school, associated with Cambridge and particularly with Professor Kaldor[1] assumes, in direct contrast to Keynes, that variations in the money supply are entirely endogenous: money is increased chiefly as the result of banks' accommodating would-be borrowers, who are dominated, in aggregate, by firms wishing to invest. The first of these approaches is closer to the *General Theory*, for Keynes gave the banking system scant treatment there, in sharp contrast to the extensive analysis in the *Treatise*.

It may be that he played down bank finance because its chief importance lies in satisfying the finance motive, which fits in better with dynamic stories than with the static method of the main argument. Or perhaps he felt that the subject was so thoroughly explored in the *Treatise* as to make further discussion unnecessary. This is doubtful, however, for his views on the role of the banks change substantially between the two books: his analysis in the *General Theory* is chiefly directed against the doctrine of 'forced saving', an idea which he *supports* (as a theoretical proposition, though he may have had doubts about its policy relevance) in the *Treatise*.

The term 'forced saving' rarely occurs these days. It refers to processes by which unintended saving takes place when banks create credit. It is a problem which is still being discussed, but in rather different language, so different as to divorce the discussion from its antecedents in economic thought. The issue is an interesting one and we devote much of this chapter to it.

Another section is devoted to the concept of the banks as providing a 'revolving fund' of finance, a conception only spelt out, and even there not entirely clearly, in two articles published after the *General Theory* (Keynes 1937, 1939). The concept has made no mark on accepted macroeconomics but it seems a valuable one to reconsider.

But first let us integrate the banks into the financial nexus in the most obvious way: through the rate at which they are prepared to lend.

Bank Assets, Interest and the Money Supply

The asset side of a bank's balance sheet lists a portfolio of 'investments' and shorter-dated securities as well as 'advances'. There are all sorts of reasons dictating the balance between these things; only one concerns us: the interest rate. It is obvious that as rates on financial assets rise, the rate at which banks will be prepared to lend must also rise, as banks have the option of holding a greater proportion of financial assets. In that way, rates on financial assets can be said to set the level (with some flexibility) of bank lending rates. Thus one does little damage in speaking of 'the' rate of interest as the cost of borrowing without specifying the source.

Earlier we discussed the possibility that waves of optimism and pessimism would be likely to affect entrepreneurs and speculators in a similar way, which could result in changes in investment without any change in the rate of interest. The same possibility exists with regard to bank lending. The willingness to lend depends not only on the rate of interest on advances, but also on the banks' sense of bad-debt risk. One would expect the actual risk to fall in times of expansion and to rise in recession, so, if you like, the supply curve of new credit shifts outward (other things being equal) in booms and back when confidence falters. The demand for funds is meanwhile likely to be behaving in a similar manner.

The shift in supply will do no good, however, if banks are constrained by their liquidity position and can risk no further expansion. This situation is portrayed in Figure 12.1, where the upward-sloping position of the supply of advances function (S_A) shifts rightward (S_A') but to no avail, since it becomes inelastic. The banks were already 'loaned-up' and cannot meet the higher level of demand (D_A').

In between these extremes is what you would expect if entrepreneurs' expectations change before those of bankers: interest rates will rise in booms and fall in recessions — interest rates, that is, untainted by inflationary expectations.

The monetary authorities of course can intervene to alter these results. At

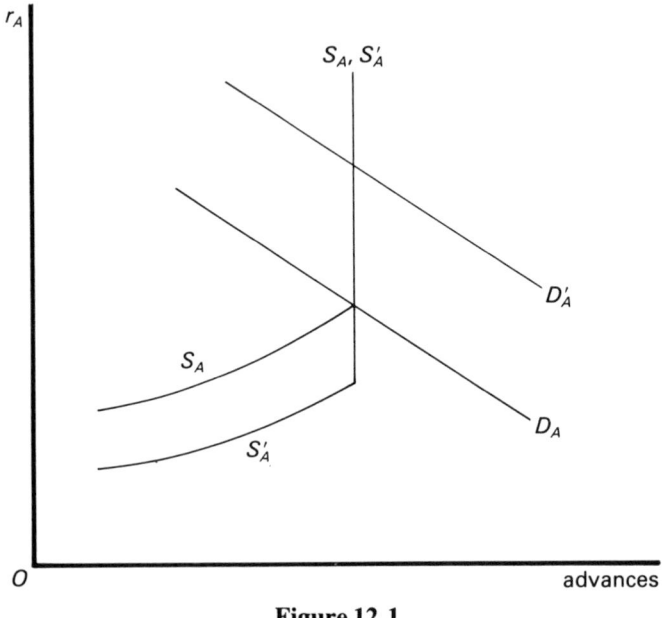

Figure 12.1

the extreme, they may act to stabilise interest rates, which effectively means supplying the banks and financial asset markets with sufficient liquidity to meet rises in demand for credit (and removing that liquidity by open market sales when demand falls off — though this implies more symmetry than there is in practice). This action strengthens the effect of the model of simultaneous optimism and pessimism, for the banks do not now face an effective liquidity constraint.

Exogeneity

Borrowing from banks causes deposits to rise [2] (and paying back overdrafts causes them to fall). Because the demand for bank credit is likely to rise with investment (or deficit spending generally), some Keynesians have argued that the money supply is determined by the level of economic activity or more specifically by investment and is therefore 'endogenous' — by which is meant 'controlled by the private sector'.[3]

This is of course an extreme view, as extreme as Keynes's assumption that the money supply could be taken as given. (One could argue that Keynes was inconsistent since, as will be shown in Chapter 14, the conclusion that an autonomous rise in investment is financed by bank credit is inescapable.) Friedman maintains (1963, 1980) equally extremely, that the Keynesian view is a 'confusion' of money with credit, as if the two were totally unrelated.

It is a question of finding the right balance. Not all the money supply is created by bank credit, though a good portion of it may be. (It rather depends on how you define money, which these days is a major question.) Banks create deposits also when they buy financial assets, whether seasoned or not, and the purchase of seasoned securities is no new credit, as previously explained.

This assumes that banks can expand their balance sheets more or less at will. But if so, what stops them from expanding indefinitely? (Perhaps nothing does stop them anymore.) The theory used to be that their contract to supply cash on demand constrained them to expand deposits by no more than some multiple of their command over cash (whether that be vault cash, money at call, or deposits with the central bank which were never used, but placated the authorities so that they would make money available). (Other assets may be included in formally required reserves, depending on the country and the period. The list in England at the moment is quite broad.) Insofar as the authorities could control the quantity of these reserve assets there was thought to be a definite stop to the expansion of bank deposits (as in Figure 12.1). If the authorities could control bank deposits, then (it was argued) surely deposits could be regarded as exogenous even though supplied by the private sector.

The argument looks simplest and most correct where bank reserve assets are cash (notes and coin) and banks' deposits with the central bank, for these are surely assets which the authorities can control. The argument has an ancient lineage. It was designed initially to allay fears that paper credit would have dire (inflationary) consequences: paper credit convertible on demand into proper money (gold) could not, so the theory went, be 'overissued'. Bank credit (and hence deposits) was similarly constrained. (There is a confident and elegant exposition of this view in the *Treatise*.)

The case is muddier when one acknowledges that banks hold assets which are realisable for cash, muddier still when some of these assets which are not under the direct control of the authorities count as reserves. There is no direct control over money at call, for example, and although the Bank of England should, one would think, be able to control the volume of Treasury bills outstanding, they can hardly control who owns them.

The authorities have for many years supplied cash on demand, in the explicit belief that this is essential to maintaining confidence in the liquidity of deposits and, apparently, in the implicit belief that the demand for cash is governed only by the convenience needs of the public and fluctuates seasonally. The possibility of supplying cash on demand where an unidentifiable part of that demand has been created by banks' overissue of credit, and the upward bias inherent in such action, is something the authorities either do not realise (this is hard to credit) or do not discuss. Insofar as it happens, bank credit expansion bears little relationship to the reserves they possess at any particular time and if they count on reserves being supplied there is no control on expansion.

This is of course an extreme case, but to the extent that the authorities' cash supply is perfectly elastic, any hope of control must rest elsewhere. The remainder of bank reserves consists of some assets, the total supply of which is in principle controlled by the authorities, and other assets created by the banks themselves. One concludes that about the most the Bank can do is manipulate the interest rate to make selling off liquid assets to meet requirements more costly.

Suppose, however, that for other reasons they do not wish to allow rates to move. Insofar as they stabilise rates (they may not do so completely) the money supply is determined by the private sector and chiefly by demand, given that the authorities often, even typically, run a mixed strategy, not fixing interest rates but acting toward that end, they may influence but do not control deposits.

Thus one concludes that money is neither purely exogenous nor purely endogenous. Which is the better description depends on circumstances. Keynes's assumption that money was largely exogenous could be justified for his own time by the facts that investment was at a low ebb and that firms did not use bank finance to the extent that they have done in the last few years, even if the monetary system functioned in the same way then as it does now; but that in itself is doubtful.

Bank Credit Creation and Forced Saving

It was argued in Chapter 9 that the question of causal ordering — whether investment brought about changes in saving or saving was a precondition for investment — was answered in favour of investment as the causal agent because of the development of the banking system. The view of banking which had supported the priority of saving, namely that banks were mere conduits for saving, was suitable to banks in the early stages of the development of banking, where banks are many and small. It becomes incorrect when the banks are large enough and well-enough integrated to justify being called a banking *system* and bank liabilities become the dominant means of payment. Then banks can expand credit with little fear of losing cash reserves.

A bank loses cash when the person to whom the credit is granted spends the money and those from whom he buys deposit his cheque in other banks; the lending bank loses the equivalent in cash in the clearings. The extent to which a bank may count on funds being redeposited with itself after the borrower spends them depends on its share of total deposits. In these days of a highly concentrated banking system, cash losses are minimal. *A fortiori*, when banks tend to expand loans at roughly the same time, the individual bank can expect to recoup some of the cash losses from its own operations from cash coming in as a result of other banks' expansion. Thus the banks as a whole can extend credit to a multiple of the cash reserves they possess. They are not now merely lending on cash received as deposits.

Deposits too have changed their role. One can understand deposits being thought of as a kind of saving when cash was more widely used in payments: deposits may have been a kind of precautionary balance, not used within the income period. Hence the idea that banks were only conduits for saving might have been a useful generalisation for a particular period of the banks' historical development.

With the wider use of deposits and the integration of the banking system this idea lost its usefulness, but to supplant it came the proposition that bank lending in excess of prior saving resulted in 'forced saving'.

The Keynes of the *General Theory* dismissed this idea. No one, he argued, is forcing anyone to hold deposits; therefore there can be no forced saving. In his view the process by which the issue of new bank credit gives rise to a change in the money supply should be viewed as a two-sided transaction between the bank and its creditors — i.e. its depositors.

That is exactly what it is not. No one asked the holders of the new deposits whether they wanted a larger aggregate money supply, nor does that question occur to the receiver. No one refuses payment for a sale just because the source of payment is an overdraft — otherwise granting overdrafts would be pretty futile. But in aggregate there is now a larger quantity of money than before which *no one intended* to accumulate. In that sense it could be said to be 'forced'.

There is also a larger income, and if the credit financed investment there is also a rise in aggregate saving, which has nothing to do with intention.

The rise in income will raise M_1, but the marginal propensity to hold M_1 balances is unlikely to be unity. Therefore there are excess deposits, which may be spent in various ways — in Keynes's framework the money will flow into the bond market — temporarily, until the multiplier effects of the credit-financed expenditure draw it back into transactions balances. First the rate of interest and then the level of income adjusts so that the new money is 'willingly held' throughout, even though its acquisition was unintended.

As adjustment to the new quantity of money proceeds, prices are rising. The initial rise in income will meet a fixed supply of consumption goods. As their supply expands prices may fall back, but then rise again as returns diminish.

Classical economists and their modern counterparts would say that some of the excess money balances would be spent on goods, not bonds. That is, either an excess supply of money affects expenditure plans at a given level of income (which Keynes rejects) or the increase of financial wealth affects expenditure (this latter is acceptable within Keynes's framework provided it is presented as a shift in the propensity to consume out of income; consumption out of financial wealth is not macroeconomics).

When these effects are taken into account forced saving takes on a further meaning, for now it is not merely a matter of not having been consulted about the desirability of an increased money supply or about the direction of credit it supports; it becomes clear that, first, those who obtain the credit and, second, those who sell to the borrowers, have obtained goods at the old prices and made consumption more expensive for those who come further down the line. A rise in consumption-goods prices means a lesser ability to consume than at the old level of prices. In modern terms this is a version of 'crowding out'. Robertson called it 'automatic lacking'.

Keynes dismisses the importance of this argument:

> ...[It] is sometimes suggested that the increased saving which accompanies increased investment is undesirable and unjust because it is, as a rule, associated with rising prices. But if this were so, any upward change in the existing level of output and employment is to be deprecated. ... No one has a vested interest in being able to buy at prices which are low only because output is low.
>
> (*G.T.* p. 328)

This is not so much an argument against the proposition that unintended saving will result from an expansion of bank credit, but that the net effect is to the general benefit: incomes will rise, and the initial effect of higher prices on consumption is counterbalanced by the effect of higher incomes.

He freely admits (p. 83) that the initial ratio of saving to income will be exceptionally high. In the end, however, saving will be entirely voluntary. When he says that 'the public will exercise a "free choice" as to the proportion in which they divide their increase of income between saving and spending' and that 'the savings which result ... are just as genuine as any other savings [; no-one] can be compelled to own the additional money corresponding to new bank-credit ...' (*G.T.* pp. 82–3), he is not talking about the first stage in the argument at all, but about the disposal of income as it is generated by the investment and its later repercussions and the holding of money at the *end* of this process.

This shows the kind of muddle that timeless comparative-static analysis leads one into. The 'forced saving' doctrine was part of the proposition that actual saving, whether 'genuine' or 'forced', is a *precondition* for investment; the banking story is about the possibility of 'forcing' saving so that investment may precede the *intention* to save. Despite the fact that the banking process is essential to Keynes's story, Keynes insists that the banks cannot force saving because actual saving and investment must be equal at all times and at the end of all adjustment actual and intended saving are equal.

It also illustrates the confusion that can be created by implicit politics. Keynes's outlook is indicated by the quoted passage. The 'forced saving' contingent were concerned about the inherent loss of control by the public at large to the banks at the outset of the process of an expansion of credit. It is all an illustration of 'political economy' on both sides.

The argument concerning the 'forcing' of real non-consumption through price changes varies in relevance according to the pressure exerted by expansion of demand. This clearly depends (*inter alia* — see Chapter 15) on the extent of excess capacity of labour and equipment. The argument, and the political question underlying it, is of most importance at a time of rapidly-expanding credit and rapidly-rising prices. The monetarists, the modern inheritors of Classical thinking, were the ones to resurrect it as 'crowding out'. Their focus, however, is not bank credit and investment but government expenditure financed by new money. In other respects, the argument is exactly the same and the only genuine question is whether it is possible to gain output and employment at the expense of rising prices. The answer is not stable over time, even though the analysis is.

Banks and the Revolving Fund

The argument over the ability of banks to extend credit beyond what was previously lent to them was repeated in the late 1950s and early 1960s concerning the role of non-bank financial intermediaries. The general conclusion was that in principle they were like banks, but in practice the extent to which funds generated by their lending would find their way back to these institutions was significantly less than that experienced by the banks. This higher 'loss coefficient' for the NBFI's was related to the less important role NBFI liabilities played in the *savings* of households.

That way of putting the case misses out an important feature of banking — that deposits support consumption as much as they represent saving. Chapter 10 suggests a way of disentangling these two things analytically, but there is no way to separate them empirically: a banker receiving a deposit cannot divine the depositor's intended use of it and the intended use, in an integrated banking system, has little impact on bank liquidity.

When banks were small and isolated, whether a deposit was saving or a much more temporary abode of purchasing power was important for the expected stability of a bank's reserves: the threat of loss from withdrawals of cash was less if the deposits were 'savings'.

By Keynes's time the distinction was of little practical importance; withdrawals for expenditure were quite regularly matched by inflows from expenditure. The implication of the fact that deposits are widely used as a means of payment is that the banks' liquidity position does not depend on saving.

Keynes makes use of this fact in arguing (1937, 1939) that the equilibrium level of investment is financed by a 'revolving fund' of bank credit, revolving because as soon as the money is spent, bank liquidity is restored — i.e. the money comes back to the banking system. Only the holding of money for the 'finance motive', between the decision to invest and its implementation, he says, diminishes liquidity. He denied that the restoration of bank liquidity had anything to do with repayment to the banks.

This struck Dennis Robertson as most odd. It does me, too, though probably for different reasons. First, Keynes seems to have a vision of money held for the finance motive as bundles of notes stashed in the company's safe. If the firm had to borrow from the public, then one expects the firm's *bank deposit* to rise; and even that is not necessary if the finance motive is satisfied by a line of credit. A finance motive which does not withdraw cash from the banks does not alter bank liquidity — if the rest of the argument is correct.

Is it correct? If the spending of loans restores the banks' lending capacity to exactly the pre-loan position, what is there to put a stop to bank lending? Since there is no doubt that borrowing is undertaken for the purpose of spending, lending is always profitable to the banks.

The assumption of repayment is, I think, implicit in the process Keynes is describing and taken for granted. Recall that the revolving fund keeps a *given level* of investment going. And his investment theory is based on carrying into effect those investments which are believed to be able to generate funds adequate for repayment. There is room for error here, but there is no suggestion of systematic bias toward failure. So at any time, investment projects undertaken previously are beginning to pay off while new projects are requiring finance. At the same time, some entrepreneurs are releasing the cash held for the finance motive while others are demanding it.

With that background established, it was correct to argue that the banks, by Keynes's time, were no longer dependent on saving for their lending-power. The 'revolving fund' reflects the fact that the circular flow of income, consumption as well as investment, profits as well as wages, runs, almost in its entirety, through the banking system.

That is even more true today, with the great diminution of payment of wages in cash.

To return briefly to our opening remarks, compare the banks' position with that of the building societies. The building societies from time to time say that mortgage lending is constrained by the amount of 'saving' currently being done with them, but one never hears bankers speaking in this way (though they do compete for deposits).

When banks compete for deposits they are trying to regain 'savings' which as income payments have already circulated through their accounts once before. This competition is subsequent to the phenomenon that Keynes was talking about and is the level at which banks and NBFI's are indeed similar. The fundamental difference, resting on the use of deposits for payment, remains.

Sinking-Fund and Floating-Fund Finance

The importance to Keynes's theory of the assumption of eventual repayment of investment loans must be stressed. It was implicit, for it was an obligation basic to capitalism. An investment not expected to be capable of generating the cash flow to pay interest and providing its own sinking fund for the amortisation of principal was not undertaken: that is what the criterion of equality between the *mec* and *r* is all about.

There is, however, nothing to ensure that the profit expectations on which the *mec* is based will in fact be met. There are two quite distinct reasons for a shortfall: either the investment was not a good idea even in the best of circumstances, or the general circumstances turn out to be less favourable than anticipated. From the point of view of the firm with debt obligations financing its equipment, the effect is the same: an impaired ability to meet these obligations.

When faced with a shortfall of cash the sensible reaction is not to admit defeat (or default) immediately, but to take one of two forestalling actions in the hope that demand will soon rise again: one can scrimp the sinking fund in order to meet the more immediate demands for interest payments, or one can incur further debt to serve the same purpose. The latter is 'distress borrowing' and is likely to behave very differently from ordinary borrowing.

Taking the life of the investment, or the debt which finances it, as a whole, one can distinguish three levels of financial success or failure, depending on the extent to which interest and principal are recouped from operations. A successful investment will pay interest and provide its own sinking fund. A less successful one may be able to meet interest payments as they fall due but not provide an adequate sinking fund. An investment in real trouble does not even generate enough to pay interest costs. The financial position corresponding to these three states are called by Minsky (1982)[4] (a) hedge finance, (b) speculative finance and (c) Ponzi[5] finance, respectively. Davidson (1978)[6] calls them (a) sinking-fund finance (SFF), (b) floating-fund finance (FFF) and (c) rising-fund finance (RFF), so called because the asset-holder must increase his outstanding debt merely to service the previously-outstanding debt.

If economic conditions worsen, SFF positions can become FFF or RFF positions, increasing the 'fragility'[7] of the financial system and threatening firms with bankruptcy. However, from a macroeconomic point of view, speculative finance is not always a bad thing. Davidson (*op.cit.*) makes the important point as follows. Sinking funds are the wedge between gross and net income: supplementary cost is income not available for consumption and to the extent that funds exceed replacement expenditure they are deflationary. Thus paradoxically they can be, at the macro level, a source of the difficulty in meeting debt obligations.

It is perhaps fortunate that governments have learned to have less hesitation to engage in 'unsound' finance than was once the case.

Too much financial probity in the private sector can of course be counteracted by government engaging in 'unsound' finance to sustain demand. Indeed it was the Treasury's hesitation to so engage that provoked some of Keynes's more caustic writing in the *General Theory*. The sustained period of growth up to the mid-1960s may have much to do with FFF and even RFF gaining acceptance by government. (There is a long-term cost of course: inflation. Chapter 19 takes up that issue.)

This development has many ramifications for the monetary system, which has altered dramatically since Keynes's time. The 'revolving fund' appears to be ever-increasing. Some of the implications of that fact will be looked at in Chapter 17.

Notes

1. See, for example, Kaldor (1970).

2. The borrowers' deposits do not rise, but 'go into the red' as they spend. The overdrafts are entered on the asset side of the banks' balance sheets; they are not negative deposits. The deposits of those to whom borrowers have made payments do, however, rise.

3. For a contrast of this meaning with technical usage of the term, see Chick (1973b) pp. 84–5.

4. Minsky's precise specifications are slightly different but not, I believe, in essence.

5. Ponzi promoted a 'pyramid' finance scheme in Boston soon after the 1914–18 war.

6. Appendix to Second Edition.

7. Minsky's term.

Chapter *13*

THE STATIC MODEL: RECAPITULATION

All the elements of the static model in the *General Theory* have now been presented. There have, however, been many qualifications and discussions of side-issues; to bring out the main features of the model it is desirable to restate it, beginning with the most recently-introduced elements and working backwards. Figure 13.1 presents the model schematically and supplements the verbal exposition to follow.

Start with the determination of the rate of interest by the money supply and liquidity preference. The money supply is exogenously determined. M^D, however, is a function of *two* variables, Y and r, so we must take the expedient of assuming the level of income; say it is the same as last period's income, a sensible assumption if we are dealing with an equilibrium solution. r is then determined.

Long-term expectations are also exogenous. Production possibilities in the capital-goods industries are given by technology and the wage rate (here again we get ahead of our story), so the supply price of capital is estimable by producers contemplating investment. Therefore the *level* of investment is determined.

The consumption function is determined by households' preferences. It is a *schedule*, varying with employment or with income in wage units, which is very nearly the same thing. This schedule and the *level* of investment give aggregate demand, a function of the level of employment.

The technology of the economy is given and there is a capital stock, K_0, inherited from the past. The subscript 0 distinguishes a variable which is predetermined (given by history) from one which is exogenously determined (determined by agencies or factors not taken into account, e.g. the money supply, determined by the monetary authorities), which is indicated by a bar.

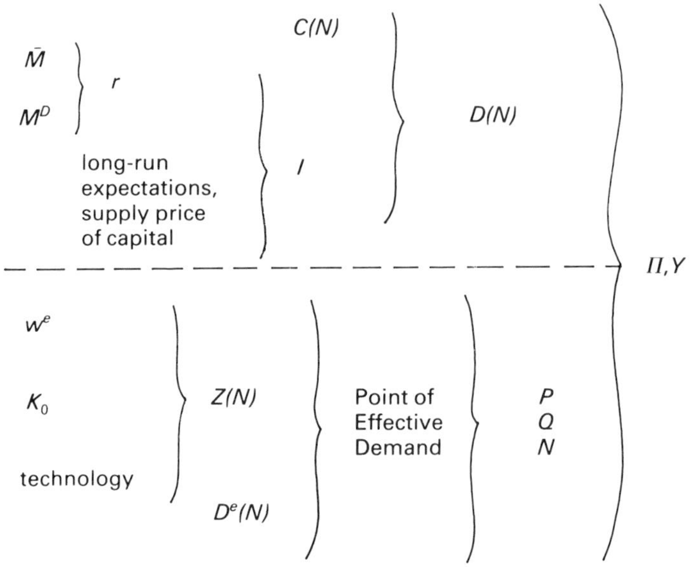

Figure 13.1

There is a wage, w^e, expected by employers as necessary to get the labour they want. The simplest assumption is that this wage is also inherited from the past — a reasonable assumption in an era of stable prices and substantial unemployment but not in general.

Unlike the assumption of an inherited capital stock, which is fundamental to the method of restriction to the short run, the assumption of inherited wages may be altered, but at the cost of greatly increased complexity of the analysis.

The wage, the capital stock and technology determine aggregate supply, a function relating the value of output to levels of employment. Technology and capital alone determine the relation between employment and the *volume* of output. Wages, the determinant of prime cost if we abstract from user cost, determine the price which will have to be charged for any given level of production to be profit-maximising. (One could substitute some other maximand here if one wishes.)

Firms have estimates of the level of demand they face. $D^e(N)$ is the aggregate demand function with which these estimates are consistent. It is a function of employment, rather than a single level, because at the aggregate level the volume of employment will alter demand, and producers know this. It is assumed that producers' estimates of their own levels of demand are derived with reference to general, overall levels of economic activity as well as to alterations, from time to time, in the composition of demand more or less favourable to their particular industry.

The intersection of $D^e(N)$ and $Z(N)$ gives the Point of Effective Demand, and that determines output and employment. Prices producers intend to charge or expect to get are also determined. We could alternatively assume that they set prices and stick to them, but the first formulation allows for adjustment by means other than by running down or building up stocks.

In the context of the model of Keynes's Chapter 3, however, the problem of price adjustment within the period does not arise, for it is there assumed that the aggregate demand function is estimated correctly. Whether estimated correctly or not, output and employment are determined for the period, for they cannot be altered within the period.

The two halves of Figure 13.1 now come together; output is produced and offered for sale. The expectation of demand is confronted with aggregate demand; sales and therefore aggregate income, and the actual level of profit, are determined.

Presenting the model in this way emphasises its causal structure, for we began with exogenous and predetermined variables. But there is one feature that upsets the scheme. Having determined income we must now loop back to the begining and see whether the level of income we got at the end is the same as the level we *assumed* when determining the rate of interest. Only if they are, and, further, if the estimate of demand is correct, have we determined an *equilibrium* level of income.

We can go on to play comparative-static games by choosing different values of the exogenous or predetermined variables (except the capital stock). Changes in wages are very messy. The best games are changing the money supply or changing long-term expectations and hence investment. We have done quite a lot of the former and in standard textbooks the latter are very popular. One can also play about with the propensity to consume by assuming that household consumption-saving preferences alter, though this is less likely than a change in policy or in investors' expectations.

In view of the fact that monetarists often claim that Keynsians believe all disturbances must arise from the volatility of investment, it is worth making explicit that from a formal point of view one is equally free to change *either* autonomous expenditure or the money supply. Which variable one chooses depends on what one thinks is important. In Keynes's time fluctuations in the money supply were, by current standards, almost non-existent. That is not true now. There is nothing to stop one using this model to analyse monetary changes *insofar as* these changes are exogenous. Of course, if one believes that the money supply is entirely endogenously determined, one must look for an alternative to Keynes when changes in M are too large to ignore.[1]

The Dynamic Process

The model just presented is static, timeless, but it represents a dynamic process, even within the confines of a single production period, for labour is hired at the beginning and sales and profits are only determined at the end. This feature constitutes the vital difference between Keynes's model and neoclassical models which 'loop back' and alter real wages until both employment and profit expectations are met. The absence of such a loop is the essence of Keynes's model. The model is static in only a limited sense: it requires that transactions balances be consistent with the income level determined at the end of an otherwise linear causal chain and in that respect the solution is simultaneous. In the formal model of the rate of interest, but *not* of output and employment, the causality is not temporal but synchronous.[2]

In the process being modelled, events, their cause and effect, are temporally ordered. A great deal happens at the beginning of the period which is irrevocable for the span of the period. The rate of interest which pertains to the investment decision, for example, may be determined afresh every day, but only the rate obtaining on the day a producer gets the finance he needs is important. From that point of view *past* income (and the expectation that income in the current period will not be vastly different) determines the amount held for transactions purposes at the beginning of the new period, and it is then that the interest rate relevant to investment is determined.

Employment, too, is determined at the beginning of the period. If prices rise during the period and labour did not expect that, there is no recontracting of the terms of work. This fact is part of the reason that employers have more control over real wages than workers do, even those workers (or their unions) who actively estimate them. At the end of the period aggregate income and its distribution are determined. (The size of the wage bill was determined at the beginning, but profit is only determined at the end along with income.) Now we know that aggregate expenditure is dependent on the distribution as well as the level of income, and if one works in static terms the distribution must be consistent with the position of the aggregate demand function, yet in the real world this cannot be known in advance. If the position of aggregate demand and the income distribution are not consistent, it will show up in alterations of both in future periods.

Similarly with estimates of demand: output and employment are determined for one period by the estimate, whether the estimate is right or not. If it is not right, futher periods are needed for adjustment. Even if it is right in one period, the general proclivity of things to contain random errors would suggest that a rational producer would not take one period's outcome as evidence of the correctness of his output policy. Thus the static equilibrium, though modelled in terms of a single period, presupposes a run of periods underlying it.

There are a number of periods, and investment is going on in all of them, but it is crucial to the method that this investment is not allowed to alter production possibilities, for then Z would shift. It is obvious therefore that the equilibria determined by this model will not, in real time, last forever. The equilibrium is defined with reference to the analytical device of the short period, which itself is not defined in terms of a length of time.

IS–LM

The static model was represented, in Hicks's famous article (1937) by two curves representing the equality of *ex ante* saving and investment and the equality of the supply of and demand for money. It is not much exaggeration to say that this model, sometimes modified to include the supply and demand for labour and a production function, has *become* Keynesian economics.

There has been much criticism of *IS–LM* in recent years.[3] My present view is that it doesn't have to be as misleading as it sometimes is — it is perfectly possible, for example, to include long-term expectations, which, when they alter, merely shift the *IS* curve — nor is it as misleading as I once thought for essentially loanable-funds reasons (Chick 1973a), but it still leaves out the all-important aspect of producers' output decisions and the short-run expectations on which they are based.

In terms of pure statics, it is fair enough to say that output is at an equilibrium level when that which is not bought by consumers (saving) equals that which is bought by the other sector (investment). What is not explained is why that level of output was ever produced in the first place.

By excluding the supply side, the value of output and income are equated and it becomes impossible to determine the division of money income between output and prices except by arbitrary assumption, e.g. prices are fixed.

Since *IS–LM* is 'pure' statics, rather than a static representation of a dynamic, historical process, the fact that wages are taken from history and may alter is also obscured from view. Fixed wages are a less extreme assumption than fixed prices, but if it is believed that the only reason for involuntary unemployment is the inability of wages to move, the blame is all too easily pinned onto the unions. Seen in an historical light, Keynes's system plainly does not assume that wages are fixed but rather gives reasons why they are unlikely to move and why, given there is no recontracting between firms and labour about either prices or the level of demand, the unemployment may stabilise until something changes long-term expectations or the government acts.

What *IS–LM* does capture very well is the separation, as a matter of method, of monetary factors as they determine the rate of interest from the rest of the model. The interaction through the transactions demand which we dealt with by 'looping back' is dealt with in *IS–LM* by strict simultaneity. Thus it is ideally suited to reflect what have become known as 'Keynes effects': effects on the rate of interest caused by variations in the level of activity, requiring more or less transactions balances.

To put it another, perhaps more familiar, way, *IS–LM* provides an easy demonstration of the proposition that to have its full effect through the multiplier, expansionary autonomous expenditure, whether investment or public works, must be financed in such a way as not to raise the rate of interest. This point comes up in the next chapter and in Chapter 18.

The Extended Model

Adding a production function and a labour market to *IS–LM* has had a disastrous consequence, for the dependence of the demand for labour on aggregate supply and anticipated demand in Keynes is transformed into a relationship of equal status (as in Patinkin, 1965) of the labour and output 'markets' or even primacy of the labour market (Warren Smith, 1956). Smith's model will serve our purposes well; it is a condensed version of the sort of model used — perhaps developed — by Modigliani in his highly influential article (1944).

Smith's system has five equations:

$$y = c(y, r) + i(y,r); \text{ the } IS \text{ curve} \tag{13.1}$$

$$\frac{M}{P} = L(y,r); \quad \text{the } LM \text{ curve} \tag{13.2}$$

$$y = f(N); \quad \text{the production function} \tag{13.3}$$

$$\frac{w}{P} = f'(N); \quad \text{the labour demand function} \tag{13.4}$$

$$N = \phi(\frac{w}{P}); \quad \text{the labour supply function.} \tag{13.5}$$

y is 'real income'. In our terminology it would be money income measured in output-units that enters as arguments in $c(.)$ and $i(.)$ and expenditure in output-units on the left-hand side of (13.1); y in equation (13.3) is physical output.

Equation (13.2) condenses the equality of an exogenous money supply, M, and a demand for real balances, M/P as a function of real income and the rate of interest, r. This transformation of Keynes's liquidity preference function presents issues I have addressed elsewhere (Chick, 1973b). Briefly, the point is that it may or may not be an improvement over Keynes's formulation, but it is *different*; therefore the case for a change must be made, and it has not been, despite (or perhaps because of) the widespread use of (13.2).

Smith starts with equations (13.4) and (13.5); their intersection determines employment and the real wage. One may elect to fix the money wage arbitrarily, cutting across these functions. Then employment is determined by intersection with the lesser of them. Then (13.3) determines output and *IS–LM* is used to determine prices and the interest rate. The market is over-determined if wages are fixed in advance. Smith defines equilibrium in that case as the happy coincidence when the price level determined by *IS–LM* is the same as that determined by the labour market.

The more important error is treating the labour market as having causal priority over aggregate supply and expected demand (despite the static, simultaneous nature of the model). The essence of the difference between Keynes's causality and neoclassical simultaneity lies here. In Keynes's theory, the demand for labour is derived from the expected demand for output: one works *from Z* and D^e *to* the labour market; the family of Z's (one Z for each wage) given by a particular technology fully determines the demand curve for labour (as shown in the Appendix to Chapter 5). Employment is a point on that demand curve elected by producers on the basis of their expectations of sales. These expectations may or may not coincide with the preferences of households for goods and leisure.

Contrary to almost universally-held belief, a lack of coincidence of firms' and households' plans is not *caused* by wage rigidity in Keynes; rather, stable wages result when producers are able to get the labour they require at yesterday's wage and sell the resulting output. Also contrary to conventional wisdom, flexible wages and prices do not solve the problem of unemployment: Keynes's Chapter 19 shows that when wages do not alter instantaneously and with perfect knowledge all round but alter through time and in uncertainty, both Z and D shift, with ambiguous results.

Notes

1. Keynes's theory of money, interest and investment is undermined if money is not exogenous. This fact has not, strangely enough, resulted in the presentation of an alternative fully worked-out theory.

2. See Hicks (1979).

3. The best-known and most extensive is Leijonhufvud (1968). For a defence of *IS–LM*, see Jackman (1974).

Part IV
THE SYSTEM IN MOTION

Chapter *14*

THE MULTIPLIER

Parts II and III have given a static analysis of the determination of the level of aggregate income, be it full or underemployment, which is uniquely consistent with prevailing expectations and given supply conditions. In this chapter we introduce the preconditions for that level of income to change — in particular, to rise.

We have seen that profit-maximising firms will not produce beyond the point of effective demand except by mistake, and that not for long. In the short run the position of Z is given unless wages change, and the outcome of a wage reduction is as problematical as the likelihood of one is low; the best hope for expansion of output and employment is for aggregate demand to rise.

Clearly consumption demand cannot be counted upon, for the bulk of consumption is induced by the very changes in income which we would like to achieve: indeed, the problem is precisely that the higher is the desired level of income, the greater is the gap between it and income-induced levels of consumption. It is to autonomous components of expenditure that one must look to fill the gap so that producing at the higher level becomes profitable. The autonomous component of consumption is presumed to be related either to factors whose influence is minor or to subjective factors ('tastes') which change only slowly. So it is to investment, or, if that cannot be adequately stimulated, to government expenditure, that one turns. Once there has been an autonomous rise in expenditure, induced consumption — so the story goes — will add to the initial expenditure, so that the cumulative change in income is, in the end, a multiple of the expenditure which sparked off its rise.

Static and Dynamic Multipliers

The multiplier is perhaps the single idea most closely associated with Keynesian macroeconomics. Textbooks are full of examples and exercises in the multiplier framework — government expenditure multipliers, taxation multipliers, foreign trade multipliers, modified later with a liquidity preference function. Yet we have, at the most elementary descriptive stage, two entirely different ways of interpreting what the multiplier means and what method of theorising it embodies.

As a description of what *will* occur if autonomous expenditure changes, the multiplier has the character of a *process*. It is dynamic. The alternative is to view the multiplier as a statement of the *necessary condition* for expansion of income to some predetermined new level or the maintenance of income at any particular level.

The latter interpretation is consistent with the straightforward comparative-static proof which begins with the statement that a level of aggregate income is sustainable when 'income' equals 'expenditure':

$$Y = C + I \tag{14.1}$$

and substitutes for C the behavioural assumption

$$C = a + bY \tag{14.2}$$

to give

$$Y = (I + a) / (1 - b). \tag{14.3}$$

If a is quite stable, i.e. the propensity to consume is fixed in position, (14.3) says exactly what the Principle of Effective Demand says: that for a given level of income to be sustainable, the gap between income and consumption must be filled with investment. (Notice an ambiguity about units of measurement. This is why 'income' and 'expenditure' have been placed in inverted commas. We shall come back to this point.)

Textbooks usually present (14.3) in first-difference form:

$$\Delta Y = \Delta I / (1 - b) \tag{14.4}$$

which suggests the more dynamic interpretation that a *rise* in investment of a given magnitude will result in a *change* in income of a certain larger magnitude.

It is said that the new sustainable (equilibrium) level of income will induce just enough saving to equal the new higher level of investment, so that the two quantities are equal *ex ante* as well as *ex post*. In the light of Chapter 9 it would be better to say that the level of investment provides (just) enough extra demand to justify producing the new, higher level of income. It is clear then that (14.3) is not dynamics but a comparison of two points of Effective Demand: the difference between the two levels of income is related by the slope of the propensity to consume to the difference in the volume of investment: pure comparative statics.

The original employment-multiplier analysis (Kahn, 1931) was, however, presented as a dynamic *process*. In the expenditure-multiplier context, over an infinite number of periods, ever-decreasing amounts of consumption expenditure are induced by the repercussions on income of an initial change in the level of autonomous expenditure. The sum of the (infinite) series of successive amounts of induced expenditure plus the one unit of autonomous expenditure is:

$$1 + b + b^2 + b^3 + \ldots + b^n = 1 / (1 - b). \tag{14.5}$$

Although the multiplier formula is the same, this interpretation relates to the question, 'how much new income will an *increase* in investment *generate* if no further exogenous changes take place?'

There is a logical equivalence to the two procedures of proof[1], but this logical property and the algebraic similarity should not mask the conceptual difference, which may even amount to a shift in the variable taken as given: the comparative-static analysis should ask how much investment is needed to sustain a new level of income; the process analysis asks: for a given change in investment, how much change in income will we get.

Keynes did not distinguish between these two interpretations: there are passages to support each. Within the space of two pages we have these statements:

> The multiplier tells us by how much their employment *has to be* increased to yield an increase in real income sufficient to induce them to do the necessary extra saving ...
>
> (*G.T.* p. 117, emphasis added)

> Let us call *k* the investment multiplier. It tells us that, when there is an increment of aggregate investment, income *will increase* by an amount which is *k* times the increment of investment.
>
> (*G.T.* p. 115, emphasis added)

The first passage supports the static interpretation, the second the process analysis.[2] An appendix to this chapter gives further quotations to illustrate the distinction.

It is not obvious why Keynes used the multiplier concept at all, if it adds nothing to the Principle of Effective Demand. Indeed one could look at the development of those two ideas as two approaches to demonstrating the same thing: that cumulative expansions or contractions come to an end. Kahn approached the matter by looking at 'leakages' from the circular flow of income, Keynes by wresting aggregate demand apart from aggregate supply and promulgating his Fundamental Psychological Law of an *mpc* less than one.

The Meaning of 'Income'

In the light of what has already been said about micro- and macroeconomic ways of looking at things, the difference in approach is not unimportant, as will be illustrated later. For the moment, the reader should recall Chapter 6: it was the slope of C_w, consumption in wage-units, that was less than one, and the slope of Z_w was unity. It is obvious that equations (14.1) to (14.4) do not apply to aggregate demand and supply in *money* terms, for the slope of Z is not unity but increases with employment and output, and the consumption function in money terms is not stable so the constant, a, cannot be taken as given, nor is one able to infer the slope with any certainty.

'Income' and 'expenditure' have quite ambiguous meanings in the conventional multiplier. Consumption is supposed to be 'real', for anything else would involve money illusion, yet the story behind the multiplier has to do with expenditure, which must be monetary. It is not clear whether 'income' is microeconomic money-flows or the value (actual or expected?) of sales of output, which is income in the macroeconomic sense.

The substitution of saving-investment equality for equality of expected and actual sales is partly responsible for the ambiguity, for it effectively allows the supply side to be dropped altogether: 'income in real terms' is simply money-income divided by the price level; one can slide comfortably, albeit disastrously, between individual real income and aggregate real output in this way. The way is made still easier if it is assumed, as it is in conventional multiplier analysis, that the price level is fixed and that it is always income in real terms that is rising (or falling).

The assumption of fixed prices in Keynesian analysis is most strange, in view of the amount of space devoted in the *General Theory* to the consequences of expansion for prices: price rises, it was reiterated again and again, are an inescapable consequence of expansion in the short run. It has, perhaps, three roots: (i) Keynes's use of the wage-unit supply curve, which has a unitary slope and therefore may have given rise to the '45° line', though there is no guarantee that Z_w goes through the origin; (ii) a rise in the belief in constant returns, which would give Z a unitary slope even in money terms and cause one to forget the original meaning of Z_w; and finally (iii) the transformation of Keynes's consumption function in wage-units (which gives an employment multiplier) to one in 'real' (output) terms. The identity (in concept) of output and price-deflated expenditure in the national income accounts, finally ties the multiplier's expenditure story to output, in a way which to say the least begs many questions, and to say the most is illegitimate.

(A comment on the 'Keynesian cross' diagram needs to be inserted here. If the 45° line is simply interpreted as a line plotting Y against Y, absolutely nothing can be said against it,[3] and we shall shortly use it. But notice that plotting an aggregate expenditure function against such a line permits one to ask only this: income being whatever it is, will demand for it be adequate, excessive, or just right? The amount of output, whether in value or volume terms, is completely arbitrary. Aggregate supply has no role to play.)

For the multiplier to describe changes in real output, output must rise *pari passu* with expenditure, i.e. firms must react within the period to produce to meet both investment demand and any increase in sales of consumption goods at constant prices. This not only assumes constant costs but also remarkable prescience.

Keynes does in fact make the assumption of prescience on the part of consumer-goods producers for part of his discussion, and we shall return to Keynes's treatment later. For now let us take the textbook multiplier on its own terms, not — as it might seem after what has just been said — to beat a dead horse, but to dissect it — a process which is instructive in revealing interior structure.

The Conventional Multiplier: Two Dynamic Interpretations

The static and dynamic concepts have been made congruent by offering two entirely different interpretations of the situation to which the process analysis is supposed to apply. On one interpretation, there is a rise in investment in the first period; subsequently this elevated level is not sustained and investment falls back to its previous level. The 'change in income' represents the cumulative sum of differences of the new income levels each period over what income would have been had the autonomous change in I and its consequences not occurred. Call this dynamic multiplier DM_1.

On the other interpretation (DM_2), the elevated level of I is sustained indefinitely and the new level of Y becomes, in the limit, permanently established. These are dramatically different stories to be represented by the same mathematics, yet a perusal of textbooks suggests that their co-existence appears to cause no great discomfort.

In Figure 14.1, representing the equations (14.1) and (14.2), a rise in investment from I_0 to I_1 raises income in the first period by its own amount, to Y_1. Subsequent periods trace the gradual restoration of Y_0 as expenditure first falls back to a point on $C + I_0$ and then along that function to the left. Periods are indicated by subscripts; Y_0 refers to the initial position. Continuous new investment, portrayed in Figure 14.2, shifts the aggregate demand curve upwards, determining the new sustainable level of income, Y_n.

The two models incorporate the same assumption about consumption behaviour but radically different assumptions about investment. In DM_1, whatever change in expectations or interest rates prompted the first period's investment, that investment is assumed to restore firms' capital stock to an optimal level, whereas DM_2 is characterised by ever-buoyant expectations,

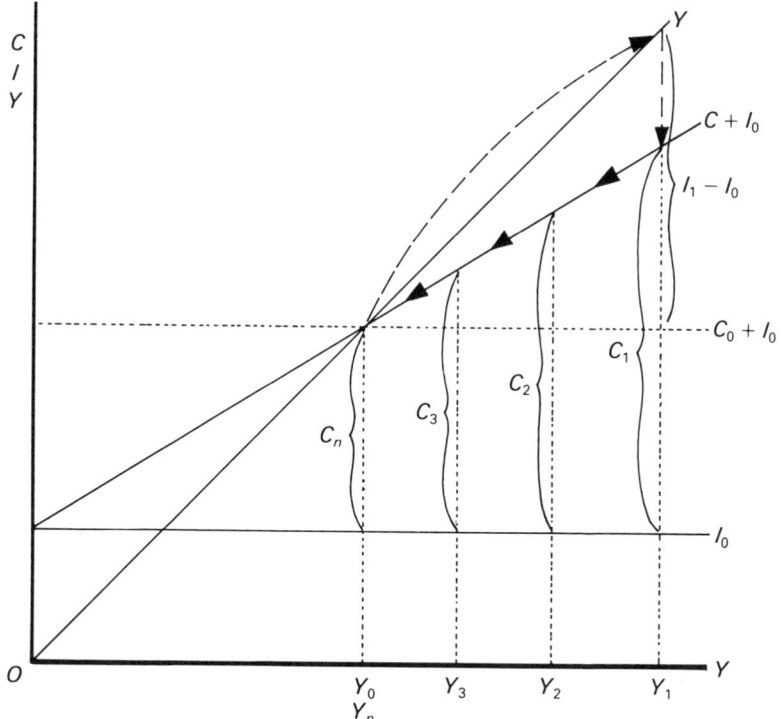

Figure 14.1

prompting continuous accumulation. Yet the two models are presented together in textbooks with no apparent sense of incongruity, no sense of there being something which deserves explanation.

We shall return to the question of investment behaviour later.

Finance

The two models have very peculiar financial implications. Accepting for a moment what was thrown into serious doubt in Chapters 9 and 12 — the identification of saving with finance, in DM_1 the once-and-for-all investment generates over the infinitely long period enough *cumulative* savings to be equal to the investment, while in DM_2 the system is supposed to come to rest when in *one period* the volume of currently-generated saving is equal to the level of one period's investment, without settling the question of what financed all the previous periods' investment. Surely these implications should have created some scepticism.

It is difficult to see how an analysis containing such contradictions could give the firm impression that autonomous investment or government expenditure is somehow self-financing. There is just enough truth in that

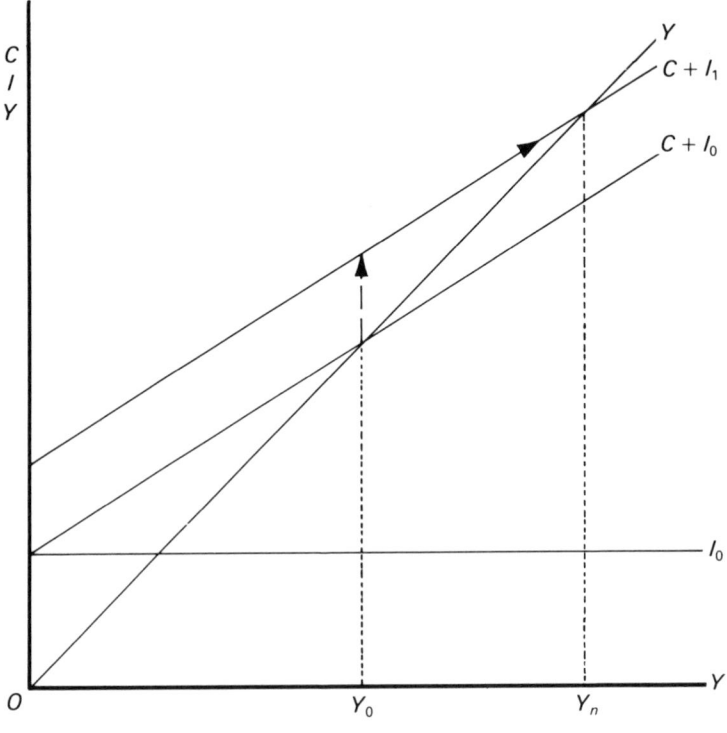

Figure 14.2

proposition to be misleading, perhaps.

The financial side of the multiplier has bothered few authors. To explore it will illustrate many points made in Part III. Characteristically, Robertson fretted over it (1940) and his model is an illuminating example of the loanable-funds approach. It is a strict period analysis, based on behaviour appropriate to individuals' decisions. Hence consumption is financed out of last period's income, and saving is free to be either a residual or a joint decision with consumption. Let b represent the marginal propensity to consume last period's income. There is an amount of investment, of unit value, presumably in addition to stationary-state replacement, which begins in period 0 and is repeated each period. Then we have the sequence given by Table 14.1, which is taken direct from Robertson (1940) except for the assumption of one unit of investment.

It is plain from the Table that Robertson identifies saving with lending for the finance of investment, in the loanable-funds manner; any gap between saving and investment must be financed by new money. The result is that a continuous stream of new investment leaves behind an increase in the money stock equal to the increase in income. The process stops when it is no longer necessary to create new money. Each period's new money creation is,

Table 14.1

1	2	3	4	5	6
Period	Investment (above previous level)	'Disposable Income', i.e. Income Received in Preceding Period	Of which Saved	Therefore New Money Created (2–4)	Income in Current Period
0	1	–	–	1	1
1	1	1	$1-b$	b	$1+b$
2	1	$1+b$	$1-b^2$	b^2	$1+b+b^2$
3	1	$1+b+b^2$	$1-b^3$	b^3	$1+b+b^2+b^3$
.					
.					
n	1	$1/(1-b)$	1	0	$1/(1-b)$
$\sum_0^n$				$1/(1-b)$	

within that period, unintended saving; the sum of columns 4 and 5 is *ex post* saving, equal to investment.

The process begins with a bank loan. (Firms cannot make the government issue notes to give them to spend; the new money must be bank money.) It can be seen that it is not possible for the multiplier process to begin without this source of finance, given that Robertson leaves no room for holdings of idle balances. Subsequent saving (= lending) then *partly* finances further new investment, with the banks taking over the remainder. Only in period n (and after, if investment is sustained at 1 in $n+1, n+2, ..., n+k$), will saving (i.e. bond purchases) provide, in each period, the funds necessary to effect the investment undertaken in those periods.

Saving, money left over from the income (cash flow to households) of last period, provides finance through a bond market which remains out of sight. The sequence proceeds without any effect on the rate of interest. (If interest were to alter, it would add to the difficulty of explaining why investment plans are unaffected.) Robertson's model, which implicitly rules out any motive for holding money idle, suggests that funds are supplied at the same rate as investors demand them from the bond market. Savers continue to lend ever-larger sums at unchanged interest rates because income (in the sense of the value of current production) is rising. The banks' supply-of-loans function is perfectly elastic.

The growth of income is matched by new money in each period. Thus Robertson's savers lend some of that new money and use the rest to finance consumption, when it accrues as income. (Here we have an example of the point made earlier that Keynes only *appeared* to ignore money circulating in the consumption sphere, taking it for granted as an aspect of (individual) income.)

If the money used to finance consumption is held as bank deposits by both consumers and the firms who received payment for goods sold, banks maintain their reserves, and hence their lending capacity, from this source, not from saving. The turnover of money balances in the cycle of consumption and income payments remains with the banks, while all Robertsonian saving is withdrawn from the banking system and channelled into the market for direct credit. If the residual from sales after the payment of wages and other costs (i.e. gross profit) is positive, some portion of the outstanding bank loans may be amortised from that source. Repayment of loans is made possible by consumption; saving (direct lending) can only provide fresh finance for additional expenditure.

In Robertson's model, the 'revolving fund' of bank liquidity is replenished entirely by expenditure, while in Keynes's model money held for whatever reason — as savings or as transactions balances — replenishes the revolving fund when it returns to the banks. Robertson, as we have said, does not allow for idle money balances.

Well-trained Keynesians will find Robertson's model jarring in its 'confusion' of a stock variable, money, with flow variables — income, saving and investment. The difficulty arises, of course, from introducing into a Keynesian framework the two awkward loanable-funds questions: how is investment financed and where does 'saving' go? These questions involve movements of stocks of assets; thus one becomes involved with the concept of the velocity of circulation, a concept inextricably involved with *time*.

Robertson avoids any technical stock-flow problem by a simple device: the example is constructed on the basis of the income period, income being received in the form of money; thus the velocity of circulation is held constant at unity.

Aggregate income, the value of production, is in principle consistent with any quantity of money, so long as money's rate of circulation can vary. Variation in the velocity of circulation of money could in principle be achieved by a variation in the average income period in relation to the average production period (or even an arbitrary length of calendar time, an accounting period), but these other periods do not appear in Robertson.

Talking as if income, investment and saving were pure 'flows' also avoids trouble if stocks are kept separate. Time is continuous or broken up only for accounting purposes. Lerner long ago (1938) declared a total separation; the multiplier was to do only with flows, monetary analysis with stocks. It was the easy solution: articles attempting to 'marry' velocity and multiplier analysis have failed.[4] But they fail not because the question is wrong-headed, as Lerner would have it; they fail because there is no convenient simplifying assumption other than constant velocity, which rules out speculative money holdings and even makes it difficult to handle changes in average transactions balances.

It is not often that a textbook treatment even attempts to integrate money with the multiplier along the lines of separation encouraged by Keynes. Table 14.2 provides a description of the results of a single money-financed injection of a unit of new investment. (As before, I and Y are taken to mean levels in excess of some previous equilibrium.) The implicit assumptions are

Table 14.2

t	I	ΔM^S	Y	ΔM_T^D	ΔM_s^D	Consumption	Saving
0	1	1	1	k	$1-k$	b	$1-b$
1	0	0	b	kb	$1-kb$	b^2	$b(1-b)$
2	0	0	b^2	kb^2	$1-kb^2$	b^3	$b^2(1-b)$
3	0	0	b^3	kb^3	$1-kb^3$	b^4	$b^3(1-b)$
.	.	.	.	.	.	.	.
.	.	.	.	.	.	.	.
n	0	0	0	0	1	0	0

clear: consumption, which generates income in periods 1 to n, is based on current income; transactions balances are related to income by equation (10.1):

$$M_T^D = kY;$$

the speculative demand is whatever is left over.

Both the initial injection and subsequent consumption are financed by the initial increase in the money supply; the velocity of circulation progressively declines (while in Robertson's example it is constant). The process stops when all newly-created money is held idle.

The last two columns show that Keynesian concepts of consumption and saving are not easily integrated into this scheme. *Ex ante* saving never equals investment, for a start. Then when one asks where saving 'goes' (a loanable-funds type of question) the serious trouble starts. One concludes that saving must encompass less than the sum of the active and idle money-holding, for this sum equals the new income. There is no scope for money to be held as bonds; in aggregate one must hold the money which is supplied.[5] Saving, however, is only equal to idle balances if $k = b$. The Keynesian will protest that k and b are not dimensionally equivalent: he sees k as relating to stocks and b to flows. That is nearly but not quite right: as demonstrated in Chapter 10, k relates to the (micro) income period while b relates to the (macro) production period, and they are not the same.

To tie that point in with the micro/macro problem raised in Chapter 9, consider the implications of this scheme for finance.

There are two senses in which saving could be understood to finance investment, and in neither sense does it do so in this schema. The first sense is that of providing the initial funds to support investment expenditure; it is obvious in period analysis that saving cannot possibly finance investment in this sense, for the money is needed beforehand (the finance motive), not at the end.

In a second sense, saving could be used to pay back the bank loan that is clearly the source of finance in the first sense. But there are two objections to this. One, raised in the context of Robertson's model, is that firms only pay back loans out of sales, not out of saving. The other is that saving is only adequate at the end, even if firms could get their hands on it. As the model stands, the loan is not paid back. (One wonders how often banks would be prepared to finance these episodes.)

Firms can capture savings by making bond issues. Let us modify the story to include bond issues subsequent to the investment. It would be convenient (though faintly absurd) to choose a bond supply equal to demand, to keep the interest rate constant. Then the whole story takes on a different appearance. Bank loans provide initial finance and the investment is progressively 'funded' as sufficient savings become available to permit long-term borrowing without excessive interest cost. (Compare this scenario with borrowing the whole amount at the outset, where the interest-rate effect would have been considerable.)

At the end of the process, the investment has been completely funded. From my reading of two of Keynes's later articles[6] I am persuaded that 'funded' is what he meant by 'financed' in this connection, and one can see the sense of saying that induced saving is the source of funding,though it cannot provide finance in the more usual sense of command over purchasing power at the outset.

Investment Behaviour

Let us return to the constrasting investment behaviour of the two textbook dynamic multipliers, for they provide a nice bridge to Keynes's own treatment. Recall that in DM_1, after the first period investment returns to its earlier level despite the fact that some of the induced consumption would come as a surprise and might be expected to stimulate further investment. In DM_2 investment is sustained at a constant rate despite the fact that income is rising at an ever-declining rate. In neither case is investment reacting to what is happening; its course is set independently of the behaviour of consumption or income.

In the case of DM_1, it is just possible that the induced consumption is enough to fulfil investors' expectations — preferably more than enough, so that they need not wait until infinity for the investment to pay off! But there is nothing to guarantee that the induced consumption *will* justify the investment, and if it did, why would the investment not be repeated, since it was successful.

In the case of DM_2, however, the investment is doomed to eventual disappointment unless consumption rises autonomously as the investment plan is being completed, for the end of investment spending will cause a collapse of income and a fall in the amount of consumption.

On the face of it, DM_1 is a possible but unproven winner and DM_2 is a certain loser. But that is to miss an aspect of Keynes's analysis which, whatever its other faults, the multiplier analysis does capture: the independence of long-run and short-run expectations. (Refer back to the discussion of Kregel's article in Chapter 2 at this point.) Investment is whatever it is despite changes that are going on while it is taking place precisely *because* the expectations which induce it and the pay-off horizon which justify it are outside the period in which the investment expenditure is taking place.

It can be seen from the last paragraph but one that this independence is just as well, especially for continued investment.

Changing Long-Term Expectations

If further proof of the usefulness of the independence of long-run expectations is wanted, consider a model in which long-term expectations depend on recent experience. The model will be crude, but effective.

A producer is contemplating an investment project at time t. He is deciding whether the desired capital stock, K^*, should be greater than the firm's existing stock, K_t. Assume that new capital could be installed to produce output — or old capital scrapped — without delay: then K^*_{t+1} depends on expected demand in the period immediately following its installation, i.e. Y^e_{t+1}, when that level is expected to continue.

Define *points* of time at the opening of *periods* of time bearing the same time-subscript. A scheme which helps to keep the time periods straight is given as Figure 14.3.

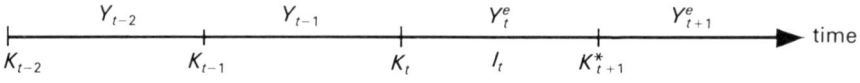

Figure 14.3

Suppose our producer is naive in the economist's technical sense: he believes that tomorrow will be exactly like today — or rather, like what he knows. At the point of time t, what he knows is Y_{t-1}. So we postulate the general principle.

$$Y^e_t = Y_{t-2}.$$

He does not know the level of income that will unfold in t either, but he forecast it at $t-1$ on the basis of Y_{t-2}, and on that forecast adjusted K to the amount K_t on the basis of a fixed capital-output ratio v.

Investment during t being the difference between K^*_{t+1} and K_t we have

$$I_t = K^*_{t-1} - K_t = v(Y^e_{t+1} - Y^e_t) = v(Y_{t-1} - Y_{t-2}): \qquad (14.6)$$

the simple accelerator! (Note that this determines gross investment, the decision to scrap or replace being integral with the decision to expand or contract.)

The assumptions of the accelerator mechanism in this simple form are rigid to the point of absurdity. There is a substantial body of literature designed to rectify this rigidity, but it is all rather beside the point we are trying to make, namely that the accelerator can be seen as an expectations hypothesis.[7] This allows us to illustrate without further ado what may happen if investment were to alter in response to recent observations. It is well known that the interaction of the multiplier and the accelerator can produce cycles or 'explosions' as well as monotonic approaches to a new equilibrium.

The accelerator model still maintains a formal separation between long-run and short-run expectations, however: Y^e_{t+1} is 'long-run' for it is outside the production period. Y^e_t *as estimated at t* for the purposes of deciding whether or not to use K_t to capacity, is short-run. Estimated at $t-1$ it was, of course, long-run.

What happens when long-run expectations are adjusted to perceived *mistakes* of the recent past is of course the subject of Harrod's 'Essay on Dynamic Theory' (1939). Although the subject is 'growth', the 'natural rate' can just as well be zero, and when it is, what we have is really a movement along Z, to higher levels of employment. Harrod's assumption that investment is purely a demand phenomenon is the essence of the short run. Harrod's famous 'knife-edge' theorem thus shows that when falsification of short-run expectations is allowed to influence investment behaviour, movement from one level of effective demand to another is a perilous business, unlikely to be successful.[8]

These two examples should put the apparently whimsical assumptions of the textbook multipliers in a somewhat more favourable light.

The Multiplier in the *General Theory*

Contrast the conventional exposition with Keynes's. While the conventional multiplier is concerned only with expenditure, Keynes's analysis begins with a rise in the output of investment goods. Until Section IV of Chapter 10 he additionally assumes that the change in aggregate investment

> has been foreseen sufficiently in advance for the consumption industries to advance *pari passu* with the capital-goods industries without more disturbance to the price of consumption-goods than is consequential, in conditions of decreasing returns, on an increase in the quantity which is produced.
>
> (*G.T.* p. 122)

Thus the connection between expenditure and output is made by the device of (*G.T.*) Chapter 3: the assumption that anticipations of demand are met. In Section IV of the same chapter, he relinquishes the assumption of foresight; the consumption-goods industries then react only with a lag to expansion in the capital-goods industries.

The words 'advance *pari passu*' suggest a process of change, a steady increase of *both* investment and consumption. Such a process is clearly not captured in either DM_1 or DM_2. The problem this model addresses is the transition from one equilibrium point of effective demand to another. The strictest interpretation would be that during an expansion from Y_0 to Y_1 (Figure 14.4), supply is continually matched to demand, in composition as well as in aggregate. The investment-goods industries 'advance' gradually to a level of investment, I_n, and consumption rises likewise from C_0 to C_n, all the while keeping exactly the pace dictated by demand, thus disturbing relative prices only to the extent that cost structures in the two industries

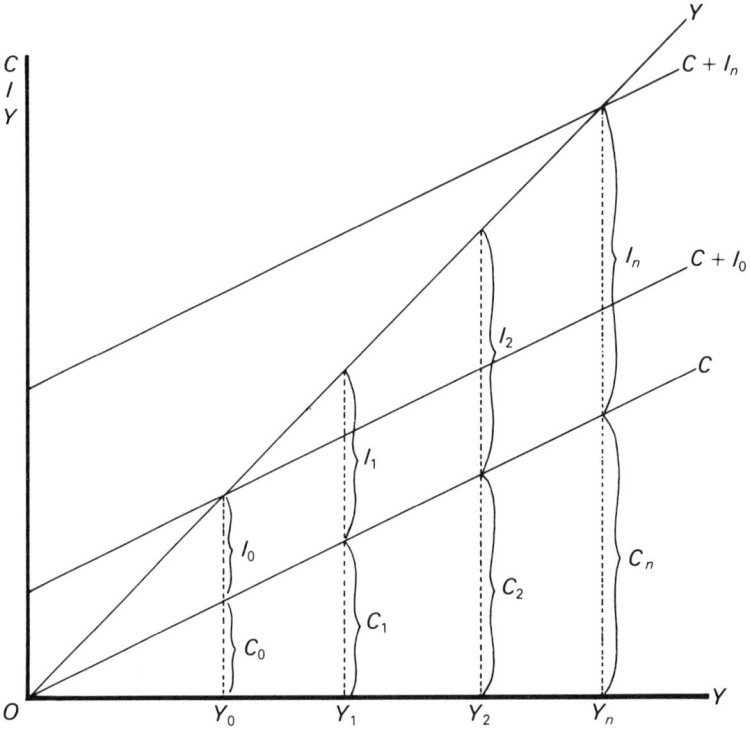

Figure 14.4

differ. (Supply conditions are not portrayed in a 45° diagram, so the course of relative prices is not determined.) In Figure 14.4, expansion is along $C + I_n$, with the position at different time periods indicated by subscripts on C and I. This is the case to which the Harrod problem pertains, but Keynes does not fret about the conditions under which such a growth path is feasible.

Later, Keynes analyses the continuous-investment case: the multiplier 'when the community has settled down to a new steady level of aggregate investment' (*G.T.* p. 123). Suppose investment has settled down to I_n. Such a point does imply continuous investment, and in some sense DM_2 is applicable, though obviously the investment cannot go on forever, as taking the multiplier to its logical conclusion implies.

'Continuous investment' could perhaps best be seen in the following light. It may be a profitable strategy for firms intending to increase their capital to some new higher level to place orders for capital goods to be delivered (or produced) *gradually*, in order to reduce the supply price. (Recall Chapter 6.) Then a stream of new investment, at a higher level than formerly, can be seen as the implementation of a single set of investment decisions. When those projects are completed, the situations alters.

Then if the *final* level of induced consumption-demand is not foreseen, but rather each rise in consumers' expenditure, period by period, *is* foreseen, we have the assumptions which justify DM_2, provided everything is specified in wage-units. If DM_2 is to be interpreted in real terms, as it usually is, then we must assume constant costs.

The extreme case of a complete absence of anticipation by the consumption-goods industries is analysed by the assumptions of Keynes's Section IV (Chapter 10). Consumption *demand* will of course increase (in the manner described in textbook expositions), and even if for a time the excess demand can be met out of inventories, eventually prices will rise, partly to clear the market and partly to cover costs of increased production to replace inventories. The analysis in Keynes (pp. 123–4) is a combination of that in (our) Chapter 4 dealing with a disparity between actual and expected demand and the remarks in (our) Chapter 6 on the redistribution effects of price changes on consumption:

> [A] temporary equilibrium [will be] brought about partly by high prices causing a postponement of consumption, partly by a redistribution in favour of the saving classes as an effect of the increased profits resulting from the higher prices, and partly by a depletion of stocks.

(*G.T.* pp. 123–4)

Postponement of consumption will, of course, cause the actual *ex post* *mpc* to diverge from its longer-run value; a change in prices will also alter the position of the consumption function. One might reasonably ask whether one will actually get to Y_n in the end.

Notes

1. Samuelson, p. 83 in Patinkin and Leith (1977).

2. There is a third interpretation, the 'logical theory of the multiplier, which holds good continuously, without time-lag, at all moments of time ...' (*G.T.* p. 122). This refers to the necessary *ex post* relation between Y and I, where the *mpc* is the relation between *actual* changes in consumption and income. If income changes unexpectedly or if consumption takes time to adjust to perceived or even anticipated income changes, this '*mpc*' bears no necessary relation to the slope of the function which indicates consumers' more considered behaviour. One would expect the *ex post* '*mpc*' to be flatter than the 'true' *mpc* (see Chapter 6), but that is all one can say. The 'logical theory' is not a theory at all but a description of a necessary *ex post* relationship. It applies to disequilibrium situations, while the multiplier applies only to equilibrium situations.

3. See Lipsey (1972) for an exposition of the confusions of standard textbook treatment.

4. For example Lutz (1955), Tsiang (1956). Archibald (1956) has declared an 'annulment'. See also Chapter 11, note 6 and the associated text.

5.   The reader should work out the implications of this for the interest rate
      throughout the multiplier process.

6.   (1937) and (1939).

7.   It was pointed out to me by David Laidler that Coddington (1979) has made
      this point, rather chiding Hicks for making it less than obvious. Perhaps it was,
      to Hicks, too obvious to point out, but looking at a good many expositions of
      the accelerator suggests it is far from obvious.

8.   Kregel (1980) has argued that Harrod's and Keynes's methods are
      incompatible and that the inference I have just made violates Harrod's
      method. Though I am convinced of Kregel's argument from a history-of-
      thought point of view, I feel that Harrod's model does tell us something
      valuable about Keynes's model and Keynes's method.

Appendix to Chapter *14*

KEYNES'S TWO VIEWS OF THE MULTIPLIER

The following page references are all to the *General Theory*; italics have been added.

I. The Multiplier as an Equilibrium Condition:

... [To] *justify* any given amount of employment there *must be* an amount of current investment sufficient to absorb the excess of total output over what the community chooses to consume when employment is at the given level. For unless there is this amount of investment, the receipts of the entrepreneurs will be less than is required to induce them to offer the given amount of employment. It follows, therefore, that, given what we shall call the community's propensity to consume, the *equilibrium* level of employment, i.e. the level at which there is no inducement to employers as a whole either to expand or to contract employment, will depend on the amount of current investment. (p. 27)

... [G]iven the propensity to consume and the rate of new investment, there will be only one level of employment *consistent with equilibrium*. (p. 28)

The effective demand associated with full employment is a special case, *only realised* when the propensity to consume and the inducement to invest stand in a particular relationship to one another. This particular relationship .... *can only exist* when, by accident or design, current investment provides an amount of demand just equal to the excess of the aggregate supply price of the output resulting from full employment over what the community will choose to spend on consumption when it is fully employed. (p. 28)

... [A] poor community will be prone to consume by far the greater part of its output, so that a very modest measure of investment will be *sufficient to provide* full employment; whereas a wealthy community will have to discover much ampler opportunities for investment if the saving propensities of its wealthier members are to be compatible with the employment of its poorer members. (p. 31)

The multiplier tells us by how much their employment *has to be* increased to yield an increase in real income sufficient to induce them to do the necessary extra saving ... (p. 117)

The relation between the increment of consumption which *has to* accompany a given increment of saving is given by the marginal propensity to consume. The ratio, thus determined, between an increment of investment and the corresponding increment of aggregate income, both measured in wage-units, is given by the investment multiplier. (p. 248)

II.   The Multiplier as a Dynamic Process:

Let us call *k* the investment multiplier. It tells us that, when there is an increment of aggregate investment, income *will increase* by an amount which is *k* times the increment of investment. (p. 115)

It is, however, to the general principle of the multiplier to which we have to look for an explanation of how fluctuations in the amount of investment, which are a comparatively small proportion of the national income, are capable of *generating fluctuations* in aggregate employment and incomes so much greater in amplitude than themselves. (p. 122)

... [We] have to take account of the case where the initiative comes from an *increase* in the output of the capital-goods industries which was not fully foreseen. It is obvious that an initiative of this description only produces its full effect on employment over a period of *time*. (p. 122)

... [The] greater the marginal propensity to consume, the greater the multiplier, and hence the greater the *disturbance* to employment corresponding to a given *change* in investment. (p. 125)

... [The] investment multiplier ... tells us by how much a given increase in investment *will increase* effective demand as a whole. (p. 298)

Where does this fit?:

This quantity [the *mpc*] is of considerable importance, because it tells us how the *next increment* of output will *have to be* divided between consumption and investment. (p. 115)

Chapter 15

PRICES AND OUTPUT

It is time to ask how an expansion of demand manifests itself: as an output change, a price increase, or some mixture of the two. A startling amount of nonsense has been written about this question by authors who claim to be interpreting Keynes — though sometimes it is clear that they refer not to Keynes but to neoclassical Keynesianism. It is held that in Keynesian economics prices are assumed to be unaffected by expansion until full employment and then *only* prices will be affected; allowance for bottlenecks modifies this proposition. The current conventional wisdom is that Keynes 'nullified the Marshallian adjustment by means of prices' and proposed quantity adjustments instead. Any reader who has got this far must realise that simply is not so.

Various ways have been found to justify fixed prices: empirical evidence is adduced to support constant costs, sometimes further backed up by a theory of non-profit-maximising behaviour; or costs of adjusting prices such as the printing and dissemination of new price information are invoked; or the intertemporal consideration of 'spoiling the market', where price rises are difficult to lower again, is deemed important. These points are not to be dismissed (especially if they are true). There is, however, no need to use them to justify an assumption Keynes did not make, nor is there anything to stop us from modifying Keynes's theory to incorporate a wide variety of beliefs or such facts as are unearthed. Taking Keynes's assumptions, we shall see that the framework he presents is broad enough to accommodate almost any empirically-based assumption about cost and about pricing policy, except bilateral bargaining. What is disallowed is the assumption of fixed prices — for there would be nothing further to say, no reason to study the *General Theory* in a period of inflation such as ours.

Keynes, as we have said before, assumed that firms were profit-maximising and small. His theory of price and output decisions, far from departing from Marshall, follows closely along Marshallian lines; the major complication is that the wage is neither given nor endogenously determined. It is not uniquely related to the level of employment independently of history. The use of the wage-unit as a deflator largely disguises the fact that the wage is, in the theory, a floating variable; its level is determined by history. However, the optimal price and quantity are determined by costs and demand; therefore, for the price level to be determined, the wage must be known. The tools of static theory which Keynes used are, because they exclude history, not adequate to the task of determining the *level* of prices (and it is doubtful that any simple dynamic system would capture enough elements of the theory to determine it either). Therefore, Keynes asked a more manageable question: how will a *change* in demand be manifest in *changes* in prices and output? This question ignores the starting point and does not determine *levels* of the variables.

To answer his question Keynes derives the relationship between three 'elasticities': the response of price, output and wages to changes in aggregate demand. The resulting equation is only a framework for analysis, to be invested with empirical assumptions which may vary according to circumstances.

The Determination of e_p

We shall need some definitions. The reader will notice a change in notation, to conform with that used in the *General Theory*: O now stands for output instead of Q. It is also suggested to memorise the definitions of the elasticities which follow.

Let:

$$e_p = \frac{dP}{dD} \cdot \frac{D}{P} = \frac{d\log P}{d\log D} \quad \text{: the response of price to (expected) } money \text{ demand}$$

$$e_O = d\log O/d\log D_w \quad \text{: the response of output to (expected) demand in wage-units}$$

$$e'_O = d\log O_w/d\log D \quad \text{: the response of output to (expected) money demand}$$

$$e_w = d\log w/d\log D \quad \text{: the response of the wage to (expected) money demand}$$

P = price of output in terms of money

P_w = price of output in terms of wage-units

D = anticipated demand in money terms

D_w = anticipated demand in wage-units

O = output

w = money wage rate.

From the definitions[1]

$D_w = P_w O$ and $P = P_w w$

we have

$$P = D_w w / O. \tag{15.1}$$

Taking logs and differentiating with respect to log D gives

$$\frac{d \log P}{d \log D} = \frac{d \log D_w}{d \log D} - \frac{d \log O}{d \log D} + \frac{d \log w}{d \log D}. \tag{15.2}$$

Now, since

$$\frac{d \log O}{d \log D} \cdot \frac{d \log D}{d \log D_w} = e_O,$$

we may write (15.2) as

$$e_p = (d \log D_w / d \log D)(1 - e_O) + e_w. \tag{15.3}$$

Taking logs of the definition[2]

$D_w = D/w$

and differentiating with respect to log D gives

$$d \log D_w / d \log D = 1 - e_w. \tag{15.4}$$

Substituting (15.4) into (15.3), we have

$$e_p = (1 - e_w)(1 - e_O) + e_w$$
$$= 1 - e_O(1 - e_w). \tag{15.5}$$

A word of warning first, about (15.5). Consulting the *General Theory*, Chapter 21, 'The Theory of Prices' one finds on p. 305 the equation

$$e_p = 1 - e_O e_e (1 - e_w) \tag{15.6}$$

and in the previous chapter, on p. 282, our equation (15.5). They cannot both be right, of course, unless $e_e \equiv 1$: which, it turns out, it can be,[3] but then it shouldn't be there.

Keynes later called the equation 'unsatisfactory' (*C.W.*XIV). In the new edition of the *General Theory* (1973), though the reader is warned about it in a mild way (p. 385), it remains to bedevil the sharp-eyed and the conscientious.

To return, feeling rather reassured, to equation (15.5) and what it means: let us first discuss the elasticities themselves. These are not elasticities in the way we are accustomed to thinking of them, for they are not necessarily measured along a single *ceteris paribus* function, but may involve points off a function or on a function which has shifted and may even involve more than one functional relationship.

Consider e_w; the response of wages in terms of the aggregate demand and supply diagram (Figure 4.1). Wages are fixed for any particular Z function, implying $e_w = 0$. But there is no need to fix e_w at zero. If wages can vary in response to increased demand for the final product, the whole set of aggregate supply curves to the left of Z_{FE} may be brought into play; expansion only follows a given Z curve if it begins with unemployment — or remains at full employment before and after expansion (when it follows Z_{FE}).

Aggregate supply and demand analysis is not, therefore, adequate to the task of determining the relative importance of price and quantity in expansion except in the restrictive case in which expansion is along a given Z. Equation (15.5) provides a starting-point.[4] First notice that any rise in demand must be absorbed in either a price or an output change, thus, if we use consistent units for the measurement of demand,

$$e_p + e_O' = 1. \tag{15.7}$$

Determining the size of e_p is, therefore, sufficient to infer the 'real' implications of expansion also.

Note that it is e_O' which appears in (15.7), not e_O which is used to derive (15.5). Precisely because one cannnot infer e_O from e_p one has the freedom to introduce the factor which brings them together, namely the behaviour of wages.

e_p and e_O have to do with the properties of movements along Z and Z_w, respectively, provoked by rises in (expected) D and D_w. If increasing returns are ruled out (some may not wish to do that), e_p is constrained to be non-negative.

The output elasticity, e_O, is essentially physical or technological. The way the units are defined it cannot exceed unity. It is zero when, no matter how much demand is expected to rise and how profitable it might be to expand production, something impedes that rise in output. There are two possible barriers: full utilisation of plant and equipment, or absolute unavailability of additional labour.[5] If labour's price expectations are static, the labour constraint corresponds to the point at which the labour supply curve bends backward: the point of absolute full employment. Raising the wage will do nothing to alleviate the shortage. Hence this cause for a zero value of e_O is independent of e_w.

Full capital capacity is a more slippery concept, as the capital does not have the choice of withdrawing its services (I nearly said its labour). There may be a point at which further additions of variable factors will achieve no greater output, but it is unnecessarily limiting to choose this purely technical or physical concept. Full capacity must also take into account user cost, unfortunately not explicit in these elasticities. Capital may be worked flat out and not maintained (as can slave labour), but its life is shortened by so doing. Full capacity is thus the point where the profit expected from the sale of additional output is exactly matched by marginal user cost on the assumption that demand will, after the shift expected in the current period, continue at the new level indefinitely. This point may be reached before the marginal product of labour attached to this capital falls to zero or before absolute full employment is reached.

The response of output to a rise in *money* demand, e_O', is not entirely technological; the elasticity of demand also enters the picture. It is possible, therefore, for e_O' to be negative: there are instances when the appropriate response of a monopolist to a rise in demand is to raise price and lower output. At the aggregate level this response is probably unlikely, even in an economy of large corporations, in the absence of rising wages.

The extent to which a rise in demand is absorbed in a rise in wages is given by e_w. $e_w = 0$ indicates expansion 'behind the labour supply curve'. When $e_w = 1$, wages absorb the whole of an increase in demand, leaving no profit as reward for expansion. If $e_w = 1$, then even if the equipment is underutilised in the above sense it will not be worth expanding; the entire product of expansion is consumed by higher prime costs. Thus, no matter what is physically possible, if $e_w = 1$ the entrepreneur gains nothing by expansion as all potential profits are absorbed by increased costs.

e_w is a complex concept, involving both the production function and the labour supply curve. Points behind the labour supply curve are also involved.
If we let

$$e_s = \frac{d \log w}{d \log N},$$

and

$$e_N = \frac{d \log N}{d \log O},$$

and e_O' is defined as before, then

$$e_w = e_s \cdot e_N \cdot e_O'. \tag{15.8}$$

Read these elasticities from right to left. For the moment e_O' shall be interpreted purely hypothetically, not as an actual or optimal reaction, and set at unity in order to pose the question, 'If we expand output *pari passu* with the increased sales we anticipate, what are the consequences?' The consequences are given by the implications of that decision for the necessary increase in offers of employment (e_N) and the wage necessary to get the labour (e_s).

e_N is a measure along the inverse of the short-run production function. Its magnitude is given by the extent of diminishing returns. Constant returns give an e_N of 1 (output rises in proportion to the proportional increase in employment) and for diminishing returns it rises until it reaches infinity at full capital capacity, where no amount of additional labour can increase output.

e_s may appear to measure the elasticity of the labour supply curve, but it is a more flexible concept than that. It may be measured from behind the labour-supply frontier to a point on it at or above the initial wage, or it may be measured along the labour supply curve itself, if we have begun with full employment. If there is unemployment to start with and, at most, just-full employment to end with, e_s is zero. Along the upward-sloping supply curve, e_s is positive. It becomes infinite only when additional labour is quite unavailable (in which case $e_O = 0$ anyway).

So in general there is nothing in $e_s \cdot e_N$ to limit e_w to 1. If $e_w > 1$, however, output will have to fall in response to a rise in demand, and prices rise more than proportionately. Now e_w may well exceed unity when the supply-of-labour curve shifts in a cost-push inflation. We shall return to that case. However, as a *response* to a rise in demand unity can be taken as the upper limit with reasonable safety.

The limits to the main elasticities can thus be seen most likely to be zero and unity. These were the limits Keynes took for granted. It is interesting to see what results one obtains from looking at the extremes.

The Extreme Cases

It can be seen from equation (15.5) that if a rise in demand is to go to waste entirely in inflation $(e_p = 1)$, then either $e_O = 0$ or $e_w = 1$. If the result is to be exclusively a real output rise $(e_p = 0)$, the conditions $e_O = 1$ and $e_w = 0$ must *both* be met.

These two extremes are often labelled the 'Classical' and 'Keynesian' cases. It can be seen that they are both quite special. It is particularly obvious that identifying 'Keynesian economics' with the assumption of fixed prices up to full employment (of labour) and 'Classical' behaviour with a fixed level of full-employment output is to assume a sharp discontinuity of short-run costs, due either to reaching capital capacity at the same level of output which fully employs the labour supply at the current wage (which would only be a coincidence), or to reaching absolute full employment (in the 'point of inflexion' sense) at the current wage — and there is no reason to presume that this can be achieved.

No wonder there have been so many *ad hoc* assumptions in defence of price stability in neoclassical Keynesianism: it is quite obvious that in the general case a rise in demand will affect *both* price and output and that the question of how much of each requires more than a mechanistic simultaneous-equation model for an intelligent reply. And all this before abandoning the assumptions of the short run and a relatively fixed money supply!

The Middle Ground

The advantage of this framework is precisely what Friedman dislikes about it (see note 4): it requires empirical information to complete the explanation of price and output changes. It is obvious that the relevant elasticities differ both as between the theoretical long and short runs, and also over the cycle and in different historical episodes. One expects e_w to be quite low in recessions and to rise in booms, though generally remaining less than one until returns diminish sufficiently to make the labour requirement excessive; it seems unlikely that labour supply will ever become completely inelastic.

Cyclical variations are also manifest in e_o when the user cost of capital is taken into account. In depressed conditions, the user cost of idle machinery is virtually zero. An expectation of more or less permanent improvement in demand makes expansion more likely, but also begins to bring user cost into the picture. User cost is still, however, very low compared to its level in boom conditions, with a high rate of utilisation and the expectation of this rate's continuing, for if output is increased, not only is necessary maintenance likely to rise more rapidly the greater the strain on the equipment, but, when its value and replacement cost in subsequent periods are also expected to be high, the desirability of prolonging the life of the equipment is greater. All these factors will increase the level of user cost in booms as compared to recessions, thus contributing to rising prices in booms and to stable prices in recessions, independently of labour costs. In addition, the behaviour of expected prices of raw materials works in the same way to contribute more to user cost in booms than in recessions.

Costs may not be constant, but they are likely to approximate constancy more closely in depressions than in booms, both because of the relative constancy of wages and raw materials prices and because of the behaviour of user cost, thus conforming to the general presumption of small price rises in depressions as compared to booms without the need to invoke either full capacity (of labour or capital) or bottlenecks (which is just full capacity in a subset of industries). Bottlenecks will of course occur and constitute an additional reason for demand to rise before full capacity is reached. But the above analysis is free from the dependence on 'full employment' which characterises the usual explanation. The framework also leaves open the possibility of cost-push factors, ignored or disallowed in the above frame of reference.

The discussion also makes clear the importance of firms' expectations: not only is next period's demand (or that of several periods hence) the starting point of the analysis, but user cost illustrates that price rises expected tomorrow, of capital goods and raw materials, are brought forward into today's prices.

Inflation, True and False

Keynes took for granted the necessity of rising prices as a concomitant to *any* expansion under short-run conditions. However, the price rises necessary to cover diminishing returns were not to be counted as inflation: only when there were price increases with *no* expansion of output had we reached the point of 'true inflation' (*G.T.* p. 303). This language was aimed at the great alarm shown in government circles by the prospect of deficit spending because of its 'inflationary' consequences. By defining 'true inflation' as the extreme in which $e_p = 1$, Keynes managed the trick of putting 'inflationary' in inverted commas, pouring scorn on those simple-minded enough to 'mean by *inflationary* merely that prices are rising' (*G.T.* p. 304). This left him room to point out that increases in employment were attainable without *some* rise in prices only under the (to him implausible) assumption of constant costs.

Shifts in the Labour Supply Curve

It is one thing, however, to say that with unemployed resources price responses to rises in demand are necessary but likely to be slight, and another to pretend that they won't occur at all. The bland assumption of prices which are constant at less than full employment and only rise at (physical) full capacity is responsible for much mischief, for it has suggested that governments can spend with impunity as long as there is slack capacity. In a sense, Keynes's political trick has worked too well. An assumption on which the analysis so far has been based, while made explicitly by Keynes, went unnoticed: the assumption of stability in the supply curve of labour. Keynes commented:

> For the purpose of the real world it is a great fault in the Quantity Theory that it does not distinguish between changes in prices which are a function of changes in output, and those which are a function of changes in the wage-unit.
>
> (*G.T.* p. 209)

Indeed, and the fault of 'Keynesian' theories as well. Keynes, while recognising the distinction, did little to drive it home, for he only elaborated the first source. It was pointed out in Chapter 7 that Keynes's labour supply function presupposed a docile labour force, which was taken by surprise if prices increased. Today's work force is different. Long experience of government commitment to full employment and the recent experience of very high rates of inflation have caused unions to take inflation expectations into account explicitly.

When labour expects prices to rise, the supply curve of labour shifts leftwards. If labour is not organised, a leftward shift in the maximum hours willingly supplied may be irrelevant, for only the maximum is determined by it: if demand remains to the left of the frontier, the obstacles to raising the wage discussed in Chapter 7 apply and e_w is zero. However, when wages are set by union bargaining, the union will usually attempt to obtain for its employed members compensation for the anticipated price rise, despite the existence of unemployed workers. If successful, $e_w > 0$ (e_w is measured between two points on different curves). And a price rise becomes a necessity if firms are to maintain their position. Similarly, if the maximum becomes operative in the non-unionised case, wages must rise and price rises will most likely follow.

Firms can only grant wage increases, however, (i) if they have excess profits and believe that allowing profits to erode by granting a wage increase is better than a strike, or (ii) if they expect demand to rise, which permits the higher prices to go forward. In the postwar history of the British economy, we have experienced quite a bit of case (ii) and some of case (i).

The essence of case (i) is that wages rise in response to an expectation of rising demand, the expectations being held, on balance, by labour. If similar expectations are held by firms (nothing guarantees that they are the same, or that either set of parties is correct) we have case (ii).

Apart from exogenous changes in private demand there are two sources of demand which firms may anticipate if they grant the wage increase. First there is the boost to consumption from the wage rise itself, on the same redistributive grounds as that argued in Chapter 6 but now in the positive direction. The *indirect* effects on demand which occupied Keynes in Chapter 19 are more problematic; it would not be wise to count on the indirect effects.

If these 'bootstrap' effects were all firms could count on, a wage rise would be quite a risk. The wages must be paid out before they have much chance of influencing demand, though some could be spent in anticipation, through the use of consumer loans. More to the point, however, is the fact that firms cannot expect demand for their own product to rise as a result of their own workers' larger incomes and they dare not depend on other firms increasing wages simultaneously, and thus providing the aggregate income necessary to support demand.

Less precarious, between Beveridge[6] and Mrs Thatcher, was the prospect of government support for demand to protect employment. Until recently, this has been forthcoming to at least some degree, whether the initiating cause of unemployment was on the demand or the cost side. (Unemployment can always be seen as a problem of insufficient demand, whatever the prime cause.) If government can be counted upon to compensate for increased costs by 'demand management', firms have less reason to resist wage increases. If government compensates exactly, $e_w = 1$, $e_O = 0$, and $e_p = 1$. (There still remains the problem, due to the fact that there are many firms each producing a limited range of products, that demand may not reach those whose costs have risen. Demand management doesn't work, either, for firms whose demand comes chiefly from abroad.)

The difficulty is that after a time government 'validation' of wage claims begins to be anticipated not just by firms but also by labour, who may adjust claims accordingly. Then one's theory of price and output changes no longer works very well, for labour is guessing (estimating, or anticipating) what they can get from firms and firms are estimating the responses of buyers and (crucially) of government policy.

(The nature of the process is slightly obscured as the bargaining begins with a figure incorporating a mark-up so that a compromise will seem to be the outcome and the government may take a tough line from which it later backs down as the consequences emerge, hoping by bluff to moderate the wage rise.)

If unions push their luck too far and firms misjudge, then $e_w > 1$, $e_O < 1$, $e_p > 1$. Although it is perfectly possible to incorporate these factors into Keynes's approach, game theory might provide a better framework. Keynes's framework is most appropriate when the disturbance arises because of a change in a single expected magnitude (e.g. demand or costs) not complicated by the relevant parties bluffing and second-guessing each other.[7]

It is, however, at least a relief that there is nothing in it which actually *impedes* understanding of the conjunction of unemployment and inflation.[8] The framework performs well compared with that provided by the *IS–LM* model, which predicts price rises only when there is excess demand for labour or an excess supply of money at full employment. Another school,[9] which claims (with justification, but not I think on this particular point) descent from the *General Theory*, asserts that Keynes's theory is that prices depend on wages plus a fixed mark-up, so that prices rise *only* when wages rise, whether wages rise in response to excess demand for labour or autonomously.

Keynes's theory of prices could be said to be based on fairly certain cost data and variable mark-up dependent on expected demand. Costs depend on technology and the prices of labour and raw materials. In the present (1980s) context, technological considerations are insignificant beside the uncertainty surrounding wages and raw materials prices. To explain price-setting in this context it would be necessary to form some view of how all the relevant expectations are formed; Keynes's framework only serves to make that requirement obvious.

Prices in the Longer Run

Outside the confines of the short run, cost functions can shift and capacity
constraints may be released, as past investment projects 'come on-stream'.
In a still longer run, social norms regarding hours of work or composition of
the work force may alter and there will be variations in the birth rate; these
factors will affect the position of the labour supply curve.

Periods of sustained economic expansion are almost always accompanied
by technical change: the rewards to pure capital-widening — increasing the
amount of already-existing types of capital — are less easy to sustain without
an exogenous stimulus to demand (e.g. population growth). Thus in a period
of sustained expansion one might expect costs to fall, as more efficient
techniques displace older ones. It is thus possible to lower supply price and
obtain the higher demand volume necessary to reach the higher level of
production optimal for the new equipment.

If this period should coincide with an influx into the labour force, wage
rises will be moderated, reinforcing the tendency for prices to fall.

As a countervailing force there is the monetary increase which
accompanied the investment and which will not be paid off until the end of
the life of the current stock of equipment, by which time there may be new
investment with an equivalent demand for new credit, or there may be a
slump, and (thinking in terms of a stable money supply as the norm) a
reduction in M as repayment or default write off outstanding credit. All this
is greatly oversimplified, ignoring the process of gradual funding discussed
in the previous chapter.

Considering a once-and-for-all alteration in the volume of investment in
the context of the short run, one can afford to ignore the money-supply
effects of the investment. But in the context of an expansion which is
sustained for any period of time, the money supply is likely to increase
significantly.

The effects of such an increase depend on whether money finds its way
into financial markets or is reflected in a rise in (money-) demand. To
analyse the effects of a monetary increase on prices or output all that is
necessary is to introduce another elasticity,

$$e_D = d \log D / d \log M, \tag{15.9}$$

the response of demand[10] to changes in M, and then proceed as before.

The effect of M on D has three components: (i) the extent to which new
money is absorbed in M_1 or M_2, (ii) the interest-rate effect associated with
absorption into M_2, (iii) the interest-elasticity of investment. Thus it is
possible for e_D to be unity either on the quantity-theoretic grounds that all
ΔM goes into M_1, or for the 'transmission mechanism' to be Keynes's route
through (ii) and (iii) with M_1 playing a purely passive role. (This thought is
developed in Chapter 18.)

If $e_D = 1$, the effects of a monetary increase on price and output depend, as before, on technology and labour-market conditions. For the quantity-theoretic proposition $d \log P/d \log M = 1$ to hold in an ongoing, production economy (as opposed to a comparative-static universe in which all money values are altered overnight), not only must $e_D = 1$ but also e_P must be unity. The short-run requirements necessary for $e_p = 1$ are rather stringent, but in the long run technical change and population growth may outweigh the short-run upward pressures on prices.

At the other extreme, if $e_D = 0$, an increase in M will have no effect at all on demand. This will be the case if (i) all the new money is held idle or (ii) investment is interest-inelastic.

One might reasonably expect e_D usually to lie between zero and one. It will be appreciated that in a sustained expansion, successive monetary increases will operate to raise money-demand and therefore usually both prices and output. Monetary influences thus relieve some or all of the need to lower prices to sell the higher volume optimal for new equipment or extended facilities: they simultaneously oppose the tendency toward lower prices contributed by technical change and enhance the possibility of the success of investment projects. The outcome for prices is of course uncertain.

> ... the long-run relationship between the national income and the quantity of money will depend on liquidity-preferences. And the long-run stability or instability of prices will depend on the strength of the upward trend in [costs] compared with the rate of increase in the efficiency of the productive system.

(*G.T.* p. 309)

The Phillips Curve

To conduct a discussion of price changes with no mention of the Phillips curve might strike the reader as downright odd; since about the mid-1960s economists discussing inflation automatically reach for this tool.

There are several reasons why I have not used it. Fundamentally I do not think it was designed for the job.[11] Secondarily I believe it was seized upon as an explanation in the belief that Keynes's model had no explanation of prices, which in turn is due to leaving out supply and profit-seeking from the *IS–LM* version of Keynes. Adding the Phillips curve (in its Lipsey interpretation) to *IS–LM* to explain prices (or wages) seems to me rather like putting the vitamins back into refined flour and calling the product 'enriched'.

Finally, the elasticities approach of Keynes makes plain to the user the necessity of making a fair number of empirical assumptions, about the state of the labour market, capital capacity and the recent history of capital accumulation and of money. The Phillips curve is a reduced form, compatible with cost-push, demand-pull and monetarist theories of inflation. As a reduced form it has the appeal of simplicity, but in that very simplicity lies the danger of looking only at labour-market factors as determinants of wages and/or prices.

Monetarists emphasise the fact that the original Phillips curve specifies a relation between unemployment (representing the extent of tightness or slack in labour markets) and *money* wages rather than real wages, thus — as they would put it — building money illusion into labour-market behaviour. They recommend adding a price-expectations term to rectify matters. This is all very well in circumstances like those since the late 1960s when price expectations become an active element in wage settlement, but it does little to restore the demand expectations of entrepreneurs to their appropriate primacy and is no better than the money-wage Phillips curve in making explicit allowance for variations in capacity or in rates of monetary expansion.

Notes

1. The derivation of (15.5) follows Friedman (1972), p. 931.

2. There is an implicit assumption of homogeneous labour here. See Chapter 4.

3. e_e is the elasticity of employment with respect to demand in wage-units. Recalling our discussion of wage-units in Chapter 4, it can be seen that $e_e \equiv 1$ provided Z_w goes through the origin, or more properly, since it cannot approach the origin, Z_w is aligned with the origin.

4. Friedman (1972), pp. 930–31) is correct to say, 'The elasticities are simply definitions; the formula connecting them … is a truism derived from … identities'. The analysis *begins* with equation (15.5); it does not end there. The reader may judge for himself Friedman's amusing assessment, 'To regard [the elasticities] as "theoretical underpinning" for Keynes's assumptions about the price level is on a par with regarding $(a + b)^2 = a^2 + 2ab + b^2$ as theoretical underpinning for the law of falling bodies'.

5. One should add for completeness the impossibility of obtaining raw materials.

6. His two Reports: *Social Insurance and Allied Services*, November 1942, and *Full Employment in a Free Society*, 1944, were influential in winning the British Government's commitment to a policy of full employment. The Employment Act of 1944 expressed a similar commitment on the part of the US Government.

7. For an exposition of the poverty of modern theory in explaining modern wage-setting, see Wiles (1973); and 'modern' theory is much less flexible than the approach outlined here.

8. For an exposition of this problem in a manner easily translated into Keynes's framework, see Chick (1973b, pp. 140–45).

9. This school may be represented by the work of S. Weintraub (see, for example, 1958).

10.   Keynes says 'effective demand' (*G. T.* p. 305), but D should refer to expected aggregate demand.

11.   I am persuaded by the argument of Desai (1975), who maintains that the curve does not pertain to events in the time domain: Phillips's technique 'cuts across' cyclical fluctuations and portrays the relation between the rate of change of wages and unemployment independently of the direction from which each level of unemployment has been approached. By taking observations around six representative levels of U such that $\dot{U}$ is on average zero within each of the six samples, the Phillips curve gives the typical relation between $\dot{w}$ and U when the level of U has been at its representative level for some time — an event rarely observed in the time domain.

   Lipsey (1960), on whose interpretation all modern understanding of the Phillips curve is based, presents a justification for Phillips's results which is in the time domain and is thus directly applicable to real-world circumstances over even a short run of data.

   The reader should consult Phillips (1958), Lipsey and Desai and make up his own mind.

Chapter 16

CYCLICAL FLUCTUATIONS

Cycles in Two Contexts

The apparently innocuous opening sentence of 'Notes on the Trade Cycle' (*G.T.* Ch.. 22) indicates the radical difference of Keynes's approach from that of Classical and neoclassical writers:

> Since we claim to have shown in the preceding chapters what determines the volume of employment at any time, it follows, if we are right, that our theory must be capable of explaining the phenomena of the Trade Cycle.
>
> (*G.T.* p. 313)

To Keynes, the Trade Cycle was an integral part of economic experience, something to be understood in the same frame of reference that, to his satisfaction, explained employment and output generally. To a Classical or neoclassical economist, cyclical fluctuations were departures from the norm, temporary aberrations. Their explanation lay in pinpointing what amongst *normal* economic relationships had gone awry. Separate explanations were found, e.g. something in the monetary/credit nexus disturbing the 'normal' relations between productivity and thrift.

Thus Trade Cycle theory could be seen also as contributing to the separation of 'monetary' and 'value' or 'real' theory, which Keynes deplored. To him the monetary system was an ever-present fact of economic life, a fact with real, and sometimes disagreeable, consequences.

Fundamentally, however, the difference can be seen as one of a separation, in the Classical mind, of the long run from events which were seen as temporary departures of no consequence to the characteristics of the long run.

Keynes's view was otherwise: though implicitly he believed in a long run which was essentially stationary, as did Classical economists, both the level

285

of economic welfare which one could attain and the speed with which one approached it were altered by the path taken toward that state. The long run was the outcome of a succession of short runs.

Depressions, therefore, were disastrous not just because of the misery suffered at the time, but for the delay, caused by leaving resources idle, in attaining a better standard of living.[1] There were those who favoured avoiding depressions by preventing overoptimism. They argued for stopping a boom before it had gone far enough to generate a reversal of expectations through disappointment of overoptimistic ones. Keynes inveighed against them on the grounds of social waste, favouring, instead of a discouraging rise in the rate of interest as the boom got underway, *lowering* the rate of interest in order to encourage the boom to continue. For Keynes had an aim:

> I am myself impressed by the great social advantages of increasing the stock of capital until it ceases to be scarce.

> (*G.T.* p. 325)

The trade cycle was an obstacle to that aim, and everything that could be done to encourage full employment should be done. These were the results he envisaged:

> It is, indeed, very possible that the prolongation of approximately full employment over a period of years would be associated in countries so wealthy as Great Britain or the United States with a volume of new investment, assuming the existing propensity to consume, so great that it would eventually lead to a state of full investment in the sense that an aggregate gross yield in excess of replacement cost could no longer be expected on a reasonable calculation from a further increment of durable goods of any type whatever. Moreover, this situation might be reached comparatively soon — say within twenty-five years or less.

> (*G.T.* pp. 323–4)

Trade Cycles

In 1968 there met in London a conference on the subject 'Is the Business Cycle Obsolete?' (Bronfenbrenner (1969)). It concluded that it was not. But that there should have been doubt is sufficient indication that the sense of regularity which had given rise to the description 'cycles' in the first place was no longer secure. It was widely believed in the 1960s that Keynesian intervention had banished cycles.

Keynes was writing with 19th century experience in mind. 19th century fluctuations were regular enough, and they were characterised also by the phenomenon of 'crisis' — a sudden break at the peak precipitating a sharp decline. A similar sharpness was not found as the slump turned into recovery. These were the facts which Keynes sought to place in the framework of his *General Theory*.

On the face of it, the exercise is improbable of success. The *General Theory* contains a full-blown static theory and the beginnings of a process analysis in the multiplier. Where is an explanation of cycles to come from?

One cannot expect a comprehensive theory in a chapter called '*Notes* on the Trade Cycle', but it is interesting to watch Keynes handle his ideas in the cyclical context, and to be able to contrast his approach with later ones (though we shall only touch on that).

The discussion is ordered around the consequences of certain physical facts, which are responsible for the regularity of the cycle, and psychological aspects, which are important in the crisis.

Some Regularities

Let us begin with a falling-off of new investment in capital equipment caused by a fall in the marginal efficiency of capital whose cause for the moment we leave unexplained. Demand is expected to fall and — if for no other reason than the drop in investment — it does so. So the expectation is confirmed and firms decide to retrench.

There are four types of capital, four sorts of investment, involved in that retrenchment and subsequent recovery: capital equipment (quite long-lived) and the three types of capital corresponding to three stages of production: raw materials, work-in-progress and stocks of finished goods.

If the recession is a deep one, the fundamental problem is the running-off of capital equipment. One does not scrap it in a physical sense, but allows it to depreciate with just enough maintenance to keep it productive. Some equipment will be left idle altogether, as production falls off in the face of declining demand. (The multiplier is now working negatively and consumption as well as investment demand is affected.)

With cash flow from sales down and fixed costs unabated there is an urgent need to run down the other forms of capital. But the work-in-progress is still being completed — production has declined, not stopped altogether — so that stocks of finished goods may initially accumulate, given the fall in demand. Orders for raw materials will be sharply curtailed.

Eventually the amount of work-in-progress is consistent with new levels of demand and output and raw materials supplies are at a minimum. If the recession is deep they will stay at these levels until further time has elapsed while capital equipment further deteriorates. When even the low level of output characterising the trough cannot be sustained with existing capital, replacement investment provides the stimulus for recovery. One can understand why the trough can be so much longer and more level than the peak, and how the shape of the cycle will vary with the durability of capital.

The reader can work out the likely course of the rest of the cycle.

Keynes is offering nothing new here. The importance of this description is to indicate the physical background of psychological and financial events. These latter, not being tied to physical wear and tear and the facts of the production line, are much more volatile. The regularity of the cycle is ascribed to the physical facts, the crisis, and one might say the inception of

the cycle, to the subjectivity and potential volatility of the marginal
efficiency of capital.

Expectations and Crisis

It is in the explanation of the downturn that Keynes sets himself against the
then-prevailing theory, which inclined to view cycles in general and the crisis
in particular in terms of the rate of interest. Now investment is a function of
the supply price of capital, the rate of interest and long-term expectations,
and Keynes admits that the rise in the first two of these as an upswing
proceeds[2] is discouraging for investment. But it is to a collapse of the
marginal efficiency of capital that Keynes directs his attention.

This is where the amusement starts, for the *mec*, in this connection, could
refer to one of two things. A problem (I see it as a problem) passed over in
Chapters 10 and 11 concerns Keynes's treatment of the demand for equities
and capital equipment, both in terms of the marginal efficiency of capital.

The case for doing so, I suppose, is that the expected income from equity-
holding is related to expected profits. In Chapters 10 and 11 dividends were
treated like interest, because the subject was the attraction of these
securities to holders. From the point of view of the firm, however, the cost of
borrowing by rights issues is represented by the price of shares. A fall in
expected profits, which is the key component of the *mec*, lowers equity
prices. From the point of view of the impact on investment, a fall in *mec* is
equivalent to a rise in the rate of interest.

The next chapter goes into detail about why they should be treated
separately, but that can wait. The important thing for present purposes is
that it is not clear whether in Keynes's view it is the collapse of stock market
prices or of entrepreneurs' long-term expectations of demand that really
causes the trouble.

One passage clearly points to producers' expectations:

> The disillusion comes because doubts suddenly arise concerning the reliability of
> the prospective yield, perhaps because the current yield shows signs of falling off,
> as the stock of newly produced durable goods steadily increases. If current costs of
> production are thought to be higher than they will be later on, that will be a
> further reason for a fall in the marginal efficiency of capital.
>
> (*G.T.* p. 317)

A rudimentary accelerator mechanism is encapsulated in that passage.

Elsewhere however, it is the stock market which is at fault:

> It is the nature of organised investment markets, under the influence of
> purchasers largely ignorant of what they are buying and of speculators who are
> more concerned with forecasting the next shift of market sentiment that with a
> reasonable estimate of the future yield of capital-assets, that, when disillusion
> falls upon an over-optimistic and over-bought market, it should fall with sudden
> and even catastrophic force.
>
> (*G.T.* pp. 315–16)

A footnote to the above passage resolves this issue:

... although the private investor is seldom himself directly responsible for new investment, nevertheless the entrepreneurs, who are directly responsible, will find it financially advantageous, and often unavoidable, to fall in with the ideas of the market, even though they themselves are better instructed.

The collapse of stock market prices has further repercussions: an adverse shift in the propensity to consume and a rise in liquidity preference because of increased uncertainty. The first further depresses demand directly and the second results in a fall in the willingness to lend which prevents a helpful fall in the rate of interest and may even cause the rate to rise.

Which way the rate of interest goes depends on the demand for funds. Keynes states that it will rise. Perhaps he had in the back of his mind that the fall in the demand for investment finance would be counterbalanced by distress borrowing from either entrepreneurs or stock market speculators.

The absolute direction of the rate of interest is a point of detail. The essential point Keynes wishes to press is that it is the collapse of profit expectations, not a rise in the rate of interest, which to his mind is the cause of the crisis. Here he opposes the monetary approach to the trade cycle and its policy conclusion: that a policy of lower interest rates is sufficient to start recovery.

Investment demand is a function of two variables, the *mec* and *r*. It is (in Keynes's view) a downward-sloping function of *r*, so in principle there is nothing perverse in a policy of low interest rates as a stimulatory device; it is just that the function has also shifted to the left, probably far enough to nullify any interest-rate effect. And the flight toward liquidity is meanwhile making a policy of low interest rates extremely difficult to carry out.

Describing the behaviour of the stock market, based on more capricious and violent expectations than those producers are likely to have, as fluctuations in the *mec*, adds great force to Keynes's argument, addressed to an audience with a clear memory of 1929.

The downturn however does not *depend* on stock-market disillusions. The short-run factor of rising supply price and the long-run factor of declining *mec* as the stock of capital rises over a substantial period would be sufficient, though the result of the operation of these factors is likely to be undramatic. It is the special contribution of the financial side to transform a gradual downturn into a sharp crisis.

Multiplier-Accelerator Interaction

Separating the 'real' influences from the financial analytically (though recognising their symbiosis) allows an evaluation by contrast of the most popular simple explanation of the cycle: the multiplier-accelerator theory. Modern trade-cycle theory is far richer than the simple models which bear that name, but they suit our purpose, which is to compare and contrast a popular theory with Keynes's framework.

Samuelson saw his celebrated article (1939) in the following terms: the multiplier was all very well but did not explain the thing to be multiplied, namely investment.

Formally, this was his model:

$$C_t = \alpha Y_{t-1} \qquad \qquad (16.1)$$

$$I_t = \beta(C_t - C_{t-1})$$

$$\quad = \alpha\beta(Y_{t-1} - Y_{t-2}). \qquad \qquad (16.2)$$

With government expenditure set at unity, the definition

$$Y_t = C_t + I_t + G_t \qquad \qquad (16.3)$$

and the two previous equations give

$$Y_t = 1 + \alpha(1 + \beta)Y_{t-1} - \alpha\beta Y_{t-2}. \qquad \qquad (16.4)$$

This model has several interesting properties. It will be seen from equation (16.1) that the consumption function is of the microeconomic, loanable-funds type. Investment is assumed to be a function of current and past levels of final demand: investment is undertaken to produce consumption goods. In terms of the scheme presented in Chapter 14, however, current investment is decided on the basis of a level of demand which· cannot possibly be known: C_t and I_t are concurrent. Producers' expectations, whether long-term or short-term, are conspicuously absent. These features are distinctly unKeynesian.

Minor modifications made in the light of previous discussions of these points (in Chapters 9 and 14) can be made without altering the crucial equation (16.4). Let us substitute the hypotheses

$$C_t = bY_t \qquad \qquad (16.1a)$$

and

$$I_t = v(Y_{t-1} - Y_{t-2}) \qquad \qquad (16.2a)$$

and retain the assumption that $G_t = 1$. Substitution into (16.3) gives

$$Y_t = \frac{1}{1-b} + \frac{v}{1-b}(Y_{t-1} - Y_{t-2}), \qquad \qquad (16.4a)$$

an equation identical in form to (16.4).

Second-order difference equations like (16.4) or (16.4a) can do most things imaginable, depending on the relationship between α and β (in 16.4) or b and v (in 16.4a): the path of Y can converge, explode, or oscillate. Because it can oscillate, this model became associated with trade cycle theory, indeed one could say it is the centrepiece of modern trade cycle theory. The fact that the model can generate an explosive path for Y was distressing, but a full-employment ceiling and a floor given by zero gross investment contained its more disagreeable results.

Now this is most unfair to cycle theory[3], as I warned, but the essential character of the theory is clear enough:

(i) It is essentially to do with expenditure decisions. Aggregate supply plays no significant role: hence the absence of any explicit treatment of short-term expectations. It must be assumed that they are met, and since prices do not enter the model, they are met by changes in output.

(ii) The question of long-term expectations is also omitted, though it can be incorporated, as we have shown.

(iii) Financial factors — speculation and anything else to do with money — are entirely absent. The cause of the asymmetry associated with the 'crisis' proposed by Keynes is not present, and there is nothing to supplant it.

(iv) Decisions to invest are geared to output by a fixed capital output ratio, v. This implies that capital is scrapped rather than left underutilised when demand falls. The story linking the length of the cycle to the average life of capital equipment cannot be told.

(v) The theory is mechanical. By this I mean that given the parameters and initial conditions (the first two levels of income) it can be entirely worked out. It is what Shackle (1965, p. 125) calls an 'engine', a theory which depends 'for its whole cycle of phases, its whole pattern of movement, on a single principle of design'. There is no learning, no alteration of the way expectations are formed (if we reconstruct the theory to admit them at all).

This failure contrasts most sharply with Keynes's treatment. Notice that consequent on the fall in *mec*, both the propensity to consume and liquidity preference shifted as well. Inventory-control policies are also changing throughout the cycle.

Keynes's cycle theory is the premier example of what in Chapter 2 we called shifting equilibrium. The interactions amongst key behavioural relations share with the financial aspect responsibility for the asymmetry between the precipitous downturn and gradual upturn. The financial and real aspects are fully integrated.

Absent, however, are the possibilities of financial implosion due to increased burden of debt, as emphasised by Irving Fisher (1933) and Hyman Minsky,[4] or of bank failures, so important in 'the Great Contraction'[5] in the United States.[6]

It may well be, as Minsky has recently argued,[7] that we have learned to avoid financial implosions by taking deliberate and quite massive steps to supply liquidity at dangerous times. The 'lifeboat' operation in England[8] in the crisis of 1974–75 is a case in point. However, it is probably premature to ask 'Is the crisis obsolete?'

Notes

1. This idea was successfully impressed on the American mind in the early 1960s by Arthur Okun, though by then continuous growth, never settling to a stationary state, had become the accepted norm.

2. The supply price of capital rises as the capital-goods industries work at close to full capacity; the interest rate rises as the demand for money to support increased activity rises.

3. For a suitable corrective read Matthews' superb book (1959) and the readings edited by Gordon and Klein (1966).

4. A collection of Minsky's essays on this topic is due to be published this year (Minsky, 1982).

5. The title of the chapter dealing with 1929–33 in Friedman and Schwartz's *Monetary History of the United States* (1965).

6. See Kindleberger (1978) for a survey and analysis of crises in Europe and America from the 18th century onwards.

7. Paper delivered to a seminar at Rutgers University, April 1981.

8. See Bank of England (1978).

Chapter *17*

MONEY

Money's influence is pervasive in Keynes's theory of production and employment. The quantity of money and liquidity preference determine the interest rate with all that entails. And its sheer *existence* is instrumental in establishing first the possibility of involuntary unemployment and then both the possibility and the *likelihood* of underemployment equilibrium — even, perhaps, its inevitability. A money economy is fundamentally different from a barter economy.

Since we live in a money economy, it is well to contemplate its fate. Keynes's answer, that the desire to save would eventually outstrip profitable outlets for saving in investment, leading to income's being depressed below the full employment level — the 'secular stagnation' hypothesis — fell very much out of favour in the 1960s, when it was believed that economic growth could go on forever. However disagreeable Keynes's forecast, his rigorous argument should be examined and its implications evaluated on the argument's own terms rather than being dismissed out of hand as has been the case for many years. The argument just might have something to reveal which the rapid technological advances of the 1950s and 60s obscured.

Before addressing this issue, which requires a long-term perspective, it seems advisable to summarise the role of money in establishing the possibility that unemployment is not merely a phenomenon of temporary dislocations.

Money and Say's Law

To establish the possibility of involuntary unemployment, Say's Law had to be refuted. The refutation proceeded in three parts, and three different

293

levels of analysis. They were discussed separately, in Chapters 4, 7 and 9 above, but it is perhaps useful to summarise the arguments of those chapters in one place, in order to concentrate on the role of money at each stage of the analysis. In the interest of brevity, however, oversimplification is inevitable.

The simplest statement of Say's Law is such as might apply to an economy close to subsistence: labour works only to consume, therefore an offer to work is equivalent to expressing an intention to buy goods, and so there can be no hesitation in offering employment to willing workers, for the demand for their output is assured.

It can be objected immediately that workers do not always spend all of their income, but that is the second phase of the story. Suppose they do. How can employers infer that offers of employment will generate demand? If workers are paid in kind, it is conceivable that they receive directly, as payment, the goods they wish to consume. In that circumstance, not only do employers know the demand implications of the labour they hire, but labour also knows the consumption potential of an hour's work; i.e. labour is demanded and supplied for a real wage which is *known* to both parties.

Under this most favourable, but completely abstract, circumstance the stop to expansion occurs when the fall in the real wage due to diminishing returns is sufficient to discourage labour from further work: the Classical full-employment equilibrium. In practical terms, however, these conditions will never be met, even in a barter economy: man, not wishing to live by bread alone, will trade the goods he receives, and he can only estimate their exchange value. In a period of great price stability the estimate will not be difficult to make, and we approximate to the first case, but one cannot generalise from that particular situation. Where workers are typically paid in *money* the entire 'real' value of the wage is, at the time of agreeing to work, a matter of conjecture. The worker cannot *know* his real wage before committing his labour.

Nor can the employer know, from the fact of being able to obtain further man-hours, that the expenditure on this labour will be reflected in sales. Workers do not buy only from their employers — indeed, if the firm produces capital goods, they do not buy from them at all. For the individual firm the profitability of expanding employment is as conjectural as the real value of the firm's wage offer is to the worker. Thus the mixture of outputs may not coincide with the composition of demand. In a money economy, however, the problem may not be only one of composition (or, as a reflection of this, relative prices of goods may not be such as to equate supply and demand). In a money economy not only may individual firms' expectations be falsified: there is no guarantee, as Say's Law requires, that *aggregate* expenditure will be as much as firms, taken on average, expected when the employment was offered.

This result depends importantly on the fact that the existence of money offers a way of 'storing wealth' additional to holding real assets. In an

economy without money the only way of securing a degree of independence
between consumption and income is to lend either one's labour or durable
goods against promises of repayment (again in kind). (These arrangements
will usually be found even in simple economies, for without them,
production would virtually be limited to the results of self-sufficient efforts,
because different things take different lengths of time both to produce and to
consume.) The offer of labour is an indication of present or future demand,
and the timing and commodity-composition of future demand is to a fair
degree specified or understood implicitly. The option of holding money
opens up the possibility of giving no signal at all about either the timing or
the composition of future demands.

Classical theory would have it that money is *not* held for the purpose of
changing the timing of consumption (i.e. 'holding wealth'), because there
exists the possibility of lending it out at interest. Money however is a safe
asset, even if it is barren, and under some expectations, the risks of holding
interest-bearing assets are not adequately compensated by interest earnings.
So it is that money can be withdrawn from the spending stream for long
enough to cause trouble, and so it is that the rate of interest may be too high
to make the full-employment volume of investment profitable to undertake.

Chapter 17: The Essential Properties of Interest and Money

In the chapter most disliked by early commentators on the *General Theory*,[1]
Keynes returns to these questions from a different perspective. The theory
of money as Keynes used it to break Say's Law could be viewed in a purely
temporary context. This in fact became an established interpretation: some
money might be siphoned off into idle balances for a time but eventually it
would return to the flow of expenditure and income, either simply because
all monetary wealth is accumulated only to be spent and the time must come
for it to be exchanged for goods, or because the persistence of a given rate of
interest consistent with a particular volume of idle balances and quantity of
money will gradually alter the normal rate of interest toward the actual rate
until the idle balances are disgorged.

The first argument is an invalid generalisation from individual behaviour:
an individual will eventually spend his savings, but rarely does society do so.
The second, which is the modern neoclassicist's main way of emasculating
speculative demand and its implications, depends on there having been
enough observations of a stable rate of interest for that rate to be taken as
'normal'. The disappearance of idle holdings of money when people are no
longer uncertain about the rate is obvious,[2] but certainty is hardly the
framework of Keynes's theory — or of reality, once rates, fixed during the
war and recovery, were freed in the early 1950s. Instead it represents the
reassertion of the conditions which led pre-Keynesian economists to deny a

rationale for idle balances. Keynes's theory depends on uncertainty, created by the rate's variability.

Equilibrium in Keynes's macroeconomics is not defined by absence of all variation, either of the variables or opinions about their future course. In the real world, variation and thus uncertainty are ever present, only rising and falling in importance with general conditions of stability, and Keynes's static and stationary models were built to accommodate that fact. Idle balances, therefore, are quite consistent with the (Marshallian) short-run equilibrium system developed in the bulk of the book. What that system says is that if aggregate demand is not adequate to produce full employment, it is no good looking to potential consumption to fill the gap. And investment will stay put as long as interest rates and the *mec* (or long-run expectations) remain unaltered. There is nothing inherent in the system which *will* alter them. Hence the unemployment will remain, in the absence of intervention, for as long as the expectations which govern investment remain as they are — and that could be quite a long time.

The 'shifting-equilibrium' model discussed in Chapter 16, though sketchy in the *General Theory*, deals with *revisions* of expectations about such things as the normal rate of interest and the marginal efficiency of capital. It admits into the analysis for the first time the effect of the gradual accumulation of capital on the rate of output and the marginal efficiency of capital.

Chapter 17 takes up in earnest this long-run phenomenon. Within this context Keynes asks, not whether unemployment equilibrium is *possible*, for that has already been established, but whether the system will tend toward this solution ultimately (even if full employment is occasionally attained in the short run).

In asking this question the Classical assertion of long-run full employment is challenged at yet another, and deeper, level. Keynes's answer was that it was highly unlikely that the profitability of investment would continue to provide sufficient incentive to invest until the aggregate desire of savers to accumulate wealth, out of a full-employment income, is satiated. This is because (Keynes argues) there is something inherent in a money economy which is likely to keep the rate of interest 'too high' to sustain the requisite profitability of investment until the desire to accumulate is satisfied at full-employment income. The problem is related to the existence of 'any asset of which the own-rate of interest is reluctant to decline as output increases' (*G.T.* p. 229). In a money economy, he concludes, that asset is most likely to be money.

The argument proceeds in a manner that is not easy to follow as Keynes developed it, partly because there are some logical difficulties, at least some of which have now been cleared up,[3] and partly because the structure of his argument is not transparently clear. Broadly, he begins with the question 'What is special about the rate of interest?' That is answered by the further questions 'What is special about money? What are money's essential properties?' From these questions he draws the implications for the functioning and long-term direction of the economic system which I think we should consider for their contemporary relevance. So I ask the reader's indulgence as we plunge into a rather arcane discussion, the object of which can only emerge at the end.

The Concept of Interest Generalised

The terms of the enquiry are entirely general: money is the medium of exchange and there exist widespread markets for claims on future sums of money which could be used by firms or individuals to enable purchases to exceed current income, and for which interest was paid as consideration.

It is this rate of interest which determines, given the marginal efficiency of capital, the pace of investment. Why? What is so special about the rate of interest on *money?* After all, any asset has an implicit rate of interest, for just as the rate of interest on money is 'the percentage excess of a sum of money contracted for forward delivery, e.g. a year hence, over ... the "spot" [current] price of the sum thus contracted for forward delivery', there is 'a definite quantity of (e.g.) wheat to be delivered a year hence which has the same exchange value today as 100 quarters of wheat for "spot" delivery' (*G.T.* p. 222).

In principle one could use any such 'rate of interest' as the standard against which to measure the marginal efficiency of capital, to determine whether the investment in question is worth undertaking. It is proper to use the highest such 'interest rate' as the test of any potential investment: if one can do better than the expected yield on the proposed investment it should not be undertaken. The argument goes on to give reasons to expect that as time goes on and capital accumulates, the rate of interest on money is likely to become the highest of these rates and thus the appropriate standard of comparison. Keynes then argues that the properties of money are such that the rate of interest is not likely to fall sufficiently to provide a full-employment level of investment in the long run.

A General Theory of Asset-Holding: If there were no durable assets, and no binding promises to deliver future goods, there would be no way to transcend current income; consumption and production would be as inseparable as they are for, say, electricity. As it is, there are three main ways of converting current resources into future assets (and sometimes *vice versa*):

(i)   borrowing and lending;

(ii) buying or making a durable asset to hold (a) for later final consumption or (b) for resale; or

(iii) using a capital asset to produce final goods for future sale.

These options are not all freely open to firms and households alike. By assumption, firms are not final consumers and households are not producers, so while both may borrow and lend, or hold assets for resale, option (ii)(a) is only open to households and (iii) is only open to firms.

An individual household or firm may, in considering the options open to it, evaluate the net rate of return to be derived from holding each asset now rather than postponing accumulation for some fixed period, say one year. The net rate of return of any asset can be calculated in principle, even where most of the elements are subjective or where resale and future markets in the asset are thin or non-existent, and converted to the dimensions of an interest rate. Again in principle, the net rate of return may be measured in terms of the asset itself or in terms of some other asset such as money. Keynes began by using the first measure, which he called the 'own-rate of interest'. It was not an auspicious beginning to the chapter: the concept attracted much criticism.[4] But with the clarifying work of Conard (1963) and a change of terminology we may begin on the same basis in comparative safety.

Three main elements enter into the determination of the net benefit of holding an asset. Each asset has a *yield, q,* in terms of direct satisfaction or capacity to produce saleable output. It also has *carrying costs, c,* arising from the need to house or store the asset safely. And it may also have a *liquidity premium, l.* Since we are dealing in own-rates, *l* is pure marketability — the ease of exchanging the asset for something else. This is determined by the asset's inherent properties, e.g. divisibility, not with the price it might fetch. The 'own-rate of interest', that is the net rate of return on holding an asset for some specified period, measured in terms of itself, is the sum

$$q - c + l,$$

each defined as a rate of return for that period.

To convert these 'own-rates' into comparable units, add a factor a to indicate the expected appreciation (or depreciation) of the asset in terms of some asset chosen as numeraire. If money is the numeraire, a is the expected change of the money price of the asset over the period. Thus l plus a resembles the more usual definition of liquidity: the ease of conversion into money without loss.

A durable final-consumption good has an expected yield in terms of direct services. Its carrying cost is likely to be high and not independent of the possession of other assets (such as a house) which provide storage. The liquidity of such assets varies: it may be quite high for antique furniture or paintings but low for more mundane household durables.

A piece of productive capital equipment has two possible sources of return, as did the consumer durable: resale of the equipment itself or sale of its product. A firm deciding to buy a piece of producer's capital for use in production does so on criteria similar to those outlined in the chapter on investment, but modified to suit a subtly different question. The theory of investment posed the question 'how much capital will it be profitable to buy now, assuming the machinery then remains in our possession indefinitely'. Now the question is 'what is the return from buying this piece of equipment today rather than next year at this time' or 'what is the return from continuing to hold this piece of equipment for the year rather than selling or scrapping it'.[5] Carrying costs were ignored in developing the *mec*; and a mention of the possibility of a positive scrap value was as close as one got to considering the liquidity of equipment. Here these factors are taken into account.

The other set of asset choices comprises various financial assets: claims on real assets (equities) or on future delivery of money (debts), and 'spot cash'. The yields are (expected) money sums, except for that on money, which has no explicit yield. Carrying costs are lower and liquidity higher than on real assets. Money is held entirely for its liquidity: its exchangeability for other things.

It follows from the principle of maximisation of net advantage[6] that resources not wanted for the current purchase of perishable commodities will be allocated amongst the available assets by comparing their net returns. Demand will fall on those assets whose rates of return are highest. The immediate effect is to raise the prices of those assets with above-average rates of return and lower the prices of those with below average returns, until rates of return are equalised.

Produced Assets and Existing Stocks

The story does not stop at equal rates of return where some of the assets are objects capable of new production. Most producers' capital is capable of being newly-produced, and the process involves the employment of labour. In contrast, financial assets, which in this framework serve as an alternative use of funds, are capable of expansion any time some economic agent wants to go into debt and can find a willing lender, but the process of expansion does not contribute to aggregate income, except to the extent of the services of the engravers, printers and merchant bankers, the latter of which market the 'product'. The face value of a financial asset is, however, no more than a *claim* on product or capital; in that sense the financial claim is not a 'produced asset'.

For simplicity, treat the volume of outstanding financial claims as fixed. Similarly, though for additional reasons which will be explored later, treat the 'stock of money' as fixed. These assets, then, are 'non-produced'.

When the price of a produced asset rises, reflecting a favourable assessment of its net rate of return, there is an incentive for its producers to expand production. If some consumer is willing to buy a durable asset at a price sufficient to induce its production, output of consumption goods will increase. Similarly, if an entrepreneur thinks it sufficiently worthwhile to 'hold' a productive asset, he may choose to use some of his own firm's labour to build the equipment or structure, or he may buy it from another firm. Thus the marginal efficiency of capital gives a criterion for the willingness to hold the asset, on the part of the firm contemplating purchase, but also embodies in the supply price of capital, the willingness to supply an asset, based on the expectation of that willingness to hold.

Conard (1963) emphasises the conceptual difference between holding an asset for final use or resale and holding it to make a profit on the output, calling the return on the first the marginal efficiency of holding and on the second the marginal efficiency of investment (which is equivalent to our *mec*). This is useful in that it distinguishes very different sources of returns, the latter of which is only open to firms.[7] But at the same time, it obscures the significance, to the producers, of the willingness to hold on the part of *others*, to whom they wish to sell. This is the critical link between the 'stock' approach of asset choice and the generation of income, for consumption as well as investment.

The Timing of Purchases: Although couched in terms of the choice among stocks of assets, the net rate of return explains not only why but *when* things are purchased. If all alternatives to holding money have a lower yield than money's liquidity premium (taking money's carrying cost to be zero), then money will be held idle rather than spent, *this year*. Its owner prefers to keep his purchasing options open for that length of time at least. Purchases occur when the net return to owning something now, for the next year, exceeds money's liquidity premium, l_m.

Similarly money is lent when the net benefit of owning a security exceeds l_m. The return on securities is 'the rate of interest' and there is virtually no carrying cost, so one may conclude that lending will continue until the rate of interest is equal to l_m. When it has reached equality with l_m, it no longer compensates for the loss of liquidity involved in parting with money: this is Keynes's theory of interest from another perspective.

Falling Rate of Return in the Short Run: Now consider the implications of the connection between asset-holding and output in a 'period' longer than the market period which first occupied our attention. In the market period, prices move so as to equate rates of return. Those firms which produce the favoured assets now have an incentive to produce more of them. This expansion involves a higher level of employment. Thus if full employment is to be attained, the gap between the return on produced assets and the rate of interest must not close before full employment is reached.

Why should it ever close? Keynes's answer was that there were reasons to believe that the rate of interest would not fall as rapidly as the rate of return on produced goods. This may be analysed in two parts: first, why are rates of return on produced goods likely to fall, and second, why is the rate of interest relatively loath to fall?

The first part of the question has both a short-run and a long-run aspect, of which only the long run is discussed in (*G.T.*) Chapter 17. This is because 'assets' have not been defined to encompass consumer durables, in accordance with the definition of consumption in the rest of the book. But here the 'durability' criterion (see Chapter 3) is relevant. In the short run the capital stock is fixed (despite the fact that investment is going on), so the adjustment of rates of return on capital assets must occur through price changes.

Now suppose output is increased. The production of additional consumption goods does not, however, guarantee their sale: the marginal propensity to consume is less than one and the gap between *C* and *Y* increases as *C* and *Y* rise. In present language, the marginal efficiency of holding consumption goods declines with the size of holdings, either because the marginal utility of their services declines or because storage costs increase. Thus the greater the output of consumption goods the more difficult these goods are to sell and the less worthwhile is further expansion of output and employment in the consumption-goods industries. In turn it becomes less profitable for the consumption-goods industries to invest and for the capital-goods industries to expand capacity to meet the other industries' demands for equipment.

In the short run, whether or not one gets full employment depends on the level of investment that equates *mec* with *r*; it was established earlier, in other language, that it is only accidental if that level gives full employment.

The translation of short-run propositions into the framework of this chapter has been done to mark clearly the methodological departure of Chapter 17. The need to lower prices as output rises is true for both the short and the long run. The salient characteristic of the long run is that the accumulation of capital (through investment) is permitted to affect the return on further additions to the capital stock (partly through the effect on prices which we have just been discussing).

Falling Rates of Return in the Long Run: The marginal efficiency of capital was calculated, in the investment chapter, on the understanding that a certain amount of capital already existed, as is appropriate to the short run. The marginal efficiency of an asset tends, however, to fall as the stock of that asset rises: the asset becomes less scarce and its quasi-rents fall. Another way to look at it is that the effect of accumulation is to increase the output of whatever the asset produces; the demand price of the output thus falls and further investment in the asset becomes less profitable.

The long-run tendency of the marginal efficiency of assets to fall is in practice mitigated or even entirely offset by technological change, which may not only improve the productivity of a kind of capital equipment (indeed it is no longer the same type of capital equipment as before) but may also, by providing new or improved final products, shore up flagging demand. Technological change was such a powerful force in the first two postwar decades that the underlying effect of accumulation on the *mec* was often forgotten or denied, and the fact that technological change is assumed away in Keynes's argument was regarded as a major weakness rather than an assumption whose importance to the argument needed to be assessed. However, technical change is neither an inevitable concommitant of accumulation nor is it explained theoretically: in growth theory it is taken as exogenous. It is best therefore to keep it in mind as a force countervailing the tendency of the marginal efficiency to fall in its absence.

Given a general tendency for the return to investment to fall as output (of capital goods) increases, net new investment will eventually come to a halt unless the rate of interest is falling at least as rapidly as the *mec*. The economy settles down to a stationary state.

The rest of the argument concerns the role of the liquidity-premium attaching to money in preventing *r* from falling below a certain level — and, Keynes thought — that level is too high to permit full employment.

The Downward-Stickiness of Interest Rates

It was established that the rate of interest must tend towards equality with the liquidity premium on money. If *r* is higher than *l*, people are prepared to part with liquidity and buy securities instead, and if it is lower, people will sell securities. (This is assuming that the carrying costs of both these types of assets are similar.) Therefore the question of what will happen to interest rates as output rises ought in principle to be capable of being analysed either from the side of securities or the side of money. Keynes, true to form, analyses from the side of money.

There are two key properties of money in the present connection: that its 'elasticity of production' and its 'elasticity of substitution' are 'zero or at any rate very small'. The first characteristic has several elements. Money is (or rather was) not readily producible by private enterprise, as distinct from the monetary authority, and the production of modern money, unlike metallic money, requires but little labour. Such labour as it does employ is not closely related to the volume of money produced: it is as easy to produce a £10 note as £1. If producing money did use labour, 'if money could be grown like a crop or manufactured like a motor-car' the progressive fall in goods prices as the output and stocks of goods rose would encourage the diversion of labour into the production of money, thus keeping labour employed.

Keynes acknowledges that while inelasticity of supply is (or was) an essential property of money, it is not unique to money. It is shared by assets which are not reproducible, such as old masters or land. Since labour cannot be diverted to their production, the depressing effect of a (long-run) rise in output on the *mec* establishes an upward pressure on the prices of non-reproducible assets, to bring the marginal efficiency of holding those assets into line with the *mec.*

> The second property is the low elasticity of substitution, which follows from the peculiarity of money that its utility is solely derived from its exchange-value, ... with the result that as the exchange value of money rises, there is no tendency to substitute some other factor for it.

(*G.T.* p. 231)

Thus, Keynes argues, the net return from holding money fails to fall while the returns from produced assets do fall as the output of the latter increases. Resources are diverted to money-holding; money can become a 'bottomless sink for purchasing power' — demand fails to continue buoyant until full employment is reached.

The argument seems to be that as the prices of non-money goods decline to enable the sale of larger quantities, people will hold more money instead, for its enhanced exchange value. Something seems wrong here. Though the proposition that money's utility derives solely from its exchange value is indisputable, surely it was a part of the story about the stabilising role of metallic money that when labour was diverted to increasing its supply, the resulting money would be spent, and the profitability of producing non-monetary goods would be restored.[8]

One of the following explanations may appeal. The first is that this is another example of Keynes's separation of money from the act of spending: consumption plans alter with income, not with available money, and the monetary preconditions of investment are not made explicit. The other possibility is that a *continual* decline in prices as output steadily rises has been taken for granted. If this future is anticipated, the incentive to hold money rather than buy things is clear. It must be stressed, however, that the point is not put that way. The assertion is made that 'there is no value for [money] (i.e. there is no level of goods-prices low enough) at which demand is diverted — as in the case of other rent-factors [goods in fixed supply] — so as to slop over into a demand for other things' (G.T. p. 231). That is an assertion about the response to current prices, not expectations.

This point is supposed, in the structure of Keynes's argument, to distinguish money from other non-reproducible goods, but it is doubtful if it in fact does so. It is just as possible for the return from holding land or old masters to rise *pari passu* with their prices. This is more likely if it is assumed that their prices are likely to continue to rise, but with objects having direct utility as well as 'liquidity', even a stable price expectation may suffice.

Any episode of property speculation will demonstrate that land is also capable of being a 'sink for purchasing power' — though whether 'bottomless' is doubtful, as indeed it is doubtful in regard to money.[9] In such an episode people are prepared to pay prices which imply a yield far below any possible direct utility, because of the liquidity premium attaching to land. If this behaviour is sustained, money is siphoned off into an asset which has no elasticity of employment. The money is simultaneously held off the

markets for various lending instruments, thus discouraging investments in
the same way as if the money were held idle.

If land or old masters can play this role, and who doubts that they can,
then the fact that money's utility derives exclusively from its exchange value
does not establish the uniqueness of money, any more than its relative fixity
of supply did. It is a matter of degree — bonds are held for their exchange
value and their income (which, being in money, is also valued for its use in
exchange), land and paintings may be held exclusively for use (by a dynastic
family or a college), exclusively for resale (pure speculation), or some
combination of these motives. The relation between these sources of value
and liquidity needs to be explored at greater length.

Liquidity, Further Examined

Money is always said to be the most liquid asset, even the 'perfectly liquid'
asset. Often, all that is meant is that money is readily marketable; it can
always be exchanged for something else. But most things are marketable,
even things which are described as illiquid, like houses. A house can be sold
very readily, if the price is low enough. It is partly the refusal to accept a
price substantially below what could be obtained by searching for the right
buyer that makes a house 'illiquid'. The other aspect is transactions costs:
selling a house involves estate agents' and solicitors' fees for the seller and
conveyancing fees and stamp duty for the buyer.

The difficulty of realising an 'appropriate' price is related to the 'thinness'
of the market, exacerbated in the case of assets like houses by heterogeneity.
An asset with many ready buyers is not, typically, going to fetch a
significantly higher price with more time spent searching for the marginally
more enthusiastic purchaser. Many financial assets have well-developed and
active 'second-hand' markets; these assets are more liquid than houses. The
shorter the term of the asset, also, the more liquid, for not only is there
certainty of realising par value at maturity, but price variability is less for any
given percentage change in interest rates than it is for long-term securities.

It can be seen from these examples that liquidity has three dimensions: a
probability, a price, and a length of time. The perfectly liquid asset has a
probability of one of realising its full value immediately. Money is the
quintessentially liquid asset in the trivial sense that it is always accepted at
face value. But that may mean nothing other than always being able to
exchange one £ note for another.

It is obvious that all homogeneous assets are perfectly liquid in the sense
that they are exchangeable at par for themselves: there must be more to it
than that. Money is accepted at face value in the sense that money is the
conventional means of payment. But prices of goods are variable; thus
money is not perfectly liquid when measured in terms of the goods it will

buy. Its exchange value is a probabilistic matter. The more stable the price of a good, the more liquid is money in terms of that good — perfectly liquid if the price is *certain* to be stable. Insofar as the variability of prices of different goods in terms of money is not uniform, uncertainty about money's exchange value, and hence an aspect of its liquidity, differs according to the goods ultimately desired.

One can easily imagine that a pair of assets other than money may be more liquid in terms of each other than in terms of money when their prices tend to vary together (e.g. goods that share the same seasonal pattern or real assets in terms of each other during inflation). What this suggests is that the liquidity premium, *l*, and the price-appreciation term, *a*, are not independent. Their interdependence is captured by the statement that a house is more liquid in a rising property market than in one which is stable or falling. If *a* and *l* are not distinct, it follows that the value attached to each is affected by the choice of the numeraire chosen to convert own-rates to a uniform standard. The choice of numeraire is *not*, as was earlier suggested, a matter of neutrality.

The reason money seems a *natural* choice as numeraire is also the source of an aspect of liquidity not exhibited by other assets, deriving from money's function as the medium of exchange. Because most goods exchange for money, prices are typically quoted in money terms, which makes calculating *a* in money terms congenial.[10] But money's general acceptability also genuinely contributes to its liquidity. Because of the wide range of assets for which it is acceptable, holders of money can avoid a loss of exchange value by changing both the timing and the composition of what they purchase to obtain the best advantage.

This property is absent for other assets whose relative prices in terms of a few other assets may even be more stable than money prices, for exchange is usually not direct between those assets; rather one asset is first sold for money and the money is then used to buy the asset desired. Holding assets other than money for their exchange value always brings *two* uncertain prices into play: the money price of the asset sold and the money price of the asset bought. This fact typically makes the exchange value of, say, a house for a yacht more uncertain than the exchange value of money for a yacht.

The transactions costs and the increased uncertainty involved in holding non-money assets for their exchange value limits their liquidity-premium, except when inflation is widely expected. When prices of most things are expected to rise, holding money as a store of value plainly is not desirable, and the property of 'low elasticity of substitution' may shift to real assets: the fact that money is held only for its exchange value does not establish a unique role for money as the 'bottomless sink of purchasing power' and the asset whose yield falls least rapidly. This is an important issue to think about at the present time, and we shall explore it.

Sticky Wages and the Liquidity Premium

Keynes proposed that 'the expectation of a relative stickiness of wages in terms of money is a corollary of the excess of liquidity-premium over carrying costs being greater for money than for any other asset' (*G.T.* p. 238). This is an intriguing proposition in the light of recent history, in which prices and wages have been far from stable and confidence in money has declined, reducing the sphere in which its liquidity premium is superior to other assets. It was implicit in the argument of the previous section that the liquidity premium of an asset is dependent on the stability of prices of goods in terms of that asset for which it might be exchanged — or, as Keynes put it, money's liquidity depends on the expectation that the value of output varies less in terms of money than in terms of other things, as output expands and contracts. For this property to attach to money, he says, two conditions must be met: money wages must be sticky and money must have low carrying costs.

This seems on the face of it a peculiar way to argue, for the first condition makes the argument circular (sticky wages are both a corollary and a precondition for the liquidity-premium to attach to money) and the second blurs the attributes distinguishing l and c. There is, however, something interesting to explore here.

The circularity inherent in the first point should be familiar to all who have puzzled over the nature of money. To 'be money', an asset must be widely acceptable. An asset becomes widely acceptable because it is believed to be liquid. It is liquid precisely because it is widely acceptable. The fact that the argument is circular does not make it less true. The properties of money are self-reinforcing.[11] To continue: money is widely acceptable when it is expected that money prices are relatively stable, and therein hangs the tale about wages. Prices are linked to wages because wages are (typically) the most important component of costs. When wages do not respond to changes in output (because there is unemployment), changes in the level of output will affect prices only[12] to the extent that there are not constant returns. Prices will vary more if changes in output result in (or coincide with) changes in wages, the less willing are workers to accept wage contracts in money terms, and the more they will attempt to fix them in real terms — that is, the less stable is the supply curve of labour with respect to money wages. The more they attempt to fix them in real terms, the more costs and therefore prices will vary, and the less liquid money will become.

If the variation is chiefly in one direction, such as during the 1970s, when the only question was how *much* inflation there would be, not whether there would be inflation or deflation, money loses still more public confidence: 'the expectation of relative stability in the future money-costs of output might not be entertained with much confidence if the standard of value were a commodity with a high elasticity of production' (*G.T.* p. 237). The result is an attempt to anticipate inflation in the wage bargain, thus producing a profit and liquidity squeeze. If the squeeze is relieved by monetary expansion, there is every prospect that the anticipation of inflation will be fulfilled, and confidence is damaged further. Yet because it is so extraordinarily difficult to usurp an established money as a medium of exchange and means of payment, the damage to its role as a store of value is not enough to 'rob the money-rate of interest of its sting' (*G.T.* p. 238).

Part of the reason that it is so difficult to find a substitute for money as a medium of exchange is that the alternatives do not have such low carrying-costs — which brings us to Keynes's second point. One might think that fixing wages in terms of money and bargaining on the basis of price anticipations (including the expectation of stability) is a roundabout method of securing a real wage. The direct method is to bargain and be paid in wage-goods. The main impediments to adopting this alternative are two: the high transactions costs of direct barter and the high carrying costs of most commodities. Given that tastes differ amongst individuals, no bundle of wage-goods could satisfy everyone, and trade will take place. The clumsiness of the resulting arrangements as compared to monetary transactions is easy to appreciate. And retaining a stock of these commodities when wishing to 'save' exposes the owner to losses due to deterioration and storage costs. Both transactions and carrying costs impair the acceptability, and hence the liquidity, of wage-goods in payment of wages. Thus l and c are to some degree interdependent, as are l and a.

Properties of an Elastic Money Supply

The properties of money on which Keynes's argument depends do not attach to money exclusively or to money in all circumstances. In particular, if money is insufficiently inelastic in supply, thus supporting or creating inflationary conditions and expectations, the liquidity premium is likely to shift to a real asset.[13]

The monetary systems of almost all countries, and now the international monetary 'system' as well, are completely free of ties to gold or any other asset whose physical supply is inelastic. This was seen as an unambiguously progressive step: the gold standard was capricious at times of discovery of new supplies, and the rest of the time it imposed, if it was made to work according to plan (which it often wasn't) a constraint on the expansion of output: particularly, export-led growth had a natural end in uncompetitive prices. The inelasticity of the supply of gold at the wrong exchange rate could give rise to prolonged unemployment.[14]

Given time, the constraints of an inelastic money can be surmounted, as history attests: substitutes for gold were created — first notes (originally claims on gold), then bank deposits (claims on coin at first, then notes).

Finally a wide range of financial intermediary debt (claims on bank deposits) has contributed to liquidity. These innovations, however, typically arose from the needs of a rapid expansion of output and investment, not the needs of an economy in the doldrums: the timing of them was no help in dealing with unemployment.

Here, an aspect of inelasticity of supply which Keynes mentions but does not develop is important: the fact that the *private sector* either cannot initiate changes in the money supply or does so at what is perhaps not the best time. The private sector clearly *has* been responsible for financial innovation. The trouble is that the incentive, the profitability of expanding money and credit or creating new financial institutions, is absent in a slump, when it is most needed. In any case, innovation usually takes too long (though ever since the war monetary institutions have grown like mushrooms — and some turned out to be poisonous, too). In the short run the private sector is confined to seeking ways of making *existing* institutions provide more money — e.g. by demanding bank credit.

In a slump, no one is clamouring for bank credit, for investment is unpromising. Even if they were clamouring, bank managers would assess their risks more pessimistically than they would do normally. The profit motive, as it applies to banks, acts to *reinforce* the ups and downs of business expectations rather than mitigate them.

The private sector may be able to change the supply of money in an upswing, but only within the limits of the banks' reserves. In principle (and at some times and places also in practice) these may be strongly influenced by the authorities. If the authorities are running a tight monetary policy (successfully) then the supply of money (consistently — and fairly narrowly — defined) does indeed become to a great degree inelastic in the sense of being outside the control of the private sector.[15] This was the burden of the distinction made by Gurley and Shaw (1960) between 'inside' and 'outside' money — inside money was whatever was created against private sector debt — i.e. manipulable by the private sector — and outside money was what was supplied, whether by government or banks, in response to anything other than private debt.[16]

The private sector has no ability to influence directly the supply of outside money, and its ability to influence the supply of inside money may be limited, in the short run, by monetary policy. These facts throw the question of inelasticity of supply on to the authorities, who, before the internationalisation of banking, could make a modern money supply as inelastic as gold, if they wished, or at the opposite extreme completely accommodate the supply to private sector demand. Managed money offered the prospect that through the operation of a wise policy which avoided both of these extremes, money might be made to fluctuate countercyclically instead of procyclically.

The release of money from the vagaries of gold mining and the balance of payments left the monetary authorities with substantial influence over money for good or ill. Some possibilities of monetary policy are explored in Chapter 18. Here is it more important to discuss the implications of the lesser degree of inelasticity of supply which the changed monetary structure has made possible. This possibility is, of course, far from hypothetical: the money supply figures of most Western countries have exhibited a strong upward trend since the war; monetary authorities now concern themselves with controlling money's rate of *growth*. Prices, too, show an upward trend with some spectacular annual observations. These phenomena, which we tend to take for granted, are from a historical perspective most unusual in peacetime.[17] Speculation in property and foreign exchange and various proposals for monetary reform suggest that confidence in money is not strong. What are the implications for the above analysis of a shift to other assets of the liquidity premium here ascribed to money? What role would the rate of interest play?

Keynes's analysis would suggest the following reasoning. The asset to which the highest liquidity premium attaches sets the standard for investment because it is pointless investing in something that has a lower rate of return than this asset. That asset's liquidity premium also sets the minimum rate of interest, for the uncertainty which, under stable prices, made securities less attractive, because less liquid, than money, now attaches to all money assets. The chief object of uncertainty is now prices or capital values in real terms, instead of the interest rate or capital values in money terms. No asset will be held in money-denominated form, including money itself, whose rate of interest does not compensate for *both* the expected price change and the risk of interest-rate changes, adjusted for the lower carrying and transactions costs of financial assets as compared to real assets.

This is not what we have observed. Non-interest-bearing money continues to be held and for a remarkable number of years since the war real rates of interest on securities and even on equity shares have been negative.

One could ascribe the negative real rates to underestimation of rates of inflation. There is probably quite a lot in that, but a theorist can do little with it.

The theoretical issue, I believe, is the 'portfolio' approach Keynes adopts in Chapter 17. Amongst other things, this approach imposes a single time period on asset-holding decisions, so that all rates of return, which can only be defined for a specific period of time, are comparable. The length of the period is arbitrary.

The single arbitrary time period makes the analysis of money in inflation extremely confusing. The liquidity of money over a year, say, is very different from the liquidity of money over the week between wage payments, although it is the same money in the same environment of inflation. If prices are expected to be stable for a year, however, this dichotomy doesn't arise. The latter was Keynes's world, the former is ours.

The two time periods also correspond to different functions of money in traditional monetary theory: the income period defines the border between transactions demand and other uses of money. The money used for recurrent, everyday transactions is typically not competitive with other assets and is unlikely to be available for the purchase of securities to any appreciable extent. Its influence on the rate of interest is therefore indirect: transactions needs absorb money which could be held for speculative purposes.

Both theory and empirical evidence[18] suggest that until the monetary system goes completely out of control, *some* liquidity premium will continue to attach to money, for money is liquid in day-to-day transactions, even when it loses some of its attractiveness as a liquid asset for holding over a longer period of time.

The asset-holding horizon relevant to money as a store of value and to the liquidity premium is of indefinite length. It is by definition longer than the income period, but its relation to the horizon governing *investment* is what matters for Keynes's argument. Undoubtedly, the monetary asset-holding horizon is shorter, for only precautionary and speculative holdings are involved; long-period money-holding is unlikely. On the other hand the possibility of holding money-denominated assets over a period even longer than the horizon of many investment projects is entirely realistic, if now quaint: e.g. saving for one's retirement in Consols.

With time horizons so variable, calculations of both net advantage and the appropriate real rate of return are slightly problematical. But not entirely so, for there is a strength, as well as the weaknesses I have just been pointing out, to the unified time horizon adopted by portfolio theory. The strength relates to one's ability to alter one's portfolio by buying and selling assets. One is not altogether 'locked in'.

On the other hand, the choice of some assets does lock one in to a considerable extent: it is not easy to buy and sell houses or businesses at whim. By treating equities as almost exactly equivalent to the firms they represent, Keynes passes over something which is extremely important, and subsequent portfolio theory has followed him in this.

It is also the case that one is in many cases 'locked out': individuals' portfolio choices do not typically cover the full range of assets. Only the very wealthy provide a link between real capital and financial assets from a portfolio perspective. ('Shall I buy out *The Times* or invest in gilt-edged?' is not the opening of breakfast conversation for most of us.) It is here I believe that most of the explanation of negative real rates of interest is to be found.

Negative real rates of interest suggest that inflation has broken the interest-rate barrier set by money (Keynes's analysis was, after all, predicated on a money supply with a low elasticity of supply) and apparently not replaced by the return on any other asset. One cannot, however, conclude that the nominal interest rate is no longer of any importance.

Its importance is better appreciated from a flow-of-funds viewpoint rather than a portfolio approach. From the perspective of the borrowing needs of the intending investor, the interest rate retains its importance as long as money is the means of payment. It is money which must be found to finance investment, and if it is to be borrowed, the expected profits must cover repayment with interest, or equivalently, the *mec* must at least equal *r*. However, the *mec* of the proposed investment must also at least equal the asset carrying the liquidity premium, for otherwise the intelligent thing to buy is that asset, not the proposed investment.

Summary

The old conundrum remains: how should monetary institutions be made to function? If paper money and deposits are made to act like gold, inelastic in supply, there is, in the absence of outside stimuli such as population growth, technical progress, or expansion of world trade, a tendency for the system to grind to a halt before full employment is reached. If the supply constraint is removed, leaving money to validate in turn the real wage expectations of labour and the profit expectations of firms, we have inflation. A third alternative, the adoption of a fixed rule for monetary expansion,[19] may avoid the rigours of completely elastic supply while not allowing free rein to inflation, or may, by its very predictability, result in monetary changes being absorbed entirely into price and wage changes, thus failing to provide the elasticity needed for growth to real output, for which the proposal was designed. Discretionary policy, because of the flexibility with which monetary changes can be timed — indeed by its very *un*predictability — ought (unless liquidity preference reacts perversely) to be able to minimise the inflationary impact of monetary changes. The history of discretionary policy is not encouraging. For this reason some favour a rule to control the authorities or a return to gold[20] while others favour dismantling the power of the state over any aspect of monetary affairs[21] and some invent ingenious schemes to make inflationary monetary expansion unprofitable.[22] The gold standard and free banking also had their faults.

To my mind active policy remains the best alternative — if it is any longer feasible. We turn in the next chapter to the appropriate use of monetary authority, though in the following chapter we question whether much control can, in the present state of development of the monetary system, be exercised.

Notes

1. The most extreme evaluation is that of Hansen (1953, p. 159): 'Immediately after the appearance of the *General Theory* there was a certain fascination about Chapter 17, due partly no doubt to its obscurity. Digging in this area, however, soon ceased after it was found that the chapter contained no gold mines.'

2. Keynes even said so. See *G.T.* p. 306.

3. See especially Conard (1963, Ch. 8), on which much of the present exposition depends.

4. See especially Lerner (1952) and Turvey (1965).

5. That is why the single q, rather than a series of quasi-rents or gross profits over the equipment's expected life, is relevant here.

6. I have not said 'utility-maximisation' because the liquidity property does not fit in well with utility analysis, though many writers on monetary theory write as if there were no difficulty.

7. It also clarifies the base appropriate to the calculation of the net rate of return: in the case of the 'non-produced' asset it is the market price which is appropriate; for the 'produced' asset, in anything 'longer' than the market period, replacement cost or supply price is the correct base.

8. See, for example, the treatment in Burstein (1963).

9. Keynes refers to this possibility (p. 241), but as a phenomenon which occurred episodically in past history. There is no suggestion that it might recur.

10. Economists who emphasise the *informative* role of money would connect this fact with increased certainty about money prices, on the grounds that direct relative prices between goods are rarely calculated. They would be calculated if (or they are calculated when) money prices become highly variable.

11. See Chick (1978).

12. Assume now that all other prime costs are linked to wages.

13. 'Money ... rapidly loses the attribute of 'liquidity' if its future supply is expected to undergo sharp changes' (*G.T.* p. 241, n.1).

14. '[The] characteristic which has been traditionally supposed to render gold especially suitable for use as the standard of value, namely its inelasticity of supply, turns out to be precisely the characteristic which is at the bottom of the trouble' (*G.T.* pp.235–6).

15. Banks may be able to manipulate the private sector's preferences for currency and deposits to gain more reserves. Until fairly recently their scope was rather limited.

16. For example, a bank purchase of government debt, a change in international reserves, or the printing of more notes.

17. For more extensive data than Table 7.1 (p. 150) provides, consult Mitchell and Deane (1962). For a dramatic chart of price behaviour in England since 1300 see Pearce (1982).

18.   The study of hyperinflations has shown that money continues to be used as the means of payment for wages and consumption goods at very high rates of inflation (Cagan, 1956).

19.   This idea originated with Henry Simons (1936) and has been generally favoured by monetarists.

20.   A gold standard pressure group was active in the last few years in the United States. In the UK the case has been put by Morgan and Morgan (1979).

21.   For example von Hayek (1976).

22.   Pearce (1982).

Part V
POLICY MATTERS

Chapter 18

POLICY IMPLICATIONS: MONETARY AND FISCAL POLICY

It is a strange irony that 'Keynesian economics' is understood as a certain set of policy prescriptions, yet in the *General Theory*, very little space is devoted to the implications of the theory for government policy. It was perhaps wise *not* to emphasise policy, as policy must be designed for specific circumstances and the theory covered a broad range of circumstances.

In the development of the policy implications in the 1940s and 1950s, however, the contingency of policy on historical circumstance was not emphasised, with a disastrous result: it became established 'Keynesian wisdom' that the economy could be 'stabilised' and growth encouraged by policies — mostly variations of government expenditure and taxation — designed to alter the level of aggregate demand, while monetary policy was dismissed as impotent, not just in the particular circumstances of the 1930s and later 1940s, but generally: 'money did not matter'.

This was Keynesian doctrine, more or less, until challenged, chiefly by economists associated with the University of Chicago who became known as 'monetarists' because of their insistence that 'money matters'. The long and somewhat fruitless debate on this issue, which has now taken other directions without being resolved, need never have occurred at all if the mechanical real-output multiplier had not been taken so seriously and if the historical background of Keynes's comments on policy had been taken into account.

The background includes not only the general circumstances prevailing when Keynes was writing but also the specific policy problem: alleviating unemployment. 'Keynesian' policy refers to much more general and comprehensive aims. It is a short, but crucial, step from the goal of increasing employment when unemployment is clearly very serious, to that of preventing the emergence of unemployment in the first place ('stabilisation'). And when the population is growing, as it was until the mid-1960s, this second goal is understood to require the growth of the capital stock to support the increasing employment need.

Now stabilisation and growth may be worthy goals, but they are much more far-reaching than the problem which urgently required solution in the 1930s, and the policies which will be most effective in their achievement are not necessarily the combination best suited to the problem facing Keynes. At the very least, the general characteristics of the economy (e.g. the level of interest rates, price expectations, the behaviour of unions) will vary both through the economy's fluctuations and as capital accumulates. Writ larger, not only is the West now relatively capital-rich, but the whole nature of the monetary system has changed and the power relations with her suppliers have altered. Disillusionment with 'Keynesianism' in recent years has been caused by the fact that 'Keynesian' policies were being applied to a world for which they were never intended.

As a result of this disillusionment with policy there is a strong probability that Keynes's *theory* will be thrown out along with 'Keynesian' policy. That would be a pity, for with suitable amendment and expansion, the theory is more serviceable than many of the suggested alternatives.

Let us remind ourselves of the features of the problem Keynes was trying to solve: unemployment high for over a decade and showing no sign of improvement, entrepreneurs discouraged, great excess capacity yet the economy generally undercapitalised:

> ... a condition where there is a shortage of houses, but where nevertheless no one can afford to live in the houses that there are.

(G.T. p. 322)

To improve employment it was necessary to raise effective demand (effective, not aggregate). In principle this could be done either by lowering Z or by raising D. In the short run however, the only way to lower Z was by reducing wages and that was likely, after allowing for the feedback on D, to be unhelpful or even counterproductive.

There are two ways to raise D: by altering the propensity to consume or by altering investment. The first might be done through redistribution of income. Though Keynes supports this policy for the maintenance of boom conditions as the boom begins to falter, he makes no mention of it in the context of the slump, probably because to achieve any noticeable effect would require too large a change.

So one concentrates on investment. In turn there are two possible ways to encourage investment: raise the *mec* — which in effect means profit expectations — or lower the rate of interest.

When the rate of interest, however, is already as low as it has ever been, there is little prospect of change there, and with considerable underutilisation of existing equipment, hope of raising investment even by improving expectations is not great. The only remaining possibility for the immediate future is to fill the gap between potential output and current demand with government expenditure.

The impact effect of the expenditure would be immediately beneficial to employment and would reduce the cost of unemployment compensation. The consumption induced by the initial expenditure (multiplier effects) would both further improve employment and, if incomes rose sufficiently, perhaps raise some taxes. So a deficit would not be as costly (to the government) as it might seem. And the effect on prices would be minimal at such very low levels of output.

As a more distant hope the rise in income might alter entrepreneurs' expectations sufficiently for a recovery of investment to follow.

That was the broad logic of Keynes's approach. It is plain that every element of it depends on the characteristics of the situation facing policy-makers. The evaluation associated with Keynesianism — that fiscal policy works and monetary policy does not — was not justified as a *general* principle.

It is of interest to speculate on the reasons why this generalisation took hold. Fundamental, I think, was the idea that the financial counterpart of autonomous spending had no role to play in the multiplier process. Recall the discussion of Chapter 14, in which financial implications were explored. Even without bringing in the consequences for the rate of interest of different modes of finance the argument got pretty turgid, so one can sympathise with the desire to ignore finance as a theorist, if not as a policy-maker.

One consequence of looking separately at government expenditure and its finance was a subtle change of language and connotation in speaking of policy options. Keynes spoke of 'public works'; 'Keynesians' speak of 'fiscal policy'.

The term 'public works' connotes government expenditure undertaken in special circumstances, as distinguished from regular expenditures. 'Fiscal policy' encompasses both government expenditure (G), the expansionary side of fiscal policy, and taxation (T), the restrictive side. Since both have a role in stabilisation policy, the broader term fiscal policy came into use. Along with that change, however, came the identification of everything involving G or T as fiscal policy, regardless of the source or use of funds attached to G or T. Keynes, in contrast, was very specific about the source of finance for his 'public works': new money.

While to a monetarist anything involving a change in the money supply may count as monetary policy, Keynes, when he spoke of monetary policy, clearly meant a policy of open market operations, designed to affect interest rates. Keynesians in the 1950s and 1960s included in monetary policy such things as variations in banks' reserves or reserve requirements, designed to affect liquidity and/or the supply of credit.

The Government 'Budget Restraint'

The above can be dealt with systematically within the framework of an income statement and a balance sheet for government. The government's income is from taxation; any expenditure in excess of tax receipts must be financed by borrowing or newly-created money.[1] In familiar symbols we write this idea

$$G - T = \Delta B + \Delta M, \tag{18.1}$$

where ΔB in this context refers to the change in government securities. This equation refers to the fact that there must be sufficient funds to finance expenditure.[2] It is usually called the government 'budget restraint', though it seems a paradoxical designation when there are the possibilities of borrowing and creating purchasing power simultaneously with the spending, and when the tax receipts are unknown at the outset: it is either a completely *ex post* relation between inflows and outflows of funds like an income statement (see Chapter 3), or it represents a consistent plan, where the financial implications are recognised.

Then there is the residue of past government action: the bonds and money outstanding. Their proportions may be altered by open market operations (or debt management policy) and their sum by increments resulting from the finance of expenditure and by the use of net surplus to retire either debt or money. So the balance sheet of outstanding claims is affected by the income statement.

Any realistic policy will be a mixture of the pure possibilities defined by the balance sheet and incomes statement, which are these:

(1) $G - T = 0$ A balanced budget
(2) $G - T = \Delta B$ A deficit financed by borrowing or a surplus used to retire debt
(3) $G - T = \Delta M$ A deficit financed by new money or a surplus used to absorb money from the economy
(4) $- \Delta B = \Delta M$ An open market purchase ($+\Delta B$, sale).

A further possibility for the fantasy-minded is a 'pure' increase in the money supply. Since to introduce the money in exchange for anything comprises the purity of *ceteris paribus* argument, it has been suggested to imagine money having been dropped on the economy by a helicopter:

(5) ΔM A 'pure' monetary increase.

The Helicopter policy could be supplemented by a Hoover policy in times of excess liquidity,

Keynesians look for G and T, call policies that involve them 'fiscal', and call the rest 'monetary'. Thus (1)–(3) are fiscal policies and only (4) counts as monetary policy. They do not countenance (5). Monetarists look at the

Table 18.1

	Fiscal Policy	*Monetary Policy*
Keynesians	(1), (2), (3)	(4)
Monetarists	(1), (2)	(3), (4), (5)
Keynes	(3)	(4)

other side of the equation as it were, and count everything involving ΔM, i.e.(3), (4) and (5), as monetary policy. Everything else, i.e. (1) and (2), is fiscal policy. Keynes specified (3) when recommending public works and envisaged (4) as monetary policy. Table 18.1 summarises the above.

It should be common sense that what is true of (3) needn't be true of (1) or (2): it is important to look at both sides of the balance sheet. And the scope for talking at cross-purposes is plain enough from considering policy (3). Note that (2) plus (4) equals (3), also.

To illustrate the confusion which this semantic tangle leads to, consider the policy of cutting government expenditure in order to hold back the money supply. (So the present British government describes its policy.) In these days of an upward trend of the money supply, slowing down the rate of increase is equivalent to a decrease in M in more stable times. Thus it can be seen that this policy is nothing other than policy (3) run in the direction of deflation.

It is called a monetarist policy, because of its ostensible aim of cutting back the rate of growth of the money supply. But since it does nothing directly to control non-government sources of money supply growth, it might better be described as 'negative Keynesianism'; a policy of deflation by the most effective means, using 'control of the money supply' as an excuse. As any close reader of the *General Theory*, or even Chapter 7 above will appreciate, there is an

> asymmetry between Inflation and Deflation. For whilst a deflation of effective demand below the level required for full employment will diminish employment as well as prices, an inflation of [demand] above this level will merely affect prices.
>
> (*G.T.* p. 291)

Finance and the Multiplier

The mechanical and equilibrium approach to the multiplier introduced three items into the substratum of economists' thinking. One was that government expenditure was somehow self-financing, so, naturally, finance could be ignored. The second was that, short of full employment, multiplier effects would fall entirely on output. The third was that since the one-shot multiplier had only transitory effects, repeated doses of government expenditure (or induced investment or consumption) were necessary to effect any significant change.

Even in the early 1960s I suppose no one confronted with these propositions put so baldly would have said he believed them without qualification. They constituted not so much a consciously-held and actively-promulgated doctrine as a kind of subconscious instinct.

So it was with something of a start that two articles by Carl Christ (1967, 1968) were received. These articles pointed out that because of the government's budget restraint a continued budget deficit implied an ever-rising public debt or monetary increase, until equilibrium. This equilibrium (determined in the usual multiplier manner) was characterised by a balanced budget. To achieve it, income would have to rise sufficiently to raise the appropriate taxes, just as it has to rise sufficiently to produce adequate saving when equilibrium is defined by $S = I$.

Introducing the government budget restraint but keeping the mechanical multiplier approach has led to Blinder and Solow's proposition (1973) that financing by borrowing is more expansionary than financing by new money, because taxes (in the $G = T$ equilibrium state which is their reference point) will have to rise by more than the rise in government expenditure: they must cover the servicing of the debt as well.

Although this conclusion is technically correct on its own terms, it would be most unfortunate if a policy-maker took this proposition seriously. It is one thing to make a hypothetical statement about what is necessary to produce an equilibrium and another to expect it to operate in practice. Common sense, superior here, indicates that finance by new money, both because it introduces new liquidity into the system and because there is no effect from the policy action itself on the rate of interest, will have a greater expansionary effect than finance by borrowing, which will push up the rate of interest and tend to discourage investment.

This effect on interest rates and investment was rediscovered in the late 1960s when it became known as 'crowding out'.[3] Government borrowing crowds out private borrowing and hence is ineffective. In that extreme form it is, needless to say, a monetarist doctrine. To support it, one must suppose that the supply of loanable funds is completely inelastic: a demand for credit cannot be made and met without displacing someone else's. In effect there are no idle balances and absolutely no slack in the banking system.

In a less extreme and characteristically more complex form, it is an effect fully acknowledged by Keynes. (For its origin he credits Kahn.) Thus:

> The method of financing the policy and the increased working cash, recognised by the increased employment and the associated rise of prices, may have the effect of increasing the rate of interest and so retarding investment in other directions, unless the monetary authority takes steps to the contrary ...
>
> (G.T. p. 119)

The argument, of course, has shifted ground, from the final equilibrium to the immediate effects of policy. Once one ceases to speak hypothetically, a short time horizon is the only possible one — a few rounds of the multiplier, so to speak. The crowding-out effect refers only to the first round. In the passage cited Keynes notes not only the effect of the initial finance but also the subsequent effects caused by the rise in M_1 holdings consequent on expansion and the need for monetary policy (i.e. interest-rate policy) to counteract them.

It is interesting that Keynes went to the trouble to caution against allowing any rise in interest rates, for one would have thought that the possibility of crowding out was at its lowest in the 1930s' sort of depression. With the interest rate already higher than the marginal efficiency of capital, new investment was minimal and much capital was not being maintained or replaced as it wore out. In that case what happens to the interest rate really doesn't matter. Furthermore, in a deep depression, very little is *likely* to happen to the interest rate. Rates are already low so there should be considerable idle money available to satisfy increased transactions needs with only a small rise in rates.[4]

Keynes did not, however, tie his policy statements so directly to the particular circumstances around him. And this caution could also be seen as a rebuttal to those who felt that even government *borrowing* might be dangerously inflationary — creating new money, far more so. (Indeed it might be if it goes on too long. This is the subject of the next chapter.)

Note too that he prepared those same inflation scaremongers for a rise in prices as a result of expansionary policy (recall the discussion of 'true' and 'false' inflation in Chapter 15), even though at the time he was writing that the probability of prices rising was at its lowest.

Interest Rates and the Multiplier

It is worth considering the behaviour of interest rates as predicted by one of our dynamic multiplier models, when there is a 'one-shot' government expenditure financed by new money. Assume no induced taxation for the moment. The new income is partly spent, partly saved. The income appears in the form of new money: there is no liquidity impediment to expenditure. There is no initial effect on interest rates.

This outcome is often represented in *IS–LM* analysis by equal shifts in the curves, but that is only the first-round effect.

Income and the money supply have risen by an equal amount, so assuming $k < 1$ there is too much money to be absorbed by transactions demand. The excess may be held idle or used to purchase securities; the proportion will depend on interest-rate expectations. The interest rate will fall as securities are demanded.

In subsequent periods there is some induced consumption to compensate for the withdrawal of government demand, but income is gradually falling

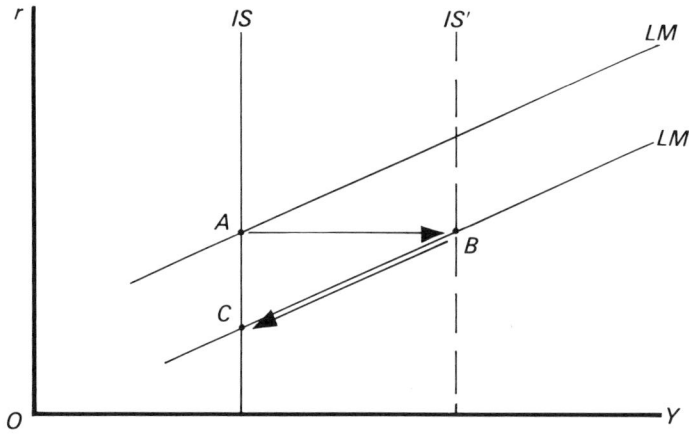

Figure 18.1

back to its original level. As this happens, some transactions balances become available to hold either as speculative cash or as securities; the interest rate falls further. Eventually, all the new money ends up as M_2 balances; at the end of the multiplier story, income has fallen back to its previous level and no net addition to M_1 is required. The interest rate will have fallen permanently to a lower level for the new money to be held idle willingly.

In *IS–LM* terms, the *IS* curve shifts outward temporarily, but the *LM* curve shifts outward permanently. The *IS* curve is vertical, since there is no interest-induced investment. In Figure 18.1 the temporary shift is indicated by a dashed line. There is a move from *A* and *B* as a consequence of the government expenditure and from *B* and *C* as a consequence of the effects on M_1 and M_2 of induced consumption as income returns to its former level.

Keynes, in contrast (*G.T.* p. 200 — this passage will be cited below in another context), allows the fall in *r* to have an effect on investment and hence income. The demand for M_1 will rise with income, perhaps even to the extent of reversing the fall in interest rates. The behaviour of the interest rate as the multiplier progresses is thus to fall and then partially, or perhaps even completely, to reverse itself.

The speed of response of investment may be expected to be somewhat irregular, giving an erratic pattern for the interest rate, and in practice the final position would be quite unpredictable. The important thing to notice, however, is that the final level of income may be higher than the initial level, in contradiction of the textbook model: a single period of government expenditure may have a lasting effect, even though the effects of capital accumulation on efficiency cannot be considered in the short run.

Figure 18.2 portrays Keynes's dynamic story in *IS–LM* terms. The *IS*

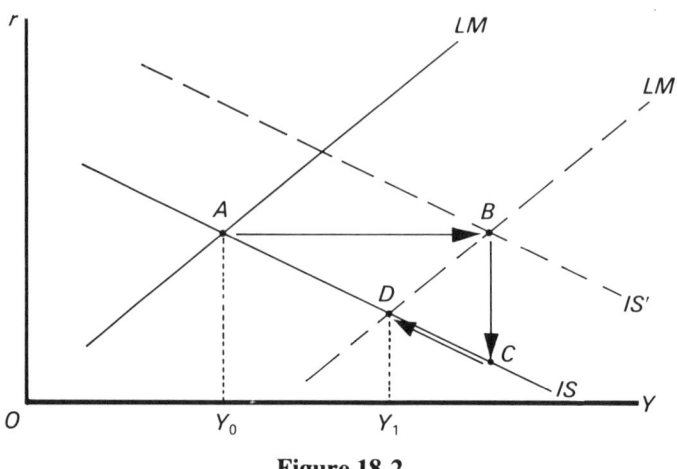

Figure 18.2

curve shifts temporarily as before, but now is negatively sloped. The *LM* curve shifts permanently. There is an initial movement from *A* to *B*, followed by a drop in interest rates to *C*, then a movement to *D* as investment rises but is outweighed by the fall in government expenditure. The permanent net effect is a rise of income from Y_0 to Y_1.

Further Prospects of Induced Investment

Investment depends on two factors: the *mec* and *r*. American economists, well before the publication of the *General Theory*, were advocating fiscal deficits on the grounds that the increased demand brought about by government expenditure would, particularly if the policy were sustained for any length of time, persuade entrepreneurs that prospects for profit were improving. If and when this happened, the *mec* would rise and investment be stimulated.

This policy was given the homespun epithet of 'pump-priming'. One — I am told — pours water down a hand-pump in order to get the well-water to rise; this procedure is called 'priming'. A nice metaphor.

Pumps, however, work on reliable physical principles. Investment does not. The responsiveness of the *mec* to government expenditure is not only likely to vary with the general state of the economy but may even be perverse: 'with the confused psychology which often prevails' (*G.T.* p. 120), the mere fact of government intervention may *diminish* confidence and lower the *mec*.

Assuming that business psychology is not perverse, one can still say that the likely success of pump-priming will vary with the general state of the economy. If expectations are deeply depressed and in addition there exists considerable excess capacity, the government may have to pursue deficit spending for a considerable time before investment picks up. A stimulus during a mild recession, say an inventory recession, when firms are selling off excess stocks but are not running down equipment, is more likely to have an effect. Thus a deep slump is exactly the time when investment is most difficult to stimulate, though production and employment may improve rapidly (particularly since the user cost of idle equipment is virtually nil).

Curiously Keynes makes no mention of the 'pump-priming' possibility — only the possibility of a perverse psychological reaction and the adverse effects on the *mec* of the rising price of capital equipment in recovery. One way to see this is that Keynes was adhering strictly to the separation of long-term profit expectations from current income observations. Another is the possibility that he omitted this form of induced investment because of its inappropriateness to the period.[5] This latter suggestion does not sit well with the fact that he allowed falls in the rate of interest to induce investment. If excess capacity or an insurmountable gap between *mec* and *r* are reasons against one, they should be reasons against both.

Whatever Keynes's reasons it seems relatively certain that disillusionment with the idea of government expenditure as a *temporary* stimulus arose from the failure of investment to respond in the 1930s.[6]

Once again we see that something regarded as a general theoretical principle is in fact shaped by historical circumstance. It is an odd twist of the history of ideas that the absence of an accelerator mechanism in the *General Theory* is widely regarded as a weakness, while the idea of fiscal policy as a stimulus to investment has given way to thinking of government expenditure as *compensation* for investment which is not occurring, despite the fact that the circumstances which invalidate pump-priming were not general.

The Mpc over the Cycle

The response of consumption to fiscal stimuli may also be variable over the cycle. First, it is plausible, though empirically not substantiated, that the *mpc* is higher at low levels of aggregate, as well as individual, income. Second, if income has been relatively stable and then begins to change, the level of consumption is likely to change little at first, adjusting slowly to a new level or rate of change of income once it is established. (These points were discussed in Chapter 6.)

In a downturn, these two considerations give conflicting interpretations. This can be seen from Figure 18.3, where the 'short-run' consumption function *SC* intersects the long-run function *LC* at a level of income Y_0 which has been stable. If consumers have not adjusted, they follow *SC* as income falls; the slope of *SC* is less than that of *LC* at Y_0, so the expenditure that would be needed to prevent a fall of income to, say, *Y*, might be regarded as unexpectedly small (if policy makers had estimated the *mpc* to be the slope

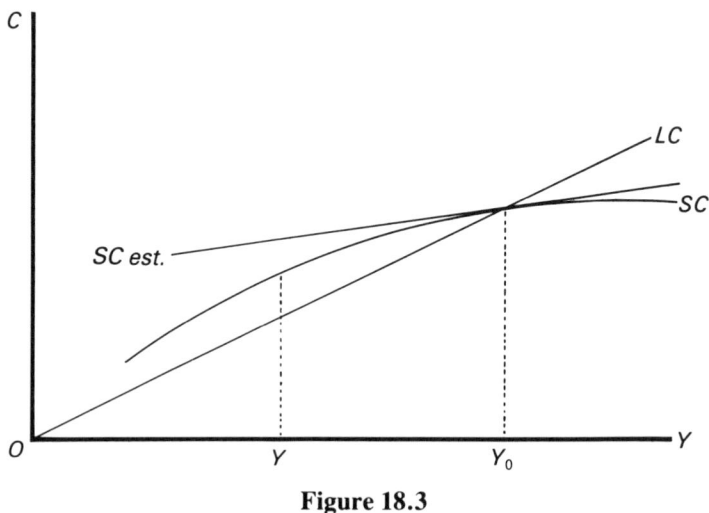

Figure 18.3

of *LC*) or unexpectedly large if the forecast was based on the slope of *SC* at Y_0 (*SC est.* in the figure). As a recession deepens, and consumers adjust, the slope of *LC* becomes relevant. The deeper the depression, the steeper that slope is likely to be — at least, so Keynes thought. This was the basis of his rejection of the *mpc* implied by Kuznets' data (US, 1919–33) which did not exceed 60 to 70 per cent: '[This is] a figure quite plausible for the boom, but surprisingly, and in my judgment, improbably low for the slump' (*G.T*.p. 128).

Empirical evidence suggests that the long-run consumption function is linear, but that does not affect the proposition that the multiplier effects of government expenditure are likely to be larger when a low level of income has been a feature of life for some time — exactly the conditions under which Keynes was writing — for consumers would have adjusted to the long-term pattern whose slope is steeper.

The conversion of policy to the aim of growth raises the same point in the upward direction, but in this context, assuming Keynes's long-term consumption function, one sees that if one takes the *mpc* estimated from recent experience (i.e. in the neighbourhood of Y_0), the multiplier effects will be overestimated, whether consumers have had time to adjust or not. This conclusion is of course modified if *LC* is linear, but in either event it can be seen that it may take some time for multiplier effects to be significant. These points, of obvious importance to policy, are not amenable to the equilibrium analysis embodied in algebraic (static) versions of the multiplier.

The Efficacy of Fiscal Policy: Summary

The aim of fiscal policy is to provide a stimulus to production by increasing demand, directly and indirectly. Just what the magnitude of its effect on demand will be depends, as we have seen, on the particular circumstances surrounding its use. And the extent to which the stimulus to demand is translated to output and employment instead of prices depends on the factors that were outlined in Chapter 15, which are also variable over time.

If there is any single principle to emerge from the first half of this chapter it is that the efficacy of fiscal policy depends, not on the size of parameters of fixed behavioural functions, but on the adroitness with which the timing of its use is judged. Though delicacy of touch is demanded in principle, in practice it is almost impossible to achieve, due to the unpredictable nature of the long-term expectations governing investment and the variability of the lags with which consumption and investment may respond.

Demand management is not only difficult, it is, without the support of exogenous stimuli to growth (technical change, population growth) doomed to eventual failure if pursued continuously. That is the subject of the next chapter. We turn now to a consideration of monetary policy, in which a fundamental difference of view between Keynes's and monetarist analysis is explored.

Monetary Policy

The history of the development of policies to act on the banks, the financial markets, credit and money and of their failures and successes is colourful and diverse and there is no time to go into it all. This section will be limited to only three interconnected aims: to explore the 'Keynesian transmission mechanism' and the related belief in the impotence of monetary policy and to sharpen the distinction between the monetarists' view of the role of money and that of Keynes. Points from Chapters 9 and 11 will unavoidably be repeated, but hopefully in a way which pulls apparently disparate points together.

The 'Transmission Mechanism'

Probably the very notion of a 'transmission mechanism' would be uncongenial to Keynes, for it suggests a dichotomy between the monetary and real aspects of the economy where he saw the economy as inherently monetary. But about the link between M and monetary aggregate demand he was in no doubt:

> The primary effect of a change in the quantity of money on the quantity of effective demand is through its influence on the rate of interest.

> (*G.T.*p. 298)

There are two levels on which this link can be discussed. The simpler has to do with the effects of monetary policy narrowly interpreted. The other is broad enough to provide a genuine confrontation with monetarism.[7]

The most congenial approach to this assertion of Keynes's is supply and demand analysis. The money supply in his theory is exogenous, therefore it is the determinants of demand which must effect a new equilibrium when the money supply changes. And Keynes did make an enormous fuss over the rate of interest and the speculative demand for money. This led to the idea that $M^D = L(r)$ was Keynes's 'Special Theory', an extreme case of his more general $M^D = L(Y,r)$. This was the interpretation in the article that has shaped our view of Keynes's system more than any other: 'Mr Keynes and the Classics' (Hicks, 1937). An alternative which is less restrictive is that r is responsible for equilibrating the supply of and demand for money before income has time to change. (Modigliani, 1944 — perhaps the second most influential interpretive article — took this view, as we did in Chapter 11.)

Keynes himself says plainly: '[It] is by playing on the speculative-motive that monetary manangement ... is brought to bear on the economic system' (*G.T.*p. 196).

So the transmission mechanism was held to depend on the existence of a significant interest-elasticity of the demand-for-money function, and the search was on.

There is nothing at all wrong with this interpretation but it seems to the present writer to play down a point which in the light of subsequent history it was unfortunate for Keynesians to have ignored: that Keynes meant by monetary management something quite specific: open market operations. Until 1971 it went without saying that open market operations supported or were supported by Bank Rate. Both the *modus operandi* and the aim of open market operations as understood at that time was to affect interest rates. Open market operations by their very nature cannot be transmitted, except they change interest rates.

The speculative motive was important because speculative holders, unlike many long-term investors, are *responsive* to interest-rate incentives and provide a market in which the government broker can buy and sell. If everyone is in 'portfolio equilibrium' and not responsive, he cannot effect the intended policy.

It is obvious, therefore, that the interest-elasticity of M_2 is of vital importance for monetary policy. But amongst all the empirical studies of this function[8] only Eisner (1963) mentions that not only is an infinite interest-elasticity not required for the Keynesian position (as was widely thought then), but rather what is important is that even a constant-elasticity function is flatter at low levels of r. That is all that is necessary for Keynes's position, that monetary policy is unlikely to succeed in a slump. The impotence of monetary policy was not intended as the *general* proposition it became.

The demand-for-money studies of the 1960s were undertaken in the context, as we have said, of the question of whether monetary policy *was* or *was not* effective, not of *when* it was and when it was not. The object of the empirical investigations was to find 'the' demand-for-money function. It was presumed to be something stable enough to be suited to econometric techniques with the data available, so a fair run of years had to be included.

Now as Keynes explained the speculative demand, stability would not, perhaps, be the most obvious thing to expect. I for one find if not surprising that income variables performed noticeably better than interest rate variables in these investigations. Shifts due both to changes in the normal rate independently of policy and in reaction to policy were allowed for in the theory, but not in subsequent interpretations or in empirical work.

An Open Market Operation:

> [It] is ... important to distinguish between the changes in the rate of interest which are due to changes in the supply of money available to satisfy the speculative-motive, without there having been any change in the liquidity function, and those which are primarily due to changes in expectation affecting the liquidity function itself. Open-market operations may, indeed, influence the rate of interest through both channels; since they may not only change the volume of money but may also give rise to changed expectations concerning the future policy of the Central Bank or of the Government.
>
> (*G.T.* pp. 196–7)

The analysis of an open market operation may proceed in two parts. First assume that expectations are unaffected by the news. This analysis is similar to the exercises of Chapter 11. The M_2 function is stable (see Figure 18.4).

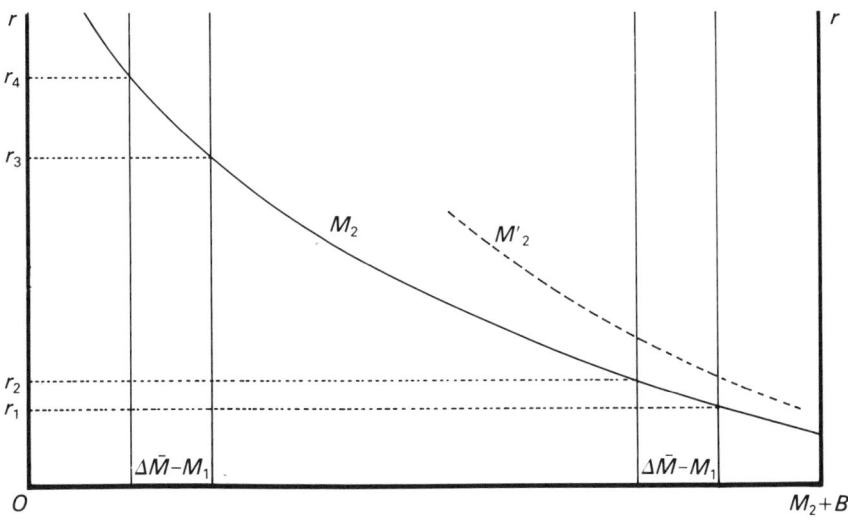

Figure 18.4

An open market purchase of securities is portrayed by a rightward shift in the line indicating the amount of money left over from M_1 and available for speculative holding: the money supply increases but M_1 is fixed, because income has not changed. The overall length of the line, measuring total funds in the speculative domain, may change slightly because of revaluation, but this is ignored.

The point made earlier about the increased difficulty of effecting interest rate changes when rates are low is brought out by postulating monetary increases of equal size. It can be seen that $r_4 - r_3 > r_2 - r_1$.

Now consider how a policy change might affect M_2 and hence the outcome.

British monetary policy has a long history of using an announcement of its intentions to achieve its policy aims with little market activity. Bank Rate was chiefly thought of as a signal of the level of interest rates the Bank wanted, and Minimum Lending Rate, after a brief period of following market rates (at least to some extent), resumed the role of guideline until its recent abolition. Expectations are bound to change when this rate is altered or indeed when any major policy change is announced.

Suppose the Bank signalled that it wished rates to rise from r_1 (without indicating the precise level it wished to see). The 'normal rate' (in Keynes's sense) would then also rise and rates previously believed safe (i.e. not likely to rise) would be thought risky. M_2 shifts to the right to M_2' (the dotted line in Figure 18.4). Those to whom the current rate now appears risky shift into money. The rate rises. An open market operation may not even be necessary.

This 'announcement effect' is likely also to be weakest when rates are low already and the authorities are trying to suppress them still further. Given the rate cannot fall below zero, belief in the authorities' success is bound to be lacking at low rates. The conclusion reached earlier, that the lower the rate the larger the required open market operation, is if anything *reinforced*.

Keynes *versus* the Monetarists

A monetarist would look at an open market purchase in quite another way. His attention would be drawn to the changes in the quantity of money brought about by the operation. He would be puzzled by Keynes's exclusive attention to r and not to ΔM.

There are two facets to Keynes's inattentiveness to ΔM. The first relates to the fact, mentioned above, that a change of policy is unlikely to leave speculators' expectations unaffected, as we have assumed up to now. Relaxing that assumption:

> If the change in the news affects the judgment and the requirements of everyone in precisely the same way, the rate of interest ... will be adjusted forthwith to the new situation without any market transactions being necessary.

Thus, in the simplest case, where everyone is similar and similarly placed, a change in circumstances or expectations will not be capable of causing any displacement of money whatever; — it will simply change the rate of interest in whatever degree is necessary to offset the desire of each individual, felt at the previous rate, to change his holding of cash in response to the new circumstances or expectations ... .

In general, however, a change in circumstances or expectations will cause some realignment in individual holdings of money ... [but this] is incidental to individual differences, ... [Even] in the general case, [where there is some change in individual holdings], the shift in the rate of interest is usually the most prominent part of the reaction to a change in the news. The movement in bond-prices is, as the newspapers are accustomed to say, 'out of all proportion to the activity of dealing'; — which is as it should be, in view of individuals being much more similar than they are dissimilar to their reaction to news.

(*G.T.* pp. 198–9)

A Monetarist Theory

The monetarist, focusing attention on ΔM, argues differently. Following Friedman and Schwartz (1963)[9], the story goes as follows. An open market purchase increases the money balance of those who sold their bonds. Now, money is only a 'temporary abode of purchasing power'; the holders of the newly-supplied money will soon demand other assets in exchange. These can be producers' goods or consumer goods, whatever the holders want (but not securities — these are now too dear). The effect on demand is direct.

There are two crucial differences with Keynes: (i) monetarists assume that there is no substantial period of time for which, individually and thus in aggregate, money is held idle in any significant amount,[10] and (ii) they assume that it follows that transactors' expenditure is constrained by liquidity (transactions balances) and that the proceeds of sales to the government broker will be spent on goods and services.

This brings us back to the fundamental break which Keynes made with the loanable-funds, circulating-money approach to economic modelling, for to him, total expenditure had little or nothing to do with the amount of money in existence — except as it affected the rate of interest. For the rest, *income* determined consumption; transactions balances were just a convenience.

It is true that Keynes assumed that idle money was often held, but that fact is not essential, for if income increased, money would most likely increase as well, whether the source of new income was government expenditure financed by new money or investment financed by bank loans. If money did not increase, the rate of interest would rise and income would rise by less. Whatever the *actual* rise in income, it was automatically supported either by the activation of idle funds through rising interest rates or by new money.

Keynes differs from the monetarists also in his assumption as to what the transactors with the government broker do with the money they obtain. In Keynes's analysis, the government broker succeeds in selling bonds because he offers a capital gain to existing holders. But although that sale increases the ready liquidity of the economy, it does not of itself generate income, and in Keynes, income and preferences alone motivate spending.

A decision to spend out of capital account, which is what spending the proceeds of a bond sale entails, requires either that some contingency for which precautionary balances were held has arrived, or that preferences to consume and save have changed. These circumstances would only appear fortuitously at the same time as an open market purchase and so cannot be said to be predictions of the theory.

Furthermore, even if individual's preferences did alter in this way, the point made in Chapter 6, that while *individuals* may spend the proceeds of bond sales, in aggregate the increment to spending is limited to capital gains, must be remembered. Here the monetarists are, I believe, simply wrong to carry their analysis through to the aggregate level.

Taken to their didactic extremes, Keynes's theory can be seen as assuming that the financing of investment is entirely dependent on the existence of a pool of idle balances, which is expanded by a monetary policy whose main purpose is to encourage entrepreneurs to draw on that pool; and the model of Friedman and Schwartz proposes a direct use of the funds thus provided, the fall in the interest rate serving to tip the balance of intertemporal choice in favour of current expenditure. Keynes rejects any influence of the interest rate on consumption, and its influence on the *timing* of investment is not explicit. On the question of timing we can find a middle ground between the two extreme positions, occupied by two sources of finance not given much attention in the *General Theory*: internal finance and the banks. Let us consider these in the light of the above contrast in theories.

Internal Finance: Firms hold liquid assets against the probability of credit squeezes, higher interest rates, etc., in order to provide some control over the finances of essential replacements and the timing of new capital expenditures. These holdings are in effect precautionary balances. And as in the case of precautionary balances held by individuals, the firm will typically hold some cash, to guard against scarce or very dear finance, or heavy capital losses if securities must be sold, when an expenditure is unavoidable. But having provided some cover in this way the rest can serve a dual purpose. By staying in marketable securities there will always be finance at a price and if the price is too high the investment is postponed. Firms large enough to support a financial management department will also speculate with these funds, so their behaviour also partakes of the characteristics of M_2 balances.

An advantageous sale to the government broker may be used to implement a capital-expenditure plan earlier than was originally envisaged. Here the increased liquidity may change the *timing* of an investment plan, bringing it forward. The proceeds of the sale, while held as money, could be thought of as satisfying the finance motive.

Since the present value of the profitability of a project is enhanced by undertaking the project sooner (*cet. par.*), 'finance' money is doubtless not held for long: it is a temporary abode of purchasing power. So internal finance provides a bridge between the two theories, providing firms have a backlog of investment projects which can be brought forward.

Again the cyclical background is decisive: the effect just described is less likely in a slump; the firms' liquid assets are then likely to behave more like M_2 balances than to conform to the Friedman–Schwartz model. The rest of the time a 'finance' effect seems quite likely.

Bank Finance: The Friedman–Schwartz scenario explicitly includes the banks. An open market purchase of securities from them, they say, increases their cash reserves. These are not held idle; rather, the banks will seek lending outlets, and the borrowers will spend the proceeds.

The relevance of this point depends on the securities involved in the purchase not being perfect substitutes for cash in banks' reserves.[11] On a cash reserve basis, a purchase from the banks would provide them with reserves and prepare the banking system for a multiple expansion of lending. On some occasions banks have held liquid assets significantly in excess of requirements, but it is not obvious that the excess liquidity has been held for speculative reasons — it is more likely due to a lack of interest and suitable borrowers. We are back to the necessity of investment expectations being reasonably buoyant if monetary policy is to have any effect.

Money, Interest and Expenditure

Keynes's view of the role of money is stated in its most general, if not its most transparent, form in the following passage:

> The relation of changes in M to Y and r depends, in the first instance, on the way in which changes in M come about ... [If] changes in M are due to the Government printing money wherewith to meet its current expenditure ... the new money accrues as someone's income. The new level of income, however, will not continue sufficiently high for the requirements of M_1 to absorb the whole of the increase in M; and some portion of the money will seek an outlet in buying securities or other assets until r has fallen so as to bring about an increase in the magnitude of M_2 and at the same time to stimulate a rise in Y to such an exent that the new money is absorbed either in M_2 or in the M_1 which corresponds to the rise in Y caused by the fall in r. Thus at one remove this case comes to the same thing as the alternative case, where the new money can only be issued in the first instance by a relaxation of the conditions of credit by the banking system, so as to induce someone to sell the banks a debt or a bond in exchange for the new cash.

It will, therefore, be safe for us to take the latter case as typical. A change in M can be assumed to operate by changing r, and a change in r will lead to a new equilibrium partly by changing M_2 and partly by changing Y and therefore M_1.

(G.T. p. 200)

Here, changes in the money supply, whether introduced as part of public works or in pursuit of lower interest rates, are given the same role to play. The apparent contradiction between the opening sentence and the resolution at the end hinges on the phrase 'at one remove'. The essence of the fiscal-policy case is that the money-flow is identical with the *initial* effect on income, but the new money continues in existence to have further effects. Those effects, however, are separated from expenditure decisions.

An extreme monetarist would, in contrast, have said that the introduction of new money produced an excess supply of money which led to increased spending, until prices or output rose to eliminate the excess supply by raising transactions demand.

The case of bank credit expansion is, of course, like the open market operation: the change in r is an initial effect. Monetary increases caused by a fiscal deficit and a credit expansion come to the same thing in the sense that the *second* stage of the fiscal policy is like the *first* stage following the relaxation of bank credit.

This passage illustrates more clearly than any other the proposition introduced in Chapter 9 that Keynes separates money in its aspect as income from money in its aspect as wealth. That separation does not deny the circulation of money in the income stream, but it puts a rather different light on much of the debate between monetarists and Keynesians.

The Long Run

While clear understanding of this methodological difference would do much to settle differences between monetarists and Keynesians, it remains doubtful that Keynes would have agreed with the monetarists that the source of monetary increase is irrelevant in the end. Keynes explicitly states that the character of the new equilibrium, defined as the circumstances in which the new money is willingly absorbed into M_1 and M_2, depends on the many factors described in his Book V — too many ideas for the monetarist method of simple models — and it is not obvious (indeed it is very unlikely) that Keynes would expect the two policies to reach the same equilibrium.

The monetarist concept of equilibrium is a 'long-run' result, not in the Marshallian sense but rather a Classical long run (with which, as is well known, Keynes had little patience),[12] in which not only initial effects but even disparities in the amount of investment stimulated along the way by different policies are made to count for nothing. The Classical notion of equilibrium entails the achievement of the optimum mix of capital, marked by uniform profit rates.

The neoclassical variant of Classical equilibrium is to make capital malleable ('putty') so that this long run does not take forever to achieve. But the world is not made of putty, and policies which, other things being equal, achieve more investment leave more capital and productive capacity behind them.

Investment was all to the good in the mid-1930s. But Keynes gave a warning:

> Each time we secure today's equilibrium by increased investment we are aggravating the difficulty of securing equilibrium tomorrow.

> (*G.T.* p. 105)

To that spectre of stagnation we now turn our attention, looking at the postwar period as a whole.

Notes

1.   The process is more complex than the phrase 'printing money', often used in this context, suggests, but the essence of the matter is captured well enough by this phrase without (I hope) being misleading.

2.   The existence of the 'budget restraint' was first acknowledged and its implications explored by Ott and Ott (1965) though the articles by Christ (1967, 1968) captured more attention. The work has been developed by Currie (1978) and extended to the private sector, in a way she would not do now, by Chick (1973a).

3.   The term was popularised by Andersen and Jordan (1968) and was probably first used by Culbertson (1963).

4.   Note that all this relates to Keynes's context, before inflationary expectations became entrenched. It is very difficult, these days, to *interpret* the rate of interest. Whether it is high or low when the nominal rate is, say 14 per cent and the actual rate of inflation is 20 per cent is, I submit, anybody's guess.

5.   Hegeland (1954), pp. 211–215 is the only author I have found to put the case that Keynes omitted the accelerator for this reason. No one to my knowledge has made the methodological suggestion.

6.   See Colm (1947, p. 463), Hansen (1938).

7.   There have been many sham battles. See Chick (1973b).

8.   Admirably summarised in Laidler (1969).

9.   A similar exposition appears in Friedman and Meiselman (1963).

10.   Following the quantity-theory view of the demand for money, money is held for transactions and precautionary purposes only.

11.   US practice is based on cash reserves; UK practice has involved various forms of liquid assets ratios, so the point holds less general force here and the particulars of the purchase and the regulations or conventions adhered to at the time would be germane.

12.   Keynes (1923), p. 65.

Chapter 19

POLICY IN A LONGER-TERM PERSPECTIVE*

Through the 1950s and early 1960s, periodic bouts of unemployment and underutilisation of resources were the chief policy concern. It was understood that expansionary policies in those times were likely to be mildly inflationary, but this was widely accepted as a price worth paying, until inflation began to accelerate in the late 1960s.

Interpretations of the higher rates of inflation of the late 1960s and 1970s have tended to focus on immediate causes — the role of 'irresponsible unions' or 'lax monetary authorities' (depending on the proponent's reading of the data and his political inclinations) and special features such as Russian wheat purchases and OPEC. These factors are, of course, important, but they should not be allowed to divert attention from a disturbing underlying pattern. Looking at the pattern of inflation in the UK and US over the period since the Korean War as a whole, a steady rise in the inflation rate at the troughs of cyclical swings is revealed. The upswing, taking off from a rising floor, has generated progressively higher peak inflation rates (in the UK the 1956 peak is an exception to this pattern). Table 19.1 gives the data.

In the 1970s it became clear that inflation was increasing and, if it was just a by-product of policies to alleviate unemployment, those policies were not working as they had done before. The idea which had begun with Keynes and was supported by some interpretations of the Phillips curve, that unemployment and inflation were evils with a trade-off — a bit more of one would gain a bit less of the other — was undermined as unemployment too showed signs of rising cycle by cycle (see Table 19.2). Though data are given for the US and UK, the problem involves the OECD countries more generally.[1]

* This chapter is a revised version of Chick (1978). Thanks are due to the *British Review of Economic Issues* for permission.

Table 19.1

Rates of Inflation at Cyclical Peaks and Troughs
Percentage Changes from Previous Year

(1) US: GNP Deflator				*(2) UK: Deflator for Total Final Expenditure*			
Trough		*Peak*		*Trough*		*Peak*	
1949	−0.6	1951	6.7			1956	5.6
1953	0.9	1957	3.7	1960	1.4	1962	3.2
1962	1.1	1970	5.5	1963	2.2	1965	4.4
1972	3.2	1974	10.0	1967	2.9	1971	8.0
				1972	6.8	1975	24.3
				1978	9.0		

(3) US: Consumer Price Index				*(4) UK: Retail Price Index*			
Trough		*Peak*		*Trough*		*Peak*	
		1951	7.9			1956	3.7
1955	0.4	1957	3.6	1959	0.6	1962	4.2
1959	0.8	1960	1.6	1963	2.0	1965	4.8
1961	1.0	1970	5.9	1967	2.5	1971	11.1
1972	3.3	1974	11.0	1972	8.9	1975	25.6
1976	5.8			1977	7.7		

Sources: (1) *The National Income and Product Accounts of the US, 1929–1965* and *Survey of Current Business,* various dates.
(2) Central Statistical Office, *National Income and Expenditure* (Blue Book): 1980, Table 2.6; 1974, Table 17; 1963, Table 16.
(3) *Economic Report of the President,* January 1980.
(4) Central Statistical Office, *Annual Abstract of Statistics:* 1982, Table 18.1; 1968, Table 379.

Table 19.2

Unemployment Rates at Peaks and Troughs
(Peak indicates low unemployment)

(1) US				*(2) UK*			
Trough		*Peak*		*Trough*		*Peak*	
1950	5.3	1953	2.9	1952	1.9	1955	1.1
1954	5.5	1956	4.1	1958	2.1	1961	1.6
1958	6.8	1960	5.5	1963	2.6	1965	1.5
1961	6.7	1969	3.5	1972	3.8	1974	2.7
1971	5.9	1973	4.9	1977	6.2	1979	5.7
1975	8.5	1979	5.8				

Sources: (1) *Economic Report of the President,* January 1980.
(2) Central Statistical Office, *Annual Abstract of Statistics:* 1982, Table 6.8; Tables 133, 142.

In my view the inflation is best understood as the culmination of a process which began at the end of the Second World War, to which the special factors mentioned above have given added impetus. My thesis is that a root cause of the current inflation is a misapplication of the policy prescription of the *General Theory*; a policy designed as a short-run remedy has been turned into a long-run stimulus to growth, without examining its long-run implications. Fundamental changes in the monetary system are essential background to the story. It is not clear whether those changes are themselves a result of policy or not; I rather think they are.

The simpler message taken from the *General Theory* was that to raise income one must invest. Hence postwar policy has offered direct or indirect encouragement to investment. Tax concessions to retain earnings and capital gains, investment allowances and grants, and accelerated depreciation allowances have been used fairly continuously; monetary policy aimed to lower interest rates and fiscal policy designed to raise demand have been used episodically.

Keynes's policy prescription was designed for a specific illness — unemployment and excess capital capacity in a world in which there was still considerable potential gain from further capital accumulation. The prescription, furthermore, was for a limited dose, designed to shock the patient into self-sustained recovery. It was not designed to sustain him over a long period.[2] In administering Keynesian medicine continuously (though in fitful doses) for 30 years, we failed to heed the warning cited at the end of the previous chapter:

> Each time we secure to-day's equilibrium by increased investment we are aggravating the difficulty of securing equilibrium tomorrow.
>
> *(G.T.* p. 105)

Recall from Chapter 16 and elsewhere that although Keynes favoured sustaining a boom, he had always at the back of his mind the stationary state as the final settling point. There is nothing inherently unpleasant about a stationary state: an economy 'ticking over' with full employment and adequate capital, including housing, would be fine. But Keynes thought it unlikely that the desire to save would be satisfied before the profitability of investment fell below the interest rate (that was the burden of the argument of Chapter 17): so the stationary state would be an unpleasant one.

The 'stagnationists' did not distinguish these two possibilities; thus *any* stationary state was viewed with alarm. In the entire postwar era, growth has been the keynote; but to sustain ever-higher levels of income, investment or government expenditure must continuously expand — at least in absolute terms and in the short term also relatively to national income — to fill the ever-widening gap between income and consumption.

Keynesians, though not Keynes, tended to assume that expansionary policy would have little effect on prices when there is unemployment. This optimistic expectation of price stability might be justified in the case of short-term or 'one-shot' use of expansionary policy, not, however, on fixprice grounds but on the grounds of conditions in the slump being particularly favourable to price stability in the short run and in the long run, there being compensation for the upward tendency in the ability to lower prices because of greater efficiency. Then one relies on the capacity of a growing economy to absorb the new money used to finance deficits or monetise the public debt.

But the long-term effect of semi-continuous expansionary policy is bound to be inflationary, for growth cannot be sustained indefinitely. Theorems of balanced growth depend on population growth and technological change; without them, the economy's equilibrium solution is the stationary state. Growth theory also ignores problems created by the residue of money and debt left in the wake of investment.

In the real world, the marginal efficiency of investment is expected to decline as the stock of capital increases, unless there is offsetting technical change. Even then there are limits to the profitability of increasingly roundabout methods of production because the incentive to *implement* inventions, embodying them in new equipment at a rate sufficient to fill the ever-widening gap between consumption and income implied by growth, requires the expectation of an ever-increasing demand for the output of such equipment. In the absence of a significant income redistribution, achievement of the required rate of growth of demand depends on population growth. With a stable population ever-greater stimuli are required to maintain profitability and the growth of demand, and these generate, over time, an increasing quantity of money which must be absorbed. Continuous deficits or ever-lower interest rates carry with them changes in the money supply which may vary in pace but not in direction.

Inflation since the war can be looked upon as the result of attempting to forestall the inevitable consequence of an increasing capital stock. It is both the concomitant of the fiscal and monetary policies designed to promote growth — indeed, to maintain the viability of corporate enterprise as we know it — and a useful instrument in its own right, for it drives down the real rate of interest and reduces the burden of corporate and public debt.

The Period of Rapid Growth and Slowdown

The postwar period began with a need for massive capital accumulation for reconstruction in Europe. Britain was particularly short of both productive capital and housing, having gone through a longer interwar slump than America or Europe due to her 1925 exchange rate decision. Indeed, rates of investment had been low even before the First World War. In the interwar period, investment as a proportion of national income had reached only 8.8 per cent in 1929 and 10.3 per cent by the comparatively healthy year of 1937.

Although not suffering the direct destruction of industrial capital and housing, America also entered the postwar period with a depleted stock of capital suitable for peacetime production. Redirection of production toward consumer goods provided a strong impetus for investment, while pent-up demand, reinforced by the baby boom, could be financed from the high levels of liquid assets acquired during the war.

Furthermore, war is a great spur to technological progress; new, more capital-intensive modes of production were waiting to be applied to peacetime uses, and the sheer habit of invention had become established. The 1950s saw many new products, which kept demand high, while the embodiment of considerable technological progress reduced costs and the relative prices of consumer durables and raised the standard of living generally. Rising profits and rising real wages were compatible.

At the level of casual empiricism, one could say that, particularly in the US, cracks in the system began to appear toward the end of the 1950s: built-in obsolescence and the creation of wants by advertising were the signs that 'genuine demand', however one might try to define that, was being less well served.

The above remark concerns the *quality* of technical change. Estimates for the UK (Schott, 1976) indicate that the overall *scale* of technical change also slowed down, though later — in the 1960s. Private industrial expenditure on research and development, deflated by an index of direct costs (manpower, materials and rent), rose steadily from 1950 to 1962, then fell for two years, recovered in the next two, and fell again from 1967 to 1970. In the US, the Council of Economic Advisors in its 1977 Report noted a fall in output per man-hour from an average of 3.3 per cent per year in 1948–66 to 2.1 per cent in 1966–73, attributed to the slowing of the growth of capital, though whether this is due to a reduction in the embodiment of technical change is not stated. Expenditure on research and development fell in the decade to 1975 (Schott, 1981).

The general picture is one in which technical change has slackened off, quantitatively and qualitatively, and in such circumstances one would expect to observe a decline in the marginal efficiency of capital. This implies a fall in the incentive to invest, unless compensated by a rising propensity to consume or an ever-falling interest rate.

The propensity to consume could be expected to respond to population growth or a redistribution of income toward lower income groups. Thus the postwar baby boom provided buoyancy for a time, but the rate of growth of population has now decreased in both countries. Evidence concerning income distribution is inconclusive. Atkinson's data (1975, pp. 51, 53) indicate an early postwar redistribution toward the middle income ranges away from both the high and low extremes in the UK. The US distribution exhibits some gain for lower income groups; however, their low absolute levels of income would limit the rise in demand in absolute terms. Overall, it

Table 19.3

Ratio of Profits to GNP

Year	UK: Profits as a Percentage of Total Final Output			US: Corporate Profits as a Per- centage of National Income	
	a	*b*	*c*	*a*	*b*
1946		25.6		n.a.	
1950		23.4		12.2	
1955		23.6		13.1	
1960		24.4		12.1	
1965		23.5		13.3	
1966	22.6	22.3		13.2	
1967	22.8	22.5		12.1	
1968	22.9	21.7		11.4	
1969	22.1			9.6	
1970	21.1		21.7	7.9	
1971	21.5		22.4	8.4	
1972	22.3		23.6	9.0	
1973	21.5		23.5	7.6	9.3
1974	18.4		20.0	4.0	7.4
1975	18.1		19.0	6.6	7.9
1976	18.5		20.0	n.a.	9.3
1977			21.6		9.8
1978			22.6		9.7
1979			21.6		9.3
1980			20.6		n.a.

Notes and Sources:

UK: Gross profits and other trading income, before providing for depreciation but after providing for stock appreciation. Source: Blue Book, Col. *a*, 1975; Col. *b*, 1969 and earlier Blue Books; Col. *c*, 1981.

US: Corporate Profits before tax and depreciation allowance but after inventory valuation adjustment. Source: Statistical Abstract of the US, Col. *a*, 1977; Col. *b*, 1980.

seems safe to say that there has been little obvious incentive to investment coming from income redistribution.

All this suggests that the general tendency of the *mec* to fall was strongly counteracted by technical change and buoyant demand at the beginning of this period, but in the middle of the 1960s these countervailing forces began to weaken.

Negative real rates of interest might have offered help for a time but obviously not as costs began to catch up with demand-inflation.

The tendency of the profitability of investment to fall is, of course, intolerable to enterprise and by the end of the 1950s probably also unacceptable to consumers, who had come to expect their incomes to grow. Investment must rise to achieve this growth but the incentive to invest formerly given by technological change had declined, and the stock of capital had by this time built up substantially. Thus to sustain a given rate of growth, greater policy action was necessary.

An indication of the fall of profits[3] is given in Table 19.3. The ratio of profits to GNP has been used instead of the theoretically preferable measure of the ratio of profits to capital because of the impossibility of measuring the latter. The roundaboutness of production has increased over the period, so the table gives an underestimate of the downward trend of the rate of profit on capital.

Table 19.4

Share of Government Spending in GNP/GDP

Quinquennial Averages

	UK	US
1950–54	14.9	19.2
1955–59	13.5	19.6
1960–64	16.7	20.5
1965–69	17.3	21.9
1970–74	18.4	22.0
1975–79	20.7	21.0

Notes and Sources:

> UK: 1950–59: Public authorities' expenditure on goods as a share of GDP in current prices. Blue Book 1962. (Break in data at dashed line)
> 1960–79: General government final consumption as a share of GDP in current prices. Blue Book 1981, Table 1.1.

> US: Government purchases of goods and services as a share of GNP. *Statistical Abstract of the United States 1980, The National Income and Product Accounts of the US, 1929–65,* and *Survey of Current Business,* various issues.

In the late 1960s, as declining profit rates became apparent, the proportion of government expenditure in GNP began to rise in the UK, and it continued its steady rise in the US (Table 19.4): if the tax, interest and demand incentives to investment prove insufficient to close the gap between income and consumption, government expenditure must close the gap instead. At the same time, in the UK the inflation rate accelerated sharply in 1968 to continue its dramatic climb to the 24 per cent rate of 1975. The US rate showed the elevated cyclical pattern pointed to earlier (Table 19.1).

The acceleration of inflation at this time, possibly already underway to recoup private sector losses on investment where return had not fulfilled expectations, would have been exacerbated by the low economic (as opposed to social) productivity or long payoff period of much government expenditure; when income-creating expenditure comes long before output, it is almost a matter of arithmetic that prices will rise.[4]

Capital Inadequacy as a Background for Policy

In Chapter 16 it was pointed out that the assumption, based on the facts of the time, that capital was far from adequate, was basic to the *General Theory*. In Keynes's view even the country with the strongest claim to capital saturation, the United States, was a long way from it in 1929 (*G.T.* pp. 322–3). This empirical assessment adds long-run desirability to short-run expediency in advocating government provision of a stimulus, not just to demand generally but to investment in particular.

It was easy to grasp the message that stimulating investment would encourage growth and employment, and Keynesians took it up with enthusiasm. A country whose capital was increasing was obviously growing, and it was seen as becoming more efficient as well. Following the American pattern, the efficiency of productive techniques was evaluated in terms of output per head: capital-intensive methods of production were systematically encouraged. Particularly, failure of British industry to compete was (and still is) blamed largely on the lack of modern (i.e. labour-saving) equipment. Fears of labour-displacement were dismissed: it was Keynesian doctrine that investment created income and employment; the significance of the short run assumption was virtually ignored.

Keynes's reasons for concentrating on investment demand in stimulating expansion were, however, somewhat different from the productivity argument. Investment expenditure, being heavily dependent on expectations, is volatile; it can be manipulated as long as expectations themselves can be changed.

Expenditure on investment goods has the added advantage that the wisdom of that expenditure is not subject to rapid falsification through immediate confrontation with the market demand for its product. There is a lag; not only is there a gestation period before any product at all appears, but profits are realised over a long run of production, during which fluctuations in demand would normally be expected. A single disappointing year would not be taken as a sign that the investment was a mistake. Therefore, a successful shift of expectations toward greater optimism may be expected to induce a flow of investment for a considerable period. In contrast, expansion of the production of consumer goods is all too quickly submitted to the market test and cannot be relied upon to sustain a boom unless demand itself can be relied upon to remain high.

The Gap between Income and Consumption

Investment was favoured, as the component of demand most easily manipulated by policy to cure a cyclical downturn. It was also essential to expansion: some portion of output must always be devoted to it if income is to be raised permanently to a new level.

> [If] there is no change in the propensity to consume, employment cannot increase, unless at the same time D_2 is increasing so as to fill the increasing gap between Z and D_1.

> (*G.T.* p. 30)

This must be one of the best-known propositions in macroeconomics, yet its long-run significance appears to have been lost entirely. Keynes himself was more perceptive:

> The consumption for which we can profitably provide in advance cannot be pushed indefinitely into the future ... The greater, moreover, the consumption for which we have provided in advance, the more difficult it is to find something further to provide for in advance, and the greater our dependence on present consumption as a source of demand. Yet the larger our incomes, the greater, unfortunately, is the margin between our incomes and our consumption ... Thus the problem of providing that new capital-investment shall always outrun capital-disinvestment sufficiently to fill the gap between net income and consumption, presents a problem which is increasingly difficult as capital increases ... [There is] no answer to the riddle, except that there must be sufficient unemployment to keep us so poor that our consumption falls short of our income by no more than the equivalent of the physical provision for future consumption which it pays to produce to-day.

> (*G.T.* pp. 104–5)

That is, the system converges to the stationary state, not the steady-state growth which we have come to expect and which postwar theory has led us to believe we could have.

Stable Consumption and the Declining Marginal Efficiency of Capital

The difference between Keynes and the steady-state growthmen has perhaps two (real) roots. One concerns the dependence of investment on expected growth of future consumption. Without population growth consumption cannot be expected to increase without limit. And the consumption-increasing potential of income redistribution has its limits, even when the redistribution itself is not opposed politically. Furthermore, there is no reason to suppose that incremental consumption will fall on the products of those industries with great scope for increasing the roundaboutness of their production methods, and it is these which must be encouraged if investment is to be maintained.

In the early postwar period the development of new products helped to keep up demand. But while firms may exercise considerable imagination in this sphere there is no guarantee that they will develop those products with the highest potential demand. Keynes remarked that this point was appreciated in the context of public expenditure, but in fact held more force in the realm of private sector investment:

> It is commonly urged as an objection to schemes for raising employment by investment under the auspices of public authority that it is laying up trouble for the future. 'What will you do', it is asked, 'when you have built all the houses and roads and town halls and electric grids and water supplies and so forth which the stationary population of the future can be expected to require?' But it is not so easily understood that the same difficulty applies to private investment and to industrial expansion; particularly to the latter, since it is much easier to see an early satiation of the demand for new factories and plant which absorb individually but little money, than of the demand for dwelling-houses.
>
> (*G.T.* p. 106)

It is expansion along well-worked lines that exhausts demand and lowers the marginal efficiency of further investment in those lines.

Falling marginal efficiency compounds the problem begun by the ever-increasing gap between consumption and income:

> Not only is the marginal propensity to consume weaker in a wealthy community, but, owing to its accumulation of capital being already larger, the opportunities for further investment are less attractive unless the rate of interest falls at a sufficiently rapid rate.
>
> (*G.T.* p. 31)

Thus the rate of interest must fall at an *ever-increasing* rate (other things being equal), until it reaches its floor, after which net investment will be zero — the stationary state — unless there is technical change.

Here lies the second source of difference with the 'growthmen'. They see growth chiefly as the embodiment of technical change, which counteracts the fall in the marginal efficiency. They appear to forget that getting new ideas is not enough: technical advances must be worth embodying. It is highly significant that in the absence of either population growth or continuous technological change, not only Keynes but modern growth theory also predicts convergence to the stationary state.

Labour-Saving Investment

Any stationary state seems bad enough to some; the 'revolution of rising expectations' is not confined to the Third World. But the probability that the economy will converge to a less-than-full-employment stationary state is exacerbated by the bias toward investment in labour-saving techniques.

Discussion of the long-run effects of the substitution of capital for labour on employment is still distinctly unfashionable. Maurice Scott (1978) has had the courage to analyse the problem.

Labour displaced by capital-intensive techniques will only find employment while the economy is growing — and to a Keynesian, investment is the cause of growth. It is the cause of growth in the short run. Yet there are such strong reasons for the bias toward capital-intensity: labour is so much more difficult to control. In the long run, why is it not reasonable to expect what Scott's analysis shows: that equilibrium employment will be lower in the more capital-intensive economy.

The Avoidance of the Stationary State

The foregoing suggests that government policy designed to stimulate investment may be helpful for a time, although it is doomed to failure in the absence of repeated shifts in the composition of output toward more profitable lines. These in turn require population growth, technical change, income redistribution, or the opening of new frontiers.

Firms which live and grow by finding new outlets for expansion will not easily accept the state of affairs to which the accumulation of stocks of capital inexorably leads: where investment covers only replacement and profit can be no more than is strictly necessary to keep the productive machine ticking over.

Households, until recently at least believing that they are getting a return for their savings, will not like it either: the scope for saving at more than zero interest was, Keynes thought, nil:

> [A] little reflection will show what enormous social changes would result from a gradual disappearance of a rate of return on accumulated wealth. A man would still be free to accumulate his earned income with a view to spending it at a later date. But his accumulation would not grow. He would simply be in the position of Pope's father, who, when he retired from business, carried a chest of guineas with him to his villa at Twickenham and met his household expenses from it as required.
>
> *(G.T.* p. 221)

This is the consumption-loan theorem for a stable population (Samuelson, 1958; Robinson, 1960). Bargaining between the non-working and working sectors of the population may make the rate of interest available to a particular cohort non-zero, but in aggregate the surplus goes into the replacement of capital.

The political and social consequences of these features of the stationary state are obviously alarming. I have not seen them debated. It is not difficult to see that the long-term end of capital accumulation threatens the present social structure, and one would expect governments to take action to avoid it.

There are contradictions, of course, between the short-run need for investment and the long-run consequences of the investments themselves. But there is a sense in which demand management or low-interest-rate policies pursued for contracyclical purposes help to forestall the long run. This effect is not due to the rise in demand or low interest themselves, for these are ultimately not adequate — but rather stem from inflationary consequences of these policies. Let us examine the mechanism more closely.

The Inflation Mechanism

When demand is raised by a tax cut or increased government expenditure, money incomes are raised in advance of output. For any given state of the economy the inflationary impact is the more pronounced the greater the proportion of the deficit financed by new money. The rise in money income shifts the aggregate demand curve upwards. The result, if the money wage is unchanged, is to raise the profit-maximising output of the industry and permit whatever rise in price is necessary to compensate for diminishing returns. Output and prices rise; profits rise and real wages fall. Expansionary policy can also be used to raise demand to cover increased wages or other costs.

Not all these price rises are 'true inflation', but price rises are essential to expansion in all but extreme cases in the short run. And policy always operates in the short run.

Its effects, however, are long-run. Here we have two conflicting influences. If the investment improves efficiency, costs will fall and prices may be reduced. But over time, to get the same amount of investment, larger and larger stimuli will be required, and in the short run, that means progressively larger price increases.

The same remarks apply to interest-rate policy through monetisation of the public debt. Over the longer term, the rate of interest must be made to fall at ever more rapid rates to achieve the same investment result. Larger and larger increases in the money supply will be necessary and this must be inflationary.

Inflation, The Real Rate of Interest and the Debt Burden: Inflation is not just a by-product of fiscal and monetary policies — (nor is it exclusively a by-product of these policies). A demand inflation has a directly beneficial effect on investment and also benefits by reducing the real rate of interest and lowering the real value of outstanding debt.

It was Keynes's despairing complaint that the rate of interest could not be pushed down indefinitely; the absolute floor was set by the existence of an acceptable non-interest-bearing asset, and for practical purposes the floor was somewhat higher, determined by belief concerning the normal rate. Inflation, however, lowers the *real* rate of interest. Real rates can be (and have been) negative and can continue to fall over time as long as inflation is not fully anticipated by savers or as long as they do not have a range of action adequate to ensure that they obtain a satisfactory rate of return. Both these factors can operate for a considerable run of years before first the anticipations and later the institutional arrangements alter. During that time, inflation permits borrowers, notably corporations and the government, to obtain funds cheaply.

Inflation achieves a permanent transfer of command over resources from surplus to deficit sectors, and a permanent destruction of some of the real value of financial wealth. (Some of that may be anticipated by creditors and the rate of interest demanded adjusted accordingly.) However, the usefulness of inflation in reducing the real rate of interest and transferring funds does have its limits, as costs catch up with demand. One might hazard a guess that the usefulness of inflation had ceased by 1972.

Wasteful and Misdirected Investment

The amount of inflation a given expansionary stimulus will generate depends on how *well* funds are channelled into productive investment. After years of concentrating on the broad Keynesian aggregates, this point finally got through to the British Government, as these remarks by Denis Healey as Chancellor of the Exchequer (1975) illustrate:

> It is no good throwing money down the drain to keep firms or industries going if they are not producing the sort of things which the world is going to buy ... The fact is that our manufacturing industry is badly wrong at present. We are producing far too many things that other people do not want and at prices they cannot afford.

The short-run implication is clear. If we are prepared to administer Keynesian medicine selectively, we should be able to maintain a given level of employment at a far lower cost in terms of inflation.

To look at the point from the opposite direction, the inflationary impact of wasteful expenditure can most easily be seen in the extreme case, when, in the short run at least, money incomes are generated but there is no additional output. This case is similar to profitable investment with a long payoff. Indeed, for a long time one cannot tell the difference between them.

Price rises can compensate for investment projects which, *ex post*, prove not to yield their expected return, hence they can be used to shift the burden of entrepreneurial error away from those directly responsible on to the public at large. The more of such investment there is, the more inflationary is any expansionary policy.

The point is so obvious that one wonders why such an unselective approach to policy has been taken heretofore. I suggest three reasons. The first is that it avoids any suggestion of planning or directing activity which, it is widely believed (especially in the United States), should be controlled by private enterprise.

The second reason derives from the environment which shaped Keynes's views: in a period of large-scale unemployment it did not much matter what was produced as long as more jobs were offered. Furthermore, even wasteful and misdirected expenditure would have multiplier effects — and these would largely affect output, not prices, in a period of slack capacity:

> It may be that [a policy of deterring over-optimism with high interest rates] overlooks the social advantage which accrues from the increased consumption which attends even on investment which proves to have been totally misdirected, so that even such investment may be more beneficial than no investment at all.
>
> (*G.T.* p. 327)

Not that he approved:

> It would, indeed, be more sensible to build houses and the like; but if there are political and practical difficulties in the way of this, the above would be better than nothing.
>
> (*G.T.* p. 129)

The third possibility is that wasteful expenditure is a blessing in disguise! It may even have been encouraged semi-consciously, to serve a real social purpose, for it postpones the day when 'the abundance of capital will interfere with the abundance of output':

> Ancient Egypt was doubly fortunate, and doubtless owed to this its fabled wealth, in that it possessed two activities, namely, pyramid-building as well as the search for the precious metals, the fruits of which, since they could not serve the needs of man by being consumed, did not stale with abundance. The Middle Ages built cathedrals and sang dirges. Two pyramids, two masses for the dead, are twice as good as one; but not so two railways from London to York.
>
> (*G.T.* p. 131)

So here we are today, with the (labour-intensive) arts starved of money and a good many airways from London to New York — which perhaps shows that one can even misdirect one's 'wasteful' expenditure. Might it not be time to ask whether a redistribution of expenditure might achieve higher employment with less inflation?

The Monetary System

It is doubtful whether the rates of inflation experienced in recent years could have occurred in the monetary framework of Keynes's time. Although Britain — and the rest of Europe — was off the gold standard by the time the *General Theory* was published, it is fairly clear that Keynes regarded something like a gold standard as the *norm*: an essential property of money, to him, was its inelasticity of supply. Indeed, that inelasticity was the source of the difficulty in achieving a sufficiently low rate of interest, and when the time came at the end of the war to reorganise the international monetary system, Keynes wanted much greater elasticity than the gold standard had allowed.

What the world got, of course, was a gold-exchange system with the dollar as the key currency.

Meanwhile, the domestic currencies were freed of their links to gold.

Now let us retrace the steps of the argument with these facts clearly in view. Beginning again at the end of the war, the remarkable fact is the very low rates of inflation in America, the Korean War year excepted. The rapid rate of real growth would partly account for that; the rest, I suggest, is explained by the international liquidity shortage. America's trade deficits were balanced by absorption of dollars into international reserves: a form of idle balances, at least from America's point of view. Domestic inflationary pressures were thus partly released through this outlet.

The desire of other countries to acquire dollars began to weaken in the late 1960s. International pressure for the US to 'do something' about its deficit seems to have had little effect on policy — deflationary measures were unpalatable. As it was, rates of inflation began to rise — at the sort of time in a period of growth when it would be quite reasonable to expect prices to begin to fall: extensive investment, embodying great technical advances, had taken place, yet the benefits in terms of price reductions were not in evidence. Keynesians apparently did not expect them and did not enquire why they were not more in evidence — whether there were inflationary pressures which past improvements in efficiency were ameliorating — and disguising.

The postwar fixed-exchange-rate system operated differently for Britain, which had lost the key-currency position. The threat of reserve losses tended periodically to thwart British expansionary policies and that factor probably partly held back UK inflation.

The constraints imposed by reserve losses have been done away with by flexible exchange rates, though balance of payments deficits can still evoke deflationary policy responses when governments are unwilling to accept currency depreciations. There is more potential flexibility of policy response, however.

While the Bretton Woods system was breaking down, the private banking system was transforming itself, freeing itself from traditional controls and becoming an international network. The money supply has become very elastic indeed, and there is no guarantee of a compensating 'sink for purchasing power' in the form of money which would absorb an excess supply. Inflationary pressures have become free to manifest themselves fully.

Summary and Conclusions

The argument of this chapter is that policies of demand management designed for the relief of unemployment when long-term expectations have collapsed have been instead directed to the goal of long-term growth and this has an inherently inflationary bias which is likely to be worse the more roundabout production becomes and the greater is the accumulated capital stock. The greater roundaboutness lengthens the gap between money income and available output but puts off the fall in the *mec*. Eventually, however, the greater accumulation makes the stimulation of private investment more difficult.

The inflationary bias was partly controlled in the early postwar years by a shortage of international liquidity and partly disguised in the leading industrial nation by the operation of that same monetary system. The banking systems of the US and UK were both then amenable to traditional controls. The monetary system, national and international, has been transformed, and the latent inflationary pressures have manifest themselves.

The emergence of serious inflation is not adequate reason for 'going into reverse', attempting to reduce inflation by cutting back expenditure as is being done in the UK at present: Keynes himself warned (*G.T*.p. 291) that the system was not symmetrical and that the effects of such action would fall more on employment than on prices. And he was thinking in terms of a stable monetary structure and fairly constant money supply.

The analysis of this chapter is offered not as an apology for present (1982) policy but as a cautionary tale: if the assumptions of one's theory are not well understood, or if the correspondence between theory and reality is not often enough assessed, one can carry out a succession of policies, each of which is reasonable from a short-sighted perspective, but which has an unexpected and undesirable long-term outcome. Stagflation is unpleasant enough in itself and is all the worse for inviting the prescription of the sort of medicine which is likely to damage the patient.

Greater selectivity and planning of investment might have forestalled some of the present difficulties. The greater use of income redistribution in place of expansion of overall money incomes might have had a similar effect. In some sense, policy thinking has been, from a longer-term perspective, too aggregative — and though the aggregates have shifted from $C + I + G$ to the Public Sector Borrowing Requirement and £M3 — still are.

Notes

1. OECD (1977), especially Table 1, p. 42 and Chart 15, p. 105.

2. Hansen (1938) also uses a medical metaphor, one which might better suit anyone put off by the homeopathic overtones of mine:

    It is of utmost importance not to be so scared of inflation as to drive headlong into stagnation. Were we not familiar with the efficacy of vaccines, it would seem utterly insane to produce a mild case of a disease in order to prevent a devastating malady. Yet it is something of this sort which it is necessary to apply in economic therapeutics today. (p. 319)

Some vaccines wear off and have to be repeated, but no one would think of them as a substitute for the basic health of the organism.

3.   For a thorough examination of the data and the issues, see King (1975).

4.   The only mitigation would come from an increased propensity to save, preferably in the form of idle balances — an unlikely coincidence.

Chapter *20*

THE RELEVANCE OF THE *GENERAL THEORY* TODAY

On the question of relevance, the position taken in the opening chapter of this book was this: the *General Theory* was a book rooted in its own time, but its analysis is far more relevant to our own time than most macroeconomic theory — including that labelled 'Keynesian' — which has been developed since. We proceeded on that basis, pointing out areas of dissonance between theory and later reality as we went along.

It is time to gather up those points and decide whether — or to what extent — the theory is still useful and to note the areas in which revision of the theory seems imperative.

Omissions

Some very important things are dealt with only tangentially in the theory — and in this book too. Government enters only as an occasional agent, engaging in policy actions when these are deemed necessary. International trade and payments also play a minor role; the theory is essentially one of a closed economy.

The latter was an unrealistic assumption even when the book was written. One could argue that international trade in the 1930s had shrunk so dramatically as to justify the assumption, but not in the context of a theory designed to hold over a wide variety of circumstances. The collapse of trade into autarky was almost universally believed to be a depression phenomenon, albeit a very serious one.

The role of government has of course altered very substantially. Government now participates in production on a long-term basis. The entrepreneur economy has become a mixed economy, neither purely

private-enterprise nor planned. Whether this makes a substantial difference
or not is an open question.

The answer depends on one's views of the motives of government — and
of corporations — in the productive sphere. If the two behave similarly, no
harm is done by treating this aspect of government as part of the firm sector.
There are many, however, who would argue that the two-sector framework
of the *General Theory* no longer suffices.

Some would argue, also, that the type of *output* produced by government
is sufficiently different to warrant special treatment. Bacon and Eltis (1976)
are extreme representatives of this view; they aver that the output associated
with government expenditure is of no economic significance (though
presumably they would admit a certain welfare content). Again, the validity
and importance of this argument is a matter for individual judgement.

Whatever the reader decides, he is enjoined to remember that it is one
thing to complain that certain features of the real world — even important
features — are missing and another to incorporate those features into a
theory without causing the theory to collapse under the weight of its own
complexity. Good theory is relevant simplification; the simplification is as
important as the relevance.

Six Key Assumptions

The *General Theory* as it stands, the theory of the interplay between the two
sides of industry in a closed economy, rests, as I see it, on six key
assumptions. They are not all equally fundamental, but they will be
discussed on an equal footing. They are all grounded in the world Keynes
was looking at; we must decide whether our world is significantly different.

(1) It is well known that Keynes dealt with the question of
unemployment. Indeed the impression is sometimes conveyed that
the theory *only* pertains to unemployment states. His claim to
generality, however, rests on the applicability of his theory to both
unemployment and full-employment states. What is true is that he
regarded unemployment as the norm and full employment as the
fortunate exception.

(2) There is a presumption of broad price stability over the sort of run of
years which would influence labour-supply decisions. There would
be cyclical variations of course, but around a stable level.

(3) Keynes took a view of the monetary system based essentially on the
gold standard, with its corollaries of a relatively inelastic money
supply and fixed exchange rates. The fact that when the *General
Theory* was written Britain was off the gold standard and exchange
rates were fluctuating does not vitiate my point: that the features
associated with the gold standard were taken as the norm.

(4) The fourth assumption is known to everybody: namely, the

Marshallian short run with a given capital stock and 'state of the arts', i.e. no technical progress.

(5), (6) Finally there are two underlying characteristics which turn out, I believe, to be quite important. One is that the population is relatively stable. The other, hardly ever mentioned, is that no Western economy in Keynes's judgement had, up to then, reached the point at which the capital stock was in any sense adequate.

In summary, these are the six assumptions which I believe to be decisive in shaping the *General Theory*:

(1) unemployment is the norm;
(2) there is broad price stability;
(3) the money supply is quite inelastic;
(4) the capital stock and techniques are given;
(5) the population is not growing substantially;
(6) the capital stock is 'inadequate'.

(1) Unemployment

Chapters 4, 5 and 7 have brought out the technical importance of 'being off the labour supply curve to the left'. This permits considerable variation in the demand for labour in either direction without a change in money wages, which in turn permits one to discuss movements along a given aggregate supply curve in money terms. Changes in w set both Z and D shifting about, the latter in a slightly unpredictable way.

The assumption of unemployment as a normal condition may have been shaped by the experience of Britain in the 1920s and 1930s. The data indicating the persistence of unemployment through those years was given in Chapter 1. Despite rates of unemployment of over 10 per cent throughout this period, the wage index fell by only 8 points from its high of 105 in 1925 to 97 in 1934–35 and rose to only 107 in 1938 as Britain prepared for war.

The American experience in this period was very different: there was no 1920s recession and wages fell much further in the depression. In the matter of empirical applicability, Keynes's assumption of unemployment as the norm and the conclusion of his theory regarding wages fitted Britain much more closely than the US.

In the 1970s, in both countries, we have witnessed the combination of high levels of unemployment and *rising* wages, a combination unthinkable in Keynes's time except perhaps in a few industries. This combination must have to do with the alteration in the monetary system discussed in Chapters 12 and 19 and is therefore related to assumption (3). The implication for theory is that we may have to come to grips with the simultaneous shifts in Z and D more fully than has yet been done. Keynes's long-lost wage-unit device might help to avoid many of the difficulties. The problem of the relation of D and income distribution is brought to the fore.

(2) Price Stability

Behind that interwar experience lay the Pax Britannica. During this long period, the hundred years from the end of the Napoleonic Wars to the First World War, economic activity fluctuated, sometimes with serious financial crises, and prices went up and down with these fluctuations. Recall that in Table 7.1 prices show considerable movement, but not the phenomenon which we have come to take for granted — that prices go in only one direction, the only question being their rate of rise.

It is plain that price stability of the 19th century kind no longer holds and that the labour supply curve has become sensitive to expected inflation. This fact has been partly responsible for the upward trend in wage rates (in money terms) throughout the period since the Second World War. And the wage rises help to raise prices.

It has been said that Keynes postulated money illusion for workers but not for firms. This charge is too shallow. The asymmetry in their responses is explicable precisely in the context outlined — cycles around a basic stability — given the nature of the decisions facing firms and households. As producers, firms *must* anticipate changes in demand and make pricing and output decisions sufficiently often to capture adequate profits.

The firm in the *General Theory* is a small firm and is a profit maximiser, but one does not have to assume continuous adjustment, extremely short-run profit-maximisation, to assert that these firms will adjust their demand for labour to perceived or anticipated fluctuations in demand for output, which is reflected in prices. The Marshallian concept of normal price, the idea that prices are not adjusted to *every* variation in demand, is quite consistent with this: cyclical variations are strong enough to require adjustment of output and labour demands to changes in demand which, by the nature of their activities, producers must forecast. The very fact that cycles in employment, output, and prices are observed corroborates this.

It seems to me that while shifts in N^s due to price expectations must now be incorporated into theory, it would be a mistake to impose the assumption that labour makes forecasts of prices over the time horizon applicable to firms. Labour is in a fundamentally different position from that of firms. Firms must anticipate changes in demand and set prices. Labour has a more passive role. It does not set prices; it only adjusts to them or to anticipations of them. In an environment in which it is perceived that, on the whole, prices go down about as often as they go up, it might not be worthwhile for labour, either individually or collectively, to renegotiate wage rates during cyclical upswings to keep real wages constant, but rather to anticipate that prices will fall subsequently and reckon on averaging out fluctuations in real wages. Firms of course would resist rises in (money) wages in any event, but especially in view of the institutional difficulty of cutting them later, and workers must be aware of this. The net result is a plausible explanation for a certain insensitivity of the labour supply curve to anticipated price changes arising both from the stickiness of the anticipations themselves and sluggishness in acting upon them.

The asymmetry between firms and the suppliers of labour is lessened when the expectation of stable prices with cyclical variation gives way to experience of a price trend which persistently undermines the validity of the money wage as a proxy for the real wage. When a rising trend of prices becomes the norm, labour cannot be expected to 'wait out a cycle', but it is not irrational for their expectation-horizon to be different from that of firms.

The more rapidly and completely labour adjusts to the possibility of inflation, the less tenable is the demand-orientation of conventional Keynesianism. When wages change, the point of effective demand becomes as much determined by shifts in aggregate supply as by shifts in aggregate demand, with unpredictable effects, as we said before.

(3) The Monetary System

It is worth asking whether the modern observation that prices only go in one direction is a myopic view, whether we are not just seeing the upward side of some long cycle.

Had that question been asked in the early 1970s the answer would have to have been far less confident. It is one thing to witness prices rising when the economies of the Western World were expanding, but quite another to come to terms with prices continuing to rise when output is falling and unemployment high and increasing.

The previous chapter was devoted to the question of secular change toward the situation in which such observations are possible. The 'real' side of the argument of that chapter could be much disputed. But it is difficult to dispute that prices cannot continue to rise over extended periods of time without a fundamental change in monetary arrangements as compared to those of Keynes's time.

The theory of managed money presupposes that the monetary authorities are both able and willing to control the money supply, standing in the stead of the somewhat adventitious constraints of the cost of gold mining and the balance of payments. This presumption has been challenged from two different directions: some have questioned the *ability* of the central bank to control the money supply or the money base, others challenge its *willingness* to do so — a point of view which usually rests on the argument that the Bank's aim is to control something else, viz. interest rates.

These ideas, while valid and interesting in themselves, fail, I believe, to deal with the essential issues: the radical transformation of the relations between monetary institutions and corporate enterprise, and the demise of any coherent international monetary system whatever. An international banking system has grown up, destroying national boundaries as the multinational corporations have done on the 'real' side. These banks now enjoy the assurance of lender-of-last-resort facilities from the major central banks, with no concomitant checks on their expansion.

The international money supply under present arrangements can expand very rapidly indeed, when such expansion is profitable for the banks, and it is difficult for the advanced Western countries to 'sterilise' the resulting monetary impact on what are quaintly called their 'domestic' economies, as if one could, any longer, shut the door on the outside world.

Domestic monetary systems, too, are now carefully protected from collapse. Given the ability of financial systems to implode (crisis), this protection is undoubtedly a good thing, but it is bound to expand the money supply. And the more rapidly the money supply increases, the greater the impact on prices relatively to output, if for no other reason than that output takes time to expand.

In the present writer's view, the elasticity of the postwar monetary system is probably the single most important area of departure from Keynes's assumptions and, with its corollaries for price expectations and the locus of the liquidity premium, represents the area of the theory most in need of thorough revamping. It is not enough merely to convert standard macro-theory from levels of the variables to rates of change. Many of the modifications needed have already been raised in the literature. The question of whether the new monetary system requires a different simplification from the one found by Keynes has not, however, received much attention. It may be that a radical revision is in order.

(4) The Short Run

Fixity of the capital stock and embodied technique is always a correct assumption for a short span of time. The length of time within which it remains 'correct' — i.e. relevant — varies from one historical episode to another. Perhaps at no time in modern British economic history was it quite as applicable as it was in the 1930s, with many years of low rates of capital accumulation preceding that time. The twenty years after the war were manifestly *not* the time for applying the short run assumption over a span of more than a few years. It may be more relevant now than it was in the heyday of Keynesianism, when it was most strikingly at variance with the world to which it was supposed to pertain.

(5) Stable Population

The assumption of a stable population has also come back into its own. With technical progress slowing down sometime in the mid-1960s, investment much reduced since the mid-1970s and population growth in Britain approaching zero, the vision of growth as normal, which marked the 1960s, should be abandoned in favour of an expectation of a high level of income with periodic bursts of high activity in response, say, to some new invention (a Schumpeterian view?) and periods of disappointment.

A British population growth rate falling gradually from an average of 1.5 per cent per year in 1821–31 and declining virtually to zero between 1911 and 1931 I believe is an important element in Keynes's assumption of a stable propensity to consume. A stable population would have been coupled in Keynes's mind with a conception of a fairly stable social pattern of consumption which has also changed. The stability of the pattern has changed and this may weaken to some extent the significance of the return in recent years to low rates of population growth.

(6) Inadequate Capital Stock

With the background of a stable consumption function in mind I come to the last key assumption. In many ways I think it is the most basic assumption, yet Keynes does not bring it out until quite late on: he believed that not in the UK nor even in the US had the capital stock reached the point of what he called full investment — that circumstance in which an increment to the capital stock cannot be expected to yield enough to cover replacement cost, *even* if full-employment demand is sustained throughout.

Keynes distinguishes between overinvestment in the sense that the yield which is expected on an investment is falsified because of a cyclical downturn, which with unemployment and decreased sales does not pay off though it would if full employment were sustained, and full investment as defined above, when further investment is not justified even in the most favourable light.

Full investment, therefore, is a notion of capital saturation or capital adequacy which is contingent on full employment. Keynes argued, very strongly, that such a situation had not been seen in any advanced economy at that time, including the US, however rich it might appear to be; that was his judgement. In such a context, where you believe that the social return from investment is almost bound to be positive, and where (perhaps) there was less reason then to question the identification of the ability of firms to make profits with the ability of firms to satisfy wants than there has been since the emergence of the giant corporation, it is an easy step to the proposition that the social rate of return on further investment is also unlikely to be zero.

This proposition is made for aggregates, of course, and that means on average. No one is suggesting that every investment made was successful in the sense defined.

In a world in which, one believes, the social return from investment is almost bound to be positive, then almost *any* investment is a Good Thing: not only does it provide employment in the short run, it is also a beneficial addition to productive capacity. Keynes admits the possibility of misdirected investment, that is, investment which mal-allocates resources because the activity does not pay off in the sense defined, but it is clearly not a possibility which alarms him.

Today, although for some individual industries capital is not adequate, is it not fair to say that for the economy as a whole we are closer to capital-saturation than we were in 1932? Indeed it is obvious that some industries are over-capitalised, in the context of world competition. In this context, the bland assumption implicit in usual macroeconomic theory and policy advice, that one investment is as good as any other, is an anachronism and a costly one. Is it not time to ask the question posed in the previous chapter: could we gain more employment for a lower inflation-cost by attending to the careful *direction* of policy-encouraged investment rather than by giving a stimulus, indiscriminately, to investment as a whole? This is a question which I believe has become extremely important now. It has not been asked since Keynes himself asked it. (It is very difficult, politically.)

Conclusion

What does one conclude from the explorations of this book? The most obvious conclusion is that economic theory is not a body of abstract logical analysis based on general principles applicable to all times and types of economic systems. This is not to say, however, that all theorising is useless and one is bound to the confines of institutional and historical description. Nor is it legitimate to conclude that the level of generality of economic theory is limited by the historical nature of the object of study: it is also limited by our imaginative powers and the youth of our discipline. But whatever the level of generality attained, the capacity of theories to capture the salient facts must remain under constant review.

It is, I think, fair to say that the macroeconomic theory we have at *present* has not moved adequately with the times. This is particularly true of the macroeconomic theory taught in textbooks, but it is true, too, of the original inspiration of that theory.

However, despite the importance of the changes which I have outlined, I believe that the *General Theory* still contains much that is useful: the idea of aggregating expenditure according to the degree of autonomy from current income (though with the rise in importance of both consumer durables and consumer credit we may wish to draw the line elsewhere), the restoration from classical authors of the periodic importance of speculation and its displacement to the financial sphere, and the integration of the consequence of asset-holding with the flows of production and investment — these ideas still hold. And the fundamental, contradictory relationship between households and producers is still the core of the problem of how capitalism functions, though now it is functioning with a degree of international integration Keynes did not foresee and with government mediation on a scale for which the theory had no place.

I believe that even in the present environment, some of the elements of Keynes's theory can, with extension — or modification — be retained. The readers of this book may take a different view. That is as it should be, for no theory is final. The student may find that fact disquieting, but he *should* find it heartening: if he becomes an economist, there will be plenty for him to discover and to do. He may not be in equilibrium, but he need not be underemployed.

REFERENCES &
REFERENCE INDEX

The numbers in square brackets at the end of each entry indicate where citations occur in the text.

Andersen L C and Jordan J L, Monetary and Fiscal Actions: A Test of Their Relative Importance in Economic Stabilization, *Federal Reserve Bank of St. Louis Review* 50, November 1968, 11–24. [335]

Archibald G C, Multiplier and Velocity Analysis: An Annulment, *Economica,* n.s. 23, August 1956, 265–69. [267]

Arrow K J, Towards a Theory of Price Adjustment, in M Abramovitz (ed.), *The Allocation of Economic Resources,* Stanford University Press, 1959. [33, 170]

Asimakopulos A, The Determination of Investment in Keynes's Model, *Canadian Journal of Economics* 4, August 1971, 382–88. [131]

Atkinson A B, *The Economics of Inequality,* Oxford University Press, 1975. [340]

Bacon R and Eltis W, *Britain's Economic Problem: Two Few Producers,* Macmillan, 1976. [354]

Bain A D, *The Economics of the Financial System,* Martin Robertson, 1981. [231]

Bank of England, The Secondary Banking Crisis and the Bank of England's Support Operations, *Bank of England Quarterly Bulletin* 18, June 1978. [292]

Barro R, Inflation, the Payments Period, and the Demand for Money, *Journal of Political Economy* 78, November/December 1970, 1228–63. [211]

Baumol W J, Say's (at least) Eight Laws, or What Say and James Mill May Really Have Meant, *Economica* 44, May 1977, 145–62. [13, 80]

Baumol W J, The Transactions Demand for Cash: An Inventory–Theoretic Approach, *Quarterly Journal of Economics* 66, November 1952, 545–56. [211]

Benavie A, Disequilibrium Static Analysis, *Western Economic Journal* (now *Economic Enquiry*) 10, 1972. [16]

Blinder A S and Solow R M, Does Fiscal Policy Matter?, *Journal of Public Economics* 2, 1973. [321]

Boulding K E, *A Reconstruction of Economics,* John Wiley, 1950. [45]

Bronfenbrenner M (ed.), *Is the Business Cycle Obsolete?,* John Wiley, 1969. [287]

Brunner K, The 'Monetarist Revolution' in Monetary Theory, *Weltwirtschaftliches Archiv* 105, 1970, 1–30. [12]

Buiter W, The Macroeconomics of Dr Pangloss: A Critical Survey of the New Macroeconomics, *Economic Journal* 90, March 1980, 34–50. [12]

Bulkley G, Personal Savings and Anticipated Inflation, *Economic Journal* 91, March 1981, 124–35. [131]

Burstein M, *Money*, Schenman, 1963. [312]

Cagan P, The Monetary Dynamics of Hyperinflation, in M Friedman (ed.), *Studies in the Quantity Theory of Money*, University of Chicago Press, 1956. [313]

Casarosa C, The Microfoundations of Keynes's Aggregate Supply and Expected Demand Analysis, *Economic Journal* 91, March 1981, 188–94. [80]

Chick V, Financial Counterparts of Savings and Investment and Inconsistency in Some Macro Models, *Weltwirtschaftliches Archiv* 109, no.4, 1973, 621–43. Referred to in text as 1973a. [231, 247, 335]

Chick V, The Nature of the Keynesian Revolution: A Reassessment. *Australian Economic Papers*, June 1978, 1–20. [131, 312, 336]

Chick V, On the Structure of the Theory of Monetary Policy, in D Currie *et al.* (eds), *Macroeconomic Analysis: Current Problems and Theories in Macroeconomics and Econometrics*, Croom Helm for the Association of University Teachers of Economics, 1981. [193]

Chick V, *The Theory of Monetary Policy*, Gray-Mills, 1973 (2nd edition, Basil Blackwell, 1977). Referred to in text as 1973b. [242, 248, 283, 335]

Christ C F, A Short-Run Aggregate-Demand Model of the Interdependence and Effects of Monetary and Fiscal Policies with Keynesian and Classical Interest Elasticities, *American Economic Review* 57, May 1967. [321, 335]

Christ C F, A Simple Macroeconomic Model with a Government Budget Restraint, *Journal of Political Economy* 76, 1968. [321, 335]

Clower R W, The Keynesian Counter-revolution: A Theoretical Appraisal, in F H Hahn and F P R Brechling (eds), *The Theory of Interest Rates*, Macmillan for the International Economic Association, 1965. Reprinted in R W Clower (ed.), *Monetary Theory: Selected Readings*, Penguin Books, 1969. [131]

Coddington A, Hicks's Contribution to Keynesian Economics, *Journal of Economic Literature* 17, September 1979, 970–88. [268]

Colm G, Fiscal Policy, in S E Harris (ed.), *The New Economics*, Dennis Dobson, 1947. [335]

Conard J W, *An Introduction to the Theory of Interest*, University of California Press, 1963. [298, 300, 312]

Culbertson J M, *Macro-economic Theory and Stabilization Policy*, McGraw-Hill, 1963. [335]

Currie D A, Macroeconomic Policy and Government Financing, in M J Artis and A R Nobay (eds), *Contemporary Economic Analysis*, Croom Helm for the Association of University Teachers of Economics, 1978. [335]

Davidson P, Keynes's Finance Motive, *Oxford Economic Papers* n.s. 17, March 1965, 47–65. [200]

Davidson P, Why Money Matters: A Postscript, in Davidson, *Money and the Real World*, 2nd edition, Macmillan, 1978. [241]

Davidson P and Smolensky E, *Aggregate Supply and Demand Analysis*, Harper and Row, 1964. [97]

Desai M, The Phillips Curve: A Revisionist Interpretation, *Economica* 42, February 1975, 1–19. [284]

Duesenberry J S, *Income, Saving and the Theory of Consumer Behavior*, Oxford University Press, 1967. [27]

Dvoretzky A, Mathematical Appendix no. 5, in Patinkin (1965). [211]

Eisner R, Another Look at Liquidity Preference, *Econometrica* 31, July 1963, 237–46. [328]

Ellis H S, Some Fundamentals in the Theory of Velocity, *Quarterly Journal of Economics* 52, 1938, 431–72. Reprinted in F A Lutz and L W Mints (eds), *Readings in Monetary Theory,* Blakiston for the American Economic Association, 1951. [210]

Eshag E, *Monetary Theory from Marshall to Keynes,* Basil Blackwell, 1963. [13]

Fisher I, The Debt-Deflation Theory of Great Depressions, *Econometrica* 1, October 1933, 337–57. [291]

Fleming M, The Timing of Payments and the Demand for Money, *Economica* n.s. 31, May 1964, 132–57. [210]

Fouraker L E, The Cambridge Didactic Style, *Journal of Political Economy* 66, February 1958. [28]

Friedman M, The Case for Flexible Exchange Rates, in Friedman (ed.), *Essays in Positive Economics,* University of Chicago Press, 1953. [212]

Friedman M, Comments on the Critics, *Journal of Political Economy* 80, September/ October 1972, 906–50. Reprinted in R J Gordon (ed.), *Milton Friedman's Monetary Framework: A Debate with his Critics,* University of Chicago Press, 1974. [283]

Friedman M, Memorandum to the Treasury and Civil Service Committee, *Memoranda on Monetary Policy,* Session 1979–80, HMSO, HC720, 1980. [234]

Friedman M, *A Theory of the Consumption Function,* Princeton University Press for the National Bureau of Economic Research, 1957. [27, 117]

Friedman M and Meiselman D, The Relative Stability of Monetary Velocity and the Investment Multiplier in the United States, in Commission on Money and Credit, *Stabilization Policies,* Prentice-Hall, 1963. [234, 335]

Friedman M and Schwartz A J, *A Monetary History of the United States, 1867–1960,* Princeton University Press for the National Bureau of Economic Research, 1963. [13, 292, 331]

Gordon R A and Klein L R (eds), *Readings in Business Cycles,* George Allen & Unwin for the American Economic Association, 1966. [292]

Gurley J G and Shaw E S, *Money in a Theory of Finance,* Brookings Institute, 1960. [308]

Haavelmo T, *A Study in the Theory of Investment,* University of Chicago Press, 1960. [126]

Hancock K, Unemployment and the Economists in the 1920s, *Economica* 27, November 1960, 305–21. [13]

Hansen A H, *Full Recovery or Stagnation?,* Black, 1938. [231, 335, 351]

Hansen A H, *A Guide to Keynes,* McGraw-Hill, 1953. [312]

Harcourt G C (ed.), *The Microeconomic Foundations of Macroeconomics,* Macmillan, 1977. [33]

Harrod R F, An Essay on Dynamic Theory, *Economic Journal* 49, March 1939, 14–33. Reprinted in Harrod, *Economic Essays,* 2nd edition, Macmillan, 1972 and in A Sen (ed.), *Growth Economics,* Penguin Books, 1970. [265]

Hawtrey R G, Keynes and Supply Functions: A Further Note, *Economic Journal* 65, September 1955, 482–84. [84]

von Hayek F A, *Denationalisation of Money — The Argument Refined,* Hobart Paper 70, Institute of Economic Affairs, 1976 (2nd edition 1978). [313]

von Hayek F A, *Prices and Production,* Routledge & Kegan Paul, 2nd edition, 1935. [5]

Healey D, May Day Speech at Corby, Northants. Reported in *The Sunday Times,* 11 May 1975. [348]

Hegeland H, *The Multiplier Theory,* W K Gleerup, Lund, 1954. [335]

Henderson H D, The Significance of the Rate of Interest, *Oxford Economic Papers* 1, October 1938, 1–13. Reprinted in T Wilson and P W S Andrews, *Oxford*

Studies in the Price Mechanism, Oxford University Press, 1951. [129]

Hicks J R, *Capital and Growth,* Oxford University Press, 1965. [193]

Hicks J R, *Causality in Economics,* Basil Blackwell, 1979. [249]

Hicks J R, *The Crisis in Keynesian Economics,* Basil Blackwell, 1974. [193]

Hicks J R, *Critical Essays in Monetary Theory,* Oxford University Press, 1967. [210, 211]

Hicks J R, IS–LM: An Explanation, *Journal of Post Keynesian Economics* 2, Winter 1980–81, 291–307. [12]

Hicks J R, Mr Keynes and the 'Classics', *Econometrica* 5, April 1937. Reprinted (*inter alia*) in Hicks (1967). [247, 328]

Hicks J R, *Value and Capital,* Oxford University Press, 1939 (2nd edition 1946). [5, 193]

Hirshleifer J, On the Theory of Optimal Investment Decision, *Journal of Political Economy* 66, August 1958, 329–52. [193]

Hirshleifer J, *Price Theory and Applications,* Prentice-Hall, 1980. [193]

Jackman R, Keynes and Leijonhufvud, *Oxford Economic Papers* 26, July 1974, 259–72. [249]

Johnson H G *Macroeconomics and Monetary Theory,* Basil Blackwell, 1971. [131]

Johnston J, *Statistical Cost Analysis,* McGraw-Hill, 1960. [94]

Kahn R F, The Relation of Home Investment to Unemployment, *Economic Journal* 41, June 1931, 173–98. [254]

Kaldor N, The New Monetarism, *Lloyd's Bank Review,* July 1970, 1–18. [242]

Kaldor N, Origins of the New Monetarism, The Page Fund Lecture, 3 December 1980, University College Cardiff Press, 1981. [177]

Keynes J M, *Collected Writings,* D E Moggridge and E Johnson (eds), Macmillan for the Royal Economic Society, various dates from 1971. [12, 13, 28, 133, 183, 273; see also other Keynes references]

Keynes J M, The 'Ex Ante' Theory of the Rate of Interest, *Economic Journal,* December 1937, 663–69. Reprinted in *Collected Writings,* vol. XIV, 215–23. [198, 199, 200, 211, 233, 239, 263]

Keynes J M, *The General Theory of Employment, Interest and Money,* Macmillan, 1936. Republished in *Collected Writings* as vol. VII. [direct quotations only: 6, 41, 56, 58, 72, 74, 79, 80, 83, 91, 105, 106, 116, 136, 139, 144, 153, 155, 156, 175, 178, 179, 193, 202, 205, 206, 208, 230, 238, 254, 265, 266, 267, 269, 270, 278, 282, 284, 285, 286, 288, 289, 296, 297, 303, 306, 307, 312, 317, 320, 321, 324, 326, 327, 328, 329, 331, 334, 335, 338, 344, 345, 346, 349]

Keynes J M, The Process of Capital Formation, *Economic Journal* 49, September 1939. Reprinted in *Collected Writings,* vol. XIV, 278–85. [3, 80, 233, 239, 263]

Keynes J M, *A Tract on Monetary Reform,* Macmillan, 1923. Republished in *Collected Writings* as vol. IV. [335]

Keynes J M, *A Treatise on Money,* 2 vols, Macmillan, 1931. Republished in *Collected Writings* as vols V and VI. [13, 35]

Kindleberger R P, *Manias, Panics and Crashes: A History of Financial Crises,* Macmillan, 1978. [292]

King M A, The United Kingdom Profits Crisis: Myth or Reality?, *Economic Journal* 85, March 1975, 33–54. [352]

Knight F H, *Risk, Uncertainty and Profit,* London School of Economics, 1937. [217]

Kregel J A, Economic Dynamics and the Theory of Steady Growth: an Historical Essay on Harrod's 'Knife-Edge', *History of Political Economy,* 12, 1980 No.1, 97–123. [268]

Kregel J A Economic Methodology in the Face of Uncertainty: The Modelling Methods of Keynes and The Post Keynesians, *Economic Journal* 86, June 1976, 209–25. [23, 24, 67, 80]

Kregel J A, *Rate of Profit, Distribution and Growth: Two Views*, Macmillan, 1971. [59]

Kuznets S, *National Product since 1869*, National Bureau of Economic Research, 1946. [116, 326]

Laidler D, *The Demand for Money*, International Textbook Company, 1969. [335]

Lange O, Say's Law: A Restatement and Criticism, in Lange *et al.* (ed.) *Studies in Mathematical Economics and Econometrics*, Chicago University Press, 1942. [80]

Leijonhufvud A, *On Keynesian Economics and the Economics of Keynes*, Oxford University Press, 1968. [111, 131, 249]

Leijonhufvud A, The Wicksell Connection: Variations on a Theme, in Leijonhufvud, *Information and Coordination: Essays in Macroeconomic Theory*, Oxford University Press, 1981. [193]

Lerner A P, The Essential Properties of Interest and Money, *Quarterly Journal of Economics*, May 1952. [312]

Lerner A P, Saving equals Investment, *Quarterly Journal of Economics* 52, February 1938, 297–309. [261]

Lipsey R G, The Foundations of the Theory of National Income: An Analysis of Some Fundamental Errors, in M H Peston and B A Corry, *Essays in Honour of Lord Robbins*, Weidenfeld and Nicolson, 1972. [193, 267]

Lipsey R G, The Relation between Unemployment and the Rate of Change of Money Wage Rates in the United Kingdom, 1861–1957: A Further Analysis, *Economica* 27, 1960, 1–31. [284]

Lutz V C, Multiplier and Velocity Analysis: A Marriage, *Economica* n.s. 22, February 1955, 29–44. See Archibald (1956). [267]

Malinvaud E, *The Theory of Unemployment Reconsidered*, Basil Blackwell, 1977. [98, 193]

Markowitz H, Portfolio Selection, *Journal of Finance* 7, March 1952, 77–91. [213]

Marx K, *Capital*, Otto Meissner, Hamburg, 1867. Page reference in text to Modern Library edition, Random House, 1906. [12]

Matthews R C O, *The Trade Cycle*, Cambridge University Press, 1959. [292]

Mayer T, Some Reflections on the Current State of the Monetarist Debate, *Zeitschrift für Nationalökonomie* 38, 1978, nos 1–2, 61–84. [13]

Miller M and Orr D, A Model of the Demand for Money by Firms, *Quarterly Journal of Economics* 80, August 1966, 413–35. [211]

Minsky H P, *Can 'It' Happen Again?* M E Sharp, 1982 (forthcoming). [241, 242, 292]

Minsky H P, Economics of Money: Debt Deflation Processes in Today's Environment. Paper to a Symposium on Post Keynesian Theory, Livingstone College. Rutgers University, April 1981. [292]

Minsky H P, *John Maynard Keynes*, Macmillan, 1975. [126]

Mitchell B R and Deane P, *Abstract of British Historical Statistics*, Cambridge University Press, 1962. [312]

Modigliani F, Liquidity Preference and the Theory of Interest and Money, *Econometrica* 12, 1944, 45–88. Reprinted in F A Lutz and L W Mints (eds), *Readings in Monetary Theory*, Blakiston for the American Economic Association, 1951. [248, 328]

Moggridge D E, *The Return to Gold, 1925*, Cambridge University Press, 1969. [13]

Morgan E V and Morgan A D, *Gold or Paper?*, Hobart Paper 69, Institute of Economic Affairs, 1979. [313]

Mossin J, *Theory of Financial Markets*, Prentice-Hall, 1973. [217]

Niehans J, *The Theory of Money*, Johns Hopkins University Press, 1978. [211]

OECD (Organisation for European Cooperation and Development), *Towards Full Employment and Price Stability* ('McCracken Report'), June 1977. [351]

Ohlin B, Some Notes on the Stockholm Theory of Savings and Investment, *Economic Journal* 47, March 1937, 53–69 and June 1937, 221–40, and Alternative Theories of the Rate of Interest: Rejoinder, *Economic Journal* 47, September 1937, 426–7. [198]

Okun A, *The Battle Against Unemployment*, Norton, 1965. [292]

Ott D J and Ott A F, Budget Balance and Equilibrium Income, *Journal of Finance*, 20, 1965, 71–7. [335]

Parker R H and Harcourt G C (eds), *Readings in the Concept and Measurement of Income*, Cambridge University Press, 1969. [59]

Patinkin D, Keynes' Monetary Thought: A Study of its Development, *History of Political Economy* 8, Spring 1976, 1–150. [80, 82]

Patinkin D, *Money, Interest and Prices*, 2nd edition, Harper and Row, 1965 (1st edition 1958). [171, 248]

Patinkin D, A Study of Keynes's Theory of Effective Demand, *Economic Inquiry* 17, April 1979, 155–76. [80]

Patinkin D and Leith J C (eds), *Keynes, Cambridge and 'The General Theory'*, Macmillan, 1977. [12, 267]

Pearce I F, The Time is Not Yet Ripe. Paper delivered to the Conference on Demand, Trade and Equilibrium, in Honour of Professor Pearce, Southampton 1982 and due to be published by Macmillan, editors A M Ulph and G W McKenzie. [312, 313]

Phillips A W, The Relation between Unemployment and The Rate of Change of Money Wage Rates in the United Kingdom, 1861–1957, *Economica* 25, 1958, 283–99. [284]

Pigou A C, Wage Policy and Unemployment, *Economic Journal* 37, 1927. [9]

'Radcliffe Report': Committee on the Working of the Monetary System, *Report*, HMSO, Cmnd. 827, 1959. [228]

Robertson D H, Effective Demand and the Multiplier, in Robertson, *Essays in Monetary Theory*, P S King, 1940. [189, 258]

Robertson D H, Mr Keynes and 'Finance', *Economic Journal* 48, June 1938, 314–18. [211]

Robinson J, The Rate of Interest, in Robinson, *The Rate of Interest and Other Essays*, Macmillan, 1952. Reprinted in Robinson, *The Generalisation of the General Theory and Other Essays*, Macmillan, 1979. [16]

Robinson J, Saving without Investment, in Robinson, *Collected Economic Papers*, vol. II, Basil Blackwell, 1960. [346]

Rothschild K W, Price Theory and Oligopoly, *Economic Journal* 57, 1947. Reprinted in K E Boulding and G J Stigler (eds), *Readings in Price Theory*, George Allen & Unwin for the American Economic Association, 1953. [170]

Rousseas S W, *Monetary Theory*, Knopf, 1972. [217]

Routh G, *Occupation and Pay in Great Britain*, 1906–1960, Cambridge University Press, 1965. [13]

Samuelson P A, An Exact Consumption–Loan Model of Interest, With and Without the Social Contrivance of Money, *Journal of Political Economy*, December 1958. [346]

Samuelson P A, Interactions between the Multiplier Analysis and the Principle of Acceleration, *Review of Economics and Statistics* 21, 1939, 75–8. Reprinted (*inter alia*) in J Lindauer (ed.), *Macroeconomic Readings*, Free Press, 1968. [290]

Sayers R S, Business Men and the Terms of Borrowing, *Oxford Economic Papers* 3, February 1940, 23–31. Reprinted in T Wilson and P W S Andrews, *Oxford Studies in the Price Mechanism*, Oxford University Press, 1951. [129]

Sayers R S, Monetary Thought and Monetary Policy in England, *Economic Journal*

70, 1960, 710–24. [211]

Schott K, *Industrial Innovation in the United Kingdom, Canada and The United States,* British North-American Committee, 1981. [340]

Schott K, Investment in Private Industrial Research and Development in Britain, *Journal of Industrial Economics,* December 1976. [340]

Scott M FG, *Can We Get Back to Full Employment?,* Macmillan, 1978. [346]

Shackle G L S , *Expectations, Investment and Income,* 2nd edition, Oxford University Press, 1968. [200, 228]

Shackle G L S, Recent Theories Concerning the Nature and Role of Interest, *Economic Journal* 71, 1961. Reprinted in *Surveys of Economic Theory* vol. I, Macmillan for the Royal Economic Society and the American Economic Association, 1968. [28]

Shackle G L S , *A Scheme of Economic Theory,* Cambridge University Press, 1965. [291]

Sharpe W F, *Portfolio Theory and Capital Markets,* McGraw-Hill, 1970. [217]

Simons H C, Rules versus Authorities in Monetary Policy, *Journal of Political Economy* 44, 1936, 1–30. Reprinted in F A Lutz and L W Mints (eds), *Readings in Monetary Theory,* Blakiston for the American Economic Association, 1951. [313]

Smith W L, A Graphical Exposition of the Complete Keynesian System, *Southern Economic Journal* 23, October 1956, 115–25. Reprinted in W L Smith and R L Teigen (eds), *Readings in Money, National Income and Stabilization Policy,* Richard D Irwin, 1965. [248]

Sowell T, *Classical Economics Reconsidered,* Princeton University Press, 1974. [13]

Sowell T, *Say's Law: An Historical Analysis,* Princeton University Press, 1972. [13, 80]

Stigler G J, *The Theory of Price,* 3rd edition, Macmillan, 1966. [97]

Tarshis L, The Aggregate Supply Function in Keynes's 'General Theory', in M J Boskin (ed.), *Economics and Human Welfare: Essays in Honour of Tibor Scitovsky,* Academic Press, 1979. [80, 98]

Taylor J, The Unemployment Gap in Britain's Productive Sector, 1953–73, in G D N Worswick (ed.), *The Concept and Measurement of Involuntary Unemployment,* George Allen & Unwin for the Royal Economic Society, 1976. [157]

Tobin J, An Essay on the Principles of Debt Management, in Commission on Money and Credit, *Fiscal and Debt Management Policies,* Prentice-Hall, 1963. [218]

Tobin J, The Interest-Elasticity of the Demand for Cash, *Review of Economics and Statistics* 38, August 1956, 241–47. [211]

Tobin J, Liquidity Preference as Behaviour toward Risk, *Review of Economic Studies* 25, February 1958, 65–86. [211, 212, 213, 217]

Torr C S W, Microfoundations for Keynes's Point of Effective Demand, *South African Journal of Economics* 49, 1982, 335–48. [80]

Tsiang S C, Liquidity Preference and Loanable Funds Theories, Multiplier and Velocity Analysis: A Synthesis, *American Economic Review* 46, September 1956, 539–64. [267]

Tsiang S C, Walras' Law, Say's Law and Liquidity Preference in General Equilibrium Analysis, *International Economic Review* 7, September 1966, 329–45. [211]

Turvey R, Does the Rate of Interest Rule the Roost?, in F H Hahn and F P R Brechling (eds), *The Theory of Interest Rates,* Macmillan, 1965. [312]

Walras L , *Elements of Pure Economics,* definitive edition 1926 (1st edition 1874), translated by W Jaffe, George Allen & Unwin for the American Economic Association and the Royal Economic Society, 1954. [142]

Weintraub S, *An Approach to the Theory of Income Distribution,* Chilton, 1958. [91, 283]

Wells P, Output and the Demand for Capital in the Short Run, *Southern Economic Journal* 32, 1965, 146–52. [126]

Wiles P , Cost Inflation and the State of Economic Theory, *Economic Journal* 83, June 1973, 377–98. [283]

'Wilson Report': Committee to Review the Functioning of Financial Institutions, *Report*, HMSO, Cmnd. 7937, 1980. [231]

Winch D , *Economics and Policy,* Hodder and Stoughton, 1969. [13]

Witte J G, The Microfoundations of the Social Investment Function, *Journal of Political Economy* 71, October 1963. [126]

SUBJECT INDEX